THE SOCIAL BASIS
OF THE FEMALE QUESTION

THE
SOCIAL
BASIS
OF THE
FEMALE
QUESTION

TRANSLATED BY ÉLISE HENDRICK
FOREWORD BY JULIANA GLEESON AND FAEZA YULDASHEVA

ALEXANDRA KOLLONTAI

Haymarket Books
Chicago, IL

First published by the Znanie (Knowledge) Cooperative (St. Petersburg, Nevsky 92), 1909.

This translation © 2025 Élise Hendrick,
published in 2025 by
Haymarket Books
P.O. Box 180165
Chicago, IL 60618
773-583-7884
www.haymarketbooks.org
info@haymarketbooks.org

ISBN: 979-8-88890-378-0

Distributed to the trade in the US through Consortium Book Sales and Distribution (www.cbsd.com) and internationally through Ingram Publisher Services International (www.ingramcontent.com).

This book was published with the generous support of Lannan Foundation, Wallace Action Fund, and the Marguerite Casey Foundation.

Special discounts are available for bulk purchases by organizations and institutions. Please email info@haymarketbooks.org for more information.

Cover and book design by Jamie Kerry.

Library of Congress Cataloging-in-Publication data is available.

10 9 8 7 6 5 4 3 2 1

CONTENTS

For my wonderful nieces, E. and L.

FOREWORD

Juliana Gleeson and Faeza Yuldasheva

Is feminism worth bothering with?

Addressing her Bolshevik comrades in 1909, Alexandra Kollontai argued it was not. Closing her report *On the Female Question* by addressing the feminist efforts to advance the shared political rights of women, Kollontai concluded that class divides formed a chasm of interests that could not be bridged through struggle: 'The women of the bourgeoisie do not intend to abolish contemporary class society with the aid of the rights they expect to win, but to further strengthen it.' In other words, the so-called women's movement was not only misguided but antagonistic towards the politics of class struggle. International gatherings that purported to gather worldwide congresses of feminists to advance the rights of women proved more hostile towards internationalism: As this report notes, those women advancing class struggle were the only group explicitly barred from such a gathering in London. The text's introduction specifically targets the slogan 'Women of all social classes – unite!' Through analysis of social struggles across national contexts and economic analysis of sex divisions within early twentieth-century workforces, Kollontai builds the case that any fabricated unity of that kind could arise *only* through muting class struggle.

As a partisan of revolutionary worker consciousness, by this point Kollontai's ambitions were rather grander than conference resolutions for unity or reforms of legal codes: The Russian communist left sought to grasp historic oppressions as a necessary means to overturning their nation's nascently capitalist society. Notably, Kollontai did not advocate for 'transitional' goals such as equal pay to bridge the wage gap faced by women. Instead, she proposed revolution as the sole means for the advancement of collective female liberation. That Kollontai's report was well received is shown by her pre-eminent standing within the ascendant party: Within a decade of the report, the regime led by the Bolsheviks would appoint her the first female cabinet member in history, the people's commissar for welfare in their new Soviet government.

Given our own times are seemingly more barren for revolutionary prospects, does Kollontai's harsh stance towards feminist organising still hold true? While our impulse may be to offer an apologia for feminism (if only Kollontai had encountered the variety which we practice!), perhaps instead we should pause to consider whether she was right – then and now.

When dealing with a political text more than a century old – as Alexandra Kollontai's *Social Basis of the Female Question* now is – some questions can be resolved by straightforward historical contextualisation. In this case, references made by Kollontai throughout to 'social democracy' refer not to the likes of the United States' DSA, and less still to nation states such as Sweden or Norway. Rather, across the early twentieth century, *social democrat* was a term interchangeable with *communist*, and a platform that followed *The Communist Manifesto*. In other words, those loosely affiliated with Karl Marx and other luminaries of the First International. As Kollontai spells out, those in her movement were distinguished even from other socialists by their persistent references to class struggle and found themselves exiled by political regimes and closed out of even emancipatory movements (including the early twentieth-century women's movement). Kollontai's meaning here is clear and uncontroversial enough among experts of the early twentieth-century workers' movement that failure to mention this to a twenty-first-century reader fresh to the topic would be a matter of neglect.

By contrast, some questions are beyond the work of either the most rigorous historical introductions or of skilled translation (and that provided here by Élise Hendrick is skilled indeed). Whether Kollontai's refutation of *feminism* refers to the movement as we encounter it today seems a thorny question. Since the 2010s, feminist theory has unmistakably reorientated to address limits that had previously stymied the movement. Contemporary efforts to render feminism more suitable for revolutionary purposes have often followed a process of purposefully bolstering inclusivity and encouraging hesitancy in those deemed 'privileged' by the existing order of society. This intersectional moment has tended to frame the failures of feminism since the nineteenth century in terms of its limiting composition: A movement that drew itself overbearingly from the white ruling classes was accordingly delimited in their vision of unity. As much as *political* terms, these internal critiques are often couched in *epistemic* terms.

But Kollontai's argument is of a qualitatively different kind: Her position is not that the women's movement lacked the necessary diversity but, rather, that unifying women was the *wrong commitment*. Rather than arguing for a more inclusive women's movement, *On the Female Question* calls into question the strategic prospect of unity between women. The report provides an account of female oppression that finds it tethered to the development of productive forces: Capitalism both demands the denigration of women's labour and makes a mockery of ideals around maternity and the accompanying duties women were tasked with. It was not the role of communists to denigrate maternal ideals or duties. Nor was it their task to draw women into workforces they'd previously been excluded from. Capitalism would do this harshly enough that social democrats could simply observe these contractions and organise in their wake.

If Iris Marion Young once drolly defined a socialist feminist as 'a socialist who goes to twice as many meetings', Kollontai might have pre-emptively replied: and twice as many as she *needs* to.

Was this a typical stance to expect from any Bolshevik (whatever her sex)? Perhaps not. Kollontai's intransigent rejection of feminism seems a clear precursor to her later positioning as not only a prominent Bolshevik but a leading figure within the *Left Communist* faction. While her cause for departing from her cabinet post was opposing the Brest-Litovsk pact along with her comrades, this was only one of several points of dissent within the party. Contrasting with the expedient promiscuity of Stalinism, Left Communists strictly opposed concessions and coalitions between communists and nationalist parties. By the end of the interwar period, the Left Communists resisted both the theoretical and strategic moves made by the party's Stalinist majority.

But years prior to the Russian Revolution, this report clearly viewed the feminist movement in similar terms to how Kollontai's faction treated nationalism: Developing *unity* between women could only come at the cost of clarity pursuing class politics. For Kollontai such a conceptual lapse could not be countenanced, at any turn. Writing from what would become the left wing of the Bolsheviks, Kollontai was predictably unmoved by many feminists who attempted to assert their socialist credentials. Her observations on the left wing of Britain's suffragettes were disdainful, reproducing a quote from Emmeline Pankhurst that revealed a milquetoast agenda to expand the electoral franchise:

> And even Miss Pankhurst, the socialist, one of the leaders of the 'combat division' of the suffragists, did not fail to inform the *Daily Mail* of the following: 'Many think that we are seeking suffrage for *all* women; *this is completely untrue*. To the contrary, our exceedingly moderate demands do not go beyond calling for women in secure positions and the same responsibilities as male voters to be included on the electoral rolls.'

Kollontai's report is quite unmoved by the typical divides understood to separate British feminism (divided then between the parliamentary advocacy of the NUWs and the window-smashing antics of the WSPU), and she becomes quite mocking in her assessment of the local attempts at *militancy*: 'This touching unity of the suffragists and the suffragettes confirmed that, no matter how "revolutionary" and "militant" the methods of struggle of the left wing of the feminists may be, they are fundamentally just as much a bourgeois class organisation as the NUWs.' Clearly, it took more than a few smashed windows to impress her. One can only imagine that second wave feminism's division into liberal and purportedly *radical* varieties might have left Kollontai equally cold.

While not suffering as harshly as the many 'Old Bolsheviks' killed on Stalin's orders, this intransigence was the direct cause of Kollontai's later political downfall and marginalisation. Departing the revolutionary government on point of principle after the signing of the Brest-Litovsk pact alongside her fellow Left Communists, with Stalin's rise, her

strident stance came to run decidedly against the grain of her party. Kollontai ended her political career as an ambassador to Norway (following
her youthful efforts to foment revolt in Scandinavia) and trade envoy
to Mexico, only briefly returning to prominence while negotiating the
Finno-Soviet peace pact in 1940 (five years prior to her final retirement).
By this point, her position on women had been thoroughly marginal-
ised across the Soviet Union, and her Left Communist tendency entirely
routed. At this time, Stalin had even dispensed with the term *Bolshevik*
(majority), given there was no longer a 'Menshevik' minority worth mentioning. In such a narrowed political context, the social revolutionary
vision found in this report's family chapter was not so much unimple-
mented as beyond clear memory.

So what to make of this hardliners' hardliner, writing still in her
prime?

While we may be inclined to perceive Kollontai's wholesale refusal
of feminism as an overly severe (even 'mechanical') stance, the travails
of twenty-first-century feminists bear comparison. In nations previously
styled as the most 'advanced' with regard to women's rights (especially
Britain), local feminist movements have suffered conceptual and strategic
collapse into protracted debates over what *constitutes* a woman. Whether
trans women are to be included as active and legitimate participants in
feminist debates is seen as a shibboleth – to the point of total preoccupa-
tion. Unlike many feminists on either side of the current debate around
transsexuality, this text refuses detailed consideration of either biology or
identity. Kollontai dryly observes one of the benefits of Marxism as being
precisely the remove from anatomical disputation: 'The followers of historical materialism leave it to the esteemed bourgeois scholars to ponder
the superiority of one sex over another or to weigh the physical brains
and mental make-up of men and women . . . ' Kollontai seems equally
aloof from either physiological comparison or any *essence* of womanhood
(be that observed through explicit self-avowal, or spiritual alignment).
Throughout, Kollontai holds in tacit contempt those whose views of the
sexes are reducible to sentimental or 'ladylike' displays of courtesy, or affinity. It's clear that Kollontai was willing to entertain neither a biological

basis for womanhood's oppressive social conditions nor any notion of revolution as featuring a vindication of femininity.

So if not through unity amongst themselves, how *would* women emancipate themselves? In Kollontai's account, the advancement of women will proceed through both revolutionary *struggle* and by the objective forces of economic *development*. Between these two historical forces, she could see little place for political organising orientated towards women *as such*. Put another way: Worker self-organisation formed a 'rising tide that lifts all boats', while the travails of capitalist political economy ravaged the supposedly sacred foundations of society (marriage, childhood, and even intimacy itself) in ways that made fools of those still naively attached to them. This aspect of Kollontai's report would appear fully vindicated not only by the political struggles she surveys but by her own later track record: At the height of Kollontai's influence, the new political order installed by the Russian Revolution would achieve newfound breakthroughs around abortion, divorce, and the decriminalisation of homosexuality. True to Kollontai's strategic convictions, these breakthroughs were achieved across the early years of a strident worker regime, rather than through any cross-class collaborations that might have threatened to undermine it.

As a leader of this revolt, Kollontai did not strictly rely on statistics: At this stage in her career as a revolutionary, she was well travelled, and had even been exiled from Sweden for her organising there. She was savvy to the limitations of existing social science research ('The available statistics cannot provide an accurate picture of the number of "broken marriages"', she explains when addressing families, 'because an enormous number of spouses part ways without seeking a formal divorce.') However, her argument's thrust is always directed towards what by today's standards would be received as an unabashedly *humanist* approach to feminism. As Kollontai puts it in the introduction, the Bolshevik position was to 'demand only one thing: for every person, whether male or female, to be given a real opportunity for the greatest, freest self-determination, for the greatest space to be opened up for the development and application of all their natural aptitudes.'

Far from a lofty ideal, Kollontai argues that women's liberation is founded in an extension of existing capitalist social *development*. Taking a broad overview of industries transformed by centuries of industrialisation shaped around the demands of Capital, she concludes that female permeation of workforces was thoroughgoing and decisive. This had obvious strategic consequences: Any notion of women being collectively advanced by elite institutions changing internal policies was a farce, given the dependence industrial labour had long established upon labour from each sex. While the concerns of the women's movement were typically about targeting the lofty reaches of ruling class institutions, which were *least* receptive to full integration of the sexes (from the civil services that typically banned women, to medical schools that refused to allow them entry or graduation, to parliaments that neither accepted them as Members nor voters), from Kollontai's view economic integration was already a done deal! The demands of capitalist industry clearly drew women (and children) into workforces, even as they might be excluded from voter rolls and graduate honour calls. As the report's introduction has it:

> To us, women's emancipation is not a dream or even a principle, but a concrete reality that is becoming fact every day. Current economic conditions and the entire further developmental path of the productive forces gradually facilitate, and will continue to facilitate, women's liberation from centuries of oppression and enslavement. Indeed, you need only have a look around: Everywhere, in nearly all areas of labour, you will see women working side by side with men.

A variation on this argument was found in Kollontai's approach to matrimony. Whereas typical feminist arguments of her era (and since) have focused on opposing the *reduction* of women to motherhood and wifely duties, Kollontai instead turned to the travails of proletarian parenting to repudiate it. Specifically she drew on accounts of child labour to emphasise the hollow nature of appeals to the family. Far from nurturing their children through to adulthood, capitalist economies demanded each generation work alongside the next on the shop floor:

> What mockery, what sacrilege the sentimental bleating of the bourgeoisie about 'the sanctity of home and hearth' and 'motherhood'

sounds like when millions, tens of millions of mothers are unable to carry out even their most elementary duties! At the commanding call of capital, mothers tear from their breasts children who have not yet even learnt to tell light from darkness, obediently massing at the factory gates. The bourgeois defenders of contemporary marriage and motherhood are perfectly well informed of how children are crippled and deformed already in their mothers' wombs by hazardous gases and vapours, how millions of young lives are lost when they drink toxic substances from their mothers' milk, how children thrown upon the mercy of fate at harvest time burn to death in their hundreds in village huts, how mothers gradually poison their children, their beloved children, with opium so that their cries will not get in the way of completing rush orders.

This considered, proletarian families of the early twentieth century faced down circumstances which made a mockery out of any efforts to provide care across generations:

> Bourgeois society oppresses women with intolerable economic hardships, paying absurdly little for their work; it deprives them of the citizen's right to raise their voices in defence of their trodden-on interests, obligingly offering them one choice: either marital bondage or the embrace of prostitution, which is publicly scorned and persecuted, but secretly promoted and supported.

That Kollontai described capitalism so unabashedly as diabolical was explicitly informed by *The Communist Manifesto*, which had also proposed the family's abolition. By the early 1900s, it was also informed by the prospect of abolishing and replacing capitalism itself (today often taken to be a mad or bygone prospect).

It's not only her revolutionary optimism that gives us pause integrating Kollontai's work into contemporary research around gender. By today's mores, Kollontai's writing on sex work (which she would refer to solely as *prostitution*) might be taken as grounds for dismissing her report. As already mentioned, intersectional approaches to feminism generally assess views in terms of inclusivity, leaving Kollontai firmly in the camp of 'sex worker exclusive' perspectives (typically referred to as SWERFs . . . although by any measure, Kollontai would hardly rank as a radical feminist!).

To most of her contemporaries, by contrast, the report's chapter on the family would be shocking moreover for outright *equating* the labour done by sex work with the supposedly sacred institution of marriage. In Kollontai's view, each of these served as one means of confining both *women* and *intimacy* itself. Sex work did so by reducing erotic acts to parcels of labour sold by the act or hour (in the context of overarching *separation* that set the stage for all labour), while marriage did so through dowries, legal restrictions, inheritances, and the rest. Sex work and matrimony were not moral opposites but variations on a theme. Each form set the limits of love around the needs of class society. Neither would be expected to continue in the order Kollontai directed her movement towards.

Later in her report, Kollontai undercut typical feminist moralising around sex work through stressing its equivalence to both marriage and the rest of proletarian labour. As is typical across her writing, her most forceful and florid text focused on the horrors that capital imposed across the whole proletariat:

> The dark picture of the lives of prostitutes chills the heart . . . What horrors they have occasion to see! What suffering they are forced to experience! Grief, humiliation, beatings, the contempt of society, poverty, and a lonely death . . . It would seem that a woman who has had even the slightest glance into this hell ought to run away without giving the dark abyss a second look. But is the life of a female craft worker, a domestic servant, or even a female factory worker any better, particularly here in Russia, where the working conditions, even in large-scale operations, are repugnant? Do they – the hundreds of thousands of proletarian women who sell their labour power to capital – live any better? Are their lives any brighter, any freer? Have a look at the dismal basements, the dark corners with their 'bunks for two', where most of the women of the working class are housed, breathe in, even just once, the stuffy air, saturated with all manner of vapours and impurities that working-class women must breathe at 'home'; try to nourish yourselves for even a day on the meagre, unhealthful, stale food with which the women of the working class still their hunger, and you will understand that the hell of an 'honest living' is worthy of the other hell, that of prostitution.

While hardly a repudiation of the 'abolitionist' approach to the sex industry taken by her contemporary feminists (and so many 'radical feminists' today), Kollontai's extension showed up the one-sidedness of scandalised accounts of the industry. London slang of the time referred to those in this particular industry as 'working girls', a euphemism which Kollontai seemed of a mind to extend to its logical conclusion. For Kollontai, the choices made within proletarian labour were a sideshow next to the horrors of being coerced into any kind at all. Closing off her account, Kollontai mockingly distinguished between the early twentieth-century feminist movement's successes in introducing *regulation* (most notably in the capital of the poster child of European progress: Austria) and the actual *abolition* they purported to aim for.

Clearly in the viewpoint advanced by the report, the commercialisation of sex acts was no more reprehensible in the form of prostitution than it was through the founding of monogamous private households, and the worst conditions faced by sex workers were continuous with those of female workers more generally. And as applied everywhere else: Feminist reforms only offered a *reinstitution* of capitalist relations.

In short: there was no such thing as good work for women, nor a good way for us to 'have a man' (whether husband or client).

Overall, Kollontai's chapter on family sounds radical even by 2025's standards. Today, book-length treatments of 'family abolitionist' politics by M. E. O'Brien, Sophie Lewis, and others have revived the tradition which this text provides a high watermark for. With positions such as Kollontai's now unfamiliar, these perspectives drew disparaging reactions from others in worker movements. So this full translation seems especially timely: Both the lines of solidarity which Kollontai makes obvious, and threatens to obscure, can hopefully be understood anew. Fully opening a vision of a communist future requires us to take a backward glance at this high tide, and also observe where the wave broke.

(And at very least, with this skilful translation from Russian to English now published, anti-family politics need be detained no longer by German philological exercises concerning the valences of *aufheben*. Revolution is as beautiful in any tongue.)

With this much apologia for dear Alexandra done, we have to admit freely to some failings: As rigorous an example of movement writing as it was, Kollontai's historical account cannot be relied upon implicitly. The subsequent century of historical scholarship can hardly leave its courageous claims assumed to be verified. One incongruence with her narration of bourgeois marital mores appears when Kollontai argues that the ruling classes in the seventeenth and eighteenth centuries used religion to sanctify the marriage. The reverse seems more easily shown: The Reformation set the stage for abolition of marriage as sacred, allowing for divorce and many other piecemeal reforms (including the previously mentioned legalisation of sex work in Austria and Holland).

While *The Social Basis of the Female Question* avoided the tiresome pitfalls that detain contemporary feminism's paroxysms around 'biological realism' (both across the left and in dominating the global right), Kollontai's scrupulous use of economic comparisons can also seem stifling. In the opening of the report's third chapter, she explicitly denounces feminists who favour idealistic justifications for equality of the sexes, calling it 'touching cries of the suffering feminine soul'. She later presses the contrast between the women's movement approach and her own: 'Feminists indifferently pass by the data accumulated by socio-economic scholarship on the role of the economic factor in the gradual emancipation of women . . . for the equality of the sexes.'

Perhaps the communist movement has no use of feminism, but can femininity be so quickly dispensed with? Kollontai's limited approach leaves her unable to frame such questions. How far Kollontai favours the supersensual over the sensual register is demonstrated by one of the few moments she turns her attention to the extensive work done by literature to address affairs of the heart and household strife:

> Fiction is full of grave images of our marital and family troubles. How many psychological tragedies have originated from this, how many ruined lives and mangled existences! For our current purposes, it is important merely to note that the contemporary family structure oppresses women of all classes and social strata to some extent or other.

But this material is addressed only to be quickly passed over (remarkably enough allowing a rare concession towards womanhood as a unifying plight!). *The Social Basis of the Female Question* clearly rests little weight on literary or dramatic canon. This contrasts notably with an earlier worker movement pamphlet written by Eleanor Marx and her lover Edward Aveling. These star-crossed lovers proved much more willing to engage with literary and theatrical approaches to sexual difference. While their defence of monogamy was strikingly more conservative than Kollontai's (staging a bitterly ironic defence of western conventions, given Aveling's personal infidelity to Marx), the couple deployed Alfred Lord Tennyson and Henrik Ibsen to buttress their position. The conventions of today's critical theory stress the need to harvest or even offer 'reparative' approaches to insights offered by class enemies. Yet Kollontai instead came to more thoroughgoing social conclusions than many of her First International predecessors – while using a considerably less refined base of evidence.

While our own political commitments obviously lie closer to those of Kollontai than those of Eleanor Marx and her treacherous Edward, we have to question whether this report's refusal of the full scope of experience deployed by the First International was altogether for the better. Kollontai's report was neither informed by the literary efforts to instil worker *consciousness* with the riches of their Gymnasium educations found in Marx (Sr and Jr), nor the probing analysis of the *unconscious* that would later come to preoccupy communist writings around sex following the ascendancy of psychoanalysis. (The report was published the same year as Sigmund Freud's case studies of Little Hans and Rat Man and of his introduction of parental unavailability in *Family Romances*, a decade before his treatment of masochism and death drive in 'A Child Is Being Beaten' and *Beyond the Pleasure Principle*.) Between these two stools, and at such a pointed remove from any recognisable *wave* of feminism, today Kollontai can seem 'neither fish nor fowl' to even the most sympathetic readers.

Rather than embracing the full weight of human culture's grappling with the erotic and marital, Kollontai favours dry empirical work, economic surveys, and headlong rhetoric to rouse the reader into further revolt. In this light, we can at least read *The Social Basis of the Female Question* as a fruitful exercise in minimalism.

Kollontai's aversion to the sensual register and to literary treatments of clashes between the sexes could be read as a perceived need to impress her fellow Bolsheviks with her theoretical prowess. But both in tone and repetitions, the emphatic refusal of the sentimental found throughout *The Social Basis of the Female Question* seems more like a personal intellectual commitment. Surveying the theoretical chops of the women's movement, Kollontai mockingly contrasts their methods with her own hard-nosed stance: 'Such fragile tools . . . will achieve nothing in the cruel struggle for social rights.' Kollontai's own strategic vision was shared along with her style among her social-democratic peers (whatever their sex). We can tell this from Kollontai's use of Russian, which at times is very expressive in a peculiar turn-of-the-century manner. Read together, the style sits quite close to how her male Bolshevik colleagues, such as Lenin or Trotsky, wrote. Making these allusions much easier to follow, Élise has made a truly enormous effort in supplying all of the references that are missing in Kollontai's text (a glaring contrast with the Russian edition). Especially appreciated are the quotes in the original languages (with translations). A lot of academic translations attempted by tenured scholars do not achieve such a level of exactitude.

On a more biographical level, the use of quotes illustrates Kollontai's own language ability: She did read the texts she mentions often, in their original language. The report was published more than a decade into her political career and bears the traces of the formidable education she received at home. Albeit less concerned with the literary canon, the Second International's intellectuals still held themselves to a standard of polyglot rigour which today's scholars (outside of India) might find breathtaking. With this translation, both Kollontai's contribution to the revolutionary movement of her time and her outstanding challenges to today's left can come to be better appreciated by today's readers.

Besides the *political* question with which we opened this text, there remain a few substantive questions for today's readers. Firstly, Kollontai's historical point about ruling class morals seems an open question: How did the bourgeois family emerge and extend its stifling conventions across other classes? How did this idealism disrupt the organising of the workers' movement? Secondly, does the *bourgeois* family specifically lose its role when economic ties no longer bind all of its members? (Kollontai's writing on the proletarian case is admirably ferocious, but seems lopsided in comparison . . . as much so as contemporary psychoanalysis was to the contrary over-reliant on ruling-class Austrian households!) Financially independent women often still engage in bourgeois family structures, and have for quite a long time. That considered, does she underestimate the power of pure patriarchy? Or is this merely the subjective decision of the few to stick with archaic convention, one that does not contradict the general trend? What conventions exactly should we understand to be relics of the past that are bound to die out, and which are load-bearing for the capitalist system? (Are these the same aspects which reactionaries are concerned about, or is that defensiveness incidental?) These questions seem pressing for both today's social revolutionaries and subversives – if only to tell each other apart.

Thirdly, Kollontai raises more points than she could fully address with her transnational comparisons. From the introduction for instance, what made Austria such an outlier in all of the statistics she is quoting? Why is Austria (now most famous for its femicides and incestuous basements) no longer remotely in this position? What can be made of the aspects of sex work in Austria that Kollontai would fully have predicted (with fully legalised workers there expected to pay onerous taxes, rents, and health insurance fees)? And of those she would clearly not have predicted (the lively underground trade in sex mostly performed by racialised migrants and refugees, as represented by the sex workers' group Red Edition)?

One does not have to believe in 'inclusivity' fixes to feminist thinking to appreciate that Kollontai's report was sorely lacking in references to racism. While stressing the uniquely high levels of immersion in industry found among female workers in the United States, Kollontai does not bring into view the 'colour line' divides that defined labour relations in the wake of slavery. And her treatment of Australian feminism overlooks the necessarily *partial* nature of the female franchise, given the exclusion of Aboriginal people (regardless of sex). Here as elsewhere, the report is keen to stress divisions that existed along class lines while passing over other divides (that would potentially delimit the fortunes of local worker organising). Within the Russian context, she wrote some fifty years after the Empire's conquest of central Asia, but reports from these provinces were so scarce that she passed over mention of either class or sex relations there. This contrasted with both the centrality that the 'National Question' would come to pose during the ascendancy of Stalin in the 1920s and today's theoretical landscape. One of the most elaborate queer communist manifestos not only reflected upon but originated from Kyrgyzstan. There, pioneering post-Soviet intellectuals from the School of Theory and Activism Bishkek (STAB) recently paid perverse tribute to Kollontai with their fictitious *Queer in Space – The Kollontai Commune Archive*, extending her achievements far beyond where this historical report reached.*

Recent progressions within the new Russian Federation have cast this report in a curious light: both timely in analysis and distant in optimism. By the early twentieth century, Russia had crashed out of the 'exceptional' progressive beacon for legal protections of women identified by Eleanor Marx, appearing to have become a backwater. In the early twenty-first century, Russia became the forefront of reaction: pioneering bans on 'promoting homosexuality' and decriminalising domestic violence. Yet also since the mid-2010s, Russian feminist discussions about the list of professions closed to women have pursued precisely the formerly feminist requirement of the Mannheim program that Kollontai's report highlights. In the twenty-first-century Russian Federation, laws still exist that bar women from entering jobs that might prove dangerous to their offspring. The retort from Russia's feminists was that not every woman wants to bear a child, that a lot of women who enter these dangerous jobs like digging coal do so precisely to provide for the children they already have, and that, even when the work is officially prohibited, women are still employed in those positions, just unofficially or under the false title of secretaries and cleaners. The law was often called a relic of the patronising Soviet political stance towards women. Only rarely was

---

* Juliet Jacques, 'Juliet Jacques on the School of Theory and Activism's "Queer in Space",' *Frieze Magazine*, 7 January 2019; Owen Hatherley, "Make Way For Queer Communism: Owen Hatherley In Bishkek," *Quietus*, 2 December 2018.

it pointed out that the laws in question were once the goal of the female workers' movement. However, the general mood was to call this legislation outdated, whatever the roots of it were.

Do we still have a use for feminism today, however much it includes? Even those who can never be convinced otherwise can gain rich insights from digesting the work of this fraught historical moment, which Kollontai's report originated from and so boldly transformed. At the very least, today's revolutionaries can take some notes in style.

TRANSLATOR'S PREFACE

About This Translation, Introduction to the Crowdfunded Translation Project, and Vindication of an Oft-Misunderstood and Undervalued Profession

The book you are holding in your hand (or displaying on your screen) is a first in two senses. It is the first full-length English translation of Alexandra Kollontai's 1909 book *The Social Basis of the Female Question* (*Социальные основы женского вопроса*), as well as the first book-length translation completed by my Crowdfunded Translation Project.

Before you begin reading the actual translation, there are a few things worth knowing about the translation and how it has come to be, things that will help you understand how to get the most use out of it and, perhaps, will help you rely on this book above the number of other English translations of a work by Kollontai bearing the same title or some variation thereof. Also, as a representative of the oft-misunderstood profession that is translation, I'm taking this opportunity to help non-translators understand what we actually do and why our work cannot be simply replaced by large language models and machine-learning algorithms (certainly not at the current developmental stage of the technology).

Alexandra Kollontai published two works bearing the title *Социальные основы женского вопроса* (*The social basis of the female/woman question*). The first, published in 1908, was a pamphlet.[*] The next year, she published a book by the same name, in which she greatly expanded on the

---

[*] This pamphlet was also the only version acknowledged on the English-language Wikipedia entry for Kollontai as of 23 January 2024.

themes she had touched upon in the pamphlet. As far as I have been able to determine, all existing English translations with this title or some variation thereon are either translations of the pamphlet or heavily abridged translations of the book.

Announcing that you are working on 'the first full-length English translation' of a book by a well-known and respected theorist such as Kollontai is rather nerve-racking; it feels like a countdown to the moment when someone finds the translation that makes a liar of you. Indeed, since I first announced in January 2023 that I was beginning work on this translation, numerous people have asked me about other English translations they found. How, then, can I say that this is the first?

In the original Russian, this book comprises just over 90,000 words. Because Russian, like German, has a strong affinity for compound words, the general tendency is for the word count of an English translation to exceed that of the original, as single words such as *взаимноблаготворительный* and *шелкопрядильня* become *mutual philanthropic* and *silk spinnery*, respectively. Indeed, not counting this preface, the English translation of this book amounts to more than 113,000 words, or 23,000 more than the original. The extant translations, however, have considerably lower word counts, in some cases less than half the word count of the original. I found in full-text searches that entire sections of this book are absent from those translations. As such, I am confident in saying that no other full-length translation of this book currently exists, if one ever did.

One of the greatest challenges in translating a work as old as this one is the use of obsolete terminology. In many cases, Kollontai refers to trades and concepts that have so long since fallen into disuse that standard dictionaries and terminology resources do not include them, or include them only in senses clearly different to those in which Kollontai used them. Sometimes, no well-attested English translation can be found at all. Other times, verifiable English translations can only be found through lengthy research and recourse to rather unconventional resources, including, in one case, a Russian translation of Shakespeare's *Julius Caesar*. Most examples of this occur in Kollontai's discussion in the introduction and chapter 1 of women's occupations in the Middle Ages and the late nineteenth and early twentieth centuries, a field in which I claim no expertise. I have done my best to verify the translations I have used, but if anyone who *does* have such specific expertise believes they see terminological choices they could improve upon, I would be most grateful to hear their thoughts.

On a related note, in her discussion of the struggle for suffrage and the bourgeois and proletarian women's movements, Kollontai refers to numerous organisations, most of them long since defunct. Where I have been able to locate generally accepted English renderings of their names, I have used them; otherwise, I have translated them myself. In order to facilitate the research of those so inclined, I have always noted the names used by these groups in their local languages.

In order to make the lives of those wishing to do further research easier, full-text editions of the works cited by Kollontai in the original and/or English are linked in the translator's notes.

For those like me who prefer to be able to verify the original of a translated quote, I have tracked down most of the sources quoted by Kollontai and included them in translator's notes. In the process, a few errors and omissions in the translations she used have become apparent. Those, too, are noted. All English translations are mine unless otherwise noted.

In Kollontai's day, citations were approached with a distinct devil-may-care attitude, and she was no exception. Often, the complete title of the source is not cited. Indeed, sometimes only the author's name is provided. Anyone wishing to look into the works Kollontai relied on will be relieved to know that I have – to the extent possible – not left them to deal with this alone. Where incomplete citations could be probably or positively identified, they are cited and linked in the translator's notes.

For ease of use, I have made two relatively minor formatting changes. Kollontai's footnotes have been converted from asterisks restarting each page to endnotes with continuous numbering. I have also placed larger quotes in block quote format. Other than these sorts of formatting changes, the work is as printed in the 1909 Znanie edition. All ellipses are Kollontai's, as are a number of unclosed quotes. One must say that Kollontai could have done with a copyeditor. Russian spellings in quotes

xxviii   THE SOCIAL BASIS OF THE FEMALE QUESTION

are as found in the respective source; where the source uses pre-revolutionary spellings, these have been maintained.

Translating Kollontai has been a singular professional challenge for me as a translator with over twenty years of experience translating highly complicated, technical, obscure, and, not infrequently, boring texts to and from numerous languages. It has put me back in touch with what our widely misunderstood and undervalued profession is all about. With over a 60 percent female work force, translation can also reasonably deemed an example of feminised labour, therefore, the first full-length English translation of Kollontai's *Social Basis of the Female Question* seems a particularly apt place to briefly answer the *Office Space* question: 'What would you say it is you do here?'

Many people seem to think that translators are merely human dictionaries (a view that manages to get both translators *and* dictionaries wrong at the same time), simply inhaling words in one language and exhaling them in another through a purely objective process that could easily be carried out by anyone with sufficient time and access to the right reference works—or by, say, machine-learning algorithms that are even now hard at work cracking the mystery of the average number of fingers on a human hand.

This view is – putting it with the utmost delicacy and charity – nonsense. Translation is rarely straightforward, and dictionaries are, at best, incomplete accounts of human language. Often, dictionaries and other terminology resources offer multiple possible renderings of the same term; sometimes (particularly when translating works over a century old) they offer implausible answers or no answers at all. In those cases, translation requires an understanding both of how to do primary source research and of how to judge the results of that research against the context of the document being translated. Human language is deeply contextual and vibe-based; a good translator is one who has a clear understanding of the context and uses this understanding to produce a translation whose semantic meaning and metalinguistic vibe approximate those of the original as nearly as possible.

One good example of this can be found in chapter 3. In Kollontai's discussion of electoral reform and women's suffrage, the term *обладать цензом* (*obladat' tsyenzom*) makes repeated appearances. Literally, this translates as *to be in possession of a/the census*, a phrase that is at long odds to break any world sense-making records. From an investigation of Russian sources using the term in an electoral context, we find that it is meant to refer to a person being recorded in a census as being in possession of a certain amount of property or paying a certain amount in tax or rates. In other words, *ценз* (*tsyenz*), as used in this context, refers not so much to a census per se as to a *property qualification* for voting. This, to answer the *Office Space* question, is what we do here.

Under what conditions do we – the majority female workforce of translators – do what we do? Suffice it to say that it is hard not to feel a certain resonance upon reading Kollontai's explication of the term *одиночки* (*odinochki*, or 'independent' female workers) in a statistical breakdown of persons living on their own income in Saint Petersburg:

> Who exactly are these 'independent' female workers? They are, of course, the most severely exploited amongst the small craft workers: dressmakers, knitters, and florists, who, as independent workers, work at home for capitalist intermediaries, and, as a result of their atomisation and separation from one another, are subjected to the harshest enslavement by capital.

In other words, these *odinochki* are home-based piecework subcontractors, combining the definite advantages of not having to be in any particular place at any particular time (I once finished translating a patent on board a coach in the middle of the Peruvian Atacama Desert) with the equally definite *dis*advantages of lacking a guaranteed regular income, benefits, or pension; being at the bottom of a food chain, where one or more bigger fish take more or less substantial cuts of the compensation for your work; the difficulties of organising an atomised workforce; and, in the United States, the joys of paying a double helping of payroll tax even in years when you have made little enough to have zero taxable income. The legions of other gig economy workers toiling in solitude whilst contributing a hefty chunk of their compensation to the care and feeding of 'disruptive' app billionaires will doubtless also recognise themselves in the description. Move fast, break things, and 'miraculously' end up with a late-Victorian business model that suits no one better than oneself.

David Graeber wrote in *Bullshit Jobs* that modern capitalism has created a situation in which the opportunity to use one's skills for socially useful purposes is treated as some sort of favour to the worker:

> In the business world, it's worse. For instance, Geoff Shullenberger, a writing professor at New York University, reacted to my original 2013 essay with a blog pointing out that many businesses now feel that if there's work that's gratifying in any way at all, they really shouldn't have to pay for it:
>
> 'For Graeber, bullshit jobs carry with them a moral imperative: "If you're not busy all the time doing something, anything – doesn't really matter what it is – you're a bad person." But the flipside of that logic seems to be: if you actually like doing X activity, if it is valuable, meaningful, and carries intrinsic rewards for you, it is wrong for you to expect to be paid (well) for it; you should give it freely, even (especially) if by doing so you are allowing others to profit. In other words, we'll make a living from you doing what you love (for free), but we'll keep you in check by making sure you have to make a living doing what you hate."[*]

I am certain I am not the only freelance translator on the planet to have considered that there are many applications for our skills that would be both more interesting to work on and more worthwhile to the general public than translating trademark renewal applications or boilerplate adhesion contracts that nobody reads and that hopefully will be invalidated in court, if only there were a way to cover the cost of living whilst doing so. It is this train of thought that led to the Crowdfunded Translation Project and to the translation you are now reading.

A couple of years ago, whilst lamenting the fact that there are so many translations I would like to do, and that others would benefit from my doing, for which no single client could be found to cover the cost at a rate of pay sufficient to cover my expenses (thus allowing me to give the task the attention it deserved), it occurred to me that, if *one* client could not be found to pay for translations of, say, the works of Ōsugi Sakae or the final reports of the German parliamentary inquiries into state collusion with fascist paramilitaries, then perhaps *many* 'clients' could be found who

---

[*]   David Graeber, *Bullshit Jobs* (2018), p. 218.

would each contribute a little to the cost. The resultant translation would then be freely available to all (with attribution to me as translator and the Crowdfunded Translation Project as having funded it). The only requirements would be the absence of any legal restrictions on translation and reproduction and the presence, on my part, of interest in working on it.

By the time you're reading this, I will likely have another crowdfunded translation project on the go (for more information, check patreon. com/elisehendrick). Your support, should you be so inclined, is greatly appreciated.

At this point, I would like to give my heartfelt thanks to everyone who contributed to making this translation possible, in particular:

> Erika Whelan, whose perennial frustration at the lack of a full-length English translation of this book led her to approach me with the idea of creating one

> Haymarket, who believed in this project and were open to working with my decidedly unconventional funding model and doing a nonexclusive publication arrangement

> Susan Pashkoff, whose idea it was to approach Haymarket in the first place

> All the comrades who contributed to the realisation of this project, whether with small donations, not-so-small donations, or by promoting it on social media

> All of my small but reliable group of supporters on Patreon

> Last but not least, everyone who came to my aid with terminological conundrums

If you expected to find yourself mentioned here and did not, please be assured that it is due entirely to an oversight whilst writing this and certainly not to any lack of appreciation on my part. All Contributions Are Beautiful.

THE SOCIAL BASIS
OF THE FEMALE QUESTION

INTRODUCTION

This is a pivotal moment for the 'women's movement' in Russia: In December 1908, it will be time to take stock of the creative activities of women's organisations over the last few years, and to map out the 'course of action' for feminists in the coming years of the struggle for women's emancipation at the All-Russia Women's Congress (*Всероссийский Женский Съезд*). Under the pressure of the events that have occurred in Russia, the complex social and political issues that had only recently been consigned to the realm of the abstract, 'cursed questions', are increasingly becoming the pressing issues of the day, requiring real, practical participation and resolution. These issues include the so-called female question. Every day, more and more women here eagerly seek an answer to such disturbing questions as: Where do we go from here? What is to be done? How can we ensure that the fruits of the protracted, persistent, lethally difficult struggle for new types of political structures for our country will also be guaranteed to Russia's female population?

Together with the suffrage section of the Russian Women's Mutual Philanthropic Society (*Русское Женское Взаимноблаготворительное Общество*, WMPS), the Alliance for Women's Equality (*Союз Равноправности*, AWE) has decided to give a comprehensive answer to these questions that plague women by convening the first All-Russia Women's Congress.

The agenda of the upcoming women's congress is quite broad: The first section is to carry out an evaluation of women's activities in various arenas of Russian life. The second section shall concern itself with the economic position of women, gain an understanding of working conditions in trade and industry and in domestic service, touch on women's occupational safety, and so on. A special subsection is being created to deal with matters related to family, marriage, and prostitution. The tasks

1

of the third section shall include: the contemporary civil and political position of women and the means of women's struggle for equal rights in these areas. Lastly, a fourth section will be dedicated to issues of women's education.

Such a comprehensive programme for the All-Russia Women's Congress can only be welcomed, particularly compared to the initial draft, which was printed in issue number 3 of the journal *Soyuz Zhenshchin* (*Союзъ Женщин*) in 1907. This draft completely ignored such an essential matter as the economic position of women in relation to legislation for women's occupational safety. Was this a chance oversight? If it was indeed an oversight, it was certainly a characteristic one: Forgetting the economic side of the female question – the position and protection of women's labour – this is the sort of 'accident' that would have immediately established the contours of the upcoming congress and made it impossible and pointless for women from those social strata for whom the 'female question' is most tightly and inextricably bound up with contemporary workers' issues to participate in it. This oversight has now been corrected: The second section is entirely dedicated to the issue of women's labour and women's economic position. As such, perhaps it would not be worth tarrying on such an insignificant incident as a temporary omission, were it not characteristic of our bourgeois equal-rights campaigners.

With the caution that lies in the nature of bourgeois feminists, the organisers of the congress long wavered over what sort of face to put on it. To us, the omission of women's economic position from the draft programme appears closely related to this vacillation. In one of the meetings concerning the upcoming congress, quite influential figures in women's society insisted on not being distracted with 'campaigning activities', preferring to concentrate all of their attention on purely concrete issues, such as combating alcoholism. Thus, even relatively recently, during the creation of the draft programme, the congress organisers themselves did not know whether to give it a virtuous, 'ladylike' character, centring on moral or charitable tasks, or to actually strive to shake women out of their indifference to their own fate and recruit them to the ranks of those struggling for women's emancipation.

Gradually, however, under the influence of the more conscious and thoughtful champions of equal rights, the latter tendency gained the upper hand. The standard feminist rallying cry was selected to be the slogan of the upcoming congress: Uniting all women in struggle for specifically female rights and interests.

The congress served as an impetus for feminist organisations: The anthill of women came to life; one after another, feminists (Pokrovskaya, Kalmanovich, Shchepkina, Vakhtina, etc.) appeared with presentations and lectures, the *leitmotiv* of which boiled down to the same feminist rallying cry: 'Women of all social classes – unite!'

As attractive as this 'peaceful' slogan sounds, as promising as it may seem to the 'poor little sisters' of bourgeois women, the women of the proletariat, it is this slogan, this favourite rallying cry of the feminists, that requires us to take a closer look at the upcoming women's congress and carefully evaluate its tasks and fundamental aspirations from the vantage point of the interests of working-class women.

Specifically, the question is as follows: Should working-class women answer the feminists' call and actively, directly participate in the struggle for women's equality, or should they remain true to the traditions of their own class and go their own way, struggling by different means for the liberation not only of women but of all humanity from oppression and enslavement by modern capitalist ways of life?

However, before answering the question posed above, I believe it necessary to state the underlying premises from which the following discussion will proceed.

The followers of historical materialism leave it to the esteemed bourgeois scholars to ponder the superiority of one sex over another or to weigh the physical brains and mental make-up of men and women, and demand only one thing: for every person, whether male or female, to be given a real opportunity for the greatest, freest self-determination, for the greatest space to be opened up for the development and application of all their natural aptitudes. At the same time, the followers of historical materialism reject the existence of a special female question, separate from the general social question of our time. Specific economic causes have resulted over time in the subordinate position of woman; her natural properties played a merely *secondary* role in this. Only the complete disappearance of these causes, only the evolution of those same economic forms that once gave rise to the enslavement of women can effect a fundamental change in their social position. In other words, women can only truly gain freedom and equal rights in a world transformed by new social and productive foundations . . . *

This statement does not, however, rule out the possibility of a partial improvement in women's lives within the current structure. Indeed, a fundamental solution to the workers' question is only possible by completely transforming the contemporary relations of production, but surely this consideration should not obstruct reform work that serves to satisfy the immediate interests of the proletariat. To the contrary, every new victory of the working class serves as a stepping stone that leads humanity to the realm of freedom and social equality; each right newly acquired by women brings them closer to the established objective: their complete emancipation.

One more caveat: In dealing with the issue of women's emancipation, as when discussing any socio-political issue, we must stand firmly on the basis of the real conditions of life; everything falling within the realm of 'moral desires' or other ideological constructions we gladly leave completely at the disposal of bourgeois liberalism. To us, women's emancipation is not a dream or even a principle, but a concrete reality that is becoming fact every day. Current economic conditions and the entire further developmental path of the productive forces gradually facilitate, and will continue to facilitate, women's liberation from centuries of oppression and enslavement. Indeed, you need only have a look around: Everywhere, in nearly all areas of labour, you will see women working side by side with men. In England, France, Germany, Italy, and Austria, of the 81 million people working in industry, 27 million are women.[1] The following figures illustrate just how many women, and what proportion of the overall female population of civilised countries, live independent lives: According to the most recent census figures, the following percentages of men and women, relative to the male and female populations, respectively, lived on their own wages:[2]

---

*   All ellipses so in original. —Trans.

Country	Women	Men
Austria	47%	63%
Italy	40%	66%
Switzerland	29%	61%
France	27%	57%
Great Britain and Ireland	27%	62%
Belgium	26%	60%
Germany	25%	61%
US	13%	59%
Russia	10%	43%

Going from these percentages to absolute figures, we see that, although the number of women in Russia living on their own income is lower than in other countries, it is nonetheless quite large. According to the data of the most recent census, of a female population of 63 million in Russia, over 6 million were reported as living on their own income; in cities, 2 million out of 8 million women (i.e., 25 percent) earn their own living; in rural localities, there are 4 million independent women out of a total female population of 55 million. Taking into account the whole economically active population of Russia (i.e., those living on their own income), we find that, of 33 million economically active people, 27 million are men and 6 million are women. To better illustrate the ratio prevailing in Russia between the male and female portions of the population of persons living on their own income, the following characteristic figures will show the true extent of female participation in the industrial life of our country.[3]

Branch of Industry	Women		Men		Total
	In thousands	As % of total	In thousands	As % of total	In thousands
Mining and metalworking	10.8	5%	218.0	95%	228.8
Ceramic production	10.4	8%	115.3	92%	125.7
Processing of fibrous materials	508.7	53%	450.9	47%	959.6
Wood processing	14.6	4%	395.5	96%	910.1
Processing of animal products	9.5	6%	144.7	94%	154.2
Processing of foodstuffs	30.3	9%	318.5	91%	343.8
Metal processing	9.6	2%	615.3	98%	624.9

Garment production	319.6	28%	839.3	72%	1,158.9
Construction	2.1	0%	714.8	100%	716.9
Other areas of manufacturing	66.5	15%	380.3	85%	446.8
Communications	6.7	1%	445.9	99%	452.6
Railways	15.4	6%	246.8	94%	262.2
Trade	192.1	13%	1,303.0	87%	1,495.1
Other sources of income	2,978.5	39%	4,598.0	61%	7,576.5
Total	4,174.8	28%	10,781.3	72%	14,956.1

Here in Russia, women's labour is particularly well represented in the textile industry. According to the 1900 data, in cotton production, there were 201,000 male workers and 17,000 female workers; in wool production, there were 46,457 women to 81,339 men; in linen, hemp, and jute production, there were 33,616 women to 33,899 men; and 12,337 men and 12,437 women were employed in silk production. In all fields of the textile industry listed in the table below, female labour predominates over male.[4]

Enterprises	Number of female workers	Number of male workers
Combined spinning and weaving mills	52,317	45,599
Weaving mills	26,283	24,806
Spinning mills	15,151	14,081
Jute factories	6,810	3,686
Complete silk processing companies	4,444	1,672
Cloth and light woollens factories	4,085	3,652
Tulle and lace factories	3,636	2,500
Wool-washing plants	3,535	1,105
Canvas, fire hose, knitted fabric factories, etc.	3,090	1,370
Ribbon, bandage, galloon, agréments, etc.	2,365	2,450
Silk carding plants	2,204	482
Linen threshing floors	688	578

The female workforce is also larger than the male workforce in dye-works, with 1,206 female workers to only 561 male workers, 1,178 female and 439 male workers in linen workshops, gold embroidery shops, and other such workshops, and 679 women to 639 men in button production, etc. In absolute terms, a large number of women can also be found in weaving mills with dyeing departments (14,500 women and 19,500 men), in wool weaving mills (7,500 female workers and 11,500 male workers), in wool spinning and worsting mills (almost 5,000 women and 6,000 men), in cloth factories (approximately 15,000 female workers and 33,500 male workers), in linen spinning mills (8,000 women and 8,200 men), and at complete linen and hemp factories (roughly 9,500 of each).

Outside of textile production, here in Russia, female labour is also widespread in other branches of industry, such as food processing, particularly in bakeries (4,391 women and 8,868 men); in chemical production, particularly in cosmetics manufacturing (4,074 women and 4,508 men); in glass production (approximately 5,000 women); in porcelain production (approximately 4,000); and in ceramics and brick production (approximately 6,000), etc. Only in the metal processing industry is female labour employed to a small extent.

The above data should suffice to demonstrate how widespread female labour is in Russian industry. However, we should not lose sight of the fact that Russia has only relatively recently begun to follow the path of large-scale capitalist production and that, as the extent of capitalist industrial organisation increases, it will continue to draw in and employ more and more female workers.

Nonetheless, even in present-day Russia, in the larger cities, where large-scale capitalist enterprise is concentrated, female labour, particularly proletarian female labour, is quite solidly represented. Let us take Saint Petersburg as an example: There, according to the 1900 census, for every 100 men living on their own labour, there were 40 women.[5] A closer look at the ratio of male to female labour in the capital reveals the following picture:

Number of Persons Living from Their Own Labour in Saint Petersburg[6]

	In thousands			As % of total	
	Total	Men	Women	Men	Women
Persons employed in trades					
Proprietors	4.4	30.9	13.5	70	30
Administration	28.0	23.7	4.3	85	15
Labourers	342.3	268.6	73.7	78	22
Independent	69.2	39.5	29.7	57	43
Persons employed in other professions					
Civil service and private employment in liberal professions	87.8	74.8	13.0	85	15
Domestic service	51.4	41.1	10.3	80	20
Total	623.1	478.6	144.5	77	23

The above table shows that women are primarily to be found amongst the proletarian occupations: For 269,000 male workers, there are 74,000 female workers, and there are 40,000 male and 30,000 female 'independent' workers. Who exactly are these 'independent' female workers? They are, of course, the most severely exploited amongst the small craft workers: dressmakers, knitters, and florists, who, as independent workers, work at home for capitalist intermediaries, and, as a result of their atomisation and separation from one another, are subjected to the harshest enslavement by capital. There are significantly fewer women in the intellectual professions, and the rubric 'proprietors' counts 13,000 women compared to 31,000 men.

The following figures show the ratios in the area of female labour between the various social groups of the populations of other countries and the position of proletarian men and women amongst wage earners:

Country	Census year	Total population		Economically active population		Of which	
		Men	Women	Men	Women	Male workers	Female workers
		in millions					
Austria	1890	11.7	12.2	7.8	6.2	4.4	5.3

Germany	1895	25.4	26.4	15.5	6.6	9.3	5.3
France	1891	18.9	19.2	11.1	5.2	5.0	3.6
England and Wales	1891	14.1	14.9	8.9	4.0	5.4	3.1
US	1890	32.1	30.6	18.8	3.9	8.7	2.9
Total		102.2	103.3	62.1	25.3	32.8	20.2

In Austria, as can be seen from this table, the number of female workers exceeds that of male workers: There are 4.5 million male workers compared to 5 million female workers. In Germany, there are more than 50 percent as many female workers as male workers; the same can be seen in France and England, and only in the US is this ratio somewhat less favourable to women.

The fact of women's constantly progressing emancipation in the area of work is placed in even clearer relief when the relative quantity of women wage earners is shown over a certain period of time. The share of female labour is relentlessly increasing, at a speed greater than that of men in many fields. The figures below demonstrate the rapid quantitative growth of the female workforce in various countries.[7]

Growth in Population Living from Own Wages

	Period	In millions		As % of total population of respective sex	
		Men	Women	Men	Women
Austria	1880–90	1.0	1.6	14	33
France	1881–96	1.2	1.1	12	22
Germany	1882–95	2.1	1.0	16	19
US	1880–90	4.1	1.3	28	48
England and Wales	1881–91	1.1	0.6	12	15

As can be seen, the quantity of women wage earners increased relative to the total number of persons of the same sex faster than the population of male wage earners. This process is particularly noticeable in the US and Austria.[8]

Here in Russia, too, the number of employed women – once again, primarily women of the working class – is increasing without interruption. Thus, in 1885, 600,000 female workers constituted 30 percent of the total number of Russians employed in industry; in 1899, 1.5 million female workers already constituted 44 percent of this population.[9]

Of course, the share of women's participation in the productive activities of the country is increasing together with female labour; even now, women produce approximately one-third of the total volume of commodities brought to market in the world.

The aforementioned fact of the uninterrupted growth in female labour is cause for concern to many bourgeois economists, causing them to see women as dangerous competitors for men on the labour market and to view the expansion of women's labour with hostility. Is there any substance to this view? Are women truly always men's 'pernicious' competitors?

The number of working women is increasing without interruption, but the constant development of the productive forces also requires an ever-greater number of workers. Only in certain moments of technical breakthroughs is there either a decrease in the demand for new workers or the replacement of one category of workers by another: Women replace men to be displaced, in turn, by children and adolescents. However, every step on the path of technological progress results in increased production speeds over defined periods, and this new volume of industrial activity is inextricably linked with new demand for workers of all categories. Thus, notwithstanding temporary delays and occasionally quite dramatic fluctuations, the number of workers employed in industry ultimately grows together with the growth of the world's productive forces. The growth in the number of both categories of workers – men and women – is *absolute*, whilst the growth in female labour only *relatively* exceeds that of male labour. In point of fact, a glance at the last of the above tables suffices to show that, when comparing the absolute numbers of male and female workers, the growth of the former is by no means at the expense of the latter. Thus, we see that, in Germany, the number of men employed in industry increased by over 2 million over 13 years, whilst the number of women only increased by 1 million; in France, the number of men grew by 1.2 million, whilst that of women grew by 1.1 million; in the US, the number of men increased by over 4 million, and that of women by only slightly more than 1 million, etc. Only in Austria do we see more or less equal growth of the workforce of both sexes.[10]

In general, what is happening on the labour market is not so much the displacement of male labour by female labour as much as the grouping of the two categories by professions: Some industries are indeed increasingly filling with women (domestic service, textile industry, garment production); others are primarily relying on the labour of men (mining, metal and mechanical production), etc. The quantitative growth in female industrial labour is doubtlessly going at the expense of child labour, a phenomenon that, in any case, can only be welcomed. As legislative protection for minors develops, and the age at which children are permitted to be employed in industrial labour increases, there is undoubtedly a regrouping of the workforce in terms of an increase in the number of female workers.

Thus, the claim that women are men's most dangerous competitors on the labour market is subject to a whole list of caveats. Leaving aside the issue of the competition existing in the area of professional and intellectual work, we merely see that, in the proletarian milieu, female workers only compete with male workers in those cases where they stand in isolation and are not included within the overall proletarian struggle. Proletarian women are only men's competitors, those 'pernicious' competitors who lower men's wages and steal the fruits of their successes in organised struggle with capital where they are not brought into the broader class and trade-union struggle. But surely any *unorganised* proletarian, be they the starving 'grey muzhiks' of the countryside, the 'former humans' thrown overboard by the intellectual professions, or simply workers deprived of stable wages, are competitors to the very same extent. Female workers adversely influence working conditions to the extent that they are currently still the less organised sector of the working class. Capital gladly uses them to counteract the more conscious, more cohesive sector of the working class. But from the moment in which female workers join the ranks of organised struggle for the liberation of their class, the claim that they – proletarian women – are the worst competitors of proletarian men can no longer be made categorically. Organised proletarians lose the capacity to harm their class comrades.

Limiting ourselves to these preliminary caveats and brief statistical examples, let us now seek answers to the questions posed above. Those wishing to better acquaint themselves with the working conditions of women, the growth of the female workforce, and the significance thereof in the economic life of peoples are referred to the specialised works on the subject. What mattered here was to note once again the intimate connection that doubtlessly exists between the emancipatory efforts of women and the economic development tendencies of society. By not losing sight of this tendency, it will be easier for us to clarify the path to be followed by women who broadly understand the task of complete and comprehensive liberation for women.

To the question of what women wishing to stand up for their trodden-on rights and interests should do, bourgeois ideologues hasten to reply: 'join a general women's organisation'. Women, like other socially weak elements, must organise and struggle together against their oppressors: men. 'In modern Russia,' says Prof. Khvostov, 'we find quite a few energetic women, despite the countless obstacles standing in the path to knowledge and freedom, but we do not find the sort of organisations here that are so well represented in the women's movement, and all movements, abroad.[11] Meanwhile, serious success in social matters is only possible on the basis of organised, cohesive efforts. Thus, if Russian women, too, wish to achieve anything, they must organise and seek to bring out in themselves the properties necessary for social activity.'

Such advice was not given in vain: Over the past few years, we have seen women's feminist organisations appear one after another. Feminism in Russia, in the sense in which we are accustomed to understanding it, is certainly a new phenomenon. The first feminist journal, *Zhenskoye Dyelo* (Women's Cause) began being published in 1899.[12] For many years, the emancipatory efforts of Russian women were limited to the slogan of 'equal education rights to men'. Starting in the 1860s, when the female question first made itself known here, and up until the last few years, the women's movement was nothing other than a history of struggle for the expansion and broader availability of education to women, particularly higher education. Not without justification, women of the bourgeois classes saw in the success of these first efforts one of the most important ways to broaden the sphere of women's intellectual work, which served as the principal guarantee of their economic independence. When the emancipation of the peasantry fundamentally changed economic and so-cial relations in Russia, requiring a significant portion of the population to seek out the means to survive, the 'female question' was born in Russia. Together with intellectual workers, the reformed structure threw a there-tofore unknown type of woman onto the labour market, who, like her brothers, sought work that would provide her daily bread. In the mouths of Russian women, the common women's slogan – 'freedom to work' – transformed into a demand for freedom of education, given that, without it, all the doors to paid intellectual work would remain closed to them. Of course, after completing higher education, women also demanded free access to state and private employment, and this demand was imple-mented on the basis of a simple economic calculation, by which private entrepreneurs and state institutions became aware of the benefit of using cheaper and more compliant female labour.

The scope of application of women's intellectual work gradually broad-ened, but for women, the slogan remained: 'freedom of education and occupation'. Equal political rights were not even up for discussion; after all, men were just as disenfranchised at the time. As for civil legal ca-pacity, the position of Russian women in this area was relatively tolerable compared to their comrades in western Europe;[13] as such, there were no particular impulses for feminist campaigning in this regard.

It goes without saying that the women's movement currently under discussion was clearly bourgeois in character; it encompassed a relatively narrow group of women, predominantly of the nobility, with an admix-ture of elements of the 'other orders' that were then arising. No socialist ideals can be found in the demands of the leading campaigners for wom-en's equality in Russia. To be sure, Russian industry recruited thousands and thousands of new proletarian women each year, but there was appar-ently such a gulf between emancipated female intellectuals and female workers with callused hands that there was simply no question of any points of convergence between them.

The women of the two opposed social camps only came into contact in the field of philanthropy. From the very beginnings of the women's movement in Russia, philanthropy has been at the centre, as indeed it has everywhere else where women's organisations have not yet achieved self-definition.[14] All women's organisations that existed in Russia until the last few years were primarily philanthropic in character. Women organised and formed societies not in order to win reforms in the area of women's equality, but to carry out private acts of charity. From the most active groups, the 'societies for the provision of means for women's higher education', to the first women's club, founded by the Women's Mutual Philanthropic Society, all such organisations pursued philanthropic ends, as can be seen from their very names.

In noting this, we do not wish to accuse Russian women of indifference to social and political matters. Can any other country boast such a number of truly majestic and engaging female exemplars of 'nameless heroines', giving of their strength, youth, indeed their whole life to the struggle for the ideals of social justice and political liberation for their country? What in history can be compared with the appeal of the inner beauty of the 'repentant noblewomen' of the 1870s, who, together with their courtly clothing, threw away all of the privileges of 'blue blood' to join with the people and pay them even part of the debts owed them by their class . . . And later, when repression inevitably turned every protest into a fierce battle with the old authorities, how many heroines arose from the midst of Russian women to astound the world with their selflessness, their mental strength, their immeasurable devotion to the people . . . The 'repentant noblewoman', that delicate, spiritually beautiful face of womanhood, was followed by the majestic fearlessness of the women of the 'other orders', who were followed by an uninterrupted, endless procession of martyred working-class women, who fought for the liberation of their class . . . The ranks of female martyrs in the struggle for the ideals of social justice are constantly filled with new sacrifices, and future historians of our time can only bow down before these shining examples of female fighters and martyrs . . .

But they are not the subject at hand. We are speaking here exclusively of women struggling for so-called women's emancipation. In this specific field, the tasks and efforts of our first feminists were quite narrow and limited.

Charity and education – that was the sphere of activity of women's organisations until the last few years. Even the first women's congress, which was proposed in 1905, intended to limit its tasks to matters of philanthropy and education.[15]

The picture dramatically changes following those memorable days in January. The revolutionary current affecting all strata of the population carried off even the feminists, whose demands had previously been modest. Women's circles raised their heads, came to life with new enthusiasm. Courageous speeches and radical demands could be heard. Statements, demands, and petitions flew into *zemstvo* and city government, and into radical union organisations. There followed a series of assemblies and meetings with decisive political resolutions. In 1905, it seems, there was no corner of Russian life where the voices of women could not be heard, making their presence known and demanding new civil rights for themselves as well. The feminists, whose aims had been modest not long before, felt that the rebirth of the country and the creation of a new state structure were also indispensable prerequisites for women's emancipation. 'Until now,' we read in one women's declaration,

> woman had been able to accept the inadequacies of her position and find an explanation for her disenfranchisement in the disenfranchisement of all. Now, however, on the eve of an overall reassessment of rights, she must not be silent. She has the right to stand together with everyone and demand the recognition of her equality, particularly given that life itself has already demonstrated her capacity for labour. We firmly believe that a time is beginning in our homeland in which the initiative and energy of all citizens will have an opportunity to be applied. It is time to put an end to the abnormal legal position of woman, which restricts her even in the sphere of property rights. Though she is subject to all duties and pays all taxes, she has no voice in their allocation and distribution, and is deprived of an opportunity to provide that benefit to her homeland of which she feels capable.[16]

The women's movement is abandoning its previously humble direction and taking a new social path. This, of course, did not occur without friction. Amongst the new elements rushing to join the ranks of women's organisations, two tendencies have become clearly identifiable: Some, more left-leaning elements, insisted on the need to precisely define their general political credo, and brought the struggle for *political* equality for women to the fore; the right-wing elements, on the other hand, held fast to old traditions and did not wish to bring 'politics' into their narrow feminist efforts. In April 1905, the Alliance for Women's Equality was formed by the more left-leaning elements: the first women's organisation in Russia to adopt a specific political platform. Meanwhile, the right wing carried on coalescing around the Women's Mutual Philanthropic Society and the *Zhenskiy Vyestnik*, implementing the idea of a politically neutral feminism. The AWE spread its branches throughout Russia, and within only one year, by May 1906, according to the bureau's figures, counted around eight thousand members in their ranks.[17] In accordance with their vague slogans, the organisation sought to recruit women from all social classes. And just as, in their youth, the Cadets spoke in the name of the people as a whole, the AWE presented themselves as expressing the demands of all Russian women. However, the constant growth of class consciousness and the inevitable differentiation of the social strata of the population resulted in further restructuring, including that of female elements of society. The political block that was suited to the well-known objectives in the heyday of the 'Alliance of Alliances' increasingly became an obstacle, particularly given that many equal-rights campaigners had political convictions that positioned them adjacent to specific political parties.

Already in spring 1906, the following tendencies split from the Saint Petersburg branch of the AWE: On the one hand, 'leftist' equal-rights campaigners, whose political convictions positioned them adjacent to the revolutionary parties, and on the other, the 'right', which founded the Women's Progressive Party (*Женская прогрессивная партия*, WPP),[18] were kindred spirits of the 'peaceful renovationists', and were just as weak in numbers and strength as the latter. Both of these breakaway women's organisations made their activities known by forming political clubs, the former more or less democratic in nature,[19] the latter maintaining their bourgeois colouring with high membership dues, etc.

The coalescence of women of different social strata around politically heterogeneous banners took place on its own, independently of the will

---

*   Members of the Party of Peaceful Renovation – *Партия мирного обновления* —Trans.

and desires of the passionate champions of the unification of all women in a single organisation. The Women's Progressive Party expressed the demands and petitions of women of the upper strata of the bourgeoisie, and, whilst continuing to proclaim the necessity of uniting all women without regard to class and political convictions, they developed their own political programme that responded to the aspirations of the social stratum whose spokespersons they were in reality. The AWE brought together representatives of the 'Cadet'-type liberal opposition; those who coalesced – and continue to do so today – around the AWE were women of the middle bourgeoisie, primarily intellectuals. The Women's Political Club in Saint Petersburg was endorsed by significantly more radical elements, but, here, too, the political bloc was rendered accessible by the vagueness of the objectives and of the character of the organisation as a whole.[20] Having dissociated themselves from all of the more moderately inclined women's organisations, however, the members of the Women's Political Club were unable to clarify to themselves or others what class of the population they represented and what their most immediate objectives were. Should they stand in defence of the interests of proletarian and peasant women, or of 'working women' as a whole? Should they pursue specific feminist goals or operate on the broader political terrain? The short-lived activity of the WPC was characterised by their vacillation between these fundamental objectives. When the question arose in the Club of whether to submit to the first State Duma a petition calling for the extension of the franchise to women, a petition primarily bearing the signatures of urban working-class women, there was serious confusion amongst the Club's members: The Club were utterly able to clarify to themselves what political party was actually closer to them ideologically, and ultimately sent the petition to the Trudoviks.

At a time when women still spoke of the need for a women's block, reality demonstrated the illusory nature of such a plan in the most obvious and irreversible way. Just like the men, the female elements in society quickly and inexorably divided up and differentiated. The coalescence of women in feminist organisations of varying degrees of political radicalism occurred on its own, quite independently of the will of the advocates of women's unity, as a result of the inexorable growth in the class consciousness of Russian society as a whole. The era of the women's political bloc came to an end not long after that of the men's liberal bloc. Nonetheless, feminists and equal-rights campaigners of all stripes continue to shout that all women need to unite closely and that an all-women's party, pursuing specifically female objectives, is possible. 'How should we be, what should we do, when men are only willing to move closer together to give us space at their side under a concentrated onslaught from us?' argue the equal-rights campaigners who defend the need for the formation of an all-women's organisation.

However, it would only make sense to pose the question in this way if *not one* of the existing political parties had included demands for women's full emancipation in its programme.

Arming themselves against the indifference, or even hostility, of men to the issue of women's equality, feminists only take into account representatives of bourgeois liberalism of all stripes, ignoring the existence of a numerically strong political party that goes further on the issue of women's equality than even the most vehement equal-rights campaigners. Ever since the *Communist Manifesto* appeared in 1848, social democracy has always stood in defence of women's interests. The *Communist Manifesto* was the first to note the intimate connection existing between the problem of the proletariat as a whole and the female question; it tracked the way in which capitalism increasingly brings women into production and makes them participants in the great struggle of the proletariat against oppression and exploitation. Social-democratic parties were the first to include in their programmes the demand for women's rights to be equal to those of men; orally and in print, social democracy has always called for an end to all restrictions to which women are subject; and only under social-democratic pressure have other parties and governments been forced to carry out reforms in the interest of the female population.[21] In Russia, too, this party not only defends women's interests in theory, but puts the principle of women's equality into practice everywhere and at all times.

What, then, prevents our 'equal-rights campaigners' seeking the protection of this powerful and experienced party? Though right-wing feminists are scared off by the 'extremism' of social democracy, the AWE, who call for a Constituent Assembly – the political position of the social democrats – ought to be quite pleased with it. But . . . therein lies the rub! For all their political 'radicalism', our equal-rights campaigners never depart from the yearnings of their own bourgeois class. Political freedom is now a *conditio sine qua non* of the growth and power of the Russian bourgeoisie; without it, all of their economic prosperity is built on sand. Capital requires certain standards and safeguards in order to grow and prosper; these standards can only be provided if representatives of the bourgeoisie participate in the running of the country. The conquest of equal political rights, which are as valuable to men as to women, is now on the agenda. For women, the demand for political equality is a necessity dictated by life itself.

Women no longer see the slogan 'free choice of occupation' as a catch-all; only women's direct participation in the political life of the country promises to bring about an improvement in their economic well-being. Hence the passionate desire of women of the middle bourgeoisie at last to be granted access to the ballot box, hence their hostility to the contemporary bureaucratic structure . . .

However, our feminists' demands for political equality go no further, as is the case with their sisters abroad; the broad horizons opened up by the teachings of social democracy remain alien and incomprehensible to them. The feminists seek to obtain equality within the context of the existing class society, and in no way fundamentally oppose the latter; they are struggling for their prerogatives as women, and by no means seek to put an end to all existing prerogatives and privileges . . .

We do not blame the representatives of bourgeois feminism for this 'involuntary transgression.' It arises inevitably from their class position. Nor do we wish to detract from the significance of feminist organisations in the successes of the purely bourgeois women's movement. We would, however, like to warn the female proletariat against getting caught up in narrow feminist objectives.

As long as bourgeois women limit their activities to raising the consciousness of their own sisters, their activities can only be welcomed; however, the moment they begin calling proletarian women to their ranks, social democrats cannot, indeed must not, be silent. We cannot be indifferent to the pointless waste of the strength of the proletariat; in this case, we must pose the question directly: What do proletarian women have to gain from uniting with their bourgeois 'sisters', and what do working-class women stand to gain by relying on the organisation of their own class?

Above all, we ask: Can there be *one* women's movement in a society based on class antagonism? It is clear to any unbiased observer that the women participating in the movement for their liberation are not a homogeneous mass.[22]

The world of women, like that of men, is divided into two camps: One has objectives, efforts, and interests positioning it adjacent to the bourgeois classes; the other is closely linked to the proletariat, whose liberatory efforts also include a solution to all aspects of the female question. The objectives, interests, and means of struggle of the two categories of women in the struggle are different, although they are both guided by the shared slogan of 'women's liberation'. Each of the groups in the struggle unconsciously aligns itself with the interests of its own class, which, en masse, gives their efforts and tasks a specific class character. An individual woman may stand above her class interests and neglect them for the sake of another class, but not a cohesive women's organisation that reflects all of the real needs and interests of the social group that created it. However radical the demands of the feminists might appear, we must not lose sight of the fact that, by virtue of their class position, they cannot fight for the fundamental reconstruction of the economic and social structure of the society, without which women's liberation cannot be complete.

Although the most immediate tasks of women of all classes may coincide in individual cases, the ultimate goals of the two camps, which define the direction they take, and even their tactics, differ drastically. For the feminists, the objective of winning rights equal to men's, within the confines of our present capitalist world, is an entirely concrete 'end in itself';[23] for proletarian women, equality now is merely the *means* for further struggle against the economic enslavement of the working class. For the feminists, the immediate adversary is men in general, who unjustly hoard for themselves all rights and privileges, leaving women with only chains and obligations. Every feminist victory marks a concession by men of their exclusive prerogatives to the benefit of the 'fair sex'. Proletarian women relate to their position in a totally different way: Men in their eyes are by no means adversaries and oppressors; above all, they are comrades sharing in the same joyless lot, loyal allies in the struggle for a better future. The very same social relations enslave women and their male comrades; the same odious chains of capitalism shackle their will and deprive them of the joys and beauties of life. To be sure, some particular aspects of the present system weigh doubly on women; likewise, the conditions of wage labour convert women from men's friends into their pernicious competitors. But the working class know who is to blame for these adverse conditions . . .

Working-class women, no less than their brothers in misfortune, hate the insatiable monster with the gilded maw that falls upon men, women, and children with equal greed so as to siphon off their juices and live high on the hog, growing at the expense of millions of human lives . . . Thousands of threads durably link working-class women to their male comrades, whilst the efforts of bourgeois women appear alien and incomprehensible to them; they do not warm the suffering proletarian soul; they do not promise women the bright future upon which all of exploited humanity looks with hope and expectation . . . At the same time as feminists, speaking of the need for a women's bloc, reach out to their little sisters, proletarian women, these 'churlish creatures' look upon their remote and alien fellow women with distrust, coalescing more tightly around the purely proletarian organisations near and dear to them that they understand.

Political rights, access to the ballot box and the deputy's seat—those are the real objectives of the bourgeois women's movement. But can political equality grant the women of the working class liberation from the abyss of evil and suffering that persecutes and oppresses them as women and as human beings whilst the exploitative capitalist structure remains intact?

The most conscious proletarian women know that neither political nor legal equality can solve the female question as a whole. As long as women are forced to sell their labour power and live in capitalist bondage, as long as the present exploitative manner of producing new value remains alive, they will not be free, independent human beings, wives who choose husbands based only on their hearts' desires, mothers who look upon their children's future without fear . . . The ultimate goal of proletarian women is the abolition of the old world of class antagonism and the construction of a new, better world in which the means of exploitation of human beings by human beings will no longer exist.

Of course, this ultimate goal does not mean that proletarian women cannot struggle for emancipation even within the current bourgeois way of life, but the realisation of such demands always runs into obstacles erected by the capitalist structure itself. Women can only become truly free and equal in a world of socialised labour, harmony, and justice.

The feminists neither desire this, nor can they understand it: In their view, the achievement of formal equality, guaranteed by the letter of the law, would suit them perfectly even within the 'old world of oppression, enslavement, groaning, and tears'. And, to a certain degree, this is true: Although equal rights to men for most proletarian women would merely mean 'equal disenfranchisement', for the 'select few', the bourgeois women, it would indeed open the door to new, never-before-seen rights and privileges, heretofore available only to men of the bourgeois class. However, every such victory, every new prerogative acquired by bourgeois women would merely give them a new tool by which to exploit their little sisters, and further deepen the abyss that separates the women of the two opposing social camps. Their interests would conflict more drastically, more acutely; their respective efforts would counteract each other.

Where, then, is this shared 'female question', this unity of tasks and efforts about which the feminists have so much to say? A sober look at reality shows that such unity does not exist and cannot exist. In vain, feminists seek to convince themselves that 'the female question is by no means a partisan political issue' and that 'it can be solved only with the participation of all parties and all women', as the German radical feminist Minna Cauer says; the logic of the facts refutes this self-aggrandisement that is so comforting to the feminists.

It would be pointless to prove to all bourgeois women that the victory of the cause of women depends on the victory of the proletariat as a whole, but, to those of them who can forsake the narrow tasks of the 'politics of the moment' and can take a broader view of women's shared fate, we strongly advise them not to recruit their proletarian sisters, whose minds are alien to them, into their ranks. Rid yourselves of the lush veneer of idealistic phraseology with which you – the women of the bourgeois classes – so like to drape yourselves, and, armed with the sober lessons of history, defend your own class rights and interests, allowing proletarian women to go another way and struggle by different means for women's rights and happiness. Life itself will show whose path is the shortest and whose methods the most reliable . . .

CHAPTER 1

WOMEN'S STRUGGLE FOR ECONOMIC INDEPENDENCE

> The female question, like the modern labour question, is a creature
> of large-scale production, revolutionised by the application of
> the mechanical power of steam and electricity. It is neither a
> political nor a moral question (although it does include political
> and moral elements), but rather an economic question.
>
> *Clara Zetkin*

The female question is ultimately a question of bread. It is deeply rooted in economics. In order to decide to demand equality with men, above all, women had to become economically independent.

Why is it that women began their journey of liberation specifically in the nineteenth century? Why is it that the 'female question' only became a constant concern when female labour became ubiquitous? Surely, there were remarkable women before? Surely, they felt the horror of their oppression just as acutely? Surely, they – these women of the past – were no less worthy of freedom and equality? Let us recall the days of antiquity, the notable *hetairai*, women who taught the ancient philosophers, advisers of the great men of Greece . . . Let us recall the images of the women at the beginning of the Middle Ages, full of delicate, spiritual beauty, the titanic characters of the Renaissance . . . Women were placed on a pedestal, *dithyrambs* were sung to them, they were hated, feared, and nonetheless, it never would have seriously occurred to anyone to demand that they be granted equal rights with men. Though individual great thinkers, foreshadowing the course of human history, occasionally came out in defence of the 'fair sex', their voices remained shouts in the desert. The conditions and forms of production have enslaved women over the entire length of human history, and gradually relegated to the degree of oppression and dependency in which the majority of them find themselves even today.

It took a colossal upheaval of the entire socio-economic structure of society to return to women the significance and independence that they had lost. That which was beyond the power of the most ingenious thinkers has now been achieved by the soulless, but all-powerful conditions of production. The same forces that once consigned woman to millennia of slavery, are, in the latest phase of their development, leading her back to the road of freedom and independence.

The female question, i.e., the conflict between the current disenfranchised position of women and their awakening consciousness of their personhood and their equality with men, could only arise as the result of a collision between the encrusted forms of social life and the relations of production that have grown beyond them. As long as women did not directly participate in commodity production, as long as their labour was largely limited to the acquisition of goods for domestic needs, a 'female question' was completely inconceivable. In remote villages not yet caught up in the all-powerful commodity cycle, there is no 'female question' even now. In order for it to arise, specific objective conditions are indispensable: Women must be economically independent, whilst their socio-political disenfranchisement remains unchanged. Only when women began producing commodities for the domestic or world market could their work become subject to social valuation, and a substantial change in their social position became necessary.

Leaving aside the entire long, highly instructive history of the legal and social position of women in relation to the development and evolution of economic forms, we will merely cast a glance at the Middle Ages to catch the first glimpses of women's struggle for economic independence. In the small-scale craftwork of the Middle Ages, we encounter not only the first proletarians to throw off feudal bondage and bring their 'free' labour power to the labour market, but also the first 'free' women trading their labour en masse.

The pauperisation of the villages, the impoverishment of the peasantry, the endless wars, the horrifying mortality of the most mobile element of the population, men, who were subject to the thousands of dangers, diseases, and other hazards that abounded in the Middle Ages, made possible the rapid growth in the number of solitary women, lacking economic security, who were thrown onto the general labour market.[1] Driven by hunger, loneliness, and the need to feed their blood relations, women in the second half of the Middle Ages knocked on the workshop door as insistently as they now knock on the doors of the factory offices, taking their place alongside apprentices, journeymen, and even master craftsmen.

Women not only entered the most diverse branches of production, but even took over entire workshops. Textile production had been considered a female speciality since ancient times, and, although weaving in the twelfth century was a predominantly male field, spinning and carding wool, and winding it onto coils, remained in the hands of women. In the late Middle Ages, we find an enormous contingent of female carders, spinners, winders, and spoolers in some cities (e.g., Frankfurt) who were under special observation by the members of the municipality. In the same time period, there was a special workshop of female winders in Cologne, who were required by the workshop charter to remain apprenticed for six years, whilst the female masters were not permitted to have more than three workers. The weaving trade itself did not exclude female workers everywhere; thus, for example, in Munich, a weavers' workshop even recruited women in an effort to put a stop to competition by unorganised female labour.[2] Canvas weaving and veil weaving and washing were trades that already belonged to women *in toto*.[3] In the fourteenth and even the fifteenth century, the production of ropes and braids was still a primarily female speciality. French women silk weavers and spinners, knitters, and milliners in the thirteenth and fourteenth centuries were united in independent, almost exclusively female, workshops; in thirteenth-century Cologne, there were a number of 'women's guilds': seamstresses, spinners, embroiderers, and wool and gold spinners. In the tailoring trade, to be sure, women were constantly displaced by men, and lengthy disputes arose between tailors and seamstresses. However, even in the fourteenth century in Frankfurt, Mainz, and other cities on the

Rhine, seamstresses were even allowed access to workshops on relatively generous terms; thus, women wishing to engage in tailoring were required to contribute only 30 shillings rather than 3 pounds and only half a quarter rather than a full quarter of wine upon entering the workshop. Women were allowed access on equal terms to the following workshops: skinners (Silesia, Frankfurt), belt makers, heraldry weavers (Strasbourg, Cologne), rosary makers (Lübeck), clothiers (Frankfurt), tanners, and gold spinners and goldsmiths (Cologne).

Female labour in the Middle Ages was most widespread in the following, partially guild-based, partially 'free' branches of production: candle making, felt making, fullery, linen spinning and weaving, gold embroidery, white embroidery, tailoring, baking, and strap making. Additionally, women could also be found in a whole array of other professions: lace makers, trimming makers, knitters, patchworkers, furriers, laundresses, burlap makers, basket weavers, bath attendants, and even barbers.[4]

Women were also employed in commerce: Female market traders, food traders (fruits, cheeses, eggs, hens, salt, etc.), dealers, and rag traders were by no means rare in the deep Middle Ages.

The extent of women's participation in medieval production can be seen from city records recording the taxable population, which at the time only included persons occupied in some trade. In Frankfurt from 1354 to 1463, women made up 18 to 25 percent of the taxable population.[5]

Women sought to enter every field of labour accessible to them: Where there was no space for them in the workshops, they sought salvation from their defenceless isolation and poverty under the protection of the convents, the dedicated women's workshops for *béguines*, 'houses of God', etc.

But as female labour spread from one trade to the next, the natural hostility of men to their dangerous, cheap female competition grew. Initially, men tried to neutralise unorganised female labour by requiring women to join the workshops. However, as competition grew within the workshops, as independent female guilds and workshops formed to defend their economic interests, the tactics of their male competitors changed. One after another, the workshops began limiting women's access, persecuting and severely punishing masters who recruited persons of the female sex to their shops.[6] Masters tenaciously clung to the privileges of the workshops and, in order to deny access to the trades to 'vagabonds' seeking salvation from the horrors of arbitrary feudal rule, issued more and more restrictive regulations: The apprenticeship periods became longer, the expenses of acquiring the title of journeyman were increased, any hope of becoming an independent master was definitively dashed. Female labour was eradicated in the most shameless manner.

However, as strict and inventive as the workshop statutes were, the restrictive tactics of men would have been useless in the struggle against cheap female labour had a powerful ally not come to their aid: the *productive forces*. On the cusp of new eras, new types of production that evades the restrictive regulations of the workshops are found more and more. The countless idle hands of starving proletarians sought employment outside of the workshops: There appeared the method of distributing work to be done at home via intermediaries or masters. Women grabbed onto this form of work, which was particularly accessible to them, with the covetousness born of hunger. The new form of production evicted women from the masters' shops and, by all appearances, returned them forever to home and hearth. But this 'homecoming' was nothing short of ruinous for women. After all, women had already reached the threshold of economic independence; it seemed that one more push was all they needed in order to be recognised as fully fledged workers. And yet, at that very moment, the blind forces of economics unilaterally decided their fate. The most horrible, most outrageous form of exploitation of wage labour took root side by side with regulated, dignified workshop-based production. Examples of such an exploitative system of production exist even today in the form of the sweating system.* Home-based labour drained women of all of their life force, dumping double work – professional and strictly domestic – on their weak shoulders.

Over the entire artisanal production period, we see women in their own dark, smoky huts, their hands silently and invisibly supplying the world market with luxuries and basic necessities. Only on the condition that they hunched their backs over their weaving, spinning, embroidery, leather gouging, etc. could women's work endure competition with the hated workshops, the monopolists, the darlings of fate, the aristocrats of

---

* 'Sweeting system' in original —Trans.

labour. This is why proletarian women in France so insisted on the abolition of workshop restrictions and greeted their abolition with such joy in 1791, considering it the first step on the way to their economic liberation. However, in order for such an upheaval in social and legal relations to take place, the productive forces once again had to intervene. The exclusivity of the trades and workshops drove women into the home; the grey lord steam called her back to the road of open labour.

Machines played an enormous role in women's assertion of their economic independence. 'Anyone wishing to write the history of proletarian women's labour in the nineteenth century', says Lily Braun, 'would have to write the history of machines at the same time; it was the machine that, like a master sorcerer, called endless droves of pallid women away from the quiet domestic hearth with its monotonous rattling noise and its fiery breath and bound them to be its servants.'[7] It was factory work that, for the first time since the Middle Ages, once again gave women the opportunity to exist independently, with the sole difference that, whilst only a relatively small number of women had previously been involved in producing goods, now, the number of wage-earning women, already quite significant, is constantly growing every day and in every country. However, as soon as women felt the solid ground of economic independence under their feet, their former disenfranchisement in society, their former subjugation in the family, became twice as bitter and intolerable. As early as the days of the great French Revolution, dissatisfaction amongst women with their social and economic position reached such levels of tension that the 'daughters of the people' joined in those great events with all the passion of impulsive female hearts. Poverty in Paris and Lyon – those leading industrial centres – reached gigantic proportions;[8] prostitution grew to a horrible degree. In Paris at the end of the eighteenth century, up to seventy thousand prostitutes were counted. Hunger and poverty held sway in proletarian neighbourhoods; children dropped like flies. Women's suffering, for themselves and their children, exceeded all tolerances. 'Of two workers' delegations that appeared before the National Assembly seeking aid,' Lily Braun tells us, 'one was made up of and sent by women. They came like children to their fathers:* They complained of their poverty, asked for help, but they themselves did not even know how they could be helped.'[9] The opportunity to acquire the means to live, the right to an 'honest crust' – that was the basic slogan of the proletarian women in the days of the Revolution. In one of the women's petitions to the king, they sought the same rights to work as men, for men to be denied access to areas of female labour, in exchange for which they were willing to commit to refrain from working in specifically male trades. 'We want work not to usurp men's authority, but in order somehow to make a living.'

Women's wish was fulfilled to a greater extent than they could have expected. But it was not the king who answered their entreaties. It was that force that, albeit soulless, was mightier than any king: *capitalism*, which tirelessly carried on with the work of destroying and creating at the same time, incorporating women into one area of production after another like a force of nature. By subjecting and enslaving women to its will, capitalism steadily put them on the road to their economic independence. It was not the feminists with their proud rallying cry to 'make way for women', but proletarian women who cleared this thorny path for women with their own bosoms.

Proletarian women fought for the freedom to work at a time when working at all was considered a disgrace by bourgeois women. Bourgeois women comfortably sheltered in the domestic shell, prospering from the labour of their husbands, fathers, or lovers, at the same time as proletarian women in the merciless struggle for their daily bread were making the feminist battle cry – 'right to work' – a practical reality.

* * *

For women of the bourgeois classes, the female question arose significantly later than proletarian women's entry into the path of labour, approximately in the mid-nineteenth century. When, under the influence

---

* The translation Kollontai relies on omits a sentence immediately before this one: *Ihr Auftreten war so naiv und ungeschickt wie möglich* (Their attitude was as naive and inept as possible). —Trans.

of the monstrous successes of capitalism, the wave of insecurity reached the middle classes of the population, when the economic upheaval in progress rendered precarious and unreliable the economic welfare of the petit and middle bourgeoisie, bourgeois women found themselves confronted by a terrible dilemma: Either descend into poverty or win the right to work. The daughters and wives of the middle and petite bourgeoisie began knocking at the doors of the universities, artists' ateliers, editorial offices, offices, etc., flooding every branch of the 'liberal professions'. Their aspiration to learning, to the higher spiritual values, was not a need that suddenly erupted amongst bourgeois women; it was once again just the question of 'a crust'.

From the first steps they took on the path of labour, the women of the bourgeoisie found their efforts met with the harshest opposition by men. There followed a hard and silent struggle between male professionals defending their 'warm spot' and female newcomers to the winning of bread. It is this struggle that gave rise to 'feminism', bourgeois women's involuntary urge to come together, lean on one another, and join forces to resist a common enemy: men. But the feminists who entered the workforce, proudly proclaiming themselves the 'vanguard of the women's movement', forget in vain that, in the conquest of economic independence, as in all other areas, they merely follow in the footsteps of their little sisters and benefit from the labour of their callused hands.

In point of fact, it is impossible to claim seriously that the feminists 'made way' for women to enter the workforce, when, in every country, the bourgeois women's movement has come into being at a time when proletarian women were already flooding the factories and workshops in their hundreds of thousands, taking over one branch of industry after another. It is only the recognition of the value of working-class women's labour on the world market that made it possible for bourgeois women to occupy that independent position in society that is the pride of the feminists.

We need only look to England, a country at the forefront of the bourgeois women's movement. What do we see there? At the end of the eighteenth century, there were 142 paper spinneries, employing 35,000 children and 31,000 women alongside 26,000 men; at the same time, not a peep could yet be heard of a struggle of bourgeois women for the 'freedom to work'. On the cusp of the nineteenth century, only the solitary voice of Mary Wollstonecraft demanded that the standards of women's and girls' education be raised and women be allowed to share in the benefits of culture in order to prepare them to be 'better mothers'. In 1841, English industry already employed approximately half a million female workers (of 464,000 female workers, 258,000 were employed in textile production and 177,000 in garment production); they participated most actively in the class struggle, and fought in the ranks of the Chartist movement. Already in 1842, the trade unions counted many female weavers in Lancashire amongst their members, and a fair number of women participated in Owen's Grand National Consolidated Trades Union.[10]

The proletarian women of England are experiencing all the adversity of the class struggle, and occupying a prominent place amongst the wage-earning population at a time when their bourgeois sisters are only taking their first timid steps on the path to economic emancipation.

Above all, access to the worst-paid professions—teachers and civil servants in the postal and telegraph services—was opened to the women of the bourgeoisie; the demand for cheap intellectual labour on the part of the state, municipal institutions, and industrial and commercial enterprises, which had expanded due to the increased tempo of life, played a significant role in attracting bourgeois women to independent labour. In 1858, the international telegraph agency hired women for the first time; in 1846, the first institution of higher education – the women's teaching seminary—opened its doors to women. 'The English census of 1881 does not mention a single occupation belonging to women outside the category of domestic service; the 1881 census, on the other hand, already lists 331 different women's occupations.'[11] Slowly, positions as teachers, bookkeepers, civil servants, stenographers, etc. gradually opened up to women. Women's economic independence gave rise to a natural dissatisfaction with their political disenfranchisement and social subordination. Only in the 1860s did the bourgeois women's movement take any serious measures, that is, at a time when the proletarian women's movement, closely linked to the class struggle of the proletariat, could already look back on an entire history.

In France, the famous *nouvelle femme* of the Third Estate, who had begun to walk the path of liberation in the '80s, merely repeated the slogans of the 'daughters of the people', who had defended their right to work and bread in the face of the most terrible convent. Opening the doors of the intellectual professions and the universities – those were the basic demands of French bourgeois women. In other words, they stood in defence of the slogan of 'freedom to work' at a time when the women of the working class had already come to curse this freedom and reminded society in the bloody events in Lyon that 'the free exploitation of male and female labour does have its limits'.[12]

In Germany, the bourgeois women's movement, pursuing the same goals as in other countries – access to the intellectual professions – came into being in the '60s. Meanwhile, the rise of large-scale industry in Germany had long since created vast cadres of wage-earning proletarian women, and these women, particularly the weavers, had already managed to taste the full sweetness of the 'right to work' in the contemporary exploitative structure.

In the United States, the bourgeois women's movement has achieved particularly fast victories. However, we must not lose sight of the sui generis conditions of economic life in the US. There is no other country where women have participated in production to the same extent as in the US. The colonist farmers, the early legislators of social and legal standards in the US, required the labour power of their wives and daughters; their welfare depended on the labour of their families. Women were workers not only in the home, but in the fields, the pastures, and the forest. They suffered all of the vagaries of the struggle with strange and wild nature; they defended their families' property from plunder by the natives with rifles in their hands. The fact that American women were not only consumers and distributors of goods acquired by men, but independent producers of them, granted them an entirely special position. In societal consciousness, they were seen as social units equal in value to men. As such, they felt their political disenfranchisement all the more acutely; they felt the injustice of being ignored as citizens by state institutions that much more. In the US, the influence of the proletariat on women's access to the various fields of labour was observed less than anywhere else. Nonetheless, the women's movement never would have reached such intensity if, at the time it arose, it did not rely on the enormous and rapidly growing contingent of working-class women. In 1816, in just a few Massachusetts spinneries, sixty-six thousand women were employed alongside ten thousand men, and at the dawn of the American feminist movement in the '60s, when the first women's colleges were founded and the doors of the intellectual professions were opened to women, working-class women already looked back on a long and grim history of the development of professional proletarian labour.

The emancipatory aspirations of Russian bourgeois women coincided with the enlivening of economic and state life in Russia in the '60s. Worker shortages in the professions – physicians, teachers, civil servants, etc. – granted women access to these professions and temporarily allowed them through the tightly guarded doors of the institutions of higher education. But the female professionals surely were not the first women to enter the path of labour and conquer one occupation after another. Even in the days of serfdom in Russia, proletarian labour was already widespread amongst women; in many factories, particularly in textile production, the number of women already exceeded that of men at the beginning of the century.[13] Cursing the dreary fate that had opened such space for the exploitation of women's labour, female manufacturing workers worked eighteen hours a day; in their huts, female artisans went blind over their spinning, weaving, embroidery, not suspecting that they – proletarian women cursed by fate – were opening up the path for the free, equal women of the future. And yet this downtrodden, apparently resigned and obedient female 'slave of labour' was always able to fight amicably and fearlessly for the needs of the proletariat as a whole, to raise her voice every time the cup of working-class tolerance overflowed with terrible force on the horrified exploiters. Women's participation in the 'factory riots' of the '40s and '50s was as unavoidable as their participation in factory work. However, in defending their economic interests in this way, and fighting for more bearable working conditions, female workers also laid a solid foundation for the economic independence of bourgeois women. Proletarian women's labour convinced the world of women's ability to produce commodities; since then, the doors of independent incomes also began to open to women of other social classes.

* * *

As the first to walk the path of labour, proletarian women dominate the ranks of wage-earning women to this day.

Let us acquaint ourselves with the distribution of the wage-earning female population over the basic branches of labour and the ratio of bourgeois and proletarian labour by women based on the most recent census data.

Country	Census year	Female wage labour		Women in liberal professions, intellectual labour		All wage-earning women
		In thous.	In %	In thous.	In %	
Austria	1890	5,310	85	935	15	6,245
Germany	1895	5,293	80	180	3	6,578
France	1891	3,584	69	300	6	5,191
England	1891	3,113	78	307	8	4,016
US	1890	2,865	74	312	8	3,915

In Germany, female labour is most widespread in the agricultural field: Thus, according to the 1895 census, 2.758 million women were working in this field. This is followed by industry, which employs 1.521 million female workers, followed in turn by trade and transport, in which 579,500 women were counted. Lastly, in the professions and the civil service, there were only 180,000 women; the remainder in the statistics represents 'unspecified' or 'variable' occupations. In France, too, agriculture still employs the greatest number of female workers; of the total number of wage-earning women in France, 1.8 million were employed in agriculture, 1.4 million in industry, 600,000 in trade and transport, and only 300,000 in the professions. In England, industry recruits the greatest number of women, employing 2.382 million women (of which 845,000 in textile production and 884,000 in garment production); 2.170 million are employed in domestic and personal service and 172,000 in agriculture and fisheries; 48,000 are employed in trade, and 307,000 in intellectual labour. In the US, the largest female contingent is found in domestic and personal service, 1.7 million in all. Approximately 1 million are employed in industry, 680,000 in agriculture, 228,000 in trade and transport, and 312,000 in the liberal professions and other intellectual professions.

Compared to the total mass of wage-earning women in the civilised countries, the wage-earning bourgeois women are a mere handful!

Let us now examine the relationship here in Russia between female bourgeois and proletarian labour.

The 6,260,976 wage-earning women are employed as follows:[14]

Agriculture, fisheries, and forestry	2,086,169
Contingent labour, service, and other similar occupations	1,673,605
Industry and mining	982,098
Trade	299,403
Liberal professions, civil service and private sector	126,016
Transport	22,116

Of 2.086 million women wage earners in agriculture, according to Chernyshev's figures,[15] the proletarian contingent comprises only 753,000, or 36.1 percent; however, the actual figure is considerably higher, given that, apart from female labourers and servants, this figure should also include landless peasants working in casual labour, fishing, handicrafts, etc., who are erroneously counted in the statistics as non-proletarian labour, whilst, in point of fact, it is these women, who have no other source of income in agriculture, who are the most deprived and exploited elements of the female population.

In industry, the proletarian element is somewhat larger: Of 982,000 women, it accounts for 389,000, or 39.6 percent. However, even this figure does not entirely correspond to reality; really, a significant number of proletarian women making a living from one sort of industrial labour or another should have been counted here rather than under 'other occupations'.

With regard to the rubric covering 'other occupations or sources of income', here, we see a repetition of the error discussed above: Of 2.186 million women, only 1.622 are attributed in the statistics to the category of proletarian labour, whilst the elastic category of 'other occupations' includes, alongside 564,000 purportedly independent, non-wage workers, many women working for capitalists in their own homes. As such, in point of fact, their work constitutes a mere variant of proletarian labour. In order to demonstrate the truth of the above, it is worth breaking down the groups included in the rubric 'other occupations' in detail. Let us take the independent contingent of at least the largest cities in Russia that is included in this rubric and examine its composition:[16]

Service and day labour	506,000
Persons living on income from assets, funds from institutions, family, etc.	232,000
Persons employed in liberal professions, civil service, etc.	73,000
Persons living on other sources of income	87,000
Total	898,000

Even with this flawed classification, the predominance of proletarians over women having independent bourgeois occupations, i.e. over those women who swell the ranks of the feminists, is impossible to overlook. Women included in the 'wage-earning' category, but living on income from assets, constitute incomparably less propitious material for the emancipatory efforts of the feminists.

In Saint Petersburg, according to the 1900 census, for 13,175 independent women employed in medicine, literature, teaching, etc., as well as those employed in the civil service and private institutions, there were (73,724 + 10,281 =) 84,005 female workers and servants, 13,478 'owners', and 29,702 'independent'. In percent terms, this ratio is expressed as follows:[17]

Owners	11.00%	15.04%
Administrative posts	3.95%	
Female labourers	59.52%	84.94%
Independent	25.42%	

This comparison clearly illustrates the predominance of proletarian groups of women over the remaining categories of wage-earning women. However, this phenomenon is placed in even starker relief by a detailed analysis of female labour in Saint Petersburg in the largest areas of production. Thus, in 1900, wage-earning women broke down into the following groups:

Field	Owner	Adminis-trative posts	Labourers	Independent
Garment and footwear production	2,479	57	19,298	11,449
Processing of fibrous materials	120	20	11,304	576
Food processing and tobacco	79	26	7,505	126
Bathhouse attendants, laundresses	398	49	5,371	5,138
Leather, paper, resin production	92	19	4,139	38
Trade	1,238	1,638	3,146	2,192
Hospitality	5,268	109	2,395	19
Printing trades	66	383	756	9
Transport	243	1,669	132	—
Field unknown	9	6	6,626	7,179

As can be seen from the figures above, the number of independent women owners is only relatively high in those fields of labour where small-scale production still predominates, e.g., trade and hospitality; in all other areas, on the other hand, wage labour and closely related 'independent' labour numerically overwhelm not only the category of owners, but also that of professional or semi-professional women employed in business administration and bookkeeping, as cashiers, clerks, etc.

These cursory figures seem sufficient to give an idea of the significance of the role played in the various countries by the labour of working-class women and its predominant position over that of bourgeois women.

However, for the ever-growing army of millions of female industrial workers winning the 'right to work' step by step for all women, this right is a curse rather than a blessing. At the same time as bourgeois women rejoice with each new profession that opens its doors to them, proletarian women approach new machines with a sense of profound resignation.[18] 'Freedom to work for women', that urgent dream of bourgeois women, has long since become a bitter reality for proletarian women.

Labour took women on a straight path to their economic independence, but the contemporary capitalist relations made working conditions intolerable, indeed disastrous for them. These conditions drove them into the most abysmal poverty; they acquainted women with all the horrors of capitalist exploitation and forced them to plumb the depths of the cup of the suffering caused by conditions of production that are harmful both to health and life. And proletarian women cursed this 'freedom to work' that is so fiercely defended by their bourgeois 'sisters'.

Need we repeat the well-known fact that working conditions for women are in all regards even less satisfactory than those of men? It has long since been indisputably shown by statistics that, in all fields of production, female workers are paid significantly less than men.

Thus, in England, according to Griffin, the average weekly wage for men is equal to 24 shillings (s), 7 pence (d), whilst female workers are paid only half this amount: 12s, 8d. In the main industries of England that employ a large number of women, we find the following relationship between compensation for male and female workers:

Weekly wages[19]

Industry	Men		Women	
Cotton	25 s	3 d	15 s	3 d
Wool	23 s	2 d	13 s	3 d
Honey	29 s	7 d	12 s	11 d
Typography (large-scale)	33 s	8 d	11 s	9 d
Hosiery	24 s	5 d	11 s	6 d
Zinc	38 s	8 d	10 s	5 d
Linen	19 s	9 d	8 s	11 d
Coal extraction	22 s	11 d	8 s	2 d
Ore extraction	16 s	6 d	5 s	10 d

In the US, where the general status of female workers is relatively more satisfactory than in Europe, we also see considerable wage inequality. In New York, for example, the wages in the cotton industry are as follows:[20]

Weekly wages	Men (thousands)	Women (thousands)
<$5	6,298	13,004
≥$6	3,186	6,264
$6–7	2,958	4,177
$7–8	2,905	1,979
$8–9	1,945	488

$9–10	1,741	148
$10–12	1,361	52
$12–15	769	13
$15–20	577	23
≥$20	275	15

This distribution illustrates that the largest number of women are concentrated in the worst-paid fields; $7 a week is the highest standard of compensation for female labour, which is very rarely exceeded. The highest wage for men in Massachusetts is $25.41, and $8.57 for women; the lowest is $7.09 for the former and $4.62 for the latter.[21]

In France, the average wage for men, according to Pelloutier's figures, is equal to 4.85 francs a day; the average wage for women, on the other hand, is only half that amount, i.e., 2.45 francs. Female bookbinders in Paris barely make 1.75 to 2 francs for a twelve- to fourteen-hour working day, whilst male bookbinders are paid up to 7–8 francs a day. In 1900, female bookbinders went on strike, demanding an increase in their rates to at least 3 francs a day. In French linen spinneries, male weavers are paid up to 3.50 francs a day, whilst female weavers are paid up to 2.55 francs; in the hemp weaving field, the average wage for male weavers is 2.50 francs, and 1.50 francs for women; in cloth production, male weavers can make up to 6 francs a day, whilst female weavers can make no more than 5 francs, with an average wage equal to 1.85 francs at the same time as the average wage of male weavers is 2.60 francs. The difference is even more striking in the case of male and female scutchers in hemp production: The maximum wage is 5 francs for the former and 2.40 francs for the latter. In paper spinning, male spinners are paid from 4 to 5 francs a day; female spinners are paid from 1.50 to 2.75 francs; in paper weaving, male weavers are paid from 2 to 4.25 francs a day, whilst female weavers are paid from 1.50 to 3.75 francs; in wool weaving, the average wage is 4 francs for men and 3.05 francs for women. In papermaking, men are paid on average 2.35 to 4.45 francs, whilst women are paid from 1.45 to 2.35 francs.

At one of the biggest Parisian sugar refineries, female workers are paid a mere 20 centimes an hour to carry heavy boxes of sugar from one end of the facility to the other, a job men could not be hired to do even for 50 centimes an hour. On average, male workers at Parisian sugar refineries are paid 4.50 francs a day, whilst women are paid between 2 and 2.25 francs. There are a whole raft of occupations in France in which women make 50 centimes a day (approximately 20 kopecks), a wage that would be unheard-of for male workers.[22]

In Belgium, the minimum wage for men starts at 1.50 francs a day, at the same time as the minimum daily wage for women is 1 franc or even less. For men, the maximum wage is 7 francs or more; for women, it is 4 francs. "Moreover," Gertsenshtein reports,[23] "of 450,000 male workers surveyed on the subject, this maximum of 7 francs or more was paid to 400, i.e., 0.80 percent, but only 300, i.e., 0.41 percent, of 72,300 female workers were paid 4 francs or more." In other words, the proportion of women receiving this maximum wage is not even half the proportion of men. For the same number (450,000) of male workers, the most common wage was 3 to 3.50 francs, and 100,000 workers were paid this amount, or 22.22 percent; for women, the most common wage was 1 to 1.50 francs, paid to 22,398 female workers, or 31 percent. Thus, amongst women, the lower range of the wage scale predominates, whilst the middle range predominates amongst men. A similar relationship can be seen in agriculture, where male workers are paid an average of 1.98 francs (75 kopecks) a day, whilst female workers are paid 1.22 francs (45 kopecks). A halfway acceptable standard of living in Belgium requires wages in excess of 3.50 francs; however, given that, for 31 percent of female workers, wages fluctuate between 1 and 1.50 francs, it is easy to imagine in what difficult circumstances the majority of working women in Belgium are living.

In Germany, the average daily wage for a male worker is equal to 67.5 kopecks in our money; the average wage for a woman, on the other hand, is barely 45 kopecks, and adolescent girls are paid even less, 36 kopecks on average. At the maximum rate of pay, men in Germany can earn 1.35 rubles; women, on the other hand, make only 79 kopecks. In Berlin, the average daily wage is 1.08 rubles for male workers and 65 kopecks for female workers. However, there are entire areas in which women are in a position to earn 22 kopecks for adults and a mere 13 kopecks for adolescents.[24] In the spinneries of Upper Alsace in the '80s, men earned 1.80 to 4 marks a day, and women earned 1.70 to 2 marks. In the German weaving industry, whilst male workers' wages are up to 3.30 marks a day, women earn 2.40 marks at best. 'In Mannheim, 56 percent of men earned 15 to 25 marks a day; 71 percent of women earned only 8 to 10 marks; 1.5 percent of men could rely on a wage of 35 marks, and only 0.08 percent of women attained their maximum wage of 30 to 36 marks.'[25]

Female loaders working in Danzig loading ships are paid 3 marks. Male labourers in Berlin, Frankfurt, and several other German cities are paid from 2.25 to 3 marks a day, whilst female labourers are paid only 1.10 to 1.80 marks. In Darmstadt, print shop workers are paid 18 to 20 marks a week. Women doing the same work for the same number of hours are paid only 6 to 12 marks. Lithographers earn up to 40 marks a week; women employed in lithography are paid a maximum of 11 marks for the same work. In trimming factories, men are paid 15 to 25 marks and women 4 to 12 marks.[26]

In Finland, women in paper spinning and weaving factories are paid from 35 pennies to 2 markka a day; men are paid 1.80 to 2.30 markka in Tampere. In Turku, wages are somewhat higher: Female wages fluctuate between 1 and 2.50 markka, whilst male wages fluctuate between 2.50 and 3.50 markka. In Tampere linen spinneries, male workers are paid 1.60 to 2.80 markka a day, and female workers are paid from 1.15 to 1.50 markka a day; in wool spinneries, men earn up to 2 markka a day and women from 80 pennies to 1 markka. In the stationery industry, the following wages are found: 3 markka a day for men and 1.80 markka for women.[27] In Helsinki breweries, male workers earn 3 to 5 markka a day, and female workers from 2.25 to 3 markka. Pay for women's work in Finland is 50 percent or even 100 percent less than men's, and, in some cases, women's relative wages are even lower; thus, female bookbinders in Helsinki are paid only one-third as much as men.

Lastly, in Russia, according to Dementyev's figures, the monthly wage of a male worker in the central governorates was equal to 13.53 rubles, and the average wage for women, on the other hand, was 10.35 rubles; in the paper-weaving industry, the male wage was 13.27 rubles a month, and that of women 11 rubles; in the spinning/weaving and wool spinning departments of cloth factories, men were paid an average of 15.32 rubles a month, whilst women were paid 6.17 rubles; in cotton-printing factories, the average wage was 15.38 rubles for male workers and 6.07 rubles for female workers; in beer and mead breweries, the average monthly wage amounts to 12 rubles for men and 6 rubles for women; and in leather and glove production, women's average earnings were 6.64 rubles, whilst men's were 13.61 rubles.[28] In Vilna District in 1885, the average monthly wage for male workers was calculated to be 20.92 rubles, whilst that of female workers was 9.20 rubles; in Congress Poland, the textile industry paid men an average of 20 kopecks a day at the same time as women 15 kopecks a day.

In the industrial areas of central Russia, whilst men in the textile industry were paid 15 kopecks a day, women were not even paid 9 kopecks; in Kharkov District, the average daily wage in fifty factories was equal to 12 kopecks for men and 7 kopecks for women.[29]

In Russia, women are usually paid roughly half of men's wages. There are factories in which women's labour is better paid, e.g., tobacco factories, where women are usually paid around two-thirds of men's wage; however, there are also areas of labour in which women's wages are barely one-third of men's. Women's wages are particularly low in agricultural labour, where women do not always make two-fifths of the male wage.

It goes without saying that the inequality in men's and women's wages is not due to the physical nature of women, nor due to their work being qualitatively worse; rather, it is due to a series of socio-economic factors that influence the valuation of the labour power of the female sex. Chief amongst these factors is doubtless the fact that, for many years, commodities produced by women did not enter the commodity cycle; this resulted in the false conclusion, which still burdens women, that persons of the female sex had lower productive capabilities.[30] Alongside this fundamental factor, there is also another contributing factor: It is presumed that women are covering only part of their needs with their wages, with the larger part being covered by the head of the household, the husband. Thus, this minimum need that puts a floor on men's wages may, according to a widespread belief, be lowered even further for women. And, although an enormous part of the female working population lives entirely independently without support from fathers or husbands, it is always presumed for some reason that women are only working for 'pin money'. Women's low wage levels are also due in part to women being less demanding, and, ultimately, the fact that some women do indeed cover only part of their needs with their own labour.

The wage inequality between men and women is also explained in part by the fact that women's labour is predominantly used in the worse-paying occupations and in departments of companies where less qualified labour is required.

> Thus, for example, London cigar factories pay men 35 s a week and men 12 to 18 s, because the former produce the higher-quality cigars, costing 4 to 5 s for a thousand, whilst the latter only produce the cheap sorts, for which they are only paid 1 to 3 s for a thousand (1 shilling (s) = 12 pence (d) = approx. 50 kopecks). According to Sydney Webb, in nine-tenths of industrial labour, there is no competition between men and women, because each of them are working on different processes, with the worse-paid occupations falling to women.[31]

Lily Braun notes a whole series of fields where wages for equivalent work for men and women differ only slightly or not at all. In the cotton, wool, and silk industries in England, the average wage for men and women is almost equal: The weekly wage for men fluctuates from district to district between 19 s / 7 d and 21 s / 11 d, whilst women's wage is between 19 s and 21 s / 4 d. Male and female weavers in New Jersey (N. Am.) receive the same pay. However, a careful examination of the means by which the valuation of men's and women's labour is brought to the same level reveals that this 'equalisation', in most cases, benefits not the workers but the entrepreneurs. In point of fact, men's wages have an undoubted tendency to fall to the level of women's; where women's wages become equal to men's, this is due in most cases to a *decrease* in the valuation of men's labour to that of women in the relevant field. Only by organising can the proletariat of both sexes counteract this sad tendency, which is why working-class women's slogan of 'equal pay for equal work', meaning higher wage levels for women, is always vigorously supported by working men. Male workers have as much of an interest as female workers in increasing the valuation of women's labour above its current starvation level.

The low valuation of women's labour forces working-class organisations to seek out different means of struggle against this evil. Working women in England proposed setting up special wage tariffs for women, but such an approach would only worsen their position by confirming the lower valuation for women's labour, and would not only fail to eliminate, but would actually worsen, competition with men's labour. Some mixed unions have come up with a different approach: They decided that men should carry out the harder work, and women should carry out the easier, and thus worst-paid work; however, this approach does nothing more than sanction the status quo, and, in any case, it does not serve to protect female workers' interests. The weavers of Lancashire have found what may be the most correct approach, setting a specified valuation that applies equally to women and men. 'To be sure,' Lily Braun reports, 'this automatically resulted in sex segregation: Women began working in areas with less space and men in areas with more space. However, work is divided between men and women depending on the strength and agility of each individual; as such, it happens that a strong woman may work in the areas with more space, and a weak man may be found in one of the tighter areas.'

In addition to all the socio-economic factors listed above, the valuation of women's labour is lowered in part by the inadequate occupational preparation of women, which makes the latter's work less productive. When, for example, the London typesetters' union finally decided to accept women on the condition that they worked for the set tariff, it turned out that only one woman was able to meet the requirements of the organisation and work at the specified productivity level. It is not hard to find a remedy for this inadequacy of female labour — all one needs to do is ensure that female workers' level of development is raised in the occupational sphere as well as in general.

As for the other, deeper socio-economic factors resulting in the lower valuation of women's labour, proletarian women have only one reliable means of struggle against them: forming workers' organisations together with men. Obtaining a wage increase for women with the aid of a robust, cohesive union is made that much easier by the fact that, as noted above, such an increase benefits not only women, but their male comrades in the same occupation, as well. The hostility with which working-class men at one time viewed female labour, not accepting female workers into unions in hopes of reducing the supply of female labour, has long since given way to a conscious recognition of the shared interests of male and female workers.[32]

The same shared interests also exist within the working class in relation to the length of the working day. In this respect, too, women work in worse conditions than men. The working day is longer in workplaces that primarily or exclusively employ women, unless there are legislative obstacles to the endless extension of the working day. At the same time, we see that a maximum working day for women also results in a gradual shortening of men's working hours down to the standard established for women. This fact is well known; as such, we will not tarry on it further.

More hygienic working conditions are also equally desirable for workers of both categories, as is the exclusion of women from occupations that are especially harmful to women's bodies. To this day, female labour is widespread in the most harmful areas of industry.

Anyone wishing to verify for themselves what tortures working women are subjected to in modern industry, how mercilessly capital devours women's youth, strength, and even their lives, need only open the excellent chapters of Lily Braun's work specifically dedicated to the examination of this question.

What could be more horrible than working in weaving and spinning shops? And yet female labour predominates in that very industry. Festering boils on their arms, eye inflammation, furuncles, eczema – these are the normal consequences for women working in the spinneries. The manufacturing of cotton batting and the related sorting of its waste products, which have often previously been used for wound dressings, amongst other things, is a source of infection. The production of mirrors and lead paint and the painting of tin toys are destructive to women's bodies, causing diseases of the reproductive organs, miscarriages, infertility, and severe mental disorders. Even more horrible is working in mercury factories, which doom women to rot alive. Women are also predominantly employed in sugar manufacture, loading sugar beets, 'because they are more agile than men and less afraid of dirt and rain'.[33] The destructive effects of working in sugar refineries at intolerably high temperatures do not even bear mentioning. The saddest thing is that millions of women employed to do work utterly unsuited for their bodies not only destroy their own health, but kill off the next generations as well. Constant standing causes serious disorders of the female reproductive organs; in the garment industry, stitchers inevitably contract female diseases; a seamstress who has worked on the machines for ten years is ready for the hospital. Premature births,[34] miscarriages, and diseases of all types that affect childbearing are the inevitable consequence of many occupations of contemporary female slaves of capital. Women spend eleven to twelve hours a day carrying extremely heavy objects, pushing and dragging trays or wheelbarrows filled to the brim, carrying densely packed boxes from place to place, and are exhausted by the excessive weights, unsuited for the female body, at the same time as thousands of strong, healthy men search in vain for applications for their idle hands.

These abnormal conditions are, of course, the fault of the exploitative capitalist conditions of our day. Working-class women are not suffering because the doors of one or another category of labour are closed to them, but because the doors leading to noxious sources of income are open far too widely and hospitably . . .

But how are women to struggle against this ever-growing evil? How can they defend their interests? How can they make their working conditions less harmful? Can they count on their bourgeois sisters? Is it possible that they will be reliable fellow travellers in the struggle for more tolerable working conditions and a better material position? Let us see how reality itself answers this question.

* * *

We struggle to find even a single case in the history of proletarian women's struggle for their material well-being in which the pan-feminist movement's effect was beneficial to working-class women. Whatever gains proletarian women have made in terms of improving their economic position are due, above all, to the combined efforts of the working class as a whole and to themselves in particular. The history of working-class women's struggle for better working conditions and a more bearable life is the history of the liberation struggle of the proletariat.

What forces factory owners to increase the rates of pay, shorten working hours, and introduce more tolerable working conditions if not their fear of a looming explosion of the discontent of the proletariat as a whole? What causes governments to impose legislative limits on the exploitation of labour by capital if not the fear of 'workers' riots'?

Factory laws are one of the most radical means of defence of the interests of the proletariat, but is the feminist movement even indirectly to thank for the enactment of even a single protective law? Indeed, under what conditions do we see attempts at legislative regulation of women's labour? We need only cast a cursory glance at the history of the appearance and development of factory legislation in the various countries to see how little sympathy these laws found in feminist circles, and how clearly their appearance is due exclusively to the growing power of the labour movement. Every time a wave of working-class discontent threatened to reach heights dangerous to the ruling classes, they sought refuge in the shadow of factory laws. In the first stages of its development, to be sure, state occupational safety regulations brought only children and women under their 'care', but even this lopsided protection is a win for the working class as a whole. When the sanitary and hygienic conditions in women's workshops improve, when child labour is reduced, when they are banned from working at night – all of this benefits the whole proletariat.[35]

And workers understand this perfectly well. This is why they are always passionate advocates of legislative protection for female and child labour. To be sure, there was a time when the class consciousness of the workers was still poorly developed, and when both male and female proletarians looked on legislative intervention into their contractual relations with hostility, but that stage of class development has long since passed. Now, every working-class woman happily welcomes any legislation having the objective of protecting her interests as a worker. Unlike the feminists, she sees nothing humiliating to her 'female dignity' in the fact that many sections of the law provide special protection only to children and persons of the female sex: She is willing to welcome any law that restricts the appetites of the entrepreneurs.

Statutory protection for female labour is all the more important and necessary given that, under modern conditions, it is only possible to involve women in the trade-union and political movement if a specified limit is placed on the exploitation of female labour. As is known, the workers who organise the best are those who have the most leisure time and the highest pay. Women, on the other hand, belong precisely to the category of the worst-placed workers: They have lower wages and less leisure time. We must not forget that most female workers are not only workers, but also homemakers and mothers. Even the most brilliant agitation and propaganda directed at female workers will be incapable of organising the broad masses of women if women exist on an inferior social and economic level. This is a vicious circle: Women's position cannot be improved if they do not themselves decisively participate in the labour movement, but they are only able to participate if the conditions of their existence improve. The way out of this situation is for the organised working class to win factory laws that ease the wage labour of women above all.

'The female weavers of Lancashire,' Lily Braun reports, 'were just as exploited and unable to organise before the enactment of the protective law as the majority of female workers are today. Only after the law made it impossible for them to agree to bad working conditions did they begin to join trade unions and associations.'[36]

This is why the matter of legislative protection for female labour is of crucial importance for the entire working class.

Legislative protection for female labour has its origins in the powerful Chartist movement. Abject terror at the growing strength of the labour movement led in England in 1842 to the passing of a bill introduced by Lord Ashley that prohibited women and children under the age of ten from working underground. This was the first step towards limiting the exploitation of female labour. The second step was the law of 8 June 1847, which established a maximum working day of ten hours for all women working in textile manufacturing. Chartism ultimately died in the 1850s and, with it, the pliability of the propertied classes waned.

Factory legislation was only revived in the '90s, when, with a series of major strikes, workers once again began to remind capitalists that their patience had limits. An 1891 law prohibited women working for a four-week period following childbirth, and the Factory and Workshop Act 1901 limited the actual working hours for women and youth to 10 hours in the textile industry and 10.5 in other industries; work on Saturdays was required to be ended at 11 a.m. or 1 p.m. – depending on the starting time – in the textile industry, with the result that the actual working day on Saturdays was 5 to 5.5 hours. In other industries, Saturday work could last until 2 to 4 p.m., an actual working day of 7.5 hours. In general, the total weekly working hours for women was not to exceed 55.5 hours in the textile industry and 60 hours in other industries. The 1901 Act defined the night-time as the period from 9 p.m. to 6 a.m., during which women were not permitted to work. Of course, all of these laws were enacted in England under the direct pressure of the workers, as can be seen from the history of the labour movement itself. We will see in the following how English feminists related to these laws, and whether they contributed even the slightest effort to realising working-class women's demands in these areas.

The independent action of the French proletariat during the 1848 revolution brought about the March laws, which, however tenuous they were, did establish a ten-hour working day for workers of both sexes in Paris and an eleven-hour day in the provinces.[37] This law, which was 'inflicted by the Paris *banlieue*', in the words of the bourgeoisie at the time, unleashed a veritable storm of indignation; on 9 September, the maximum working day was extended to twelve hours, with an entire series of exceptions. At that time, in fact, working-class women in France bade a permanent farewell to any protection of their labour, and were once again delivered to the uncontrolled exploitation of the entrepreneurs. Only in 1874, after extensive debate, did the National Assembly enact a law banning night-time work for minors and underground work for women.

When the French socialists had established themselves more firmly in the Chamber of Deputies, the regulation of women's and child labour was returned to the agenda. On 2 November 1892, a law was enacted that brought under its protection both children and women employed in factories, mines, and workshops. Pursuant to this law, girls aged eighteen to twenty-one, as well as women having attained the age of majority, were not permitted to work more than eleven hours a day; for adolescents, on the other hand, the working day was set at sixty hours a week. Night work for women was significantly curtailed, albeit not entirely banned.

These modest protective provisions were nullified by numerous exceptions enacted in subsequent years. The dissatisfaction of the workers grew, and the socialist deputies cried out for more effective factory laws. The struggle between the Chamber of Deputies and the Senate continued until 1900. Ultimately, the lower house was able to pass protective legislation, which took effect in 1904. Currently, the working day for women is set at ten hours; night work (between 9 p.m. and 5 a.m.) is banned. In general, shift work is banned (subject to many exceptions).[38] In the same year, 1900, a short ordinance was enacted that required traders to provide female shop assistants with chairs, and, although bosses, who have chairs, still prohibit shop assistants using them, this rule nonetheless may be counted as one of the victories 'in principle' of proletarian women.

In Germany, the origin of legislation protecting female workers coincides with the growing influence of the Social-Democratic caucus in the Reichstag. As early as 1877, the Social Democratic Party (SPD) introduced a bill in the Reichstag that sought to improve the position of female workers, limit working hours, protect pregnant and postpartum women, and ban night work, underground work, etc. for women. To be sure, this proposal was voted down by the majority of the Reichstag; however, a series of laws in 1891, 1897, and 1900 later almost completely implemented the basic provisions of the SPD bill. Currently, the working day for women in Germany is set at eleven hours, with a one-hour lunch break (for those running their own households, a one-and-a-half-hour break is permitted). Work on the eve of Sundays and bank holidays may not exceed ten hours. Night work, between 8.30 p.m. and 5.30 a.m., is banned. Sunday is a day off, although this provision is significantly weakened by a large number of exceptions. Overtime is only permitted with a number of exceptions. Women are absolutely banned from working underground. Moreover, the law provides for four weeks of leave (six with a doctor's note) after childbirth and *compulsory* health, accident,

disability, and old-age pension insurance; the postpartum period is included in the category of 'illness', and entitles women to receive six weeks
of free health care whilst continuing to receive 50 to 70 percent of their
wages, as is the case with other illnesses.

A bill debated in the Reichstag that sought to protect waitresses was
also initiated by the SPD: They led the first movement of waitresses, and
required a special investigation of their situation to be undertaken. It
was also under social-democratic pressure that the first attempt at state
regulation of at-home industrial labour was made following a large strike
of male and female workers in the garment industry in 1896 that forced
society to look at an abyss of poverty and exploitation that had previously
passed without notice. 'Even Bismarck, that inveterate enemy of social
democracy,' says Lily Braun, 'was forced to acknowledge that the social
reforms would never have happened without the SPD.'[39]

Here in Russia, as in other countries, the bourgeois women's movement has had no influence – nor could it have any – on the development
of factory legislation. Miserly though they may be, the statutory provisions protecting women and children at work nonetheless impose a limit
– at least in principle – on the exploitation of the labour power of children
and women by capital. Yet even these modest protective laws had to be
wrested from the hands of the powerful with great effort and sacrifice.

The spontaneous 'epidemic' of strikes in 1878–1879, the impressive,
turbulent work stoppages that erupted throughout Russia (at the Kreen-
holm Manufacturing Company* in Narva, Estonia, in Perm, in Żyrardów,
Poland, in Saint Petersburg, and other places) in the early 1880s, forced
an anxious government to report to imposing limits on the appetites of
entrepreneurs. The law of 1 June 1882 protected some minors. It was
assumed that children, 'broken both physically and morally, will be especially receptive to revolutionary teachings' (надломленные физически и
нравственно легко поддаются воспріятію революціонныхъ ученій).
However, even the enactment of the June law could not damp the unrest of the workers; on the contrary, they continued to spread from place
to place as a result of the persistent crisis in the cotton industry. Mass

---

*   Also known as Krähnholm Manufaktur (German) / Kreenholmi Manufaktuur (Es-
    tonian). —Trans.

unemployment acted as a source of momentum for a relentless labour movement. Fearing an imminent collapse and under the influence of the problems caused by the protracted economic crisis, the factory operators of Saint Petersburg themselves turned to the mayor of Saint Petersburg to ask for a ban on night work for women and minors in the textile industry. In their view, a measure of this sort would be the only effective means of 'reducing production, which has of late reached such significant dimensions that all the markets are saturated with product'.[40] The unceasing wave of strikes provided the most compelling cause for this 'request' of the factory operators. The ubiquitous working-class agitation in 1885, the famous 'riot' at the Nikolskaya factory in Orekhovo-Zuyevo, which was accompanied by the demolition of factory buildings, forced the government to take additional steps. Factory legislation entered its second stage, and female workers were taken under its protection.

On 3 June 1885, a law was enacted banning *night work for women and adolescents* (under 17 years of age) at cotton, linen, and wool factories. According to the candid statement of the city council, this law came into being because the government was 'concerned with finding means for eliminating strikes and disorder at the factories in the future' (*озабочивалось изысканіемъ способовъ къ возможному устраненію на будущее время фабричныхъ забастовокъ и безпорядков*).

Within one year—on 3 June 1886 (with additions from 1 October 1886)—a second important law was enacted that regulated employer–worker relations. This law was a direct result of the worker agitation in Orekhovo-Zuyevo. One of the chief causes of the famous 'riot', in which eight thousand male and female workers participated, was the particular system of fines, which amounted to up to 300,000 rubles a year, or 40 percent of the workers' wages. The new law intervened in the contractual relationships between entrepreneurs and workers, imposing a series of restrictions: Accounting books were introduced, the truck system was banned, a minimum frequency of wage payment was established (no less than twice a month), the amounts of the fines had to be approved by factory inspectors, wage deductions for debts were banned, etc.

At the same time, the powers of the factory inspectorate were significantly expanded, and a special supreme inspection agency was created: the site inspectorate (*фабричное присутствие*).

Nonetheless, enough loopholes were left for capital to ensure that factory operators' power over workers was maintained. 'Thus, factory operators are allowed to sack workers from the factory for the most trivial reasons and to unilaterally terminate employment contracts for "impertinence or bad behaviour on the part of the worker", whilst workers were required to seek judicial intervention to terminate contracts, and in factory operators, behaviour had to border on the criminal in order to justify termination."[41]

The relative quiescence of the labour movement that began at the end of the industrial crisis offered an opportunity to weaken the provisions of the laws of 1882 to 1886 starting in the 1890s, as industry revived. The 1890 law permitted: 6 hours of *night* work for children aged twelve to fifteen in one of the most harmful industries, the glass industry, 6 hours of daytime work without a break or 8 hours (4.5 hours at a stretch) in workplaces operating a two-shift system. As for women's and adolescents' night work, the 1890 law added a truly substantial qualification that practically constituted a repeal of the 1885 ban: Night work was permitted for adolescents and women with the permission of the governor for good cause and in the case of joint work with the head of household. This exception was justified with 'moral concerns'; it was assumed that the morality of female workers would be in excessive 'peril' if they did not spend the night-time hours in workshops replete with harmful fumes, at hard labour, fighting to stay awake . . . Subsequently, the factory inspectorate was given the authority to allow minors to work on Sundays and bank holidays, and, with the approval of the ministers of finance and home affairs, to allow children under the age of twelve to work in factories.

---

* In original: *Такъ, фабрикантъ по самому ничтожному поводу можетъ выбросить рабочаго изъ фабрики, можетъ своей властью расторгнуть договоръ найма даже „за дерзость или дурное поведеніе рабочаго", тогда какъ рабочій для уничтоженія договора долженъ обращаться къ содѣйствію суда; да и то, чтобы имѣлся къ тому поводъ, фабрикантъ долженъ быть уличенъ чуть-ли не въ уголовщинѣ.*

It took another explosion of the labour movement, this time an organised one, to disturb the tranquillity of the ruling classes and remind them of the need for new and more effective interventions into the 'freedom' of labour relations. A series of individual strikes in Saint Petersburg in 1894–1895, agitation in the Yaroslavl factory in April 1895, and the 1898 work stoppage in Saint Petersburg, which lasted more than two weeks and in which thirty thousand weavers, both men and women, participated, had their effect.

The finance ministry convened a conference of factory operators of all industrial areas, which came to the conclusion that it was necessary to legislatively limit the working day for adults. The workers tensely awaited the promised law; workers in Saint Petersburg threatened to take strike action if the law was not enacted by 1 January 1897. In fact, when the first date went by with no signs of a law, male and female textile workers at the Maxwell factory went on strike. The agitation spread to other companies, with around eighteen thousand people going on strike; there were even discussions of a general strike. Then, the finance ministry rushed to announce that the working hours act would soon be examined by the Council of State.

Indeed, on 2 June 1897, a new law appeared that limited the working day for adults. To be sure, the workers had expected the introduction of a ten-and-a-half-hour working day, and the new law set eleven and a half hours as the standard maximum working day for factories and mines. What had been expected was a complete ban on night work for industries that did not require uninterrupted production, but the law actually only established a maximum ten-hour working day for cases in which work extended into the night-time hours. Moreover, the law was careful to permit 'overtime' work, and only required work to end at midday on Christmas Eve. In general, the working day on the eve of bank holidays and Sundays was limited to ten hours. In addition to Sundays, fourteen more compulsory bank holidays a year were established. In workplaces with uninterrupted production, the law permitted work to continue for up to sixteen to eighteen hours under certain specific conditions; in general, it permitted the working day to be extended from eleven and a half to twelve hours.

However, as pathetic as these provisions were, as elastic as the sections protecting workers were, the fact that the need for regulation of the working day was recognised in principle nonetheless constituted a new gain for the working class. All it took, however, was for worker agitation to calm down temporarily in order for the government to oblige factory operators with any number of 'explanations', 'addenda', and 'exceptions' that ultimately rendered inoperative even these weak attempts at legislative protection for workers. Given that a twelve-hour working day was permitted in workplaces with uninterrupted production, the government issued a long list of such workplaces, which had nothing in common with the name. Pursuant to the 1897 law, overtime was permitted up to 120 hours a year; now, the unlimited exploitation of overtime work was permitted administratively. The circular also eliminated the compulsory four days off a month. Under the new 1903 rules, the factory inspectorate, which had previously been under the authority of the department for trade and manufacturing at the finance ministry, was transferred to the industrial department, and was, in practice, subordinate to the governors.[42]

Having shown that workers' discontent threatened to cause new agitation, the 1902–1903 strike movement in southern Russia once again served as an impulse for the enactment of rules on injury compensation for workers on 1 July 1903. It goes without saying that the law making employers liable for workplace accidents was pervaded with class spirit; in response to agitation by industrialists, the law reduced the proposed amount of compensation, limited the scope of application of the rules, and made it completely possible for factory operators to force workers to agree to accept any pittance as compensation in order to avoid bureaucratic red tape. Nor did the 11 June 1903 worker representative law make any real contribution.

As a result, industrial labour in Russia, both for women and for men, was carried out in the most unfavourable conditions; outrageous abuses abounded, and were not mitigated even by formal statutory provisions. In a number of factories that employed a large number of female workers, night-time work was not abolished; the standard working day of eleven and a half hours, excessive in and of itself, could be arbitrarily extended as a result of a number of loopholes and exceptions provided in the law. There

is not even time off before bank holidays for female workers with households, a large and growing category of workers. Postpartum mothers are
not exempt from the requirement that they abandon the being who has
only just come into the world and spend eleven and a half hours on their
feet doing factory labour in their quasi-sick condition. Is there any other
'civilised' country in which women labour in such unfavourable conditions,
in which the state itself treats the fate of mothers, their citizens, with such
myopic brutality, and so recklessly facilitates mass infant death?

* * *

Of all the immediate tasks presenting themselves to the Russian proletariat, the development of proper protection for workers, concerning itself above all with the population of minor and female workers in Russia,
doubtless has a prominent place. Surely, we need not reiterate that this
task can only be carried out and made a reality by the proletariat itself, as
a whole. Only in the ranks of their own class party, relying on their own
specific class programme, can women workers attain better working conditions and a more bearable existence. Not one of the most radical bourgeois women's organisations, not a single one of the existing bourgeois
parties, is capable of fully responding to the petitions and demands of a
class whose economic interests are diametrically opposed to the other,
non-proletarian strata of the population.

Leaving aside those parties that are to the right of the Cadets, and, accordingly, do not even purport to collaborate and ally themselves with the
working class, let us see what the party of 'people's freedom' promises female workers in the section of their programme dedicated to labour issues.

Together with the demand for the introduction of an eight-hour working day, now where possible, 'gradually' where it is inconvenient for production, there is also a specific demand for statutory protection of female
workers: 'the development of protection for female and child labour and
the establishment of protective measures for male workers in particularly
harmful workplaces'. No further detail on the principles on which this
protective legislation is to be based can be found here: Are there to be
specific sections of the law protecting mothers? Will night-time work

be prohibited? Will the statutory protection extend to all categories of female labour? On these matters, the programme of the party of 'people's freedom' is utterly silent. Despite the fact that the representatives of this party are occasionally willing to express their sympathy even with socialism (meaning, of course, the civilised socialism abroad, and not our 'barbaric' socialism!), any further specification of the party's demands in labour matters would put the Cadets in a truly critical position and force them to put their cards on the table on a matter where it would be more advantageous for them to put out general position statements with no specifics. This 'caution' of the esteemed Cadets on the subject of protecting the workplace interests of the proletariat should reveal to the working class the true nature of the friends of 'people's freedom' and make proletarian women treat the promises disseminated by the party in the run-up to elections with circumspection.

Nor does the party of 'popular socialists' promise working-class women much more. To be sure, here, we do find the general proletarian demand for an eight-hour working day (no more than forty-eight working hours a week), a 'minimum wage' established by agreement between workers' organisations and local authorities, participation of workers in the management of industrial establishments, and, lastly, 'workplace protection in accordance with demands for scientific hygiene, to be placed under the oversight of an inspectorate elected by the workers'.* That's it. Not once did the 'socialist' party mention the need to abolish night-time work for adults, mandatory maternity leave, pre-holiday leave for women workers with households, or care for the fate of working-class infants and children on the part of the state or the local authorities. Of course, all we have is a draft programme, but surely it should at least specify the basic governing principles, leaving only the details to be worked out. To say nothing about specific protection for female and child labourers is to fail to address the most urgent needs of the working class and to ignore their most immediate petitions. Even if the programme of the 'popular socialists' suited proletarian women in Russia on the whole, this single omission of a matter so essential for female workers would suffice to show

---

* In original: *охрана труда сообразно съ требованіями научной гигіены и постановка его подъ наблюденіе избираемой рабочими инспекціи*

them whether the 'popular socialist' party is really capable of standing up for the special needs and interests of the working class as a whole, and the interests of women workers in particular.

Does the party of 'socialist revolutionaries', close kin to the 'popular socialists', promise much more to working women? Here, together with demands covering adult workers in general for an eight-hour day, mandatory insurance, minimum wages, etc., we find a specific demand in the programme: 'a ban on female and child labour in specific branches of industries and specific periods'.* This is already somewhat more specific. Nonetheless, this programme also fails to specify the standards by which the development of these protective statutory provisions is to be guided. Based on the SR programme, female workers may conclude that this party is, in principle, sympathetic to the idea of protecting the workplace interests of women. But is there any actual, comprehensive accord between the demands of this party and their own? Do the standards of both sides coincide? Working women will search in vain for an answer here. However, this phenomenon is entirely natural: Thoughtful concern for the fate of the younger generation of their own class, the working conditions of their wives, sisters, and mothers, can only come from the organisation that focusses itself on the numerous needs of the economic class from which it originates. In all countries, this organisation is the workers' own party.

Not a single party in the world extends its protection to women to the same extent as the social-democratic parties. Working women are, above all, members of the working class, and the more satisfactory the position, the greater the well-being of every member of the worldwide proletarian family, the greater the ultimate benefit for the entire working class. One need only have a look at the programme of the workers' party of any country to find demands for broad social measures specifically protecting female labour along with those protecting workers as a whole. The greatest care is taken in drafting these measures, both at the annual congresses of the parties in each country and at the international socialist congresses.

At the third international socialist congress in Zürich, resolutions were adopted on the matter of protecting the workplace interests of

---

*   In original: *запрещеніе женскаго и дѣтскаго труда въ извѣстныхъ отрасляхъ производства и въ извѣстные періоды*

women: The introduction of real, comprehensive protection for female workers employed both in small- and large-scale industry, in commercial establishments, at home, with employer liability for unlawful acts and expanded powers for large, independent factory inspectorates. The establishment of a maximum eight-hour working day for adults, with the total number of hours worked per week not to exceed forty-four. Guaranteed pre-holiday leave for female workers. A ban on giving female workers orders to fill at home after finishing work at the shop. Two weeks of leave leading up to childbirth and six weeks of leave after childbirth, with full wages, to be paid by the state during this period. The removal of women from a number of harmful workplaces during pregnancy. The enactment of specific statutes protecting the interests of female agricultural workers and servants. Equal wages for male and female workers.

These resolutions were subsequently worked out in further detail in accordance with the needs of the proletariat in the respective countries. In Germany, the matter of special protection for female labour was the subject of discussions at the Hanover Congress in 1899, where the following demands were adopted:

> A complete ban on night-time work for women. A ban on the use of female labour for work particularly harmful for the female body. A statutory eight-hour limit on the working day for women. Exemption from work for female workers on Saturdays after lunch. Extension of the period of statutory protection for pregnant and postpartum women to at least one month before childbirth and two months thereafter. A ban on any exceptions to these provisions based on medical opinions. Extension of statutory labour protection to at-home workers. Appointment of female factory inspectors. Complete freedom of organisation for female workers. Active and passive suffrage for female workers in industrial court (*Gewerbegericht*) elections.[43]

As can be seen from the resolutions set forth above, social democracy always extends its demands for statutory protection to women, not just as workers, but as mothers; the health and viability of the next generation is a matter of much greater concern to the most deprived and exploited part of humanity than to the radical proponents of the 'purely female cause'.

A woman worker in any country opening the programme of the workers' party will always find an attitude of concern for her fate, both as a member of the working class, and particularly as a woman and mother. Demands of this sort on the subject of female labour have also been raised by Russian workers in their programme. There is no space here for indirect allusions and vague, nebulous wishes that are phrased in such general terms that there is plenty of room to interpret the demands in whatever direction one desires, such as those we have seen in the programmes of other political parties. 'In the interest of protecting the working class from physical and moral degeneration, as well as that of the development of their ability to carry out the liberation struggle,'* this programme demands: The establishment of a maximum eight-hour working day for adult workers of both sexes; no less than forty-two hours a week of uninterrupted rest; a ban on overtime, as well as night-time work (from 9 p.m. to 6 a.m.) in all areas of the economy except for those in which the technical conditions of production require uninterrupted work; authorisation to do industrial labour only for those aged sixteen and up; limitation of the work day for youth (age sixteen to eighteen) to six hours a day, etc. All of these resolutions protect women's labour as a member of the working class who sells her labour power to capital, independent of sex; however, there are additional demands for the protection of female workers specifically as women:

> A ban on female labour in industries harmful to the female body; leave for women for four weeks before childbirth and six weeks thereafter with continued payment of wages in the usual amount over the entire period; establishment of crèches for infants and minor children in all factories and other enterprises in which women work; breaks for breastfeeding women at least once every three hours, to last no less than one half hour.†

---

*   In original: *Въ интересахъ охраны рабочаго класса отъ физическаго и нравственнаго вырожденія, а также въ интересахъ развитія его способности къ освободительной борьбѣ.*

†   In original: *Воспрещеніе женскаго труда въ тѣхъ отрасляхъ, гдѣ онъ вреденъ для женскаго организма; освобожденіе женщинъ отъ работы втеченіе 4-хъ недѣль до и 6-ти недѣль послѣ родовъ, съ сохраненіемъ заработной платы въ обычномъ размѣрѣ за все это время; устройство при всѣхъ заводахъ,*

Of course, these demands do not reflect all of the diverse and urgent needs and petitions of women workers. However, when the female proletariat swells the ranks of workers' organisations, when they lock arms tightly around the flag of all workers, then female workers will have the influence to expand and supplement the programmatic demands in the direction they desire; only then will the programme of the working class truly give full coverage and expression to the pressing needs of the female proletariat here as it does elsewhere.

However, even in its current form, the programmatic demands of the working class on the matter of protecting the interests of the female proletariat are more complete and more comprehensive than the programmes of all of the other political parties.

However, even if it is the case that not a single one of the existing political parties in Russia offers women workers the same degree of protection as workers' organisations do, then perhaps women workers will find true allies in the struggle for their workplace interests amongst their 'bourgeois sisters'.

In this context, first of all, the following question arises: Can the feminists a priori be sincere champions and committed allies in the protection of wage labourers? Who makes up the core of the feminist organisations? Women of the bourgeois classes, obviously. Only around that consolidated core that sets the 'tone' for the efforts and objectives of a given organisation are the less conscious, less politically mature, semi-proletarian (and, more rarely, completely proletarian) elements found. Not only the practical implementation of any issue, but also the fundamental stance on that issue is developed by an organisation depending on the predominance of one or other element of society within it. Statutory workplace protections have not had the same significance for women of the bourgeois classes as they have for proletarian women; hence bourgeois women's negative, or, at best, passive attitude towards statutory workplace protections and their slow, reluctant inclination in recent years towards

---

фабрикахъ и др. предпріятіяхъ, гдѣ работаютъ женщины, яслей для грудныхъ и малолѣтнихъ дѣтей; освобожденіе отъ работы женщинъ, кормящихъ ребенку грудью, не рѣже, чѣмъ черезъ три часа, и не менѣе, чѣмъ на 1/2 часа.

social reformism, albeit not in all countries and not in all strata of the bourgeois women's movement.

For many years, the feminists have attacked specific statutory standards for female labour with all the passion typical of the neophyte. Armed with the whole archaic arsenal of liberalism, they bolstered their conclusions with the long-buried theory of 'state non-intervention'.

Even as recently as the 1900 international women's congress in Paris, the feminists stood against special protections for female labour, and viewed laws regulating women's labour as an attack on the 'freedom' and 'equality' of the fair sex. The congress found that these laws, under the pretext of protecting women, only harm their interests, obstructing their access to all areas of labour.

'Every attack on liberty,' Frédéric Passy said at the Paris congress, 'no matter how well-intentioned, is harmful, does something worse than the evil it seeks to remedy, by harming the most sacred thing there is in a human being, his liberty, his personality, his responsibility. They seek to place both men and women under guardianship; we say: enough guardianship, enough boundaries, enough barriers!'*

The congress decisively rose up against all laws limiting women's labour, and adopted the following resolution: 'Whereas, in the current state of society, every protective law that exclusively concerns women inevitably transforms into a law oppressing them, the Congress demands full freedom of labour for women.' And further: 'Given the current position of women in society, the Congress demands the complete repeal of every law that, under the pretext of protecting women, merely restricts her freedom of labour.'

An analogous decision was taken by the London congress, one year earlier, in 1899. At that time, Miss Hicks, a factory worker, protested against this resolution in a brief but powerful speech. On the other hand, there were no working-class women at all at the Paris congress, and thus no one to protest. Miss Hicks said:

---

* The full text of the proceedings of the 1900 Paris congress is available as a free ebook (in French) at https://play.google.com/books/reader?id=nDgEAAAAYAAJ&pg=GBS.PA18&hl=en_GB. —Trans.

Much has been said here about how factory legislation has only harmed women, and how they are rising up against it. I am a worker myself, and I can tell you, ladies and gentlemen, that that is all untrue. We, working women, demonstrated our attitude towards the factory acts at the time of the enactment of the Factory Act of 1895, when all workers' associations and women's cooperative societies agitated at meetings in support of this law, and sent petitions to Parliament. Rather than concerning yourselves with saving fallen girls, you would do better to help them improve their economic position; then, they will stop falling on their own. And one of the main means of doing so is factory legislation.[44]

The same principle of unlimited freedom of labour for women has more than once been put into practice by representatives of feminism. Thus, for example, the newspaper *La Fronde* in France, published by one of the prominent champions of the women's movement, introduced night-time work in the printing shop, which employed only women, 'on general principle'. Because night-time work is banned for women in France, the authorities held the publisher to account in court several times, but, committed 'equal rights campaigner' that she was, she persistently continued to demonstrate to the world that women were just as able to work at night as men, as if the capitalist system had not already made this sad fact painfully obvious even without her helpful lesson!

In England, where the feminist movement is particularly strongly marked by bourgeois liberalism, the champions of women's equality are unable to free themselves of their hatred for statutory standards for women's labour even today. In 1903, at the congress of the most significant women's organisation in England, the Women's Liberal Federation (WLF), feminists protested against statutory protection for female workers, and, in their resolution, demanded equal working conditions for women and men! How great was the harm these passionate advocates of equal rights for women did with their one-sided, single-issue equal rights policy when, in 1895, they stood in opposition of a government bill that sought to expand the scope of statutory workplace protection! Enraged, bourgeois women then railed against this bill and agitated openly and fiercely against it. They even fought against such undoubtedly beneficial provisions such as the extension of leave for women in the last weeks of pregnancy and the postnatal period. Many will remember the struggle waged by the organised proletariat at that time against the bourgeois advocates of 'freedom of contract'. Alas, some of the female proletariat, unconscious and confounded by the combative stance of the feminists and their effective slogan *Make Way for Women*, joined with the opponents of this bill that benefited them. The clamour raised around this issue gave the bourgeoisie the opportunity to weaken a number of important provisions of the new law that had protected the interests of the workers.

Of course, the feminists justified their opposition to statutory workplace protection by stating that any separation of female labour into a special category ultimately adversely affects the material interests of women and increases competition from men, who are 'free' of such statutory protection. 'Oddly enough,' Beatrice Webb notes in this regard, 'the opponents of unequal working conditions for both sexes quite rarely stand in defence even of those pieces of legislation that extend equally both to men and women of the working class.'[45] The most honest feminists, as Webb says, do not even deny their antipathy towards factory legislation – *in general*.

Indeed, that is quite natural. Protective laws are the fruits of years of struggle of the working class against their direct antagonists: bosses. Every additional attempt to further develop, expand, or strengthen provisions that seek to protect the interests of labour, by its nature, cannot be met with sympathy by representatives of the bourgeois class, regardless of their sex. As the former, pure water of liberalism leaves the world scene, giving way to 'social reformism' with its sermons on the 'harmony of interests' and its efforts to soften, to blur the growing class antagonism, feminist attitudes towards the issue of statutory protection for female labour are also changing. The policy of open struggle is replaced by a flexible policy of accommodation; 'blunting class contradictions' is the slogan with which the bourgeois world seeks to dull the growing class consciousness of the working class. This panacea for ever-increasing class differentiation could not help but find resonance in the hearts of many feminists. It is not for nothing that the feminists feel called to serve as bridges to connect the different classes of the population.

At the 1904 international women's congress in Berlin, feminists spoke in favour of the need for statutory workplace protections for women. This was a new course for the international women's movement. Since then, more and more resolutions and decisions of bourgeois women's organisations have begun to include demands for special protections for working women. The feminists argue as follows: Although special regulations for female labour do harm the purity of the principle of 'freedom' and 'equality', on the other hand, the defence of measures that primarily benefit proletarian women ought to win over the hearts of their 'little sisters', proletarian women, to those selfless champions of women's cause, the feminists. Surely, the odd handout to the working class is the wisest way to bring peace and tranquillity to the world. That is the thinking of those feminists who have adopted protection for women's labour as a principle.

Let us see now how our compatriots view this matter, where their sympathies lie: on the side of consistent liberalism on the English model or that of the social reform brought into the world by the growing might of the working class?

Before answering this question, let us remember the circumstances, the socio-political atmosphere, in which our first political feminist organisations came into the world. The first congress of delegates of the AWE, at which the platform and statutes of the Alliance were drawn up, took place at a time of feverish activity on the part of all thinking and oppositional elements in Russia. 'Bloody Sunday' was still vividly remembered: The proletarian sea quietly boiled; there was the feeling that there was unrest 'below', that a storm was growing there, that the whole atmosphere was pervaded with revolutionary electricity . . . The congresses of all sorts of newly formed associations and parties of all stripes spoke in heightened tones, expressed brave demands and daring wishes . . . 'Constituent Assembly' was the slogan of the day. Every organisation saw it as their duty to bow and scrape before the proletariat. The AWE also echoed this general chorus. The AWE's platform states that the representatives of the Alliance for Women's Equality consider it absolutely necessary to carry out not only a series of general fundamental political reforms, not only to equalise the civil and political rights of women with those of men, but also to 'protect women's labour and provide them with mandatory insurance on equal terms with men"* (point b). The 'Statutes', for their part, state that one of the means of achieving the goals of the AWE is 'support for improving the position of working women and protection of women in the workplace'† (point c). Thus, the AWE have, in principle, declared themselves advocates of workplace protections for women. Such a position naturally flowed from the political atmosphere that surrounded the AWE, pushing it towards the greatest possible 'radicalism'. 'If our Alliance is to be an alliance of life and struggle,' we read in the third bulletin of the AWE following the October congress, 'if it is to be an alliance of women and not ladies, it must find the means to substantially push the boundaries of its work and meet women workers where they are'‡ – a common argument amongst feminists on the path of social reformism.

The need to support proletarian women and democratise their activities was acutely felt by the AWE. 'The idea of democratisation came up a few times in the work of the congress,' we also read in the third bulletin. 'Propositions of this type were raised on several occasions, but, for some reason, the issue did not attract much serious attention.'§ The equal-rights campaigners, who were not unsurprised to acknowledge this fact, immediately go on to find an explanation for it: 'The reason must lie in the nervous, tense mood caused by everything occurring beyond the walls of the conference room that did not make it possible to concentrate even on important matters. Beyond the walls of the conference room stood the proletarian masses, the very working-class women we discussed at the congress, the very working-class women whose life the

---

*   In original: *охрану труда женщинъ и обязательное страхованіе ихъ наравнѣ съ мужчинами*

†   In original: *содѣйствіе улучшенію положенія трудящейся женщины и охрана женскаго труда*

‡   In original: *Если нашъ Союзъ хочетъ быть союзомъ жизни и борьбы, если онъ хочетъ быть не дамскимъ, а женскимъ, онъ долженъ найти средства широко раздвинуть рамки своей работы и итти навстрѣчу женщинѣ-работницѣ*

§   In original: *Мысль о демократизаціи нѣсколько разъ проскальзывала въ работахъ съѣзда,—пишется въ томъ-же 3-мъ бюллетенѣ,—нѣсколько разъ были сдѣланы предложенія подобнаго рода, но почему-то большого и серьезнаго вниманія вопросъ къ себѣ не привлекъ.*

AWE has made it an objective to improve and who, alas, were not only absent from the congress, but almost entirely from the AWE as well."

Then, as now, nothing less than an abyss separated the women standing 'beyond the walls of the conference room' of the women's congress from those who were conscientiously thinking up plans to 'benefit' and win over the hearts of these annoying working-class women standing 'beyond the walls', who made it so hard to concentrate. However, despite the obvious discord and alienation between the two female camps, the representatives of the AWE continued to ponder 'the shared cause of all women'. Class differences amongst women, they wrote in their bulletin on the occasion of the congress, were by no means as irreconcilable as they were amongst men. The AWE are happy to meet all women where they are, and believe that they, and no one else, have found the 'lost keys' to women's happiness: With these keys, the AWE hopes to unlock the doors of happiness for all women, without class distinctions. In this 'optimistic' heightened mood, the inclusion of a demand for workplace protections for women was inevitable. It is more remarkable that this demand is expressed in overly indefinite terms. The bourgeois men's parties had specific reasons for their failure to be specific about their demands. Can the same be said of our radical equal-rights campaigners, who were not afraid at the time to pronounce themselves in favour of a Constituent Assembly, and yet evince such caution in dealing with the matter of workplace protections for women? Does this not lead to a whole series of thoughts and raise the suspicion that this wording was not 'by accident'? Incidentally, we note an even more characteristic fact, i.e., that not a single resolution or decision of the AWE offers greater specification of the equal-rights campaigners' demands in the area of workplace protections, thus leaving it unclear where the focus of our leftist feminists actually lies: on demanding broad statutory protection for the interests of female

---

* In original: *Надо думать, что причиной было то нервное, напряженное настроеніе, которое, благодаря всему, совершавшемуся за стѣнами залы засѣданій, не давало возможности сосредоточиться даже на важномъ. За стѣнами залы стояла пролетарская масса—-та рабочая женщина, о которой мы говорили на съѣздѣ, та рабочая женщина, улучшить жизнь которой ставитъ своей задачей „Союзъ" и которой, увы, не было не только на съѣздѣ, но почти и въ „Союзѣ".*

workers as representatives of the working class, or narrow protection of them exclusively as women and mothers? Nor have the members of the AWE dispelled these doubts in practice, given that, over the entire existence of the AWE, they have made no actual attempt to provide 'support for improving the position of working women and protection of women in the workplace', and have done nothing to facilitate their struggle for better working conditions.

This matter of vital importance for working-class women is constantly ignored by bourgeois feminists. Indeed, that is quite natural. On the one hand, the practical implementation of reforms in this area, no matter how beneficial they may be for proletarian women, would be of no benefit to most members of the AWE; on the other, any further specification of the demands, and certainly any active struggle to implement them, would inevitably have given rise to incredible unrest under the surface of the 'harmonious' alliance. Though one sector of the equal-rights campaigners, whose special position or mindset is closer to that of proletarian women, might agree to the proposals of the working class, another sector of the AWE would doubtless pronounce them 'traitors' to the cause of all women, especially given that the implementation of the new proposals would have resulted in material losses for the more 'solid' adherents of the AWE. Raising the matter of the eight-hour work day directly would already be enough to divide the AWE and destroy its much-lauded 'unity' . . . By limiting themselves to broad strokes on such an essential point of the programme as workplace protections, in any case, our equal-rights campaigners have shown that they are able to handle the 'subtleties of politics' and find a diplomatic way out of an awkward predicament. Well, well! That, too, is a valuable quality for their future 'political careers'.

Much more naïve and direct are the right-wing feminists who drew up the programme of the Women's Progressive Party. This organisation, as already noted above, consists of social elements adjacent to the upper strata of the bourgeoisie. Had the Women's Progressive Party formulated their demands a few years ago, they likely would have included the principle of pure 'liberalism' and not wasted a single word on workplace protections for women. However, the political atmosphere of those days was not conducive to such a sharp division of oppositional elements.

The wave of the liberation movement that rose from below banged on the windows of even the women of the bourgeoisie, and forced them to perceive their own dependence on the turbulent waves of widespread popular discontent. To stand stubbornly in the way, refusing to listen to the voices coming 'from below,' was to lose the opportunity to act, to relinquish the opportunity to realise their own aspirations . . .

In order to win the general struggle, it was necessary to ingratiate themselves, win over the hearts of the women of the working classes, those women with 'callused hands', who, when the time came, would not hesitate to put their bodies on the line to fight for women's demands . . . But how could these distrustful proletarian women with their alien souls be attracted? There was only one thing for it: Assure them of the broadest possible protection for their *female* interests. Of course, when the matter is posed this way, the social privileges of the core members of the Women's Progressive Party could easily suffer, especially if working-class women were to grab hold of the demands in the programme and (God forbid!) actually implement some of them . . . But what could be done? How could the wolves' hunger be sated with the sheep remaining intact?

The Women's Political Party [*sic*] did a truly remarkable job of getting out of this deeply awkward predicament. In their programme, they were careful to include demands concerning workplace protections *specifically for women*, whilst remaining utterly silent on any measures that might have served the interests of the working class as a whole! However, this tactical wisdom could hardly confuse anyone, and, though the vague, cautious wording of the demands of the AWE might still maintain some illusions of the unity of the demands and wishes of women of all social strata, the detailed discussion of the objectives and aspirations of the Women's Progressive Party does not give any false hope on this score.

The demands of the 'progressive party' on the matter of labour begin with a grand proclamation in favour of workplace protections for all types of female wage labour. This is followed by a list of measures that are reasonable, and even entirely desirable, such as: introduction of female factory inspectorates in industrial establishments, leave for women for four weeks before and six weeks after childbirth with full pay, crèches at workplaces, breaks for breastfeeding women every three hours, to last half an hour each, replacement of male supervisors with female supervisors for women workers, and, lastly, equal compensation for equal work. What else could the heart desire? As can be seen, the demands are indeed radical; it is not for nothing that most of them are plagiarised from the labour section of the social-democratic programme . . . But where, then, is the demand for an eight-hour work day, an end to night-time work, the expansion of statutory protections to include in-home production and domestic servants? Protecting women not simply as women, not simply as mothers, but as workers, as representatives of the working class, is utterly absent from the objectives of the feminists. As consistent advocates of solely female interests, our right-wing feminists are willing to take proletarian women under their wing and care and fight for them, but not their class interests – God forbid! – only their specifically female needs. 'Statutory workplace protection for all areas of wage labour,'* reads the 'progressive' party programme, but this broad position contains quite modest wishes: proper breastfeeding for the children of working-class women, rest in the perinatal period, and appointment of women as supervisors and factory inspectors. That's it! Not one word about limiting women's employment in harmful workplaces, not one word on limiting working hours! . . .

The class position of the 'progressives' obviously limits their magnanimous foray into the area of social policy, forcing them to limit the scope of their expectations to a narrow, antisocial feminism . . .

We can see from the same programme how far the members of the Women's Progressive Party are from understanding the class nature of the demands of the working class, and how inextricably intertwined their notion of purely feminist demands is with socio-political objectives and demands. Curiously, together with the demand for the establishment of a women's factory inspectorate, indeed in the same sentence, we find a call for women to be allowed to act as sanitary supervisors of the preparation and sale of food products, and, together with the call for equal compensation for equal work, the purely feminist call for occupational equality between women and men; this is followed by the demand for equal inheritance rights with women, and for women to be granted access to all areas

---

* In original: *Законодательная защита наемнаго труда во всѣхъ областяхъ*

of state, social, and private employment, and, lastly, for peasant women to be given equal plots of land to men. All of this in the same paragraph as statutory workplace protections! Apparently, the Women's Progressive Party were trying to concentrate all the benefits they promise, to satisfy women of all strata of the population, and make the strongest possible impression through the sheer quantity and compactness of their demands.

But let us leave aside the programmatic demands of right-wing and left-wing feminists and examine how this position 'beyond class' looks in real life. The true test of any women's organisation claiming to stand 'beyond classes' in defence of women's interests is its attitude towards domestic servants and their demands. As long as the petitions of proletarian women only attack the wallets of the entrepreneurs, as long as the labour movement plays out someplace off in the distance, beyond the confines of their own homes, the feminists, who largely belong to the intelligentsia, take an attitude that is in any case tolerant, albeit not always sympathetic. However, the moment their own home and hearth are concerned, things take a dramatic turn: Any effort on the part of domestic servants to free themselves of their slavish subordination and dependency is viewed by their 'mistresses', arch-feminists though they may be, as an attack on their privileges. Any accommodation to the demands of the servant is accompanied by a sacrifice on the part of the mistress; their interests are in acute, direct conflict, and all the beautiful words about a party of all women go up in smoke . . . Germany went through a period of dramatic conflict between the feminists and their slaves in 1899; for the first time, female servants raised their voice in defence of their own interests, organised, and began to struggle against their masters for an existence that was more bearable, more worthy of human beings. The hostility with which these attempts were met by the bourgeois champions of equal rights shows as clearly as anything how illusory the cross-class feminist position is. Now, when the organisation of female servants began to constitute an actual force within society, the feminists' attitude towards it naturally changed: In the interests of the victory of women's cause, it was necessary to come to terms even with the servants, and to offer them some kind of benefit in exchange for their collaboration with the champions of women's equality.

Here, in Russia, where the position of domestic servants is incomparably worse than in Germany, this discord between mistresses and domestic slaves must be felt even more vividly and directly. In the memorable year of 1905, the year of the general uprising, when all social elements oppressed and enslaved by the contemporary regime came alive, female domestic servants also made their presence known. Glance at newspapers from 1905, and you will see that they are full of breathless reports about open defiance by female servants, even in remote backwaters of Russia. This defiance took the form either of joint strikes or street demonstrations. Strikes and agitation occurred amongst cooks, laundresses, maidservants, either by occupation, or united under the umbrella term *servants*. The protest of the domestic servants was transmitted from place to place like an infection. *Unite!*, the rallying cry in times of revolutionary insurrection, was quickly taken up by the servants, and, at the first meetings in Saint Petersburg and Moscow, domestic servants were present in enormous numbers.

And how did our feminists, the vanguard of the struggle for women's liberation, react to this phenomenon of such great importance for the cause of women? The AWE, in the early days after its formation, made a few attempts to organise servants (in Vladimir, Penza, Moscow, Kharkov), but, as the equality campaigners themselves acknowledge, not without bewilderment and sadness, these attempts were not successful. How can the failure of the feminist initiatives in this area be explained, given the uncommonly favourable social climate and the exceptional inclination of the servants to organise? The following facts may shed some light on this question: In Kharkov, the AWE formed a special 'commission to study the position of female servants'. This commission came into contact with female household staff and developed a specific draft list of demands and statutes for the servants' union. At a 'fairly crowded' meeting of the union, this draft was adopted by the servants, but the nature of this draft and the extent to which it actually corresponded to the demands of the domestic slaves can be judged by the fact that the social democrats organised a number of meetings with the specific goal of explaining to servants why the draft, created as it was with the direct participation and under the leadership of the mistresses themselves, was unacceptable.

The organised workers then proposed another draft list of demands, including a minimum wage, a regulated working day, specified hours and days of rest, etc. The majority of the servants subscribed to these demands and supported the draft statutes of the social democrats, as was reported with bewilderment and frank disappointment by the benevolent equality campaigners. The same fate met the equality campaigners nearly everywhere when they approached the female factory workers in hopes of rallying them to their women's flag. 'All it took was to awaken the political self-awareness of the proletarian women for them to leave the ranks of the AWE and join the party of their own class, becoming "party workers".'*46

Under these circumstances, the leading equal-rights campaigners comforted themselves with the thought that they were merely a 'school' to awaken the self-awareness of proletarian women. But anyone familiar with the mood within the AWE, with their objectives and aspirations, understands perfectly well that this was just a way to put a happy face on it. The feminists need women workers in all industries and proletarian women as a base, the only foundation on which they will be able to erect the edifice of women's equality. For all their sincere desire to respond to the growing demands of women workers in general and domestic servants in particular, the AWE were incapable of fulfilling the mission they had taken on, and the current of the organisation that, by late 1905 and early 1906, included all strata of the working class passed right by the equality campaigners on a course unknown to bourgeois women.

In this matter, too, the representatives of the Women's Progressive Party prove more consistent and more frank. They did not even try to disguise their intentions and true objectives. 'The servant question is particularly near and dear to the mistresses,' we read in *Zhenskiy Vyestnik*, 'and, as such, great attention must be paid to it by intelligent women. They must coordinate their own convenience with that of the servants.

---

*   In original: *Стоило разбудить политическое самосознаніе пролетарокъ, чтобы онѣ, покидая ряды союза, спѣшили вступать въ собственную классовую партію и становиться „партійными работницами".*

They must establish relations with servants such that peasant girls living in alien surroundings find sympathy, humanity, and attention to their needs on the part of the educated mistress." What lovely, praiseworthy desires! But how exactly do our progressive women propose to put these noble, lofty prescriptions for 'intelligent mistresses' into practice? It turns out that the issue of the position of servants is resolved so simply that one can only be surprised that no one else had thought of it earlier: The servants need to be dailies. This immediately resolves all complexities and anomalies in the relationship between mistress and servant and puts an end to all exploitation. But this does raise the question of where exactly the servants are meant to live. A 'solution' is provided for this as well: A 'servants' cooperative' must be organised. Initially, a few mistresses will coordinate to organise dormitories for servants; thereafter, they will hire the servant 'on the condition that she is *obliged* (italics mine – A.K.) to join the servants' cooperative, live in the dormitory, come to work for a few hours, and, the rest of the time,' the *Zhenskiy Vyestnik* magnanimously explains, 'she can spend however she wishes.'† . . . 'We believe that such a cooperative could be quite successful, and would provide great convenience both for the mistresses and the servants'‡47 – above all, we add of our own accord, for the mistresses. Fully aware of all the intricacies of their solution of the servant question, the *Zhenskiy Vyestnik* adds that the main task 'of the daily servants' cooperative must be to *guarantee* to employers conscientious fulfilment of their duties (i.e., those of the servants).'§

---

* In original: *Вопросъ о прислугѣ особенно близокъ хозяйкамъ, поэтому онъ заслуживаетъ со стороны интеллигентныхъ женщинъ большаго вниманія. Имъ необходимо согласовать свои собственныя удобства съ удобствами прислуги. Имъ надо установить съ прислугой такія отношенія, чтобы крестьянская дѣвушка, живя въ чужой сторонѣ, находила со стороны образованной хозяйки участіе, гуманность и вниманіе къ ея потребностямъ.*

† In original: „*съ условіемъ чтобы она обязана была вступить въ артель прислуги, жить въ общежитіи для послѣдней, приходить къ нимъ работать на нѣсколько часовъ; а остальное время",—великодушно поясняетъ „Женскій Вѣстникъ"— „она можетъ употреблять по своему усмотрѣнію"*

‡ In original: *Мы полагаемъ, что подобная артель могла-бы имѣть большой успѣхъ и доставила-бы много удобствъ, какъ хозяевамъ, такъ и прислугѣ*

§ In original: *артели приходящей прислуги должно быть гарантированіе хозяевамъ добросовѣстнаго отношенія съ ихъ стороны (т. е. со стороны*

In setting themselves the task of improving the position of domestic slaves, the champions of women's equality unexpectedly veered off to protect their own interests, as employers. This is at least honest of them; after such an open declaration of whose interests they have at heart, there is no risk that even less conscious elements of the female proletariat will get caught up in the nets of the right-wing feminists.

We do not examine all these real-life examples to cast aspersions on the feminists for deliberately seeking to catch 'trusting' proletarian women in their nets. On the contrary: There is no doubt that the feminists are acting sincerely, and approaching proletarians in a naïve belief in the shared nature of the tasks and aspirations of women of all classes of the population. Didn't the French bourgeoisie of the late eighteenth century comfort themselves with a similar illusion in imagining that they were expressing and serving the interests of all democratically minded strata of the population? But all of the equality campaigners' benevolent attempts to unite all women under a shared banner are inevitably doomed to fail. The feminists' demands cannot simultaneously meet the economic demands of those who sell their labour power and those who buy it in their efforts to derive from that transaction the greatest possible benefit for themselves. For the feminists most sensitive to social evils, there remains one, alas, utterly imperfect path: that of bandaging the open sore of modern humanity with the help of philanthropy . . .

Most women's organisations in England have philanthropic objectives. Philanthropic activities are carried out broadly, methodically, and even according to plans. Despite this, however, the need – the acute need that eats away at the nerves and the righteous conscience of the English people – grows, grows, and grows. . . . In 1905, hunger and unemployment in London led to a grand street demonstration of proletarian women. The impressive crowd of those exhausted, tormented by overwork, poverty, and hunger, and despairing at the impossibility of their situation exploded onto the main streets of London. In the arms of some, like small children, and held up by others were banners reading: 'Unemployed! Demand the right to work!' 'Women, demand the right to vote to rebuild society!' 'Work for our husbands! Bread for our children!' The women

прислуги) къ своимъ обязанностямъ

walked to the prime minister in search of 'work, work, work . . . ' In their petition to the minister, the proletarian women described in dramatic detail how they, the women of the working class, had long remained silent, but that the cup of patience had now overflowed, and they had to make their presence known. They lacked the strength to suffer unemployment and hunger any longer. The demonstration was the only way to make their needs known, to draw attention to themselves; after all, working-class women still do not have the opportunity to defend their own interests as representatives. The British government was informed that women workers would no longer be silent and accept poverty and hunger, dependency and humiliation. If their demands were not met, they would be able to make those who so unjustly oppress the people tremble! . . .

In the face of such an explosion of desperation and determination, all the benevolent initiatives of the feminists were powerless. What good are all these lodgings for working women, dormitories for shop assistants, dining halls for poor women, homes for young girls, when cases of death by hunger are reported in the newspapers as a normal occurrence, when the residents of London experience the same hunger pains as our forefathers, who had no other tool to work with than poorly hewn stone . . . ? But in those days, hunger was natural and inevitable; in those days, nature was all-powerful, and the productivity of human labour nonexistent. But now, death by hunger in the middle of London, a city full of massive food supplies, this is the greatest indictment, the most powerful accusation that future humanity will throw at twentieth-century capitalism. In vain, bourgeois women seek by means of philanthropy to free themselves from niggling pangs of conscience at the sight of the poverty, desperation, and humiliation of their 'little sisters'. What can even the most exemplary philanthropy do against the growing proletarianisation of the masses, against the uninterrupted growth of the might of capital? The hands of even the most sensitive feminists buckle under the weight of the social evil engulfing the entire planet. The teaspoon of philanthropy will never empty the sea of suffering and poverty created by the capitalist exploitation of wage labour! . . .

Sincere champions of women's cause must stand in sad perplexity at the sight of the growing social disaster. They cannot fail to see how little proletarian women have been given thus far by the movement of all women, how powerless that movement is to change the working and living conditions of the working class for the better. How grey, gloomy, and cloudy the future of humanity must look to these women who fight for equal rights who have not adopted the proletarian worldview, who are not nourished by an uplifting faith that a more perfect social structure is drawing nearer. How incomplete, partial, and watered-down the notion of liberating women whilst maintaining the integrity of the entire contemporary capitalist world must appear to them! What despondency must pervade the ranks of the most profound and sensitive champions of women's cause! . . . Only the working class is able to avoid hanging their heads in the face of the current monstrous social relations. With measured, iron steps, the working class steadily stride towards their goal, calling women workers into their ranks. Proletarian women walk bravely on the thorny path of labour. It wounds their feet, tortures their bodies; it is full of dangerous chasms and hungry predators watchfully tracking them . . .

But only by entering this path can women reach the goal that beckons from far off – their complete liberation in the renewed world of labour . . . On her arduous journey to the bright future, the proletarian woman – who had until just recently been a humiliated, disenfranchised, beaten slave – will learn to cast away all of the servile virtues that have been imposed upon her: Step by step, she will become an independent worker, independent in personality, free in love . . . In shared struggle with the men of the proletariat, she fights to win the right to work for women; she, the 'little sister', persistently, steadily blazes the trail for the 'free', 'equal' woman of the future . . .

After that, what would working-class women want with an alliance with bourgeois feminists? And who actually benefits from such an alliance? Certainly not working-class women: Their salvation, their future is in their own hands. Standing watch over her class interests, not letting herself be flattered by grandiose speeches about the unity of the 'world of all women (*все-женского мира*)',[48] working-class women should not and cannot forget that, if the goal of bourgeois women is to guarantee their own prosperity within the existing social framework that is antagonistic to us, they have a different goal: to build in place of the old, moribund world a new shrine to shared labour, comradely solidarity, and joyful freedom . . .

CHAPTER 2

MARRIAGE AND THE FAMILY PROBLEM

> The contemporary form of the family is not the final
> form. A new society will create a new form of family.
>
> K. Kautsky, *The Class Struggle (Erfurt Program)*[*]

Let us move on to examine another aspect of the female question – the family question. Need we even mention the significance the resolution of this painful, complex issue of our day has for the actual emancipation of women? Women's struggle for equality is, of course, not limited to the struggle for political enfranchisement, access to doctorates and other academic degrees, and equal pay for equal work. In order to become actually free, women must cast off of themselves the chains of the contemporary, obsolete, coercive form of the family that weigh on them. The resolution of the family question is no less important for women than the acquisition of political equality or the assertion of their total economic independence.

In the current forms of the family structure, as they have been established by law and custom, women suffer not only as human beings, but as wives and mothers. In most civilised countries, the civil code makes

---

[*] The original reads: *Wir halten die heute bestehende Form der Familie nicht für ihre letzte und erwarten, daß eine neue Gesellschaftsform auch eine neue Familienform entwickeln wird.* (We do not consider the currently existing form of the family to be the final one, and expect that a new social form will also develop a new form of family) (https://www.marxists.org/deutsch/archiv/kautsky/1892/erfurter/2-proletariat.htm). —Trans.

women more or less dependent on men and grants husbands the right not only to dispose of their assets, but to exercise moral and physical control over them. It is worth mentioning the civil code of France, under which women lose all civil legal capacity from the day on which they conclude a marriage contract. Their assets pass into their husbands' control; they may not carry out any transaction without their husbands' consent; even a tenancy agreement must be witnessed by their 'lord and master'; and the sanctity of the family hearth is protected by the strictest of laws, completely sanctioning double standards. Adultery by the husband the law punishes with a fine, and only under certain conditions; a breach of spousal faith by the wife, on the other hand, is punished by two years' imprisonment. Unmarried women are subject to the *patria potestas* of their fathers, but, by remaining unmarried, they enjoy somewhat greater freedom and independence. On the other hand, their 'virginal purity' is carefully watched over by French law, which severely punishes single mothers by saddling them with all consequences of extramarital intercourse: As is known, art. 350*[*sic*] of the French civil code provides that 'inquiries into paternity are prohibited'.

Although the laws of some other countries are less harsh towards women, the principle of the legal subordination of the wife to her husband and master is emphasised in them to a greater or lesser degree.

Here, in Russia, married women cannot enter into personal service contracts without their husbands' permission. Likewise, promissory notes issued by a wife without her husband's sanction are deemed void. In our legal system, wives are obliged to obey their husbands, and the latter's power is greater than that of parents. Wives are also obliged to share the same residence as their spouses, and, until quite recently, the latter were entitled to demand the return of their 'recalcitrant wives', who sought to free themselves from husbands they disliked, or even hated.

And where the official, statutory enslavement of women ends, the intervention of so-called public opinion in their rights begins. This public opinion is created and supported by the bourgeoisie in order to preserve

---

* So in original. The provision in question is actually found in art. 340 of the code, which reads: *La recherche de la paternité est interdite* . . . (https://fr.wikisource.org/wiki/Code_civil_des_Fran%C3%A7ais_1804/Texte_entier) —Trans.

'the sacred institution of property'. Hypocritical 'double standards' are sanctioned. Bourgeois society oppresses women with intolerable economic hardships, paying absurdly little for their work; it deprives them of the citizen's right to raise their voices in defence of their trodden-on interests, obligingly offering them one choice: either marital bondage or the embrace of prostitution, which is publicly scorned and persecuted, but secretly promoted and supported.

Need we tarry on the dark sides of modern marital life, on the ways in which women suffer that are intimately connected to the family structure of our day? So much has already been said and written on this subject. Fiction is full of grave images of our marital and family troubles. How many psychological tragedies have originated from this, how many ruined lives and mangled existences! For our current purposes, it is important merely to note that the contemporary family structure oppresses women of all classes and social strata to some extent or other. Custom and tradition persecute unwed mothers alike, no matter what segment of society they belong to; the law places bourgeois, proletarian, and peasant women alike under the guardianship of their husbands.

Have we perhaps stumbled upon the aspect of the female question in which women of all classes may actually join hands and struggle together against the conditions oppressing them? It may be that shared woe and suffering bridge the abyss of class antagonism and create unity between the aspirations and objectives of women of the various camps? Could it be that these shared desires and objectives make cooperation between bourgeois and proletarian women possible? After all, the bourgeois feminists fight for freer forms of marriage and the 'right to motherhood', and raise their voice in defence of the universally persecuted prostitutes. Look how replete feminist literature is with the search for new forms of marital cohabitation and how courageously it rushes towards the 'moral equality' of the sexes! Indeed, whilst bourgeois women ride the coat-tails of a millions-strong army of proletarian women in the field of economic liberation that has blazed the trail for the 'new woman', is it not so that the feminists have the ones to lead the way to the resolution of the family question?

Here, in Russia, women of the middle bourgeoisie, that army of women wage earners who were suddenly thrown onto the labour market in the 1860s, have already practically resolved many convoluted aspects of the marital question for themselves by bravely striding past traditional church marriage and replacing the consolidated form of the family with an easily dissolved union that is more responsive to the needs of the mobile intelligentsia. However, the subjective solution of this question by individual women does not change the issue or overcome the overall dismal picture of family life. If anything is breaking down the contemporary form of the family, it is not the titanic efforts of people of greater individuality, but the dead, yet powerful, productive forces that inexorably, step by step, are placing the structure of life on new foundations . . .

At this point, let us try to answer two essential questions: (1) Whose efforts – those of proletarians or those of the feminists – are responsible for women's gradual liberation from familial oppression? and (2) Is there in fact unity of efforts between the feminists and proletarian women in relation to the family question, or does the class discord that divides women into two antagonistic, occasionally even hostile, camps appear here as it does in all other areas of life?

Need we also prove that all is in fact not well in the contemporary family structure, that the existing form of the purportedly monogamous family is constantly falling apart and breaking up at its very roots? With every passing day, the contemporary family, coercively established by a civil code that is complicated in the interests of bourgeois property, loses its stability, its former robustness. The natural bonds that once welded the family into an indivisible cell of society are weakening and falling away as the economic forms that gave rise to them disappear. A sturdy, cohesive, unbreakable union of the family in which all power belonged to the sole breadwinner, the sole acquirer of wealth, the father and husband —that was the ideal of family life that met the needs of the emerging 'Third Estate'. In those times, in which the Third Estate had only just embarked on its great mission – to accumulate tremendous wealth in the depths of the family – the indivisibility and stability of family structures were one of the prerequisites for the success of the bourgeoisie in their existential struggle with the other strata of the population. It is not for nothing that the bourgeoisie of the seventeenth and eighteenth centuries boasted of their morality and smugly juxtaposed their familial virtues with the morals of the wicked, frivolous aristocracy, who had not learnt the great sacrament of capitalist accumulation, and thus looked upon the family not as a way of storing accumulated wealth, but of squandering it. The Third Estate did everything in their power to make the family more stable and further elevate the prestige of familial virtues. In this, they brought to bear religion, with its preaching on the indivisibility of the holy sacrament of marriage; the law, which punished adultery on the part of the wife; and morality, which proclaimed the 'sanctity of the family hearth'. And when the bourgeoisie assumed the dominant position within society, when all threads of production worldwide began joining in their hands, their morality, their ethical and civil codes, the purpose of which was in fact to protect their class interests, gradually turned into norms that bound the other strata of the population as well. The morality of the 'Third Estate' was proclaimed the morality of all humanity. Narrow class-based material considerations forced the bourgeoisie to be concerned about the 'purity' of the marital deception and persecute the 'illegitimate', that is, those who could not and must not inherit even a single particle of the treasures accumulated by the family; this class calculation aided in the establishment of the moral 'double standards' and the 'strict' statutory provisions in the area of family law. And here we all are, raised on artificial norms of sexual morality that serve the sole purpose of protecting the interests of the bourgeoisie; even today, we bow down to these class principles as if they were supreme ideological categories, willing to declare them the normative principles of morality.

At the same time as capitalist production was proclaimed the timeless, eternal form of human economic life, monogamous marriage was declared an immutable, constant social institution. The evolutionary view of marriage was condemned and persecuted with the same vehemence and hatred with which evolutionism in the economic life of society was denied and disputed. Property and the family are too intimately intertwined to be certain that one of these pillars of the bourgeois world could be undermined without calling into question the solidity of the other. This is why the bourgeoisie have always so jealously guarded their familial origins; this is why they have always fought so passionately in defence of the contemporary, decrepit forms of marriage, and continue to do so even today.

However, the economic evolution that humanity has experienced – the death of small-scale craft production, the rise of mechanised labour, the colossal growth of cities, the fever pitch of their productive and commercial life – this evolution could not but influence the forms of family cohabitation and was bound to shake the supposedly inviolate foundations of the bourgeois family.

For an entire century now, there has been an uninterrupted conflict between the supporters of the old view of the family as an immutable social institution and the advocates of new theories, for which the contemporary form of marital cohabitation is merely a passing historical category. So many historical examples and ethnographic studies, so much lived reality testifies day by day to the instability of the contemporary family and its ongoing, constant decay. Ever more rarely do we hear voices asserting that the contemporary family is a constant, immutable institution, and the debate on family relations itself is already passing to a new plane. The question that now occupies the ideologues of the bourgeoisie is: With what 'reforms' to preserve the closed bourgeois family as a whole, with what measures prevent its further decomposition?

Nothing provokes greater disgust amongst the bourgeoisie than the claim advanced by the followers of scientific socialism that radical changes in the area of family life are inevitable as the economic foundations of society are restructured on a new, collectivistic, basis. Bourgeois ideologues then begin screaming with redoubled vehemence that the contemporary family can transfer intact into any reformed structure, and that changes in the relations of production by no means render inevitable a rupture in the forms of cohabitation of the sexes.

But is this really so?

For any form of social relations between people to be stable, the economic reasons that brought about this, and not another, form of social relations must be in place. In the days when subsistence farming predominated, the family was above all an economic unit that produced all of the goods required by a particular group of persons.[1]

As the exchange-based economy developed and established itself, the members of the family could all, to a greater or lesser extent, meet their own needs without the aid of the family as an economic unit; nonetheless, up until the nineteenth century, i.e., the dawn of large-scale capitalist production, the family maintained a whole number of minor economic functions, injecting a decisive and determinative economic aspect into the moral union of marriage. As long as the family was, to a greater or lesser extent, a producer of value, its social existence was guaranteed; solid, living bonds held its members together with much greater strength than even the strictest legal codes and coercive norms of morality. However, as soon as large-scale capitalist production wrested from the family its customary economic obligations, the family lost its significance as a necessary economic unit, and was thus condemned to slow, but inevitable, decomposition.

Indeed, where now are those economic bonds that once made the family so stable and vital? Let us first take the bourgeois family and examine which of those functions that it performed for centuries remain preserved in our time.

The productive activities of the family, in the sense of producing a long list of basic necessities, have been reduced to a minimum; the domestic sphere of the economy has been narrowed to the point that it is no longer recognisable. Where would we find a bourgeois family these days that dedicates itself to making candles, butter, and beer, spinning and knitting, making preserves for the winter, baking bread, or sewing clothes for all members of the household? Where there is no benefit, there is no need to expend the energies of the members of the family on obtaining and producing such objects, which, despite being basic necessities, are cheaply obtainable at any commercial establishment. One area of the economy after another slips out of the hands of the housewife to become an object of industrial speculation. With the growth and enthronement of large-scale capitalist production, the family loses its former role as a cell of production, and, no longer playing the role of an independent economic unit, gradually loses its significance in the economic life of society.[2]

Is it, however, possible that other economic functions of the family continue to be preserved, even if the production and acquisition of necessities in the family sphere has ceased? Indeed, over the many centuries of its existence, the family has not only been an independent creator of value, but a reliable storehouse of it. Homes, housewares, family treasures – all of this has been protected and preserved as sacred by the family.

The relatively immobile family of the recent past, tied as it was to property, land, and houses, was the most reliable apparatus for storing family wealth, and, under those circumstances, the fortress of family ties is intimately connected to the property interests of the clan. If the family breaks up, the family treasure, too, will be dispersed.

Things are different now: Banks and other savings institutions are completely taking over the saving function of the family; they, and not moral-sexual unions, take it upon themselves to preserve and protect the wealth that families have already accumulated. In addition, this wealth is ever more frequently expressed in the form of interest-bearing portable securities, whose preservation requires no particular care on the part of the household. As the mobility of life becomes ever greater, lines of communications develop ever further, thus facilitating frequent relocation of families from one place to another, and bulky assets become a burden; under such conditions, the only easily portable expression of value is money and interest-bearing securities. Thus, even the previous, customary function of the family of storing accumulated value is extracted from the sphere of domestic obligations.

And what of consumption, that integral condition of family life? Is it still practised in the family sphere to the same extent as it once was? Restaurants, clubs, furnished homes, and hotels are taking the place of the customary domestic hearth. The moneyed haute bourgeoisie spend half their lives swanning about fashionable spas, relying on the services of palatial hotels; the middle and petite bourgeoisie, in an effort to cast away burdensome economic concerns and cut 'domestic' expenditures, huddle in furnished flats, dine in restaurants, work in public libraries and laboratories, and in national galleries and museums.

As growing demand for cheap labour in all areas of labour draws women out of the narrow family unit, bringing them into the current of the independently employed population, this type of life becomes more and more widespread. As long as the husband was the sole breadwinner of the family and his income provided the family with all material goods accessible to it, as long as the welfare of the wife and children primarily depended on him, the family was held tightly together by bonds that are frequently wholly unknown to today's families. Today, in the petite bourgeoisie, and even in the middle bourgeoisie, women increasingly cover part of the family's needs from their own income; the wife's dependency on her husband, the daughter's dependency on her father, is being destroyed from the roots, and the powerful bonds that once held together the members of the bourgeois family are weakening and breaking apart, one after another.

What remains for the family in our days? What functions does it still have, what bonds still hold its members together? Child rearing, perhaps? But where are these bourgeois mothers and fathers who raise and educate their children themselves? Not only the petite and middle, but even the haute bourgeoisie do not recoil from socialised educational institutions. Kindergartens and primary schools are becoming more widespread than ever before, not to mention institutions of intermediate and higher education. Child-rearing responsibilities, just like the other functions of the family, are passing from the closed unit of the family to society or the state.

What remains for the family after that? What is its task in our current individualistic class society? None other than the direct transfer of acquired and inherited wealth. The purpose of the near-indissolubility of contemporary marriage is to facilitate this sole task of the present-day family, a family that serves not the moral needs of the person, but the interests of property. Surely the entire history of contemporary marriage shows that this institution was created based on purely utilitarian calculations, and only included a moral element such as affection in rare, particularly favourable cases.

With the establishment of their dominance, the bourgeoisie ceased to be disingenuous and began openly presenting their marital unions as a sort of commercial transaction, a profitable 'deal'. In the present conditions, the union of 'two loving hearts' that make up a marriage in the preferred portrayal of bourgeois ideologues is increasingly metamorphosing into a cynical transaction for a dowry or the sale of a title. Marriages concluded on the basis of newspaper advertisements are so common that the moral sensibilities of the punctilious bourgeois cannot be bothered to be offended. The happy outcomes of such 'pragmatic' marriages can be seen from the ever-increasing number of divorces.[3] Applications for the dissolution of marriage are so numerous that one Vienna judge cried out in desperation: 'Soon, complaints for broken marriages will be as common as complaints over broken glass!'

The available statistics cannot provide an accurate picture of the number of 'broken marriages', because an enormous number of spouses part ways without seeking a formal divorce. Nor should we forget that the laws of all states impose all manner of obstacles to the dissolution of marriages, thus forcibly preventing spouses from parting ways, and frequently preventing the dissolution of such beneficial unions as the marriage of millions to a title or land to capital . . .

However, if the family in the bourgeois class is inexorably breaking apart, if the foundations that once kept it alive are dying out with every passing day, does this mean that the same inexorable process of family decay is also taking place in the other strata of society? We know that there was a time when the aristocratic family of feudalism went into frank decay and broke up in the most public and irrefutable way, but the Third Estate that was emerging at that time sanctified family traditions, rightly seeing the integrity of the family as the beginning of a trusty stronghold for their growing social power. Could it be that, even now, it is only the families of the middle and haute bourgeoisie that are falling apart, whilst the foundations of the family in the petite bourgeoisie, e.g., in the peasantry, remain viable?

We need not even mention the western European peasantry, who are subject to the same influences that are bringing about the breakdown of the family in the other bourgeois strata, but even our 'rigid' Russian peasantry is experiencing a drastic evolution in family relations. The transition from the large, extended family to the 'nuclear family' alone, the mere fact of such mass breakups is a clear indicator of the dissolution of the previous family structures amongst the peasantry.

The 'nuclear' family, it is known, is based on completely different economic foundations; here, the woman is given greater leeway and opportunities to establish herself in the independent position of 'mistress' and housekeeper. In the 'extended' family, she is just one of many mechanically carrying out the will of others, the heads of the clan. In the absence of a specified division of labour, she is left with no room for initiative and, no matter how hard she might work, has no opportunity for recognition of all the value she contributes to the household. Thus, her work is devalued, and she is kept in total dependency. In the nuclear family, women work no less – indeed, they sometimes work more – but they are in charge of a specific area of the household; they act as individual producers, and the labour of their hands is easily acknowledged and valued. They are responsible for the maintenance of the household in the broadest sense of the word, including spinning, weaving, caring for livestock, even selling the products of the household; only at harvest time do they merely help out their husband with the fieldwork. It is for this reason that the husband does not feel entitled to interfere in his wife's housekeeping. 'In Little Russia*,' we learn from Aleksandra Yefimenko, 'where, as a result of particular local historical and domestic conditions, the extended family broke up significantly earlier than in Greater Russia, this division of labour, duties, and rights has occurred to a significant extent. The husband never intervenes in his wife's affairs, leaving them to her complete and unchecked discretion: '*Se babskoye khozyaistvo* – That is women's business,' as men in Little Russia say. But it is specifically in Little Russia that the domestic position of peasant women is significantly more bearable than in Greater Russia, where the foundations of the old extended family still hold sway.

The relatively large degree of independence that women benefit from in small families naturally made them fierce defenders of this form of family relations, and has caused peasant women to use all means at their disposal to attain division, shunning neither defamation, nor pugnaciousness. 'Both in Greater Russia,' Yefimenko states, 'and amongst the other Slavic peoples, women are considered the evil opponents of shared tribal life and the main cause of the decline of the old order.'[1] Although this statement is not entirely true, it is in any case characteristic: The decline of clan life doubtless has deeper causes than the 'pugnaciousness' and 'contentiousness' of the womenfolk. After all, women quarrelled in the past without it resulting in the ubiquitous division of extended families into 'small' families.

---

*   Ukraine —Trans.

The durability of the foundations of the family is inversely proportional to the prevalence of the exchange-based economy in the village; this is well known. Where the peasantry have not yet been caught up in the worldwide current of commercial intercourse, where the original, closed subsistence economy holds sway, the ancient form of the patriarchal family is maintained in all its archaic integrity. In this case, the family remains a primarily economic unit, the producer of all goods needed for life, a unit of extreme importance, even indispensable, for all its members. In that case, the economic ties that bind the peasant family guarantee its stability and vitality; here, divorce is not even spoken of. To be sure, marriage here is not a 'moral union', but it nonetheless rests entirely on the real foundation of the relations of production. Our extended peasant families in Russia, with all their inherited ugliness, in which women have no recourse against their enslavement, in which the 'master' holds unlimited power over the entire household, have remained preserved to this day only because our peasantry retained forms of economic relations long since overcome and abandoned by other peoples until the end of the nineteenth century.

However, the former encrusted norms of patriarchal life are losing their previous stability as the peasant economy is swept into the general current of worldwide commodity exchange. The moral principles of family life, which had seemed so firm and inviolate just a few decades ago, have begun to lose their categorical character, and are departing the peasant household together with home-knit linen shirts and homemade ploughs.

The transition of the peasant family from 'extended' to 'nuclear', a transition born of the aforementioned economic causes, is merely accelerating the process of the further breakdown of the family. Even if folk custom has brought the principles of the wife's disenfranchisement and dependency on the head of the household into the bosom of the nuclear family, the practices of everyday life stand diametrically opposed to these principles. The same economic conditions of the nuclear family grant women a certain economic independence and, even within the darkest depths of the peasantry, create a conflict between its outmoded foundations and the realities of life. This is the first step towards the appearance of the 'female question' in the peasant milieu.

The unprecedented growth in the number of women opting for monastic life demonstrates that the dissatisfaction of women of the peasant estate is growing together with the evolution of the family form. In 1855, there were 7,091 novices in the convents; in 1902, there were no fewer than 32,029. Without a doubt, the attraction of peasant women (for it is from the peasantry that novices are overwhelmingly recruited) indicates their growing desire to leave behind the hardships of peasant family life, with their constant economic insecurity and gruelling labour. The same thing can be seen from the prevalence of *chernichki** amongst peasant girls. *Chernichki,* who condemn themselves to official celibacy, nevertheless do not renounce love; to the contrary, having acquired for themselves a certain degree of independence within the family (their earnings are considered sacrosanct, and no one in the family can touch them), they also benefit from freedom in the sentimental sphere. Peasant women's desire to become nuns or *chernichki,* like their departure to the city or to industrial areas 'to earn', is an expression of their growing self-awareness, which renders their previous familial bondage unbearable. Here, in Russia, the decomposition of the peasant family is most visible in localities where women are thrown in large numbers onto the agricultural labour market.[5]

Women who travel a hundred versts† away to strange provinces to work in agriculture, women participating in seasonal work away from home, represent a new type of peasant woman. Her psychology is more reminiscent of that of the female factory worker than that of the submissive 'village woman' who obediently took upon herself all the hardships of domestic life that patriarchal tradition sanctifies. The family itself

---

*   This term, for which no good English translation exists, is defined by academic.ru as 'peasant women who did not marry due either to their parents' vow or their own. This intention had to be stated at a young age, before the age of twenty, whilst there were still willing suitors. Otherwise, their fellow villagers would consider them spinsters (*vyekobukhi*), whose unmarried state was not intentional, but accidental.' (*сельские женщины, не вступившие в брак по обету родителей или своему собственному. О таком намерении полагалось заявить смолоду, до двадцати лет, пока еще сватались женихи. В противном случае в глазах односельчан девушка была вековухой, то есть оставшейся в девичестве не намеренно, по обету, а случайно.*) (https://dic.academic.ru/dic.nsf/russian_history/11798/%D0%A7%D0%95%D0%A0%D0%9D%D0%98%D0%A7%D0%9A%D0%98) —Trans.

†   Russian traditional unit of measurement equal to 0.66 miles (1.1 km). —Trans.

takes on a new appearance in such cases, losing its insularity, its rigidity, becoming mobile, fragmented, and, accordingly, easily dissolved. Penetrating even the most remote corners of the countryside, the new relations of production are subjugating and changing the previous forms of social life. In embedding itself in the villages and penetrating all local agrarian relations, capitalism is not only changing the face of the eastern European peasant family, but delivering the decisive blows to the patriarchal way of life of our Russian peasantry. Slowly but surely, a number of serious changes are occurring in the peasant family, breaking through its previous, customary stability and inviolability . . .

That leaves the most numerous stratum of contemporary society: the proletarian class. What is the situation in this class of the population? Will we, perhaps, find conditions to ensure the vitality of the present family structure here, at least? Can this question even be seriously asked? Where is it, the family of the contemporary worker and seller of labour power?[6]

At the first glimmering of daylight, both husband and wife hurry to leave their wretched, dark home in order to obey the call of the factory horn and abjectly submit to the power of their soulless, but all-powerful mechanised overlords. The spouses remain away from home until late at night, consigning the children to the care of the good Lord; in the best of cases, their care is ensured by a neighbour's decrepit or absent ability to work . . . The street – noisy, dirty, and lewd – that is their carer, that is the first school the children of the proletariat attend . . . If the workshop is far from home, the parents do not see the inside of their abandoned abode, even at lunch. The last illusion of the insularity of the family is shattered by boarders: men and women, alcoholics, old people, and children. Meanwhile, poverty hauntingly knocks at the window, watching with the eyes of a predator for chance misfortunes – illness, unemployment, the death of a family member, the birth of a child – to tear into the proletarian family with its greedy claws, casting them asunder, spreading them over the world . . . In such conditions, marriage, even marriage entered into by mutual affection, quickly transforms into an unbearable yoke, from which both parties often seek to escape with vodka . . .

Her husband's low wages and capital's ceaseless demands for cheap female labour push the woman into the open arms of capitalist production.

But the moment the factory doors slam shut behind the woman worker, the fate of the proletarian family is sealed. Slowly, but inexorably, the family life of the worker falls into decline. The home fire goes out, ceasing to be a centre that unites the members of the family.

What mockery, what sacrilege the sentimental bleating of the bourgeoisie about 'the sanctity of home and hearth' and 'motherhood' sounds like when millions, tens of millions of mothers are unable to carry out even their most elementary duties! At the commanding call of capital, mothers tear from their breasts children who have not yet even learnt to tell light from darkness, obediently massing at the factory gates.

The bourgeois defenders of contemporary marriage and motherhood are perfectly well informed of how children are crippled and deformed already in their mothers' wombs by hazardous gases and vapours,[7] how millions of young lives are lost when they drink toxic substances from their mothers' milk, how children thrown upon the mercy of fate at harvest time burn to death in their hundreds in village huts, how mothers gradually poison their children, their beloved children, with opium so that their cries will not get in the way of completing rush orders.

But the hypocrisy of the bourgeoisie knows no bounds. What do they care that the children of working women employed in match and mercury factories, or in the production of mirrors or lead paint, are born with musculoskeletal deformities, with weakened vital functions, or are merely born to die with excruciating convulsions?! What of the fact that miscarriages and stillbirths are the inevitable result of the monstrous exploitation of women's labour by the modern industrial system?! Or the fact that mothers, driven out of their minds by hunger and poverty, abandon their children to 'angel factories', whilst the statistics show uninterrupted growth in infanticide, and the ranks of these 'criminal mothers' include not only girls abandoned by their lovers, but also the lawful wives of proletarian men, respected mothers of families?![8] The hypocritical bourgeois defenders of the modern family do not let the full screaming horror of these everyday realities dampen their enthusiasm as they carry on singing hymns to 'the sacred role of motherhood' and inveigh against women being torn away from their children's cradles to do work outside the home (though this is, of course, only lip service).

'The sacred duty of motherhood!' But what form can this role of women take in the working class given the current conditions of female wage labour? Where is the indispensable concern for children's health, where are minimal hygienic requirements for preserving infants' lives met? Infant mortality, particularly in the first year of life, reaches horrifying levels in the proletariat. At the same time as 8 percent of the infants of the bourgeois class die in the first year of life,' Lily Braun remarks, roughly 30 percent of the children of the working class die at this age. In the rich neighbourhoods of Berlin-Friedrichstadt, 148 nursing infants die out of every thousand, whilst in the poor neighbourhood of Wedding, 348 [*sic*] out of every thousand die! The mortality in the industrial centres demonstrates the close link between infant mortality and the growth in female labour.[9]

The tobacco industry is one of the most harmful in this regard; the greatest number of stillbirths amongst industrial workers occur amongst women tobacco workers. Here, even if babies are born alive, they can look forward to slow poisoning by their mothers' nicotine-laced milk. The infant mortality is also enormous amongst women employed in the paper industry; in Germany, it amounts to 48 percent. The same fate also awaits the children of women textile workers: in England, 22 percent of infants born to mothers working in fibre processing died in the first year of life; in Germany, the figure is 38 percent.

And what awaits the children of proletarian families if they do manage to survive all the mortal dangers with which their path to and after birth has been so generously sown? Hunger, cold, poverty, angry shouting, beatings by tired hands. The wish, brought about by sheer desperation: 'If only you'd suffocated!' This is followed by dismal years spent in apprenticeship or at the machine, and, in their leisure time: the street, fighting, swearing, pubs, and many, many beatings . . . This is what is meant in the present structure by an upbringing 'under mother's attentive eyes'!

No, no matter how much the tender mummies of the bourgeois milieu reject the collectivist structure of the future with its principle of socialised child rearing, no matter how much they curse socialists for their 'callousness' and their barbaric desire to take from them the 'blood of their blood', it can be said that any form of child rearing different to the contemporary one will save millions of little lives . . . There will at least be no more unfortunate children tied to the bed by their mothers so that they can go to work, there will no longer be the martyrology, to which we are accustomed, of children dead of tragic accidents, falling under carriages or out of windows, or drowning in tubs of water . . . The lives of proletarian children are so brutal, so full of the most barbaric deprivation and unchildlike suffering that the loss of their parents and their families is not infrequently a blessing to them. Orphanages founded by philanthropists or the state, with all their glaring inadequacies, are quite often a salvation for the children of the proletariat.

Let the affectionate bourgeois mothers who inveigh against socialists for their intention to 'tear children away from their mother's breast' honestly acknowledge how many proletarian mothers, in the current bourgeois system, remain at their children's cradles.[10] We certainly must not close our eyes to the constant growth in labour by married women. Over a period of twelve years in Germany, the number of married women workers increased by 300,000; in 1882, of 1,000 working women, 173 were married. In 1895, the number was already 215. According to the most recent figures, of every thousand women working in Austria, 450 are married. In Germany, the figure is roughly 220, and roughly 200 in France. Indeed, this figure is significantly greater, because the statistics only count women as married when their marriage is sanctified by the law and the church. Meanwhile, free cohabitation, in which the woman – wife and mother – has all the customary familial obligations, is more and more common amongst working-class women.

The material deprivation of the proletarian family forces married women to work in the factories, and, as long as the system of wage labour remains, as long as capital has an interest in bringing ever cheaper workers into production, there will be no reason to expect a decrease in the number of married proletarian women working in industry.

According to testimonies collected by factory inspectors in Alsace-Lorraine, 82 percent of all married working women turned to industrial labour because they lacked any other means of support; in Aachen, the number of married women condemned to the factories by desperate need was even higher at 88 percent; in Schleswig, it was as high as 96 per-cent![11] Our esteemed entrepreneurs, often the most bitter opponents of women's emancipation and independence when it comes to women of their own class, declare with cynical candour that married women are their most beloved exploitation objects. Of course they are! Working mothers will endure anything, agree even to the most outrageous work-ing conditions, so long as they do not return home with empty hands and hear the soul-crushing cries of hungry children! Factory owners consider unmarried women workers too independent, too brave and daring, and much more susceptible to the propaganda of dangerous ideas than mar-ried women who bear the burden of supporting families. It comes as no surprise that entrepreneurs do everything they can to encourage married women to work for them. And under such circumstances, where, on the one hand, economic need forces women into wage labour, and, on the other, capitalist production awaits them with open arms, it should come as no surprise that the proletarian family is rapidly and inexorably mov-ing towards complete collapse.

Thus, no matter how much the bourgeoisie shout about the indestructi-bility and constancy of the foundations of the family, the family – the con-temporary, insular, property-orientated, narrowly individualist family – is doomed to death and dissolution. In front of the eyes of the whole world, the home fire is going out in all classes and strata of the population, and, of course, this dying flame cannot be fanned by artificial means.

Marriage represents one side of the sexual life of bourgeois society; prostitution represents the other. Marriage is the obverse side of the coin and prostitution the reverse. If a man does not find satisfaction in mar-riage, he usually seeks satisfaction in prostitution. Both men who are unmarried by choice or necessity and men who are married, but disap-pointed, find it considerably easier to satisfy their sexual desires than women do.[12]

Scorned by all, shunned by all, but quietly encouraged, prostitution, with its lush, toxic blossoms, muffles all that remains of familial virtue. As if covering society in putrid mud, its stinking breath poisons the pure joys of amorous relations between the sexes. In our time, prostitution has taken on colossal dimensions heretofore unknown to humanity, even in the times of its greatest spiritual decline.

What are the semi-religious *dicterions* of Greece, the *lupanars* of Rome, the cheerful prostitution of 'camp followers' or the hierarchical prostitutes' guilds of the Middle Ages, or the publicly shunned, but quietly promoted cynical debauchery of the Reformation? What are these thousands of frivolous *grisettes* of the eighteenth century compared to the mass sale of women's bodies practised in our days?

Like a toxic infection, prostitution moves from place to place, from country to country, from the cities to the countryside, poisoning the atmosphere of modern social life. Entire professions, entire social strata are subordinated to this disastrous influence.

So much has been said and written about all the horrors of prostitution that there is no need to tarry here on the dark pictures illustrating this 'reverse side of the coin' of the modern form of family and marriage. It suffices to note the number of women forced to engage in prostitution in order to understand the full enormity of this phenomenon, the full malignancy of its effects on modern family life. In 1900–1901 in the principal cities of Europe, the following approximate number of women were found to be engaged in the sale of their bodies in one form or another:[13]

City	Population	Number of prostitutes
London	4,500,000	250,000
Paris	2,800,000	100,000
St. Petersburg	1,400,000	30,000–50,000
Berlin	2,000,000	50,000
Vienna	1,500,000	30,000
Warsaw	1,400,000	25,000

No further comment is required. These figures speak quite clearly for themselves. Of course, the extent of officially registered, 'legal' prostitution is considerably lower than that shown above; however, what matters for our purposes is not what is counted in official medical and police oversight reports, but the figures that show us the actual state of affairs. Clandestine prostitution, according to many serious researchers of the subject, always significantly exceeds open prostitution, by five to ten times; and there are even figures that suggest that the difference is even greater. Thus, in 1900 in Paris, 5,183 prostitutes were officially registered, whilst one set of figures put the number of clandestine prostitutes over 100,000, or as much as 120,000 in another. Dr Kankarevich calculates that there is 1 prostitute for every 9 women in London,[14] 1 for every 14 women in Paris, and 1 for every 20 women in Berlin and Saint Petersburg. In Russia in the '90s, according to the Home Affairs Ministry, 45,000 prostitutes were registered, when, in point of fact, approximate calculations indicate that at least 30,000 women are engaged in prostitution in Saint Petersburg alone.

Not only clandestine prostitution (which doubtless comes in first place) but registered prostitution is growing relentlessly. According to the figures of the local police administration, in Berlin, at least five or six young girls who are falling into the hands of the medical and police oversight for the first time are arrested every night; thus, every year, there are approximately two thousand newly registered prostitutes. 'In Berlin,' Hirsch writes, 'prostitution grew nearly twice as fast as the population between 1875 and 1896.'[15] And together with the prostitution that is legally regulated and sanctioned, driven by hunger, loneliness, defencelessness, temporary, casual, or 'seasonal' prostitution, as it is called in scholarship, lurks in hidden alleys.

The development of 'casual' or 'seasonal' prostitution is promoted particularly by the existence of a number of branches of industry that only employ women workers in certain times of the year. A woman working a few months a year until total exhaustion for wages that barely suffice to cover the most basic necessities of life is thrown out onto the street for the rest of the year with no provisions at all.[16] 'As if it were not enough,' Dr Blashko writes, 'for there to be thousands of working women in all major cities who are poorly paid and forced to seek a steady, more or less substantial, *secondary income* in prostitution, in some branches of industry, where seasonal work flourishes, we find prostitution in the form of a temporary, but nonetheless principal occupation, alternating with the workers' actual trade.'[17] In published reports on the wages of women workers in finished linens and garment factories, the federated governments of Germany themselves find that 'it is common for female workers of limited means with a penchant for clothes, lacking family, to become prostitutes either voluntarily or of necessity when they are deprived of means of support during periods of unemployment.'[18]

Here, in Russia, there is a special type of so-called fair prostitution. Peasant women, women artisans who sew doll clothes, servants, and other women involved in 'honest labour' year round, who usually find a palpable gap in their annual budget, go to the fairs in order to overcome the deficit hanging over their heads by selling their bodies, if not their labour power. 'We find in the reports of many physicians,' writes the woman doctor Drenteln, 'that, during the Nizhny Novgorod fair, prostitution is pervasive amongst the women from the towns near Nizhny Novgorod.'[19]

The whole horror of modern prostitution can be seen from the fact that ever broader segments of the female population are forced to resort to it. The 6,000 official prostitutes in Paris, or the 5,000 in Saint Petersburg, are nothing compared to the 100,000 or 30,000 or more women with 'honest employment' who are forced to resort to the sale of their affections.

The very thought is horrifying: It is not just lonely, unmarried women cast off by their lovers who turn to prostitution, as many prefer to believe; rather, it is not uncommonly the lawful wedded wives of workers, peasants, and artisans who are only able to support the subsistence of their loved ones by this means. 'In the past,' Hirsch correctly notes, 'only women of the lumpenproletariat turned to this shameful trade; these days, thanks to the omnipotence of capital, even women wage earners are forced to put a price on their bodies. Prostitution, once a luxury that society could afford, but whose absence would in no way call its existence into question, has now become an institution most intimately and inextricably bound up with the social structure, a sort of "necessary evil."'*[20]

---

* The original reads: *Früher gaben sich nur Lumpenproletarierinnen disem schmächlichen Gewerbe hin, heute sind selbst arbeitende Frauen dank der Allmacht des Kapitalismus gezwungen, ihren Körper für Geld preiszugeben. Die Prostitution, einst ein „Luxus, den die Gesellschaft sich erlauben konnte, dessen Verlust aber keineswegs ihren Bestand gefährdet hätte", ist heute eine mit der Gesellschaft aufs Innigste verbundene Einrichtung, ein „notwendiges Übel".* (In the past, only the women of the lumpenproletariat dedicated themselves to this shameful trade; today, thanks to the omnipotence of capitalism, even working women are forced to offer their bodies for a price. Prostitution, once a 'luxury that society could afford, but the loss of which would by no means endanger its existence,' is now an institution most intimately connected with society, a 'necessary

Examples of women supporting entire families, raising brothers and sisters, and feeding elderly parents by means of prostitution are by no means scarce. According to Parent-Duchâtelet, of 5,183 prostitutes, 1,441 were driven to the 'shameful trade' by poverty and misery; others were driven to prostitution by: losing their parents, being thrown out of their family home and becoming homeless (1,255), the desire to support weak and sick parents (87), the desire to raise their younger brothers, sisters, nephews, nieces, etc. (29), the desire of widows and women abandoned by their lovers to raise large families whose maintenance was left to them (23), arrival in Paris with the goal of establishing themselves and finding means of subsistence (280), and seduction by employers resulting in loss of employment (289). Thus, of 5,183 women, 3,354 took the 'bad path' to secure bread, clothing, and shelter for themselves or their close relations.'[21]

According to Dr Oboznenko's research, in Saint Petersburg, of 2,934 women, 1,712 referred to need, poverty, and lack of income as the factors leading them to the bad path; moreover, some dozens of women, in their words, turned to the shameful trade as a result of diseases that deprived them of their ability to work or, horrifyingly enough, 'in order to support their children'.[22]

These reports, once again, only concern official, regulated prostitution, but it is amongst the clandestine or occasional prostitutes that we find the greatest number of women forced to seek such 'ancillary income' for the sake of their families and loved ones.

The contemporary exploitative capitalist system forces mothers to turn to the 'bad path' for the sake of their children and children to turn to the 'bad path' for the sake of their mothers. Even tender age is not able to protect a child of the working class from the predatory demands of the overfed debauchery of the bourgeoisie. Girls as young as five or six are sold for defilement by bursting purses and die in their thousands, never having known the innocent joys of childhood. In Moscow, according to Shashkov, of 957 prostitutes surveyed, one started in the occupation at age eleven, five from age twelve. However, there are numerous indications that child prostitution in Russia begins at age nine. Prof. Tarnovsky

---

evil'.) The translation quoted by Kollontai omits the inverted commas around 'Luxury'. —Trans.

claims that most of the prostitutes in Russia are aged between thirteen and seventeen. In Paris, the age of the majority of prostitutes ranges between thirteen and twenty-three.[23] The most 'refined' brothers of Naples keep prostitutes aged fifteen or younger. In London, there are houses with prostitutes younger than fourteen. But those are just children! The same children who sit on school benches, for whom bourgeois families hire an entire staff of nannies and tutors, about whose proper mental and physical hygiene so much has been preached, written, said . . . One's hairs stand on end when one thinks of these babies, these children of the working class! And yet, child prostitution is an inevitable companion of the proletariat. It is a toll taken in the form of vile, rampant debauchery The most horrifying thing, however, is the fact that the ranks of child prostitutes are not only filled by orphans; children are put onto the path of 'shame and disgrace' by their very own parents . . . And these parents are by no means the 'monsters' that sentimental bourgeois fiction writers present them as; with great emotional pain, with unbearably heavy hearts, mothers throw their underage children into the crèche of debauchery. But they, proletarian mothers, have no choice when it comes to the fate of their children: They can either send their children to the factories, surrender them to the power of capital, watch how, day by day, impossibly hard work drains the health, youth, the very life out of their children, or turn them over to predators of another sort, the blood brothers of the exploiters of labour . . . What of it, if shame and condemnation fall upon the child's head! At least their pallid child, drained by deprivation, will be able to eat heartily and live someplace warm . . . The temptation is great, and a mother's heart so weak . . . [24]

Child prostitution, too, is beginning to take on horrifying, unbelievable dimensions. It is growing together with industrial child labour: The adolescent girls not swallowed up by industry due to market conditions are thrown onto the foul path of the 'shameful trade'. Dirty, disgusting, infectious waves also carry off girls seduced by 'gentlemen', along with respected mothers with families who have no other way to feed their children, and adolescent girls for whom life holds only two paths: unbearable wage labour, with more or less occasional prostitution, or 'easy bread' with inevitable disease and premature death . . . The servants of bourgeois scholarship preach that prostitution is a 'necessary evil', that it has been present throughout human history, that there is an entire contingent of women fairly aching to join the ranks of prostitutes. In their words, these are the 'born' type, 'born criminals', adding to the ranks of 'criminal types' amongst men. Relying on Lombroso, Prof. Tarnovsky finds the existence of such women quite 'handy': Thanks to this type of women, marked by nature for the sale of their affections from the day of their birth, men are able to duly satisfy their physiological needs. And this hypothesis is, supposedly, 'entirely' supported by the anatomical and pathological properties of the structure of the cranium, pelvis, etc. amongst prostitutes and criminals. But one thing remains mysterious to these respected representatives of bourgeois science: Why do we find the greatest number of these 'criminal types' amongst women of the deprived strata of the population; why are prostitutes overwhelmingly recruited from the working class and the peasantry?[25] Why do more of the prostitutes in Saint Petersburg come from Estland than come from all of Finland, whilst the remote Vitebsk province and the even more remote Smolensk province, with their poor populations, with their razed forests and swamps, with their sandy, rocky soil unsuited for agriculture, each sent nearly twice as many prostitutes than neighbouring Vyborg province?[26] Why is it that we find 'born prostitutes' in such abundance in the surroundings of Nizhny Novgorod of all places? Why, lastly, is it that such a high percentage of physically abnormal individuals, an extraordinarily high percentage compared to women from other social strata, is found amongst 'female servants'?

If truth were on Lombroso's side, women of all classes of society would be represented in prostitution in approximately the same proportion in which these classes are represented in the female population. However, as we will see, no such proportionality exists. This alone suffices to refute Lombroso's theory and prove the rightness of the view that 'external conditions of life predispose the proletariat to prostitution to a greater degree than the materially prosperous class.'[27]

Is it indeed possible to seriously dispute these passionate, false claims of the representatives of class scholarship? Does not life itself, point by point, refute these artificially cobbled-together hypotheses that serve to give the bourgeoisie the congenial conviction that 'everything is fine', that the 'civilised world' familiar to them remains stable and firm? Thus it ever was, thus it will ever be.

In order to finish off the matter of 'innate' types of prostitutes, it suffices to take even a cursory glance at the contingent of women who have been recruited by debauchery. Where do all these hundreds of thousands of women who sell their own bodies come from? What stratum of the population provides the greatest number of them?

> 'The statistics,' as Shashkov already wrote, 'show beyond a doubt that all public women, almost without exception, are of working-class or poor peasant origins. We could bury the readers in dozens of such statistical tables that provide proof of this exceedingly instructive fact.'[28]

Female domestic servants, saleswomen in the shops, female craft workers, daughters of the worst-paid workers, and, lastly, female factory workers – this is the female material from which contemporary life moulds the holders of the 'yellow card'.[†]

> Material need is particularly intense amongst: personal servants, female skilled workers, dressmakers, linen seamstresses, day labourers, laundresses, and factory workers. The pittance they receive in wages for the work they perform is incapable of covering even their most fundamental needs, short-term physical rest or even the slightest moral comfort; out of need, they become the slaves of labour and bosses. Illness and temporary job loss leave them without a kopeck to their names, and then put them out on the streets . . . And often, these women, left without protection, buffeted by sorrow and need and unable to find other work, are left with no alternative but to take the bad path and there forever to lose their human aspect . . . and there always appears a man with his lecherous urges.[29]

In Germany in 1898, the former occupations of 152 prostitutes were as follows:[30]

---

*   Closing quotation marks missing in the original —Trans.

†   An imperial Russian identification document licensing the holder to engage in sex work. —Trans.

Labourers, dressmakers, saleswomen	66	48.4%
Servants	78	51.3%
Lived with parents	7	5.3 %
Child minders	1	

In Frankfurt am Main, 30 percent of registered prostitutes had previously been domestic servants, 22 percent had been waitresses, and 13 percent had been factory workers; the remaining 35 percent were divided amongst other occupations.[31]

According to Russian statistics, 45.5 percent of registered prostitutes had previously been in service, 8.4 percent had been seamstresses and dressmakers, 3 percent factory workers, 2.4 percent labourers, and 6.4 percent had no specific occupation.[32]

In Saint Petersburg, according to Dr Oboznenko's figures, of 5,189 prostitutes: 40.4 percent had been in service, 12.2 percent dressmakers, 11 percent craft workers, and only 6 percent had been factory workers.[33] In Italy in 1878, of 10,000 registered prostitutes, 2,574 had worked as maids. In general, the statistics show that the greatest number of prostitutes come from service, restaurant service (waitresses abroad), followed by craft workers; factory workers, on the other hand, are in last place amongst officially registered prostitutes.

'Both foreign and Russian figures,' Prof. Elistratov says, 'coincide in indicating that the heavy tribute paid to regulated prostitution that is subject to statistical analysis by domestic servants is significantly greater than the sacrifice cast into the whirlpool of licensed debauchery by factory workers. Thus, according to the all-Russia figures, domestic service yields *five times* more regulated prostitutes than factory work relative to the numbers of these two occupations.'[34]

It should be added that, at the same time as the share of domestic servants in registered prostitution is constantly increasing, factory workers appear to provide ever less suitable material for recruitment to the cadres of 'living commodities'. According to Dr Blaschko's figures, over a period of 44 years, the number of registered prostitutes coming from the ranks of industrial workers decreased from 71 percent to 43 percent in Berlin. To a certain extent, this phenomenon can be explained by the fact that, compared to the situation and conditions of factory work fifty years ago, the absolute level of material well-being of male and female workers has increased, and that, of course, this increase is not conducive to the diversion of the female element to the ranks of prostitutes. Moreover, the intellectual and moral level of female factory workers, who have joined the broad course of the class movement, with its elevating and encouraging prospects doubtlessly also has an influence on the moral face of female factory workers. Even if 'darkest need' casts female factory workers onto the streets and forces them to pay for their daily bread with their bodies, greater strength to withstand the vortex of life will be preserved within them than in domestic servants, who are isolated and deprived of the encouraging awareness of comradely unity and solidarity.

However, the significance of the fact that the percentage of registered prostitutes recruited from the ranks of factory workers is so low should not be overstated. We must not forget that female industrial workers who remain at their stations are too often forced to top up their utterly meagre wages by temporarily or occasionally selling their bodies to their own 'comrades' in the shared struggle, their own allies in building a better future . . . Often, this is the only way that female workers can cover the screaming deficit in their budgets. The entire difference between the position of female servants and that of female labourers is that, in the case of labourers, prostitution serves as an 'ancillary trade', whilst it becomes the prevailing occupation of servants.

To be sure, as the persistent struggle of the working class raises their economic position, the need for female workers to resort to 'ancillary wages' decreases; however, we must not flatter ourselves with the illusion that the recruitment of women to exploitation by modern large-scale capitalist production rescues them from the need to deviate from the straight and narrow. To the contrary, women's participation in industry is all too often the reason for their moral decay. Let us linger on the purely economic causes that force female factory workers to sell their bodies. Surely there are plenty of examples of entrepreneurs, bosses, directors of industrial institutions setting themselves up with harems composed of their female employees. And foremen and overseers? It is not exactly rare for girls or women to be persecuted, fined, or have their wages docked merely for refusing to be 'biddable' and submit to the foreman's whims . . . 'Many factory operators,' reports Mrs Dobier in relation to France, 'have made a habit of not giving girls work without first robbing them of their innocence. The law and the administration take no notice.' Such are the customs in the industrialised world!. . .

The occupations with the worst pay of all, which put women in the greatest dependency on the buyers of labour power, also yield the largest contingent of prostitutes.

Given all this, need we actually prove that heredity plays no role at all here, that women's reasons for falling are entirely comprised within their economic position? According to the findings of Dr Oboznenko, of the number of prostitutes registered in the records of Kalinkinskaya Hospital in Saint Petersburg, 70 percent had previously been enslaved in hard wage labour, subject to the despotism of their bosses and in constant need. According to A. F. Kon, 83 percent of prostitutes had no means of support prior to falling.

Dr Comminge, who researches prostitution in France, a man wholly devoted to the interests of his class, finds that inadequate wages and poverty are the most common inciting factors for prostitution.

Another author, Shashkov, who is in no greater suspicion of being devoted to the materialist understanding of history, nonetheless also claims that 'the main, indeed practically the only, cause of prostitution in Europe is the horrific poverty of the masses. We have before us more than twenty learned monographs on the trade in debauchery, and their authors near-unanimously state that the true mother of prostitution is poverty. Such unanimity, which cannot be found in solving other social issues, is a testament to the indubitability of the fact.'

Need we further bolster this claim with the words of other authorities? Need we continue providing more and more evidence in support of these views? Does it not suffice to note the horrible material conditions in which the women of the working class are forced to live? Without touching on the unhealthy and physically torturous working conditions of female workers or tarrying on the nature of their home life or their housing and living conditions,[35] we note that the wage levels of female workers in themselves provide sufficient stimulus to push them into the open arms of debauchery and supply the market for living female bodies with a relentless influx of 'fresh forces'. 'The number of prostitutes,' as Bebel correctly states, 'grows in proportion to the growth in the number of women employed in different branches of industry as workers receiving wages that are too high to die, but too low to live. Prostitution is promoted by the industrial crises that have become necessary in the bourgeois world and bring poverty and need to hundreds of thousands of families.'[36] That industrial crisis are always conducive to the growth of prostitution is an indisputable fact. In England in 1865, during the cotton crisis, the number of young prostitutes recruited from the army of unemployed workers increased more in one year than in the preceding twenty-five years combined. We see this same picture wherever we look. Women being drawn into the ranks of the sellers of labour power is the source of the colossal growth and development of the trade in female bodies. And the worse the professional work of women is paid, the earlier they are pulled into the harsh struggle for existence, the sooner and more unavoidable the bad path becomes for them . . .

The labour of domestic slaves is particularly poorly paid, and it is that occupation that throws the greatest number of female bodies onto the prostitution market.[37] In our province, the monthly wage of servants ranges between 3 and 8 rubles, or 36 to 96 rubles a year. With this money, servants have to cover all their personal needs, not only dressing themselves (whilst frequently being required to be 'decently' dressed), but not infrequently also buying their own 'hots', i.e., tea and sugar; from this money, they often have to help family members, and, if they have children, send money for their maintenance; the latter regularly exceeds their entire modest income. What can a person do in such circumstances? How could one not take advantage of an 'easier' way of living? At the very least, it provides a safeguard against the constant deprivations, made particularly severe by their repetition. The slightest incident, a single false step, and, she is counted amongst the 'rejects' before she even realises.

After the servants come the small craft workers. It is difficult to say who is worse off: the linen seamstresses or the dressmakers? In Germany, the professional intermediaries have taken the exploitation of dressmakers to such a degree that even the cleverest worker is unable to make more than 8 or 9 marks (3 rubles, 70 kopecks to 4 rubles), and less experienced dressmakers make even less – 4 or 5 marks. Moreover, the manufacture of clothing is one of those trades in which the work is overwhelmingly 'seasonal'; in other words, the workers tend to be employed only some four or five months a year. Given all that, is it really surprising that prostitution finds its recruits more easily amongst this category of industrial workers than any others? Do the bitter, hopeless need, the total dependency on the boss and the intermediary, the exhaustingly long work day, and the lack of moral and material support force female craft workers to seek a living in an occupation that she initially views with contempt and revulsion? Yet, in all countries, it is this branch of industry (garment production) that employs a particularly large number of female workers.

In France, according to Gonnard, the earnings of female craft workers range from 1.60 to 4.10 francs a day; meanwhile, the most basic needs can only be satisfied with earnings of 2.75 francs, and that is without any unexpected urgent expenditures, such as those due to disease, unemployment, seasonal lulls, or the like; likewise, this amount does not include the support of elderly parents or brothers and sisters.[38]

What can be said of our Russian craftswomen? It suffices to have a look at their living and working conditions to wonder along with Prof. Herkner where the women of the working class find the reserves of courage that allow them to withstand the temptations of life. Dark, dirty, crowded, grey flats with a sepulchral supply of air per person, with the incessant noise of rowing neighbours, crying children, screaming elderly people, the sickening tedium of sitting hunched over needlework, meagre food that has often already gone off, restless nights on a hard, narrow bunk 'for two' – that is a typical picture of the existence of craftswomen.

In Saint Petersburg, seamstresses working in workshops are paid 8 to 80 rubles a month for board, without flats; as such, this wage is distributed roughly as follows.

Bodice makers	15–20
Patternmakers	25–50
Sleevemakers	10–15
Skirtmakers (less skilled)	8–15
Skirtmakers (more skilled)	15–20
Trimmers*	25–50

---

* The original *гарнировщицы*, a term for which no English translation related to the garment trades can be found, refers to women employed to add decorative

The higher wages paid to patternmakers and skirtmakers is explained by the fact that this line of work is the most skilled in the dressmaking trade, and only a very small number of craftswomen are capable of doing this work. Patternmakers, skirtmakers, and trimmers are only needed in the largest shops; in small and medium-sized workshops, these matters are usually seen to by the 'mistress' herself. Thus, most women working in the dressmaking trade make no more than 20 rubles. When we recall that this amount must cover expenses for accommodation and clothing, particularly warm clothing, without which life in Saint Petersburg is inconceivable, that the board provided is frequently inadequate or unsatisfactory, thus requiring this line item to be topped up from one's own pocket, is it really surprising that craftswomen 'fall' so often?

No better – indeed, perhaps even worse – is the situation of seamstresses: Patternmakers in workshops are paid 12 to 20 rubles to cover all living expenses; only the particularly skilled ones are able to earn up to 25 to 30 rubles a month. Female sweepers are paid 10 to 18 rubles a month plus room and board, or 70 kopecks a day. Seamstresses working not in workshops, but at home, for ready-to-wear linen and dress shops are particularly poorly paid. For a dozen women's blouses with every conceivable contrivance, fold, and insert, the shop pays between 80 kopecks and 4 rubles; meanwhile, a dozen such blouses require at least six to seven days' work. For a dozen pairs of trousers, requiring the same six days' work, the shops pay 1.80 to 3 rubles; for a dozen skirts or silk blouses, requiring at least twelve days' work, they pay around 6 rubles. The wages of bodice makers working for board without room is 8 rubles a month; only the more skilled bodice makers are able to earn 15 to 17 rubles. Even patternmakers in corset and band shops make no more than 25 rubles a month.

In ladies' milliners' shops, the most skilled workers are able to make 30 rubles a month; ordinary workers only get 10 rubles. The number of especially skilled women trimmers able to make around 60 rubles a month is quite small; but these workers, who are particularly burdensome to the

---

embellishments to otherwise finished garments. The translation used here comes from the French *garnir/garniture/garnisseur* from which the Russian term originates. —Trans.

shops, are more often than not thrown out of the workshop during the dead season.

Florists working in their own flats are paid 8 to 15 rubles a month. Cigarette girls working at home have to cover all expenses on 10 to 20 rubles. Stocking makers make 8 to 15 rubles; most of them are paid 12 rubles, with only particularly skilled stocking makers being able to increase their wages to 30 rubles. The wages of glovers even in large shops do not exceed 8 to 10 rubles a month with board. A particularly skilled glover, working at home, can produce up to ten pairs a day and earn 1 ruble a day; however, there are not many of them, and, as such, the actual wage of glovers is significantly lower.[39] Cord makers earn 4 to 18 rubles, with which they must pay for room and board. The living conditions of women making 4 rubles a month in Saint Petersburg are easily imaginable. Laundresses working in laundries are paid 12 to 18 rubles without board and 6 rubles with board; if they work on a daily basis, their usual monthly wage is as much as 6 rubles.

As striking as the insecurity of craftswomen is, the working conditions of female factory workers here in Russia are not much better. In Western Europe and the US, female factory workers not only receive higher wages, but also have the advantage of steadier pay. No such thing can be said of the situation here, particularly in the past few years of severe, protracted industrial crisis with its mass sackings and constant decreases in production in one or another field.

In the Saint Petersburg textile industry, in which female workers are particularly abundant, they are paid 0.55 to 1.20 rubles a day; female ring spinners, the most widespread category of female textile workers, mostly get 80 to 85 kopecks a day, i.e., not counting Sundays, about 20 rubles a month.[40] In the tobacco industry, in which women, according to the figures compiled by workers' professional organisations, represent approximately four-fifths of employees, female workers make 40 to 90 kopecks for a work day of 10 to 10.5 hours, but the most widespread wage is 40 to 45 kopecks a day, or 10 to 14 rubles a month. This figure does not take into account fines for absenteeism or tardiness (around 25 kopecks for every 10 minutes), which are quite common and extremely burdensome for female workers' finances.[41] At sweets factories, female workers get 45 to 50 kopecks for a twelve-hour work day, to which only 25 kopecks are added for hot pre-bank holiday work days that may last until 11 p.m.[42]

The adhesives industry also employs a significant number of women. In the factories between Beloostrov and Aleksandrovskoye, only women work in the sorting department, the department with the worst hygienic conditions, and earn 30 to 60 kopecks for a fifteen-hour work day. The air of the workshops is full of veritable pillars of dust; the dust on the ceilings, walls, and windows could be shovelled. Workers suffer from eye disorders, and most of them have pulmonary damage . . . Outside the gates in Saint Petersburg, the most common monthly wage for women employed in smaller businesses does not exceed 12 rubles. Taking into account the fact that the most modest accommodation, 'half a bunk', costs between 1.5 and 3 rubles a month, that black bread costs at least 2.5 kopecks a pound, and that female workers need that same 8 to 12 rubles to cover shoes and clothing, as well as, often enough, to support an entire family – an unemployed husband, children, elderly parents – it is plainly obvious that there is no way for them to work without an 'ancillary income' such as clandestine prostitution.

According to testimonies taken by factory inspectors in 1900–1901, female workers are paid 12 rubles a month, whilst male workers get 20 rubles. However, it does happen that female workers' wages in the countryside plumb implausible depths.[43] Thus, a Kiev district inspector reports that in one sleeve factory in Uman, women and adolescents were paid 2 to 4 rubles a month, whilst, at a tobacco factory in Zhitomir, they were paid around 2.5 rubles. Only a few female tobacco workers' monthly incomes reached 9 rubles.[44]

In the sugar refining industry, which also employs a sizeable number of women, the wages for female workers range between 4 and 15 rubles a month, without board, and between 3 and 12 rubles with board included. There are large textile factories in Moscow where women are paid no more than 6 to 8 rubles a month. 'What are we meant to live on?' women workers say, when board alone costs 3 to 8 rubles a month, and a woman has to pay 3 or 4 rubles for a flat if she's single, or 6 to 8 rubles if she's got a family; not only is nothing left – it isn't even enough. 'Like it or not, we need to be doing something on the side.'

At 149 companies in Tver province, which employ more than twenty-five thousand workers, the average wage of women in 1898 was equal to 138 rubles a year without room and board. Underage workers were paid even less, about 9 rubles a month on average, and girls under fifteen received 8.75 rubles a month.

Even sadder is the lot of women working in mining: For a twelve-hour working day, underage coal sorters get a maximum of 30 kopecks a day. On the Urals, even adult women are paid only 25 to 45 kopecks a day; female day labourers who care for the horses get no more than 80 kopecks. There are places in Perm province where the daily wage of an adult female mine worker do not exceed 20 kopecks.[45]

Is any further commentary required on these figures? Are they not a sufficiently eloquent testament to the fact that the fundamental impulse leading working-class women along the slippery path of 'easy living' is their total economic deprivation?

The dark picture of the lives of prostitutes chills the heart . . . What horrors they have occasion to see! What suffering they are forced to experience! Grief, humiliation, beatings, the contempt of society, poverty, and a lonely death . . . It would seem that a woman who has had even the slightest glance into this hell ought to run away without giving the dark abyss a second look. But is the life of a female craft worker, a domestic servant, or even a female factory worker any better, particularly here in Russia, where the working conditions, even in large-scale operations, are repugnant? Do they – the hundreds of thousands of proletarian women who sell their labour power to capital – live any better? Are their lives any brighter, any freer? Have a look at the dismal basements, the dark corners with their 'bunks for two', where most of the women of the working class are housed; breathe in, even just once, the stuffy air, saturated with all manner of vapours and impurities that working-class women must breathe at 'home'; try to nourish yourselves for even a day on the meagre, unhealthful, stale food with which the women of the working class still their hunger; and you will understand that the hell of an 'honest living' is worthy of the other hell, that of prostitution . . .

The contempt of society? Good Lord! Just how much 'respect' do they get by remaining 'honest', all these seamstresses, cigarette girls, tobacco makers, weavers, who slave away at work from morning to late night just so that, after a nearly sleepless night on a narrow bunk in a dark, over-crowded dwelling, they can begin the same unbearable life all over again? And carry on doing so, from day to day, from year to year, until they die! Would it not be better to live for even just a few years, even just a sin-gle year, in idleness, satiety, in modest happiness?! 'It's just one day, but it's mine!' How much courage, how much moral integrity and advanced consciousness is needed in order to prefer an 'honest crust', with all the hellishness it implies, to one that is dishonest, but at least 'filling'? . . .

A hypocritical, two-faced attitude to prostitution is characteristic of the bourgeoisie, and brings their class position in what would seem to be a shared human concern into sharp relief. Indeed, prostitution, that inevitable concomitant of present-day class society, this corrective for the obsolete, compulsory family form of our time, is the exclusive burden of the unpropertied classes. Here, in the dark, stale basements, it releases its doomed sprouts; it digs its venomous claws more and more into the pro-letarian's body and, though its stinking breath poisons the atmosphere of the entire society, it is primarily a scourge for the working class. This is why the bourgeoisie are in no hurry to sound the alarm: If the largest share of women available for sale came from the propertied class, their attitude towards this issue, one must assume, would be different . . .

The solution to the mystery of the ambivalent approach of governments around the world to prostitution must be sought in the class perspective that permeates this social issue. Condemned by religion, persecuted by society and even the law itself, prostitution is nonetheless not only tol-erated, but even regulated by the state. Considered necessary in order to satisfy men's natural sexual needs, prostitution has served as a 'lightning rod of debauchery', a guarantor of the basis of the family and preserver of the purity of 'honest' bourgeois women, from the time class society took shape in one form or another.

Not to speak of prostitution in the ancient, pre-Christian world. But even starting from the Middle Ages, states and magistrates, on the one hand, 'tolerated' all these 'bordellos', 'women's houses', and 'girls' houses', etc.[46] whilst, on the other hand, a whole series of inhumanely draconian laws and ordinances were issued that subjected prostitutes to all manner of humiliations, torments, and affronts.[47] Kings availed themselves of the services of prostitutes, counted them as members of their court, and appointed special officials to supervise them, and this did not stop them persecuting and tormenting women engaged in prostitution and subjecting them to all manner of humiliations, sometimes even murdering them by their hundreds at the same time, under the influence of religious ecstasy in moments of hypocritical repentance.[48] The bourgeoisie and the clergy, who make extensive use of the services of prostitutes and secretly support them, openly whipped and persecuted them. The people, seeing in them the vivid and horribly denuded expression of their own disenfranchisement, hated them with all the power of their impulsive souls and sought by all means to destroy them and wipe them off the face of the Earth, swearing at them, throwing stones at them, breaking up tolerance houses, torturing and murdering individual unfortunate victims of 'the shameful trade'. But no matter how much the people combated the sale of women's bodies, the class society that gave rise to the sale of labour power incessantly created ever more new victims of 'social temperament'.

Modern society has not moved far beyond the cruelty of the Middle Ages, replacing public torment and periodic beatings of prostitutes with psychological beatings of prostitutes by means of strict legislative regulation. In the age of the consuls, the 'Third Estate', with their characteristic 'rationalism' and penchant for legislative protection of their interests, first proclaimed the principle of state regulation of prostitution. In France in 1800, medical and police supervision was introduced, and, in 1802, the first 'yellow card' was issued.

Prostitution, which, until then, had only been tolerated by the state, became a legislatively regulated phenomenon recognised by the authorities. And, nonetheless, the customary hypocrisy does not allow for open recognition of the bankruptcy of the obsolete family forms and the inevitable growth of prostitution on the basis of capitalist relations. All Russian legislation on 'the shameful trade' is suffused with this hypocritical spirit. In the interest of preserving the bourgeois family, the nursery of the heirs of capital, the trade in women's bodies is promoted, but, from the point of view of 'official morality', it is strictly condemned without leniency; and, in order to preserve the prestige of their 'high moral purity' in their own eyes, bourgeois society, with its sham virtue, always rushes to blast prostitutes with abuse, finding numerous ways to poison the lives of these unhappy 'priestesses of vice', which were not exactly sweet to begin with.[49]

When the formation of a medical-police committee was planned in Moscow, it was first proposed to collect funds from public houses for the treasury. However, this was then deemed inappropriate, 'in particular because carrying out any sort of collection from public women would be inconsistent with the spirit of our laws, because it could be seen as the government approving licentiousness, which is strictly prosecuted by the law'.[50]

In Germany, we encounter the same double standard: The criminal law prosecutes landlords who house prostitutes. And,

> on the other hand, the police are forced to tolerate thousands of women engaged in prostitution and preserve them in their trade as soon as they are listed in the prostitutes' registry and submit to the rules established for them, e.g., periodic medical examinations. However, if the state permits prostitutes and thus supports their trade, then it must also allow for flats for them and even, in the interests of public health and order, allow there to be houses where prostitutes can engage in their trade. What a contradiction! On the one hand, the state officially acknowledges that prostitution is necessary; on the other hand, it punishes prostitutes and procurers. This attitude of the state shows that, for modern society, prostitution is a sphinx, the riddle of which it cannot solve.[51]

Yes, this is how consistent modern bourgeois society is!

But as if it were not enough that prostitution as a social phenomenon is the natural fruit of modern class society, the very acts regulating prostitution are permeated with class perspective. 'The common thread,' says Prof. Elistratov, 'running through the local regulations is the class demarcation of prostitution, which is also strictly observed by the practices of the vice police.'[52] Our legislation permits obligatory inspection and incarceration in hospitals only for the category of 'vagabond', 'common' (i.e., of the lower class) and 'suspect girls'. This is the text of § 158 of the 1890 ordinance. Almost identical is the language of the old senate decree of 1763: 'Be it ordered . . . women found to be licentious shall be inspected, and only those who are *lowly* and *vagabond* shall be sent away upon being cured.'

Even more specific is the decree of the Minister for Home Affairs issued to the provincial governors on 17 October 1844, on the basis of which there has been, and continues to be, de facto supervision of prostitution in Russia's provinces:

> It goes without saying that only those persons shall be subject to the effects of any measures that may be deemed necessary in this case who, on the basis of their way of life, as well as their *rank* and other *social relations* may be subjected to them.

The same principle is also reflected in the special regulations of individual cities; although there are exceptions, their very random and lenient character, created for women of the affluent classes, puts the class character of these ordinances into especially sharp relief.[53]

The whole horror of the regulation lies in the fact that its weight falls entirely on women of the unpropertied classes; in the face of wealthy prostitutes, on the other hand, both the police and the regulations merely doff their hats in deference.

> Everywhere, it may be said, it is the less affluent prostitutes who fall under state supervision. The agents of the police are not sufficiently skilled to identify high-end prostitutes, and at times do not even have the opportunity to do so. This requires a great deal of tact; sometimes, significant payments must be made. Moreover, prostitutes of this sort always find defence counsel willing to help them and, if the worst comes, to bail them out. Prostitutes of the lower classes predominate in all cities. The worse the oversight, the fewer the wealthier, intelligent prostitutes. The police, wishing to avoid excessive work and unpleasantness, only go after seedy and vagabond women.[54]

Given that 'high-end' prostitutes mostly come from the bourgeois class, the vigilant eye of medical-police oversight calmly passes them by and falls with redoubled zeal upon those women whose social position does not inspire the trust of the ruling authorities.

In the slums where the women of the working class dwell, misfortune and vice are so intimately intertwined that it is impossible to distinguish between them at a glance. To the contrary, the constable has neither the time nor the desire to give the matter any thought; he resolves the matter rapidly and unappealably: Any woman he arrests on the street, in a corner flat, or a night shelter, is deemed a prostitute; he treats her as a fallen woman, even if there is no suggestion that she is engaged in debauchery other than her lack of a fixed residence and occupation.[55]

The existing rules of medical-police supervision constitute a dangerous threat to the entire female proletariat, especially those living on the margins. We need not even tarry on periods of acute unemployment, in which women naturally find themselves on the streets without 'due cause'; proletarian women risk humiliating inspections on any bank holiday. The loss of a passport or another such accident aggravates their already difficult position and often forces female workers to choose between either being sent back to their hometowns on a prisoner transport or submitting to medical-police supervision (in this, and *only this* case, the medical committee take upon themselves all the difficulties involved in acquiring a new passport). Of course, this state of affairs exists not only in Russia, but in all bourgeois countries. 'Not subject to inspection,' Dr Blaschko says, 'are nearly all of the elegant prostitutes, the so-called ladies of the *demi-monde*, who constitute a sort of *noli me tangere* ("do not touch") for the police. The masses subject to inspection almost everywhere consist of the most unfortunate and underprivileged riffraff. Obediently and stupidly, from year to year, over decades, these stepdaughters of fate make their usual "walk" to the inspection site.'[56]

Modern class society contrives to divide all women even suspected of prostitution into two classes. The 'better sort', the more affluent prostitutes, are included within the bourgeois class, serve them, live side by side with them, and, to a certain extent, share in their privileges. The 'worse sort', flesh of the flesh of the working class or the poor peasantry, drinks from the cup of disenfranchisement, humiliation, and sorrow down to the very dregs . . .

It is clear that the problem of eliminating prostitution, the problem of fostering healthier relations between the sexes, is a problem of the proletarian class, a problem that is intimately and inextricably intertwined with the conditions of work and production. Whilst for the other classes and strata of the population, solving the 'marital' problem, and thus that of prostitution, is primarily of psychological and moral interest; for the proletariat, it is one of the fundamental problems of life, one of the moments that define the future. The struggle against prostitution and the ugly forms of the modern family, in other words, is a struggle against the class institutions of the modern bourgeois world, and flows directly from the struggle of the proletariat as a whole, constituting an integral part thereof.

Hunger and exploitation are the inexhaustible wellsprings feeding prostitution, and class society is the source of the evils accompanying it. Is it really surprising, given that, that outrages to women's dignity in this area most often fall on representatives of the working class? The sale of women's bodies is intimately linked to the sale of women's labour power; prostitution can only definitively disappear together with the disappearance of wage labour.

But surely there must be ways of mitigating and alleviating the suffering and horror arising both from the very existence of prostitution and its regulation by law within the limits of our exploitative class society? The struggle against prostitution and the hypocritical laws governing it is one of the liveliest aspects of the activities of bourgeois women. The issue of prostitution and the improvement of public morality is given particular attention at all international women's congresses. As champions of the abolitionist movement, demanding the total repeal of regulations on prostitution as a trade, the feminists have come to the defence of their oppressed sisters and essentially acted as exponents of a shared, 'cross-class' female interest. But is this really so?

On the issue of prostitution and the abusive formalities associated with it for women, the interests of women of all classes do coincide to a certain degree; of this, there can be no doubt. The abyss separating female intellectuals from proletarian women lies immediately before the possibility of finding oneself in the ranks of the pariahs of the female population. A chance misfortune – illness, setbacks – and the independent female intellectual wage earner is subject to all of the allures of 'easy living', and from there, the distance to making the acquaintance of the caring eyes of medical-police supervision is not great . . . This regulation is equally hateful to women of all strata of the population. However, the women of bourgeois outlook and those of proletarian outlook differ radically in regard to the methods of struggle, both with prostitution itself and with the rules governing it. For the women of the bourgeoisie, the task of struggling against prostitution almost entirely comes down to the repeal of the existing regulations and the issuance of new 'rules' that are less abusive to women, but just as vigilant in the sense of protecting 'public morality'. The evil at the root of prostitution remains hidden to most feminists; they are willing to believe that the matter of prostitution can be resolved within the confines of the modern class world by repealing the shameful regulations, and taking 'strict measures' against 'entertainment' facilities and, ultimately, introducing social and political reforms facilitating early marriages. With the naïvety of the bourgeois ideologues of the eighteenth century, bourgeois women still believe that the 'female question', and, specifically, the 'family question' can be resolved with a few wisely drafted regulations! . . .

However, the apparent naïvety of this view stands on firm class ground. In protesting against women being placed under the arrogant, unchecked power of medical-police supervision, the feminists limit themselves to timid half measures, constantly fearing that complete, unregulated freedom of private sexual relations might ultimately subvert the 'family foundations' of the bourgeoisie and affect the virtues of their husbands and sons . . .

With complete transparency, the German feminists stated their bourgeois concerns at the women's congress in Halle (October 1905). On the one hand, they demand that society recognise a 'single moral standard' for men and women, denying the state any right to intervene in matters of private sexual morality; on the other, however, they insist on the need for that very state to take measures for the *protection of social mores*; but this protection was not meant to protect exploited or corrupted young people. To the contrary, they proposed to remove from the path of 'decent society' all manner of obscene phenomena that 'offend public morality and decency'. It would follow from the opinion of the strict guardians of 'decency' in Halle that anyone guilty of such transgressions should be held liable and appropriately punished.

In preaching the principle of state non-intervention in matters of sexual morality and championing abolitionism, bourgeois women contradict themselves by rushing to limit the principles of freedom they only just proclaimed and wrapping themselves in customary moral principles. Marriage, the modern coercive union of two individuals, with all its imperfections, remains the most reliable bastion of economic well-being for the average bourgeois woman, causing her to cling reflexively to the preservation of this institute and all its legal inviolacy.

On this matter, the German women in Halle issued a resolution that read as follows: All theories proclaiming equal rights for fathers and mothers in marriage, establishing equal responsibility of husbands and wives, etc., but subverting the moral responsibility of the spouses arising from marriage must be considered untenable and thus rejected. Theories 'subverting moral responsibility' apparently refers to the 'free principles' of social democracy, its highly 'amoral' assertion of the inevitability of the decay of the contemporary family, and other such stone-throwing.

But in that case, what is the actual position of feminists on the subject of prostitution? On the one hand, abolitionism; on the other, protection of the contemporary marital union together with the criminalisation of acts 'offending public morality', and all of this is seasoned with naïve belief in the possibility of eliminating all of the evils of the relations of the sexes by revising the current civil code . . . The contradiction is obvious, but inevitable for those who are not able to renounce the bourgeois class perspective. All of the benevolent initiatives of the feminists in the struggle against prostitution normally remain within the area of minor palliative measures. No matter how admirable the intentions of its champions, abolition in itself is just as powerless to end prostitution at its roots as even the broadest philanthropic initiative is to stop the growing proletarianisation of the masses. One need only look at the countries (England, Australia, Norway, Denmark, part of Switzerland, and the Netherlands), where prostitution is unregulated, to see whether the women cast into the ranks of the prostitutes there live better, and, most importantly, whether fewer young beings are forced by need, powerlessness, and disenfranchisement to join the ranks of the trade that is unregulated, but no less despised, despite its 'toleration'.

Legislation is even less capable of protecting the family hearth of the comfortable bourgeoisie from the deleterious influence of street debauchery. At the same time as the feminists faithfully struggle for the victory of the abolitionist principle, they go on about 'strict police prosecution' of *cafés-chantants* and other institutions that sow debauchery and 'offend decency'; whilst the best of them build virtuous 'Magdalene shelters' and shelters for single young girls, capitalist production, concentrated in the hands of the magnates of capital, tirelessly goes about its business, daily casting out millions of new victims to satisfy 'public temperament'. That will inevitably continue so long as the productive forces solely serve the owners of capital and not society as a whole. Whether driven underground or boldly on display, whether clad in rags and covered in bruises, or in silk and velvet, prostitution will continue to poison the social atmosphere, serving as a source of pleasure for some, and bringing sickness, desperation, and sorrow to others . . . On this matter, as on all other dark problems of her life, woman can only expect liberation from the growing power of the working class. Only the working class is capable of dealing with the hundred-headed hydra of our days . . . Combating prostitution does not only mean destroying its current regulation by the police; no, it means struggling against the foundations of the capitalist system, striving for the destruction of the division of society into classes, clearing the way for new ways in which human beings can live together.

Prostitution seeks its victims above all amongst the proletariat. By struggling for the cause of their class, workers are also protecting the interests of the most humiliated and deprived member of their class – working women, who are led by exploitation and disenfranchisement to the forced sale of their bodies. Each victorious stride the proletariat makes also brings women closer to their coveted goal and promises them salvation from the monster that maliciously lurks in the corner, lying in wait for her with its venomous, stinking breath . . . Instead of the offensive, burdensome sale of affections, the proletariat will win free relations between free individuals; the coercive form of marital cohabitation it will replace with the unhindered pursuit of direct, sincere attraction, free from narrow, worldly calculations . . . There, in the new word of social-ised labour, the hypocritical double standards of our time will disappear, and sexual morality will truly become a personal matter of conscience for each individual.

One might think that this would spur the feminists to join the ranks of the supporters of the new social structure. But class instinct is invinci-ble. And the feminists, who push away the ugly spectre of women trading in their bodies with one hand, strive with the other to support the very class structure that gives rise to and maintains prostitution. The fem-inists operate in a vicious cycle, and proletarian women cannot expect liberation from the horrors of forced prostitution from them.

Working-class women can only combat this evil with their own means, by remaining on the foundations of the class politics of the working class as a whole. Increasing wages, shortening the work day, greater wealth and greater leisure to dedicate to wide-ranging intellectual interests – those are the measures that the working class mobilises in the struggle against the humiliating trade in women's bodies and that in practice will yield more real results than all the noise made by the feminists around the matter of repealing regulations. Of course, the working class is also a committed champion of abolitionism, but it cannot ascribe to this move-ment the primary significance that it has in the eyes of bourgeois women. And, practically speaking, the achievements of the feminists in this area are hardly more significant than the gains won by the workers them-selves. It is quite doubtful whether the abolitionist movement would have been able to remain standing through its worst times in England if the working class had not risen up in defence of it. The powerful petition movement against the regulation established in England in 1866 was primarily supported by the working class. The proper actions were also taken by the workers' delegation sent to the Home Secretary in 1872 to deliver to him the workers' protest, which stated, inter alia, as follows: 'It is regrettable that, despite 1,279 petitions filled with more than a million signatures and submitted to Parliament over the past two sessions, the laws protested by the people continue to exist.'[57]

Let the feminists of any country show where their active struggle against prostitution or the evil that makes it worse – legislative regulation – has led to tangible results for women.

And here in Russia, what has the bourgeois women's movement done in its struggle against prostitution? Individual voices of champions of women's equality have, to be sure, been raised in defence of the victims of 'social temperament', with Mrs Pokrovskaya making a particularly passionate stand in their defence, as she continues to do today; it is also true that 'shelters for repentant Magdelenes'[58] and 'societies for the rescue of maidens' exist here in Russia, as well.

However, the women's liberation movement as a whole has not taken even a single noticeable step in this direction, and we must note that Russian feminists look upon this ulcer on the body of modern society with surprising indifference.

The champions of women's equality abroad can at least boast that they, following in the footsteps of Josephine Butler, have everywhere and always energetically and actively supported the abolitionist movement and, have, in their own way, combated the causes giving rise to prostitution. There are a number of specialised women's societies that have the objective of struggling in one way or another against the sale of women's bodies.

The few attempts that are made here in this area, such as creating cheap hostels for young girls, evening and Sunday entertainment for the daughters of the proletariat, etc. are mere toys compared to such initiatives. To be sure, all manner of cultural and educational activities can be found here, which are all too often subject to arbitrary administrative and police restrictions; however, independently of these purely external efforts, we cannot but observe that neither the women's societies nor the women's parties here in Russia pay this serious issue the attention due to it.

One need only have a glance at the reports on the activities of such major women's organisations as the Women's Mutual Philanthropic Society and see whether even a kopeck of their substantial 15,000-ruble budget is dedicated to the struggle against prostitution. To be sure, the Society does have a 'hostel' and an office for seeking accommodations, as well as a 'mutual aid fund', not to mention children's homes, a library, etc. But who is served by all these numerous operations of the first feminist organisation in Russia? Not proletarian women, of course. Proletarian women cannot even become members of the Women's 'Mutual Philanthropic' Society, because the high membership subscriptions only open the Society's doors to wealthy women.[59] Proletarian women, by the very nature of the first women's feminist organisation, were only to be the objects of 'charity from above'. However, judging from the Society's reports, the 'philanthropy' mostly goes to women in intellectual occupations. It is they – teachers, office workers, stenographers, etc. – who live in the hostels, make use of the information provided by the accommodation search office, and receive benefits from the Society's funds. As we have already seen, it is women labourers who are cast onto the market for 'female commodities', and, as such, all of the 'mutual philanthropy' of the Russian women's society, which absolutely does not reach the social strata that provide the constant supply of women for sale, does not combat prostitution directly or indirectly.

Another society – the 'Society for the Care of Young Working Women' (*Общество попеченія о молодыхъ работницахъ*), which exists in Saint Petersburg and a few provincial cities (Odessa, Nizhny Novgorod) has the following stated objective in its articles of association: 'to safeguard young girls, overwhelmingly belonging to the working class, such as craftswomen, factory workers, and servants, from the effects of the morally harmful conditions of life in their environment and aid in their moral development'.* The objectives of this society, thus, completely correspond to the activities of the organisations abroad that have the objective of combating the corruption of young girls. But how exactly does the Society put its important objective into practice? With nine departments in Saint Petersburg that are readily dedicated to female factory workers, servants, craftswomen, and female staff in general,[60] the Society, in their efforts to raise the cultural interests of the visitors, meticulously protects from every living word and everything that might turn girls to the disastrous path of 'class struggle'. In their most sincere desire to help working women in their daily struggle, this Society nonetheless constitutes a

---

*   In original: *предохранять молодыхъ дѣвицъ, преимущественно рабочаго класса, какъ-то ремесленницъ, фабричныхъ и служанокъ, отъ дѣйствія окружающихъ ихъ вредныхъ въ нравственномъ отношеніи условій жизни и содѣйствовать ихъ нравственному развитію*

'living contradiction'. On the one hand, they raise the cultural and moral level of proletarian girls, their visitors, and thus increase their intellectual interests; on the other, they place an impenetrable wall between them and the only paths, the only methods and means of struggle with which proletarian women can improve their position. At the lessons given by the Society, 'harmful teachings' are meticulously expurgated and eliminated, and neither the professional nor the political needs of working women are discussed within the walls of the Society. What exactly can the 'cultural and educational' activities of the Society provide? Can mere 'education' and 'moral training' save young women from prostitution, which is unescapable in fifty out of a hundred cases? It goes without saying that despite all their best intentions, with these cultural and educational offerings, the Society not only fail to accomplish their mission, but doubtlessly cause or worsen the mental tragedy of proletarian girls whose mental and intellectual demands are totally at variance with the sad reality surrounding them.

The only real accomplishment of the Society for the Care of Young Girls is the provision of cheap hostels for working-class girls, unlike the aristocratic hostel of the Mutual Philanthropic Society. These hostels at least alleviate the daily struggle to survive for the slaves of labour, and make them more resistant and less susceptible to the temptation of 'easy income'.[61] But even in this area, the inadequacies of the Society's activities must be noted: All its initiatives are based not on the vital principle of 'self-help' or 'autonomy', but on the principles of philanthropy and charity.

Nonetheless, the Society for the Care of Young Female Workers is the only one in Russia that in one way or another actually seeks to combat the corruption of young working-class girls, which absolutely cannot be said, for example, of the 'Russian Society for the Protection of Women', which is officially recognised and even promoted by the authorities. Nor need we mention that the latter is blatantly characterised by aristocratic philanthropy; it is also known for its total passivity. Just recently, it decided at last to build a settlement in Okhta, where twenty women who have entered the slippery path can find refugee and engage in 'honest agricultural labour'.[62] A refuge for twenty prostitutes in Saint Petersburg! That is such a drop in the ocean of desperation and poverty, especially given the growing unemployment of the past several years, that it is actually rather embarrassing to even discuss such an initiative. After all, it is no secret that, over the past several years of simultaneous economic and political crisis, the 'export of living commodities' from Russia has reached colossal levels. Half of the inhabitants of brothels in South America are natives of Russia, a particularly large number of them Jewish. In Vilna, prostitution of minors has reached unprecedented levels. This phenomenon must have reached such monstrous levels if even the ministry for justice has decided to introduce into the Duma a bill on 'measures for combating the trade in women for the purposes of debauchery (*о мерахъ пресеченія торговли женщинами въ цѣляхъ разврата*)'.

And our feminists, our women's parties and organisations have nothing to say. It would seem that this would be the place for them to show what they do, to show their 'little sisters', the women of the proletariat, that they stand in solidarity with them, that their concern is about them and for them. But apparently, 'political equality' is such an elephantine matter as to overshadow all other issues facing all women. Never mind practical struggle against prostitution; even the 'platforms' and 'programmes' of our women's organisations give a decidedly modest amount of space to the matter of prostitution.

Point 'e' (*д*) of the 'platform' of the Equality Alliance reads as follows: 'repeal of all exclusive laws concerning prostitution and offending the human dignity of women (*отмѣна всѣхъ исключительныхъ законовъ, касающихся проституціи, унижающихъ человѣческое достоинство женщины*)'. But having expressed this general wish, our left feminists rest on their laurels and never return to the matter.

Demands to repeal regulations and other expressions of protest against the trade in women's bodies can be found neither in the resolutions or the numerous decisions, nor in the equality campaigners' house organ *Soyuz Zhenshchin*. Even the left feminists were not active enough to submit a petition demanding the repeal of the regulations to the Duma, as they had done concerning the political equality of women. One gets the impression that this issue does not particularly captivate our equal-rights campaigners, that it does not weigh heavily on their minds. After all, it does not directly affect their interests, but merely those of working-class women. The issue of prostitution is truly a purely proletarian matter; therein lies the solution to the mystery of why our 'extreme' feminists take such a cold-blooded attitude towards it.

But, in this case, the mystery is why the more right-leaning feminists of the Women's Progressive Party are more sensitive and attentive to this issue. In their programme, their demands are much more concrete:

> Enacting laws prohibiting the establishment and maintenance of all brothels, tolerance houses, and establishments trading in women's bodies, and establishing severe punishments for intermediaries, procurers, and other persons deriving material benefits from the trade in women or facilitating their reduction to prostitution. Eliminating medical-police supervision of prostitution and repealing the marriage ban for soldiers.[*]

The Progressives did not merely declare their wishes in their programme; over the past several years, they have returned to the matter of prostitution and discussed ways of combating it at several of their meetings. At one such meeting, it was even decided to submit to the Duma a proposal to enact a law repealing the regulation. Why are they so active? What has given rise to such a lively interest in the 'private matter' of women's lives? Could it be due in part to the fact that the Progressive Party is led by M. I. Pokrovskaya, who is known for her work on the matter of prostitution and has dedicated much sincere effort and energy to the struggle against the regulations that darken the lives of prostitutes, which were already lacking in light to begin with? But is there not another, more general motive that leads the Progressives to follow their leader? The Progressives approached the matter of prostitution in the same way as their bourgeois sisters abroad. Although prostitution as a social phenomenon does not affect them directly, it does, by its nature, also cast a shadow on the existence of the bourgeois strata of society. In order to preserve

---

* In original: *Изданіе законовъ, запрещающихъ устройство и содержаніе всякихъ притоновъ проституціи, домовъ терпимости и торговли женскимъ тѣломъ, и устанавливающихъ строгое наказаніе посредникамъ, сутенерамъ и другимъ лицамъ, извлекающимъ матеріальныя выгоды изъ торговли женщинами или содѣйствующимъ совращенію ихъ въ проституцію. Отмѣна врачебно-полицейскаго над-.зора за проституціей и отмѣна запрещенія браковъ военнымъ*

the purity of bourgeois family life, to avoid bourgeois mothers having to worry about the promiscuity of their sons, in order to allow wives not to tremble in fear of betrayal by their husbands, it is necessary to eradicate the disease, in other words, *strictly* prosecute everything that facilitates debauchery. Pay attention to the demands in the Progressive programme. There is much talk of 'laws forbidding', 'laws establishing severe punishment', and not a single word of the living sources of the struggle with prostitution: Measures to improve the economic position of the working class. The Progressives still cling to the naïve faith that a couple of strict laws against *souteneurs* and tolerance houses will suffice to eradicate prostitution; they would not be averse to medieval-style persecution and exile for prostitutes themselves, were it not for the principle of 'equal rights' getting in the way. This 'banner' must be held high, and nothing else remains but to add the call for the repeal of the regulations to the 'strictly penal' demands. The Progressives can support this demand bona fide given that even the bourgeois luminaries of the medical world acknowledge that the regulations are far from achieving their purpose and are not saving the bourgeoisie from the spread of venereal diseases.

Thus, the Progressives stand on the side of abolitionism and, at the same time, join in the struggle against the 'debauchery' that takes away their husbands, lovers, and sons. Because, for the Progressives, prostitution is a phenomenon that is not so much economic as moral in nature, they do not wage their struggle against the causes that lead women to trade in their bodies, but with prostitution as it already exists. In other words, when it comes to the matter of prostitution, the Progressives do the same thing that feminists usually do in relation to economic evils: They pay no attention to the source of the evil, and seek by means of charitable donations to patch up the gaping wounds of the social problems of the modern capitalist world.

No, if the abolitionist movement in Russia actually were to triumph, if the army of prostitutes were to grow more slowly, no one would be less responsible for this than the feminists. It is not the anodyne resolutions of the feminists, but the workers' party struggling for the abolition of the existing socio-economic relations that women would have to thank for this. It can be reliably stated that the cadres coerced by material dependency into prostitution will become fewer with every new victory of the working class in the economic and legal areas.

The family, the contemporary bourgeois family, with all its moral traditions and civil foundations, is going through a protracted crisis. Marriages are becoming less and less stable, as prostitution takes on threatening dimensions. This is acknowledged both by the bourgeois feminists and people sharing the proletarian worldview. The troubles of contemporary married life weigh to a greater or lesser extent on women of all strata of the population; this, too, is indisputable. Thus, it remains to see whether there are shared goals between the feminists and working-class women in terms of the methods of discussing the family problem and the solution thereof, and whose efforts – those of the proletariat as a whole or those of the feminists – will be capable of emancipating women from the heavy yoke of the family.

Let us first see what the feminists have achieved in the area of marital and family relations.

The more right-leaning feminists, whose social position is adjacent to that of the *haute bourgeoisie*, raise, first and foremost, two issues: (1) replacing religious marriage with civil marriage and facilitating divorce accordingly, and (2) enacting complete separation of the assets of the spouses in those countries where this has not yet been established.

Both of these demands are doubtless of great importance to women of the middle and *haute bourgeoisie*, who represent capital in one or other form; by this means, they will be better able to defend their pecuniary interests, on the one hand, and to provide for their children with the assets of mother and father unified by means of lawful marriage, on the other, preserving their complete economic independence from their husbands.

As representatives of the upper layer of the bourgeoisie, our Progressives naturally had to develop their demands on the family problem in that spirit. The programme of the Women's Progressive Party reads:

> Marriage witnessed by a notary, which shall be made compulsory for all, shall be introduced into family law. The question of religious solemnisation of marriage shall be left to the discretion of the individual.
>
> The divorce process shall be simplified and facilitated. Both parents shall have equal authority over their children. Wives shall be equal to

husbands in all matters, shall have the right to one-half of the family
savings, and shall be legislatively made economically independent of
their husbands if they are unable to have an income of their own due
to family circumstances. There shall be broad legislative protection for
children, particularly extramarital children.*

Based on the assumption that the existing socio-economic structure
cannot be abolished, the Progressives merely wish to introduce a few
improvements to family and marital relations, improvements that do not,
however, eliminate the roots of the bourgeois family. The correctives introduced seek not only to improve the relations between persons united
by legal marriage, but to make the family in its contemporary form more
stable and more viable. Marriage and family are institutions that are no
less holy and inviolate than private property. And right-wing feminists
the world over emerge as their vehement defenders, seeking to eliminate
from marriage and the family only those aspects that contradict the principle of equality of the sexes and primarily harm the material interests
of women.

The 'left' feminists take a different view of this matter. We must not
forget that this group is made up primarily of independent female intellectuals, women not backed by inherited or other wealth, who build
their independence in life by means of an independent income. For
these women, the family problem loses its foundational character and is
transferred from the area of substantive law to the area of morality par
excellence; for them, the preservation of the institution of marriage, as
a means of transferring wealth from parents to children, does not play
the same role that it has amongst the women of the *haute bourgeoisie*.
Marriage, even reformed marriage, even with easier divorce, bears no

---

* In original: *Въ семейное право вводится бракъ нотаріальнымъ порядкомъ,
который признается обязательнымъ для всѣхъ. Религіозное освященіе брака
должно быть предоставлено доброй волѣ каждаго.*

*Упрощается и облегчается порядокъ разводовъ. Родители пользуются
одинаковой властью надъ дѣтьми. Жены во всемъ равны мужьямъ, имѣютъ
право на половину семейныхъ сбереженій и законодательнымъ путемъ
должны быть поставлены въ экономическую независимость отъ мужей,
если не могутъ имѣть своего заработка по семейнымъ обстоятельствамъ.
Должна быть установлена широкая защита дѣтей, особенно внѣбрачныхъ,
законодательнымъ путемъ.*

attraction for them. Legalised marriage is, above all, a means of finding a reliable breadwinner and provider in the form of a lawful spouse.
However, independent female intellectuals have no need for marriage as
an economic transaction: Even without husbands, they have sufficient
material independence; any formalisation and legal sanction of the bond
can only reduce their independence and take away part of the freedom
that is usually the pride of the emancipated *bourgeois woman*. Thus, the
slogan of left feminists in relation to the family problem is not reform of
marriage laws, but the triumph of the principle of 'free marriage', 'free
love'. This slogan, first coined by socialists in the early nineteenth century,
remains a favourite battle cry of the more emancipated feminists even
today; many of them even make 'free love' the centre of the female question. Making a brave stand against the hypocrisy of the double standard,
they fearlessly enter the battle against maliciously and venomously seething mobs of bourgeois philistines. No official formalisation of the bond
between lovers, no rituals or formalities! A free contract is the panacea
for all evils oppressing women: Love is the only foundation sanctifying
the union. Let women follow their hearts without having to worry about
bourgeois prejudices – this is their most reliable path to moral liberation,
the only solution to the family problem. This is the reasoning of the foremost bourgeois women of all countries.

Our most emancipated equal-rights campaigners are following in their
footsteps in practice, in any case, if not in theory. It is, however, of interest to mention that neither the platform of the AWE nor the 'statutes'
of these equal-rights campaigners say a single word about the necessity
of one or the other reform of marital relations. The AWE recruit their
members primarily from the ranks of women wage earners with a certain
degree of material independence, and perhaps for that reason, the matter
of marriage and the regulation of marital and family relations does not
have the same primary significance for the members of the AWE as it
does for the members of the Progressive Party. In any case, the fact is
that the AWE pays no attention to the matter of marriage. Our Russian intellectual women, independent as they are, have been accustomed
since the 1860s to resolve the matter of marriage 'for themselves', and
thus, they address it *in practice* in the same manner as their Western

European sisters address it *in theory*. Nowhere in the world is the matter of marriage and family debated so little in *feminist* circles as it is in Russia, and yet, nowhere has the principle of 'free marriage' been so widely put into practice. This phenomenon was doubtlessly unexpectedly promoted by the rapid growth of the intellectual proletariat, with their constant insecurity and uncertainty about tomorrow, their forced mobility, and the habit both amongst men and women to rely only on themselves and bear the burden of life without outside aid, under the post-reform regime. Hence the sui generis psychology that leads to a negative attitude towards 'nesting', a habit of freedom and independence that does not permit them to accept any chains. This relative 'moral freedom', this conscious disregard of bourgeois traditions and prejudices, the 'extramarital cohabitation' that has become customary amongst the intellectual strata is particularly at odds with the bleak, dependant position of women in the peasant and bourgeois milieux, where the old attitudes remain strong, where women are yet to be caught up in the worldwide flow of capitalist production and carried into the broad sea of general human labour and independent activity. But capitalism is creeping up on even these impregnable fortresses of good, old Russian traditions and subjugating the hardened, immutable customs by which peasant, merchant, and bourgeois families wall themselves off from the world.

What a curious and beautiful procession of new sorts of 'women who did' the foreign literature of the last twenty years has given us. Here, we find the circumspect heroine of Grant-Allen, a principled opponent of legal marriage, and the driven soul of Renate Fuchs (Wassermann), and the youthful and brave Dora Syk (Mackay),* the doctor Lancelevée

---

* Given the time and effort that was involved in tracking down the original spelling of the name of this more or less forgotten character of the 'new woman' genre, which is rendered phonetically as *Дора Сик* in Kollontai's book, I would like to save future readers and researchers some time by noting that Dora Syk is a character from individualist anarchist novelist John Henry Mackay's 1892 novel *Die Menschen der Ehe* (The people of marriage), who is described as having her 'true home' in the great wide world, in the bustle of the gigantic city, in its unlimited circumstances, whose physiognomy varied with the changing day, in the great intellectual movement'. (Mackay, J. H. [translated in 2001 by Hubert Kennedy], *The People of Marriage* in *Three Novels*, p. 47). The novel can be found in translation at https://www.google.com/books/edition/Three_Novels/2L0GBIYqpREC?hl=en&gbpv=1&dq=three+novels+mackay+hubert+kennedy&printsec=frontcover and in the original German at

of *Princesses de Science*, a woman proud of her independence and full of consciousness of the great value of her rich individuality, that image of the 'idle woman' that is charming in its own way. Our Russian literature offered much less attractive examples of women and girls 'who did', given that the whole atmosphere of specifically intellectual experiences offered too little space for such 'boldness' and that that which emancipated feminists in Germany or France are still struggling to win is long since taken for granted by independent Russian women intellectuals. But these specific victories of a very limited stratum of the Russian population are a drop in the ocean compared to the ocean of familial suffering in which millions of women of other social strata drown every day.

Thus, the indifference of the members of the AWE who would lead a 'cross-class' women's movement in Russia to the reform of family and marital relations is entirely characteristic. The question that gnaws sharply and painfully away at every proletarian woman, especially here in Russia, is met with silence, as if it were unworthy of particular attention on the part of such serious 'political actors', as our equality campaigners wish to appear. The demand for reforms in the area of marital relations and motherhood is too trivial a task for an organisation dedicated to 'larger political matters', as the AWE claims to be. But if the most immediate demands of the Alliance do not include a demand for reorganising the family, then surely our 'leftist' equality campaigners must have some sort of general ideal of marital relations? What exactly is this ideal?

The heroic struggle of individual girls of the bourgeois world, who have thrown down the gauntlet at society for the right to 'dare to love' without decrees or chains that is meant to serve as an example for all women drowning in familial restrictions, this is what is preached by the most emancipated feminists abroad, and it is also the opinion of our most advanced equal-rights campaigners. In other words, as the feminists see it, the matter of marriage is resolved independently of environmental conditions, independently of any change in the economic structure of

---

https://www.gutenberg.org/cache/epub/14700/pg14700.html . I am indebted to Niall Spooner-Harvey for having succeeded in tracking down this name where a number of others, myself included, had failed.—Trans.

society, simply through the power of discrete, individual heroic efforts. Women need only 'dare', and the problem of marriage will sort itself out.

But the less heroic women shake their heads in disbelief: 'It's easy for you, you novel heroines who have been blessed by a prudent author with a nice nest-egg, a couple of selfless friends, and unusually attractive qualities that cause each and every person to help you out, it's easy for you to throw down the gauntlet at the world. But what about those of us who have neither capital, nor sufficient income, nor friends, nor attractive qualities?' And the matter of motherhood rises before the concerned eye of women fighting their way to freedom. 'Free love' – is that possible, feasible, not as an individual, exclusive phenomenon, but as a normal phenomenon, in the existing economic structure of society, as something generally recognised as the dominant norm? Is it possible to ignore that which defines the contemporary form of marriage and the family – private property? Is it possible, in an individualistic world, to eliminate the formalisation of marriage contracts – the only guarantee that the entire burden of motherhood will not fall on them alone – without harming the interests of women?[63] Is what is happening with women not the same as what happened with working-class men at a certain point? Repealing the suffocating workshop regulations without providing new obligations on the part of employers delivered workers to the uncontrolled power of capital, and the tempting slogan of 'freedom of contract between labour and capital' became a means for capital to exploit labour with impunity. In present-day class society, would 'free love', taken to its logical consequences, not place upon woman's shoulders yet another burden – caring for children – rather than freeing her from former familial burdens? 'A private contract for women,' as Bebel correctly notes,

> would be as insignificant as the fact that women can obtain the means of subsistence in any branch of labour suited to her strength and skills. In both cases, she is oppressed, because not only the recognition of her economic freedom, but even the facility of marriage and its dissolution, cannot protect her from economic and social oppression and exploitation. Until the social position of women (specifically their economic position) is completely independent and equal to that of men, until the political rights of both sexes are equal, the private nature of marriage

will be of as little use to her as even the most beautiful constitution can be to a people whose rights and freedoms are at the disposal of the government and the ruling classes, who have in their hands not only wealth, but also physical and intellectual power.[64]

Only a whole series of fundamental reforms of social relations, reforms that transfer the former obligations of the family to society and the state would create the foundation on which the principle of 'free love' could become implementable to a certain degree. But can we seriously expect the modern class state, no matter how democratic its structure, to take upon itself all of the obligations in relation to mothers, and even more—to the next generation—currently assumed by that individualistic cell that is the modern family? Only a fundamental restructuring of all relations of production would establish the societal prerequisites that alone can safeguard women from the negative sides of the elastic formula of 'free love'. Is it not clear that the promiscuity and chaos of sexual mores under contemporary conditions are lurking behind that formula? Look at all these esteemed entrepreneurs and administrators of industrial institutions: Are they not availing themselves of their own form of 'free love' in forcing female workers, office workers, and servants to accede to their sexual whims under threat of the sack? Are not all these 'masters' who have their way with their female servants and then throw the pregnant women onto the street already adhering to the formula of 'free love'?

'But that's not the sort of freedom we mean!' the champions of free marriage object. To the contrary, 'we demand the establishment of a "single morality" equally binding on men and on women, we stand up against modern sexual promiscuity and proclaim that only that "free" marital union is pure which is founded on "true love"!' But, my dear friends, do you not think that your ideal of 'free marriage', when applied to the present socio-economic system, might give results quite similar to the twisted formula of sexual freedom? The principle of 'free love' can only be put into practice without bringing more sorrow to women when the material chains currently giving rise to dual dependency – on capital and their husbands – are removed from the last woman. As women are recruited into independent labour and declared economically independent, some possibility for 'free love' does arise, particularly for the best paid intellectual professionals. But there remains the dependency of women on capital, and that dependency grows as proletarian women join the ranks of the sellers of labour power. Can the slogan of 'free love' improve the sad fate of these women, who only make just enough to avoid dying of starvation? Is 'free love' not being widely practised amongst the working class, so much so that the bourgeoisie has more than once raised a hue and cry about it, shouting about the 'promiscuity' and 'immorality' of the proletariat? But pay attention: When the feminists deliriously speak of new forms of extramarital cohabitation for emancipated bourgeois women, they call that marriage by the beautiful name of 'free love'; when speaking of the working class, extramarital relations are contemptuously branded 'disorderly sexual relations'. That is typical enough.

Meanwhile, under current conditions, for proletarian women, the consequences of religiously sanctified and free cohabitation are equally burdensome. The centre of the problem of marriage and the family for women, for proletarian mothers, does not lie in the external ritualistic or civil forms, but in the surrounding socio-economic conditions determining the complex family obligations of women of the working class. Of course, the question of whether her husband can control her wages, whether he has the legal right to force her to live with him if she herself does not wish to do so, whether he can forcibly take the children from her, etc., is also significant to proletarian women. But the actual position of women in the family is not determined by these sections of the civil code; they are not what will solve the complex family problem. Whether witnessed by a notary, sanctified by the church, or established on the basis of contractual freedom, the problem of marriage will become less acute for most women only when society takes from women all the petty household concerns that are currently inevitable for the management of atomised individual households, if society were to take upon itself the concern for the younger generation, if it were to protect motherhood and give the mother to the child for at least the first months of its life.

The feminists are fighting against the fetish of the marriage contract, legalised and sanctified by the church; proletarian women are at war with the factors giving rise to the contemporary form of marriage and the family, and, as they strive to fundamentally change these conditions, they are aware that, in so doing, they are promoting the reform of relations between the sexes as well. Therein lies the fundamental difference between the bourgeois and proletarian approaches to the complex problem of the family.

In the naïve belief that new forms of family and marital relations can be created against the dismal background of contemporary class society, the feminists and social reformers of the bourgeois camp are at great pains to find these new forms of marriage. If life itself has not given rise to them, then they will have to be made up somehow. There must be such a perfect form of relations between the sexes that could solve the complex problem of the family even within the contemporary regime. One after another, the ideologues of the bourgeois world – writers, novelists, forward-thinking women, emancipation campaigners – put forward their 'patent remedy for the family', their new 'formula for marriage'.

Marriage, according to some, is the free, unobstructed pursuit of the natural attraction encompassing the body and soul of human beings; it is a union of two individuals, both free and equal in rights, having no obligations to one another, not being answerable to one another; it is a union that may last for years, but may also last just one short, but bright and ecstatic, moment. The main thing is that there should be no chains, no bonds other than the personal feelings of the parties to the marriage.

Marriage, as others would have it, even free marriage, even with no external bonds, must remain a closed familial cell even in the future. Fanning the dying flames of the home fire – that is the goal of the new, free, ideal marital union, based not on unvarnished material calculation, not on external, ritualistic cohabitation of two alienated individuals, but on the harmonious merger of two souls, two bodies, the merger of the spouses in spiritual friendship and physical love. The basis of such a marriage is harmony in physical and moral feelings; its task is to reproduce a posterity that is healthy in all senses of the word.

Marriage, says old man Björnsen (who is followed in this by some feminists), the stringent denouncer of sexual promiscuity, the naïve reformer of sexual morality, is the sacred institution which only the 'pure' and 'sinless' must and may approach. Complete abstinence before marriage, preservation of sexual innocence until the age of 25 for men and

until the age of 20 for women, followed by strictly monogamous marriage, monogamy in the full sense of the word, without any exceptions
or indulgences. This is how Björnsen solves the family problem; this is
how, in one fell swoop, he brings light and joy into the marital union and
ends prostitution for evermore! But the world of exploitation, a world full
of injustice, with its narrow class-based morality and the immeasurable
power of capital, must remain whole and intact. Monogamy in our existing system! An end to prostitution! The naïve faith that it is possible
to simply turn the line of demarcation in the field of sexual morality in
the direction opposite the one in which it is, by all appearances, inclined.

How utopian all these marriage formulas sound! What bland palliatives
they are against the dismal background of our present family structure!
'Free marriage', 'free love!' In order for these formulas to be implemented,
it would first be necessary to carry out a fundamental reform of all social
relations between people; moreover, it would be necessary for the norms
of sexual morality, and with them the entire psychology of humanity, to
undergo a profound, fundamental evolution. Can the psychology of contemporary human beings really be capable of perceiving the principles of
'free love'? What of the jealousy that eats away at even the best human
souls?! What of the deeply rooted right of ownership not only of the body,
but also the soul of another person? What of the inability to respectfully
bow before the expression of individuality in others, the habit of either
'subjugating' or 'serving' one's beloved? And the bitter, fatally bitter feeling of abandonment and boundless loneliness when one's beloved falls
out of love and leaves. Where is the head of the 'lonely' person, the true
individualist at heart, to turn? The 'collective' with its joys, sorrows, and
efforts is, at best, an 'object' on which to expend one's spiritual and intellectual strength. But can contemporary human beings merge with this
collective so as to feel themselves realised in it and it realised in themselves? Can the life of the collective replace their minor personal joys?
Without the 'one' kindred spirit, even socialists, even collectivists are
boundlessly lonely in this contemporary world that is hostile to us, and
only in the working class do we catch faint glimpses of the future of more
joined, more socially minded relations between people.

The family problem is as complex, confused, and multifaceted as life itself, and solving it is beyond the capabilities of our current system . . .

But there are still other marriage formulas. The marital union, some advanced women and social thinkers say, is merely a way of reproducing posterity. Marriage in itself has no particular value for women; *motherhood* is its purpose, its ultimate goal and task. Thanks to such inspired champions of motherhood as Ruth Bré or Ellen Key, motherhood is a bourgeois ideal that sees in woman not, first and foremost, a human being, but primarily the female of the species, and it has assumed the special halo of progressiveness. Foreign literature enthusiastically adopted this slogan raised by 'advanced' women. Even here in Russia, in a time preceding the political storm, in examining a number of social values, the matter of motherhood caught the attention of the daily press. The sincere and brave approach taken by Irina De in her article *The Right to Motherhood* (*Право на материнство*) (*Rus*, 1904) heralded an entire series of articles dedicated to the matter. The slogan 'right to motherhood' could not but find lively resonance in the broadest segments of the female population, and although all the proposals made by the feminist camp suffered from utopian naïvety, it was in itself so much of a live issue, so immediate that it could not help but concern women's hearts.

'The right to motherhood' belongs to a category of issues that concern and weigh not only on women of the bourgeois class, but even more so on proletarian women. *The right to be a mother* is a golden phrase that goes straight to the heart and makes every 'feminine heart' beat. The right to feed 'one's own' child with one's breast, the right to follow the first glimpse of its awakening consciousness, the right to protect its little body and tender soul on its first steps into life from thorns and unnecessary suffering – what woman who is a mother does not subscribe to those demands? It would seem that we have again stumbled upon a point that might serve to unite women of the different social strata; it would seem that we have at last found a bridge that connects women of two mutually hostile worlds. But let us take a closer look at what these advanced bourgeois women mean by a 'right to motherhood', how the problem is posed and solved by its inspired champions à la Ruth Bré or Ellen Key. Then, we will make clear to ourselves whether women of the working class agree with the definition and solution of the problem of motherhood proposed by bourgeois equality campaigners. Motherhood, in the eyes of its enthusiastic apologists, has almost sacred properties. In an effort to do away with the false prejudice that brands women for a natural act, giving birth to a child without legal sanction, the champions of the right to motherhood go too far in the other direction: To them, motherhood is the goal of a woman's life.

The 'new mother', she who is to build the world anew, to purify and sanctify the marital union that has been perverted by false ideas, cannot – must not – share her right to a child with anyone. Men, husbands, lovers for her are nothing but passing apparitions, means to achieve her natural purpose, realise her raison d'être. In relation to men, husbands, the fathers of their children, women have no obligations; as for society, her only duty to it is to bear, feed, and raise her child.

But surely this transformation of motherhood into an end in itself borders on the truly bourgeois conviction that a woman's only 'profession' is to be a mother. What about the fact that the 'new woman/mother' gives the best of herself, her mind, the strength of her spirit not to the family cell as such, but only to the flesh of her flesh – her child? 'Will the world be saved' by this 'new, strong mother, who takes responsibility for herself, by raising children on her own in her own spirit, teaching them to clarify their future obligations, and will be closer to them than the mother who was robbed of her *greatest achievement* by the stork?'[65] (italics mine). What does a woman win by being granted the 'right to motherhood' whilst the present social structure remains intact? Can a woman who has given all of herself to her child remain a 'free personality' under present conditions? Does the child's very existence not wrap her in an entire net of unavoidable, pressing concerns that overshadow all the wide, bright world, with its wealth of experiences with the tiny, selfish little world of her child?

In the present capitalist society, freeing women by realising the slogan of 'free motherhood' is a more naïve utopia than the dream of solving the family problem by merely preaching 'free love'.

The right to motherhood as interpreted by the feminists already exists, in all of its harsh reality, for the numerically largest class of the population – the proletariat. Look at the long line of unmarried mothers who bear the entire weight of free motherhood on their shoulders not with their heads held high in pride, but with their backs hunched over. Does this cruel right serve to liberate them? Is it not actually too often the cause that pushes them to crime, or even infanticide?

To the contrary, even the defenders of free motherhood as a patent remedy for all family ills and a means of 'healing' the relations between the sexes sense the weakness of their position. Ruth Bré herself, who ecstatically proclaims the 'eternal, ancient right of motherhood', who wishes to 'create space for that most ancient and eternal dyad – mother and child' takes her demands to a quite modest and prudent objectives: 'The free woman, who demands matrilineal marriage, wishes to own her children as her own property; as such, she must be able to support them, at least halfway. The other half, as well as the expenses of his own maintenance, must be borne by the husband.'[66] In other words, half of the responsibility in the marital union, even under free motherhood, falls upon the father. Well, that is quite normal and just indeed! But what of this 'new, strong mother, who takes responsibility for herself, and must save the world', what of the 'desire to *own* her children like her own property?' And then, an objective dictated by a purely bourgeois attitude:

> All children of the same father shall inherit equally from him, even if they were born from different marriages. A child born in free marriage shall inherit equally with one born in legal marriage. Additionally, every child shall inherit from its mother. This measure completely fits the legal consciousness of the people.[67]

These are all great bourgeois truths. But why, then, should we cross swords for free motherhood if it ultimately amounts to such modest and anodyne reforms? In this context, it should be noted that these advanced bourgeois women transfer the concern for the growing generation to husbands and fathers, and by no means to society. Such is the strength of custom, such is the power of individualist psychology even for an advanced person of our time!

It is difficult for bourgeois feminists to place responsibility on society as a whole rather than the individual responsibility of a single person. Ruth Bré, however, does incidentally mention 'the state'; from the state, she demands that free motherhood be guaranteed by financial insurance. 'When a woman becomes a mother, excessive family concerns make further service impossible; as such, a serving woman must be guaranteed a pension just in case.'[68]

Do you think that 'insuring motherhood' refers to a pension for 'citizen-mothers'? No, what she is referring to is that women in the intellectual professions – civil servants, teachers, actresses, etc. – should not be deprived of the *employment-based* pension that they have earned and that is not infrequently taken away from them by sacking them. It is proposed to add another 'privilege' – pensions for married women. But what sort of insurance for motherhood is this? It is also proposed for the state not to terminate the employment of married women, and to provide a fixed period of pre- and postnatal leave for women. At last, a demand that directly touches the interests of proletarian women as well! But we rejoiced too early; it turns out that she is by no means referring to all women, but only to representatives of the 'middle stratum'. 'To date,' Ruth Bré says,

> such protection for pregnant and postnatal women has only been put
> into practice in factories, as is the case with many other similar measures. No one gives any thought to the human interests of the middle
> class, especially those in the civil service. It is the state, which should
> set an example in this regard, that sees in its employees only employees,
> but not human beings.[69]

Thus, the most advanced campaigners for mothers' rights, it turns out, go on about granting these rights primarily to representatives of their own class, that is, 'the middle stratum'. At least they are open and honest about it.

Another passionate champion of motherhood, Ellen Key, takes her immense passion even farther than Bré. Ruth Bré – no socialist, she – is simply an advanced bourgeois woman who has not renounced her class psychology; for her, what is important is to solve the problem of motherhood within the confines of present-day society, and she shows very little hope of transforming the world based on new principles. Ellen Key *is* a socialist; she condemns the feminists with their narrow-class psychology, utilitarianism, and inability to take a deeper, broader look at their own 'women's cause'. Ellen Key strives for a promised land of socialised labour and warmly greets women's liberation. And yet, the old bourgeois yeast has left its indelible imprint of bias on her fresh, independent, and at times astonishingly healthy judgments.

Ellen Key is an exemplar of that sort of reformers of the marital question for whom the solution of the family problem consists of reforming and healing the family. As a counterweight to those feminists who see the centre of gravity of the female question in marriage and love, she locates it in motherhood. For Key, marriage and love must become synonyms; the foundation and purpose of marriage itself is children and family.[70] The ideal of a healthy, normal woman should be a home full of bright joys and sunny smiles, a home, in whose centre she, the mother, stands. Here, in the foundations of the joined, harmonious family, children are raised lovingly and attentively by father and mother. By no means impervious to the relatively dark sides of the modern family structure, she demands its fundamental reform from within that much more insistently; but, despite all Key's radicalism, the family is just as sacred for her as it is for any bourgeois philistine.

Of course, Key is a fervent opponent of socialised child rearing: 'Do not take from all children their lawful birthright – familial feelings and family memories, family sorrows and joys, all that which gives human nature its special tone, colour, and scent!' 'Do not destroy the most important of all systems of joint education – the system of children raising parents and parents raising children!'[71] With her characteristic passion, she defends the contemporary closed cell of the family and calls not for its destruction, but for its transformation: 'Rather than destroying the family; family law should be transformed. We should not move away from child rearing by parents; rather, we must introduce education of the parents themselves; we should not destroy the home, but eliminate homelessness.'[72]

Contemporary economic conditions diverted women from the home, took them away from their primary duties; now, humanity must consider how to return mothers to children and the home.[73] Women joyfully take the opportunity to serve society as mothers and carers; after all, children are the purpose of a woman's existence: 'Through the child, she must give all the wealth of her individuality and the individuality of her beloved to posterity; she must give her developed personality and the independence that she was has won through work wholly over to the raising of the child.'[74]

Of course, women should be granted the freedom to choose the purpose of their lives themselves, whether to become a professional or a mother and carer; but woe betide those mothers in whom social instincts, love for scholarship and the arts block their natural calling and kill the passionate desire to give the world a child and dedicate themselves to it.[75] Professional women, women who expend their mental strength outside of child rearing, do great evil to humanity.

> Many women, in recognising the need to select one or the other – a profession or motherhood, opt for the former and completely avoid or limit the latter, because they believe that they are obliged to make another, richer contribution to the cause of culture. But surely humanity would have won more from the geniuses who might be born from these talented women?[76]

And these are the words of a vehement and passionate champion of women's complete liberation; these are the words of the socialist Ellen Key! But how, then, does her 'progressive ideal' of new marital relations and a 'new woman' differ from the wise old prescriptions of the virtuous bourgeois? Surely, this is just a narrower version of the sermon of the German Kaiser, who believed that the intellectual and spiritual outlook of a 'reasonable' woman was more than fully covered by the 'four Ks' (*Kinder, Kirche, Kleider und Küche*).[77] Listening to all these verbose odes to 'motherhood' as an end in itself, it is hard not to remember the wise words of Clara Zetkin, who noted that

> the claim that women's natural purpose is child rearing is a remnant of antiquity that has no place in modern social conditions. Mothers are indeed the 'natural' carers of children during nursing as a result of the natural connection existing between them and children, but nothing more. The task of society is to protect and preserve the child's access to maternal care during this period and give the child the possibility of developing normally during the mother's pregnancy. But as soon as the period of nursing has ended, it is of no importance to the child's development whether it is cared for by the mother or someone else. Here, the decisive influence is not that of 'natural', immutable factors,

but, to the contrary, the ever-changing social conditions. What is important is not maternal, but generally reasonable, loving care, based on a knowledge of the laws of child development.[78]

In her measureless worship of motherhood, Key is ready to ignore the obvious and claim that unmarried female workers will soon completely displace married ones from the labour market, and that the complete return of women to the home is merely a 'matter of time'.[79] Key bases these claims on the fact that, somewhere in the US, unmarried female workers united to struggle against the employment of married female workers; Key has no other facts from real life to offer, but this does not stop her drawing her premature conclusions.[80] By means of legal provisions and the struggle between married and unmarried female workers on the labour market (Key apparently believes that, as socialism draws nearer, it is not solidarity that will grow and become more acute in the working class, but competition!), women will be returned to the family, especially 'if their domestic work is given the character of paid labour . . .'[81]

Housekeeping will become less labour-intensive when handled cooperatively; however, women will nonetheless concern themselves with home and hearth and manage their exemplary households with the aid of 'comfortable and pleasant tools'. Domestic labour will eventually regain its previous respected position, but only under the condition that 'society values women's care for the household, and they will no longer feel that their husbands support them so that they can do second-class work, work that is not worthy of the value currently unconditionally assigned to economic values—i.e., cash.'[82]

'Women's dependency,' Key states, 'can only be eliminated by assigning their domestic work an economic value.' But how, exactly, is women's domestic work to be valued? In Key's view, this is not difficult at all; one need only compensate women for the earnings they lose by renouncing their prior professions. 'If this criterion is not met, then she should receive the amount that would have been paid to a housekeeper under similar circumstances.'[83]

Women are to be paid for domestic work.

But by whom? Their husbands? Society? Apparently by their husbands, because Key proposes this measure independently of the achievement of socialism. Also characteristic is the following caveat from Key: Those women who have assets or dowries and can cover their portion of the household and childcare expenses from their own pockets are *not required* to dedicate themselves exclusively to their households; accordingly, they retain the right to opt for a profession outside of the home without any particular compensation. What a conceptual mess! How narrowly bourgeois these quasi-reforms are!

In order to rehabilitate the foundation of the family, Key additionally considers the following immediate measures necessary: above all, of course, complete division of assets between spouses, obligatory transfer of one-half of the responsibility for children to the father, who is obliged to care for them and cover one-half of the maintenance of his posterity until they reach the age of eighteen. But here, Key also mentions a role for 'society' – it's not for nothing that she's a socialist! Enter maternity insurance. At one time, this principle was only advocated by socialists, but these days, this demand has found a home in the broadest segments of the female population. Women, Key proposes, who are doing their female version of military service, that is, 'due to looking after children, and, if possible, looking after the sick, has learnt public hygiene, and has neither personal assets nor sufficient income to cover her half of the child's expenses, shall receive from society a subsidy for a period not to exceed the first three years of the child's life'. In this context, there is to be a special 'children's inspectorate' that distributes the subsidies and oversees the care of infants and children.[84] And these 'half-socialist-half-bourgeois' demands Ellen Key proposes as a panacea for the ills of modern marital relations! And whom does she give the responsibility for carrying out these measures? Contemporary class society!

Key's commitment to the duties of motherhood and the foundation of the family causes her to declare with certainty that the closed-off family cell will continue to exist within a society transformed on the basis of socialist principles. The only changes to be made in this area amount to excluding any rational or material calculation as a motive for marriage, with the marital union being concluded based on mutual affection without any rituals or formalities, so that 'love' and 'marriage' become synonymous. The closed-off family cell is a creature of the contemporary individualistic world, with its merciless battle for survival, its atomised and lonely souls; it is a creature of the monstrous capitalist system. And this Key hopes to bequeath intact into the socialist society. But will there then be a moral and social need for such blood- and kinship-based ties that, in the current state of fragmentation, often act as the sole bastion in life, the only refuge in moments of great adversity? Key has no answer to this question. Too great is her love for the 'ideal family', this egoistic cell of the middle class upon which the female champions of the bourgeois social structure look with hope and awe.

But it is not just a few erratic, albeit talented, minds like Key who get caught up in social contradictions in their efforts to solve the family problem.

It seems there is not a single question in the field of the mutual social relations of people that evinces such divergence of opinion even amongst socialists as that of marriage and the family. If we were to try to organise a survey, the results would likely be quite interesting. Is the family in decay, or is there reason to believe that the current family troubles are merely a temporary crisis that the family is undergoing? Will the present form of the family be preserved in the society of the future, or will it be irrevocably buried under the rubble of the contemporary capitalist regime? These are questions that might yield the most divergent answers.

As recently in 1869, at one of the conferences of the German trade unions, the socialist Bracke submitted a motion calling for a ban on professional labour by married women as distracting them from the home and causing the inexorable decay of the proletarian family. The conference, aware that no legislative regulation could save women from exploitation by capital under the contemporary relations of production, immediately rejected Bracke's proposal: The workers understood perfectly well that banning work outside the home would not give children their mothers back, that capital, inventive as it was, would find a cunning way into the proletarian home, and would continue to drain them of their vital juices in the guise of 'domestic industry'. Surely this is not unknown in the annals of female labour. It is worth remembering the late Middle Ages, when women were forced to return home by the exclusionary rules of the workshops after widespread female participation in the trades. The ban on open work in workshops would have increased the labour burden ten-fold for women, and would not have helped them escape the web of capital. Isolated and disconnected from their workplace comrades, women would once again bow down under the oppression of increasing exploitation, and instead of light and relief, the ban on working in the factories and workshops would have merely resulted in new suffering and sorrow for women with children.

But the gravitational force of the customary family hearth is so strong that it forces even socialists to raise their voices in defence of the contemporary family structure.

Almost simultaneously with Bracke's proposal, at the second congress of the International, in 1868, during the discussion of female and child labour, the French socialist faction pronounced themselves in favour of 'returning women to the family'. Coullery, in support of the memorandum of the Proudhonists, sang a pretentious hymn in praise of women's emancipation, but his eulogy ultimately led to philistine praise of women who remained 'at the hearth'. Some of the French delegates even introduced a resolution declaring women's place to be in the family as mothers and carers for children, condemning female labour and proposing a protest against it, 'the evil that results in physical, moral, and social degeneration.'[85]

Karl Marx took a completely different approach to the matter of female and child labour. Protesting against the barbaric exploitation of women's and children's labour in contemporary capitalist society and speaking in favour of the need for broad legislative protection, Marx did, however, welcome women's entry onto the path of social production. Only work could free women from the suffocating atmosphere of family life; only work could make whole human beings about of them. Work in hygienic conditions was not only not harmful to women; to the contrary, it would facilitate the development of her physical strength and help her become an independent, autonomous personality. The International immediately adopted a resolution in the spirit of Marx's proposal, and yet, again and again, we hear voices in the socialist world raised in defence of women who live at the family hearth. A few years ago, an article by Fischer appeared in the *Sozialistische Monatshefte* that basically reiterated the argument made by the Proudhonists at the congresses of the International. Female industrial labour was an unalloyed evil against which it would be necessary to struggle actively unless the tendency of capitalist production itself did not show any favourable signs in this regard and did not promise the disappearance of this evil in the future. Fischer seeks to prove that the decay of the working-class family is merely a temporary phenomenon brought about by the specific relations of production of our days, primarily low wages for fathers making it necessary for women to earn an ancillary income. As the degree of organisation and significance of the working class grows and the scope of social legislation increases, wages will gradually increase, and may reach a level at which women will leave the factories of their own volition in order to once again become 'good wives, attentive mothers, and dedicated housekeepers.' The customary picture of the comforts of home of the German *Bürgertum* is painted before Fischer's enchanted eye: The husband, the sole breadwinner of the family, returns tired in the evening to his attractively glowing hearth, where his family waits to welcome him affectionately; well-dressed, healthy little children and the caring housewife, proud of her culinary skills, with hot soup already steaming on the table! Yes, for the contemporary proletarian man, who, day by day, has to eat dried food, 'hot soup' doubtlessly is occasionally the subject of 'secret sighs'. But why must he imagine this 'hot soup' on 'his' table, in the tight circle of 'his' blood heirs? How far is the psychology of contemporary people, the entire structure of their souls, from the collectivist consciousness in which, one must think, they will be re-educated by different relations of production . . .

But let us return to Fischer's argument. What is this standard of wages that could be considered sufficient to cover all of the most urgent needs of a proletarian family? Where is this limit of material well-being, at which a working-class man can, with full conviction, tell his wife: 'Now, I'm earning for two; so you go back home and handle your domestic matters'? Do the needs of the working class not grow as their income grows; do the former not in fact grow even faster than the latter? Surely this is the basis for the Marxian 'theory of impoverishment'! Surely it is the relations of production themselves that set the limit to the uninterrupted increase in wages. What, then, is the point of modern technology if, at the critical moment, it does not come to the rescue of capitalists with its usual alacrity to increase the productivity of labour with new machines in order to reduce the number of workers, once again giving factory owners whose backs are to the wall the opportunity to emerge victorious?

But regardless of purely objective conditions, are there not already elements in the psychology of the proletariat, particularly the female part of it, that prevent the revival of the former foundations of the family? A woman who has, by the very process of habituation to social production, imperceptibly but irreversibly emancipated and removed herself from the home will no longer be capable of turning her back to the liberatory path along which she has walked 'on one fine day', and, of course, does not wish to voluntarily take upon herself the uncomfortable domestic burden. Look how quickly the psyche of women workers, women professionals participating in social production, and, thus, in class struggle, has been transformed! What valuable traits are developing in them that had in the past been completely foreign to them: independence, love of freedom, the ability to join with the collective. Women workers, who have over a few generations passed through the hard school of proletarian labour and struggle, women 'forged in the factory boiler', who are used to being looked upon above all as equal comrades and human beings, and only thereafter as sexual beings, will never make peace with family bondage, even if it is embellished with a number of civil and social reforms, and will be even less able to return to the dependent position of being kept by her husband or lover.

This important aspect is all too often overlooked when examining the marital and family questions of the future. Even socialist women underestimate the change in women's psychology under the influence of the change in social conditions. When the matter of motherhood was under discussion at the fourth conference of the social-democratic women of Germany, voices – albeit only individual ones – were raised in defence of the family and the domestic obligations of women. Thus, the delegate from Magdeburg, in relation to a resolution concerning protections for pregnant and postnatal women of the working class, stated that woman can only be safeguarded from harm to her health and that of the child by means of one radical measure, i.e., joint struggle to win a wage level at which women's work outside the home would become superfluous.[86] However, the social-democratic women's conference did not share the views of the delegate from Magdeburg, and adopted a resolution (below), in which the exact opposite view was expressed.

The conditions of production pushed women out of the home and required them to forget their maternal and household obligations, but those very conditions are what mould a human being out of her. 'Workers,' Lafargue says,

> were the first to draw the logical conclusion from women's participation in social production: They replaced the ideal of the craftsman, the ideal of the woman homemaker, with a new ideal, that of women as comrades in the economic struggle to increase wages and liberate labour; only the bourgeoisie have yet to comprehend that their ideal has long since become obsolete and must be renewed in order for it to be consistent with the current conditions of the social environment.[87]

And no matter how much it outrages the supporters of the family principle and the enslavement of women, no matter how much they call women back to the joys of the family, the woman who has tasted other, broader joys, who is conscious of being an independent human being and a valuable worker comrade, will not wish to sell her liberated personality for lentil soup, for the closed shell of home and hearth . . . No, no matter what the believers in the contemporary foundations of the family say, the tendency of social development shows that the present closed family is living through its final days, that it is irrevocably condemned to die together with the contemporary world of class antagonism.

We have examined the most characteristic feminist formulas for marriage. Which of them is the most acceptable? Which of them comes closest to the ideal for future relations between the sexes that is gestating in the subsoil of the working masses? Is this really a matter of choosing one formula or another for marriage, of evaluating different standards for family relations? Surely the solution to the family problem does not actually lie in simply '*inventing*' a more congenial form of marital union.

Anyone who is familiar with the basic postulates of historical materialism knows that people are powerless to arbitrarily modify the form of their social coexistence because these forms flow logically from the economic relations and relations of production in their environment. All that they can do is detect the tendency of the evolution that is already occurring in the social organism and accelerate this often painful process of transformation. Anyone who wishes to get a sense of what marital relations will be possible in the future must, first and foremost, carefully follow the evolution of the foundations of the contemporary family. Capitalism is breaking up the family, but the further process of socialisation of production is facilitating the creation of new forms of social coexistence. Slowly, but inexorably, one obligation after another is being transferred from the family to society and the state. Those functions of the family that, just recently, appeared inextricably tied to the family cell are gradually becoming the tasks of one collective or another. The separate, closed-off individual households are giving way to grandiose cooperative enterprises where, together with collective heating and lighting for scores of individual households, there are also shared kitchens, dining areas, and restaurants.[88] Crèches, kindergartens, and primary schools will take the heavy task of the rational, healthy education of the younger generation off of the overburdened shoulders of the working mother. In the smiling, hygienic, moral environment of crèches and kindergartens, under the supervision of professional teachers and carers, kids will be free of the infectious air of contemporary working-class neighbourhoods, from chewed-up crusts instead of milk, from cold, hunger, fighting, and the other unavoidable attributes of the contemporary 'child rearing' that is loudly referred to as 'being raised under mother's eye'. Of course, today, all these crèches, kindergartens, and primary schools in the hands of 'charity from above', rather than the class of the population served by them, are full of inadequacies and shortcomings; therefore, they can be viewed only as the pale prototypes of the forms of social coexistence that not only will be created in the future, but in which a new humanity will likely be able to breathe in new content, a new spirit. In these nurseries of the growing generation, the little forming souls will be instilled from the first years of life with the precious abilities of solidarity and community, the habit of looking at the world through the prism of the collective, rather than that of their own solitary, selfish ego.

Loving bourgeois mummies clutch their pearls in horror when they are shown that life itself, step by step, is taking child rearing out of their hands in favour of the better prepared hands of specialists. 'In order to stitch boots, one must go through an apprenticeship, but in order to lead such fragile creations as the souls of children, maternal instinct is supposedly enough,' Zetkin exclaims. How many people are destroyed by this blind instinct that they believe is capable of replacing scientific knowledge and special training. The bourgeois mummies should not hypocritically dismiss the spectre of socialised child rearing; let them tell us whether it is in fact their shoulders that bear all the burdens of contemporary child rearing. What of the omnipresent governesses, tutors, nannies, and even nurses? With an easy heart, bourgeois women throw all the burdensome concerns of having children onto women of another, 'lower', class, even going so far as to offer the greedy mouths of their babies another woman's breast, that of a proletarian woman. Socialised child rearing is the constant bugbear of bourgeois women, when the future society comes up for discussion. As if it did not exist even now, albeit in a monstrously distorted form!

But bourgeois women do not want to acknowledge the insignificance of their role in the modern family; they understand all too well that, if they openly acknowledge how little actual content lurks behind the grand phrase 'maternal duties', there will no longer be any moral justification for the lives that these days are proudly led by the bourgeois matrons 'kept' by their lawful husbands.

With the transfer of the child-rearing function from the family to society, the last of the foundations of the modern closed family cell will disappear; the old bourgeois family will begin to break apart even faster, and the vague silhouettes of the marital relations of the future will become ever more clearly visible through the surrounding atmosphere. What are these vague silhouettes that hide behind the fog of contemporary influences?

Need we repeat that the coercive present-day form of marriage will be replaced by a free union of free individuals? The ideal of free love that is painted by the starved imaginations of women fighting for emancipation will doubtlessly correspond to the norm of relations between the sexes that will be established by a collectivist society. Societal influences are so complex, their effects too diverse for anyone now to be able to clearly imagine the form that marital relations will take after the entire structure has fundamentally changed; it is currently impossible. However, the slow evolution in relations between the sexes is a clear testament to the fact that ritualised marriage and the forcibly closed-off family are doomed to disappear.

The feminists are ready for their victory celebration: After all, without their ideal of free love and free marriage, we never would have managed it! But is this really 'their' ideal? Surely it came into the world and matured in the very foundations of the working class under the influence of 'sad necessity' and the oppressive force of the all-powerful economic conditions? Slowly, but continuously, without noise or slogans, familial norms are evolving in the proletarian milieu day by day, clearing the way for a viable principle, that of the free union.

Proletarian men are necessarily deprived of the option of an early marriage; if their wages aren't enough for their own maintenance, how can they possibly think of starting a family? But the heart refuses to wait. It begins to express its demands independently of wage levels. The result of this is free intercourse, intercourse in which, under current conditions, the full burden of the consequences fall upon the woman, but which give proletarian women at least the satisfaction of knowing that her husband will not gain the power of 'lord and master' over her. And proletarian women, who have learnt to cherish their independence, value their relative freedom, are increasingly reluctant to submit to family bondage and cherish marriage only as a means of transferring part of the cost of maintaining their shared child to their husbands.

As cohabitation based on cooperative principles becomes more widespread, the economic functions of individual families will become less and less significance, facilitating the transformation of marriage into a purely moral union. Under the influence of changing economic conditions, the psychology of the working class will fundamentally change. If any class is able, under the current economic regime, to perceive the as-yet barely recognisable norms of the sexual morality of the future, it is, of course, most likely the proletariat.

Despite being poisoned by widespread prostitution, relations between the sexes in the proletarian milieu come substantially closer to the psychology of future humanity that paints itself in our imaginations. Here, the 'double standard' that poisons so many women's lives no longer plays the decisive role that it does in the bourgeois milieu, and no longer distorts and mutilates so many young existences. Do unwed mothers really see themselves as the despised, rejected beings that they remain even today in the eyes of the hypocritical morality of the bourgeoisie? The innocence of a girl – a quality necessary for a husband-as-owner, a guarantee that the woman will not bring into the family 'elements of strange blood' – is losing its significance in the working class, where the question of inheritance is of no importance, and girls with 'a past' marry as easily as girls without one, as long as they do not bear the mark of legalised prostitution. 'In the working class,' Dr Blaschko notes,

> men and women between 18 and 25 years of age mostly enter into sexual relations without concerning themselves with marriage. This class never considered free love a great sin. In the proletarian milieu, where there is no inheritance to be found no matter how hard one looks, there is no need for lawful heirs; in cases where people are united not by financial or other calculations, but the pure attraction of the heart, people naturally are less worried about whether a marriage is 'real'. And were it not for the existence in the present day of the simplified form of civil marriage and – on the other hand – the difficult position in which society places extramarital children and unwed mothers, who knows? Perhaps the institution of marriage would be even weaker.[89]

Infidelity by one's wife – that source of intense drama and mandatory grounds for separation amongst the bourgeoisie – is not seen by workers as an indelible stain on the 'honour' of the husband. Industrial workers find it much easier than peasants to make their peace with unfaithful wives, as only moral aspects matter in evaluating this fact; for peasant men, on the other hand, with their owner psychology, infidelity on the part of their wives is further exacerbated by additional, unconscious economic calculations. Of course, the bourgeois defenders of freer morals, unable to renounce their class bias, usually recoil in sacred horror at descriptions of the 'free' or, according to their terminology, 'bestially licentious' morals of the working class. Particular horror is inspired by the statistics showing a growing number of 'illegitimate' babies, but instead of renouncing the bureaucratic formula of 'legitimate' and 'illegitimate' children, they prefer to lament the decline of morality and the need to 'raise the moral standards' of the proletariat. And, behind the bourgeois ideologues, we find the feminists, the same feminists who demand a reassessment of all moral values *for themselves*. It is of course undeniable that the harmful effects of capitalism and the unbearable working and living conditions of the working class bring many abnormal and immoral elements into the moral environment of working-class men and women, sometimes irreparably distorting the moral appearance of the proletariat. Overcrowded dwellings, starvation wages for women, extremely long, strenuous labour, children living on the streets, and the lack of cultural interests all lead to a number of extremely sad consequences, promoting the growth of prostitution, drunkenness, and child molestation, which result in the coarsening of morals. But even in this poisoned atmosphere, there is doubtlessly a more favourable basis for the development of the psychology of the future than in the bourgeois milieu; it is only here, in the working class, that the young seedlings of the future, freer relations between the sexes, can sprout even weakly. The proletariat is the only class for whom economic calculations are excluded to a greater or lesser extent from the marital union, and for whom marriage is the very psycho-physiological act the feminists would like to see it as.

However, they would hardly agree. Why? Surely they – the emancipated women – are the bearers of the new morality, surely they are the vanguard, on the front lines of the struggle for women's liberation from familial oppression! It is difficult, very difficult for bourgeois women to imagine that the bearer of the new social and moral truth is not they, but that proletarian 'little sister' to whom they have made an incorrigible habit of patronising and condescending to.

The new moral standards taking shape in the working class under the influence of the process of socio-economic transformation are spreading to the other strata of the population. As the puritan, and simultaneously rawly sensual, morality of the Third Estate displaced the more spiritual, but less constraining moral norms of feudal chivalry, in our time, the morality of the bourgeoisie, which had appeared inviolate until just recently, is gradually being pushed aside by the ethics taking shape within the working class. Ultimately, the dominant morality is the morality that grows up within the class that grows together with the relations of production in a given period.

But these positions are not shared by the feminists. After all, it is their firm conviction that the torch of women's liberation is in their hands. We shall not argue with them over who was the first come up with it, particularly since the 'it' in question, i.e., 'free marriage' and 'free love', are interpreted totally differently by us and the feminists. This is not the place to tarry on the differences in these concepts; we will return to this matter elsewhere. What matters here is to emphasise that, in fighting for women's liberation from familial oppression, one must take aim *not at the forms of marital relations themselves, but at the causes that have given rise to them.*

Only by carrying on the class struggle day by day in the ranks of the working class can women rightly believe in the creation of a social structure in which they will be able to freely choose their occupation and dedicate themselves to motherhood or use their strength to serve society or the arts and sciences, one in which the lively attractions of young hearts will no longer be distorted and mutilated in the interests of prejudices and traditions. A liberated humanity will know truly free love and the joys of free, healthy motherhood.

'But,' realistic souls exclaim, 'all of this is in the future, the distant future, cloaked in the fog of long, dark years. And what about us? We want to live now, we want to live and struggle not just for the happiness of future generations, but for our own, as well!' A lawful and just demand! But who other than the socialists can meet it? Turn to the feminists and ask them what women today should do in order to avoid the full weight of familial oppression falling upon them. They will start offering the same advice we already know: 'Demand easier divorce,' 'Demand the abolition of religious marriage and separation of assets,' 'Ignore the external forms of marriage and bravely follow your heart!' Working-class women, however, will throw up their hands in perplexity at this cascade of feminist *desiderata*. 'But all these "reforms" will have only the slightest effect on the most immediate and essential interests of working-class women!'

Let us now look at what the workers' party proposes as the immediate measures to be taken for working-class women who are crushed under the dual burdens of domestic duties and work on the shop floor. Unlike the feminists, this party does not delude itself with the hope of attaining a fundamental solution of the family question and the problem of motherhood within contemporary capitalist society; as such, it has no 'patent remedies' like those the feminists bandy about so lavishly. But it knows that the difficult position of women and mothers can be alleviated, and the health and very life of the next generation protected, by a number of socio-political measures. These measures are meant, firstly, to facilitate the acceleration of the economic process that is breaking up the small economic unit of the family and taking the concerns of household management from the overburdened shoulders of working women to place them in the hands of a specially qualified collective; secondly, they seek to protect the interests of mother and child, to develop broad, comprehensive protective legislation, to include maternity insurance; thirdly, these measures lastly seek to transfer the care of the younger generation from the family to the state or local authorities, conditioned, of course, on the complete democratisation of both the former and the latter. However, of course, these demands can only have the necessary effect if, at the same time, the well-being of the working class is improved as a result of the general gains made by the proletariat; otherwise, in a setting of poverty and disenfranchisement, neither protective legislation, nor maternity insurance, nor anything else will be capable of tangibly lightening the load of married women.

The protection of motherhood and the defence of the interests of mothers and children are constant concerns of socialists. At the fourth social-democratic women's conference in Mannheim, particular attention was given this matter. The resolution set forth below, which was unanimously adopted following heated debate, may serve as an indicator of the most immediate, minimal demands of social democracy on the matter of the protection of motherhood.

Protection of Women in Pregnancy and after Childbirth*

As women's participation in economic life grows, the question becomes more urgent: How can women's industrial labour be made compatible with motherhood? Proletarian women and their children suffer particularly under this dual burden; gynaecological diseases, complicated pregnancies and deliveries, stillbirths and premature births, as well as infant morbidity and mortality are caused by the unfavourable conditions under which women work.

The path of restricting (half-day work) or even forbidding work by married women is unacceptable for us. Working women do not turn to wage labour for pleasure, but under the influence of economic need, and making work outside the home difficult, or banning it outright, would result in significantly greater numbers of women being forced into the unprotected zone of working from home.

Moreover, unwed mothers and their children, who are even more likely to be exposed to the risks set forth above, would have no protection at all. Lastly, we are by no means in favour of such a restriction on women's labour because we see it as the only path to women's liberation.

For us, the matter comes down to the following:†

I. Establish working conditions for women that do not prevent them becoming healthy mothers of healthy children

    and

II. Create institutions that would alleviate the burden of motherhood for women.

In order to meet the first of these two objectives, we demand:

1. The introduction of an eight-hour working day for all female workers over the age of 18 (a six-hour day for adolescents from 14 to 18 years of age), the introduction of which may be prepared by means of a gradual shorting of the existing working day to 10 and 9 hours for a brief transition period to be established by law. Because all monotonous work is harmful to health when it lasts long.

---

* See the appendix for the original German text, *Schwangeren- und Wöchnerinnenschutz*, in full. —Ed.

† The original reads: *Für uns kommt nur in Frage* (For us, only the following is acceptable) —Trans.

2. A ban on women working in industries that are especially harmful to maternal and child health.

   Above all, we are referring to the following: Trades involving the risk of poisoning; industries in which lead, mercury, phosphorus, sulphur,* and similar poisons are used; as well as lifting and carrying heavy objects and other activities particularly harmful for the female body and the health of posterity.

3. A ban on methods of work that are dangerous for the female body, and, above all, the replacement of pedal-driven machines (presses, binding machines, and embroidering machines) with mechanically driven machines. Where this demand might serve to promote home industries, e.g., in garment production, this must be counteracted by a duty on the part of employers to establish special workshops.

To meet the second objective, we demand:

In the area of legislative workplace protections:

1. A right to leave in the 8 weeks prior to childbirth.

2. A ban on working for women for 8 weeks following childbirth when the child is alive, and for 6 weeks in the event of a miscarriage or stillbirth, or when the child dies during this period.

In the area of health insurance:

1. Mandatory support for pregnant women (which the Health Insurance Act [Krankenversicherungsgesetz] leaves to the absolute discretion of the insurer) for 8 weeks in the event of unemployment resulting from pregnancy.

2. Free midwifery services and medical aid in case of complications of pregnancy.

3. Extension of the duration of postnatal support from 6 to 8 weeks if the child is alive and, if the mother is able and willing to breastfeed her child, for a period of no less than 13 weeks; free medical assistance for 8 weeks.

4. An increase in the benefits paid to women during and after pregnancy and during nursing for the duration of the support up to the full amount of the average daily income.

---

* The original reads: *Schwefelkohlenstoff* (carbon disulphide) —Trans.

5. Mandatory extension of the provisions set forth in §§ I – III to the wives of insureds.

6. Extension of mandatory health insurance to all female waged workers, including agricultural workers, home workers, and domestic servants, as well as all women whose annual income does not exceed 3,000 marks.

From the local authorities:

1. The establishment of care homes for women during and after pregnancy and during nursing, the organisation of postnatal home care, the distribution of healthy milk for infants, as well as the distribution of bonuses to nursing women to the extent that support for them is not yet covered by the responsible health insurer.

From the state:

1. Education of women on how to properly carry out their maternal duties by including care for infants in the compulsory education curriculum.

2. Distribution of leaflets with rules for the care and feeding of infants, as well as the care of postnatal women by municipal employees.

Although I completely agree with the overall spirit of this resolution, for my part, I feel it necessary to note two matters on which I disagree with it.

The first, and most essential, matter on which I differ with the resolution concerns the organisation of maternity insurance with the aid of the general health insurers. K. Dunker, who was responsible for discussing the matter of the protection of women in and following pregnancy, spoke out against organising separate maternity insurance funds, because this would result in the entire burden of insurance falling exclusively on the members of the fund, i.e., women; meanwhile, if women's inability to work in the perinatal period is viewed as a particular type of disease, support for women during and after pregnancy could be organised on a general basis using the health insurance funds, whose members include both women and men. This would be fairer, given that, under the form of organisation she proposed, the maternity insurance burden would fall not only on women, but on men as well, who are at fault for this particular disease of women that deprives them of their income. The state would merely be required to support the insurance fund with specified contributions, and thus the entire burden of supporting and caring for motherhood would lie on the shoulders of the working class itself. 'Self-help' is indisputably a wonderful thing, but is it appropriate in this case? Would it not be more proper to transfer the care for mothers from the health insurance funds to the state itself, at least in those countries where there is the hope, with the aid of democratic representation of the people, to implement such a measure? Part of the amounts levied by the state by means of progressive taxation of wealth could be used to form the necessary capital, and then the burden for providing for mothers amongst the part of the population in greatest need of such support, the proletariat, could be distributed over all strata of society. Maternity insurance could be organised similarly to the bill introduced in the last Finnish Seim by the social-democratic deputy Persinen, which proposed that all mothers whose family income does not exceed a specified minimum amount (for Finland, 1,500 to 2,000 markka per annum), in addition to free medical assistance in the perinatal period, must receive from the state specified support from the state budget for a period of six weeks in advance of and eight weeks following childbirth. Of course, the duration of the subsidy and the standard of financial support could be changed. I personally would call for the state subsidy to be extended to a greater period of time; however, this is a personal view, and there is no need to insist on it currently. It is more important to discuss general principles and address the question of whether maternity insurance should be considered a function of the state, or whether it is preferable for the interests of the proletariat to provide for it by means of health insurance or other mutual aid funds.[90]

Another observation that must be made in relation to the resolution quoted above concerns the means by which leave in the last weeks of pregnancy is determined. The resolution speaks of the provision of a 'right of working women to stop working for eight weeks in advance of birth without notice'.* The reason given by Dunker for this provision was that a *ban* on work for eight weeks in advance of childbirth would result in a penalty in the form of a fine for noncompliance. Meanwhile, who would bear the burden of this fine?

---

*   *Kündigungslos* – i.e., 'without termination' – in the original. —Trans.

The worker? Given how easy it is to make mistakes and miscalculations when determining the perinatal period, this would be unjust and would only further burden the already modest budgets of working women. The employer? The notion that employers would willingly grant working women leave significantly before time, of course, has no sufficient basis. Meanwhile, replacing a *categorical ban* with the provision of an elastic 'right' would, were this demand to become law, mean that, for most working women, leave during the last weeks of pregnancy would, in point of fact, remain a pious wish. What does the 'right to stop working' mean for working women under the current conditions? There is no doubt that most working women, fearing conflicts with management, would only avail themselves of this generously granted right in rare, extreme cases. If one is to decide to protect mothers, it is more rational to demand a *complete ban* on work for eight weeks leading up to childbirth, as was noted by Lily Braun in Mannheim; however, her amendment was not adopted, and the resolution remained unchanged.

With the above exceptions, the Mannheim resolution is quite a valuable document of the demands of social democracy on a matter as important as motherhood. No matter how minimal the measures proposed are compared to the fundamental objectives of this party, there is no doubt that their implementation would have the most salutary effect on the position of women and mothers, and that to a considerably greater extent than all of the clever formulas for marriage of the inventive feminists would be able to solve the matter of marriage.

Not deceiving themselves with the hope of fundamentally solving the family problem within the confines of our class society, the followers of scientific socialism take up only a modest task – showing women the path to their full liberation. Following the historical path of humanity with eyes wide open as it runs into the centuries of the distant future, they tell women with conviction: 'The contemporary conditions of production will lead you through a dark maze of suffering and travail to a new, bright future. Go without fear, go and remember that it is you, the modest callused-handed woman worker and not your proud feminist sister who blazes the path of the new woman, the free lover, citizen, and mother . . . '

CHAPTER 3

WOMEN'S STRUGGLE FOR POLITICAL RIGHTS

> The emancipation of proletarian women cannot be the task of
> women of all classes. This task can only be achieved by the combined
> efforts of the entire proletariat without distinction as to sex.
>
> *The Gotha Programme, as quoted by Lily Braun**

Without a doubt, the issue of political equality for women is a matter of
cardinal importance for the bourgeois feminist movement. In its urgency,

---

* Quoted in *Die Frauenfrage*. The original, as quoted by Braun, reads:

*Als Kämpferin im Klassenkampf bedarf die Proletarierin ebenso der rechtlichen und poli-
tischen Gleichstellung mit dem Manne, als die Klein- und Mittelbürgerin und die Frau der
bürgerlichen Intelligenz. Als selbständige Arbeiterin bedarf sie ebenso der freien Verfügung
über ihr Einkommen (Lohn) und ihre Person als die Frau der großen Bourgeoisie. Aber
trotz aller Berührungspunkte in rechtlichen und politischen Reformforderungen hat die
Proletarierin in den entscheidenden ökonomischen Interessen nichts Gemeinsames mit den
Frauen der anderen Klassen. Die Emanzipation der proletarischen Frau kann deshalb nicht
das Werk sein der Frauen aller Klassen, sondern ist allein das Werk des gesamten Proletari-
ats ohne Unterschied des Geschlechts.*

('As combatants in the class struggle, proletarian women have the same need for
political equality with men as women of the petite and middle bourgeoisie and the
women of the bourgeois intelligentsia. As independent workers, they have the same
need to freely control their income (wages) and their person as women of the haute
bourgeoisie. However, despite all the commonalities in their demands for legal and
political reforms, proletarian women have nothing in common with women of the
other classes in relation to the decisive economic interests. Thus, the emancipation of
proletarian women cannot be the work of women of all classes; rather, it is solely the
task of the entire proletariat without distinction as to sex.')

The full text of the programme and the proceedings of the Gotha conference of
the SPD (in German) can be found at http://library.fes.de/parteitage/pdf/pt-jahr/pt-
1896.pdf —Trans.

this demand overshadows even the complexities of the family issue and the difficulties of the everyday struggle of women for their economic independence, forcing them to recede to the background.

Surely, political equality, access to the ballot box and seats in parliament 'on the basis of equality with men,' is the culmination of the feminists' aspirations. As more and more women join the ranks of the independently employed population, this demand becomes more and more vital for women. As one of the greatest obstacles on the road to women's emancipation, political disenfranchisement overshadows all other phenomena, which are no less burdensome for women, of the contemporary structure of society. All feminist literature primarily revolves around the demand for political equality, seeking to offer a logical rationale for the 'right' of women to participate in the political life of their countries. The feminists seek to bolster the legitimacy of their demands with a series of ideological premises that were already widely used in the days when the Third Estate were struggling for their emancipation. Forgotten arguments of bourgeois ideology, long since consigned to the very bottom of Grandmother's jewellery box with references to 'natural law', 'innate concepts' are once again being dragged back to the light of day by feminists.

The feminist movement, as accurately defined by Clara Zetkin, is the last echo of the Third Estate's struggle for emancipation. Is it not natural that the contemporary successors of the 'best traditions' of the bourgeoisie would seek to use the same means and deploy the same tools of struggle, albeit somewhat rustier, as were repeatedly used by their class comrades? According to the feminists and bourgeois defenders of women's equality, the reason for the gradual entry of women into political life is not the fact that economic relations are changing in real life, but the 'intellectual insight' of a society that has realised that 'women are people, too' and that 'higher justice' and 'humanity' compel contemporary civilised humanity to recognise women as having the same rights as men.

Feminists indifferently pass by the data accumulated by socio-economic scholarship on the role of the economic factor in the gradual emancipation of women, and continue to cling to purely idealistic evidence for the equality of the sexes: What arguments will the ideologues of women's equality not deploy in support of their argument, what will they not use to defend the legitimacy of their demands? Here, we find the principle of 'justice' and 'good conscience', and the 'vitalising influence of culture and knowledge', and the evaluation of the moral qualities of the sexes, and the likening of women to 'lower races' to whom legal scholarship does not deny rights, whether civil or political.

An economic basis for women's equality is either not provided at all, or offered in a distorted form. When the declaration of the newly formed International Woman Suffrage Alliance (IWSA) was drafted at the 1904 feminist conference in Berlin, the feminists decided to 'rely' on the economic factor in order to give their arguments greater weight. But what a unique use they made of it! The feminists derived their demand for women's suffrage from the fact of the 'growing prosperity' of that part of the female population that is gradually joining various fields of labour. How typical! 'The true, principal foundation of the demand for suffrage cannot be found in the growing prosperity of a negligible stratum of the female population, but in the poverty, misery, and exploitation of the broad masses of women,' Clara Zetkin correctly observes. 'We vehemently protest the aforementioned basis provided by the feminists for women's suffrage. In this form, it is a mere variation on the old liberal theme of national wealth and political rights delineated by property.'[1]

Of course, it is not just the feminists abroad who rely on purely ideological premises for their defence of political equality for women. Just open any resolution adopted by our equality campaigners, any article concerning the matter of women's suffrage, and you will find the same familiar principles of 'law and justice' that so abound in the feminist agitprop of the West.

The champions of women's equality hope to convince contemporary class society of the legitimacy of their demands not with factual data from the social and economic sciences, but with ardent, heartfelt speeches. However, such fragile tools as touching cries of the suffering feminine soul and heartwrenching appeals to the feelings of 'justice and humanity' will achieve nothing in the cruel struggle for social rights. For all their selfless devotion to women's cause, the feminists, in their struggle with the inexorable facts of life, could not expect to be victorious if the truth of life were not on their side, that truth that they* so often ignore in their one-sided defence of the cause of women. The principle of equality for women has long since ceased to be a pet idea of well-meaning thinkers who wish to see a just order established on Earth: It has ceased to be 'ideological' in nature, and has become the expression of an indisputable fact of reality with which *realpolitik* must reckon, whether it wishes to do so or not.

To be sure, the demand for women's equality has also been raised in the past as one of the inalienable principles of democracy, and, to a certain extent, it has received support from the bourgeoisie in the struggle to establish their rule; however, the demand for political equality for women could only become a serious social phenomenon that could no longer be ignored when the broad masses of women had been recruited into capitalist production.[2]

The upheaval of the economic life of society over the past century made it possible to recruit women into production, and helped them occupy a specific place in modern society. Any further growth of the productive forces of civilised humanity became unthinkable without women's participation. However, just as the evolution of the ideological superstructure of law has, in other cases, constantly lagged behind the economic relations giving rise to it, here, women, having become economically independent and acquired a certain value in the eyes of society as independent producers, remain socially dependent and politically disenfranchised.

In order to secure their newly won economic independence, women must also struggle for the recognition of their political and civil rights. The matter of women's ability to participate in the life of the state has gone from a pious wish belonging to the realm of abstract principles to a vital necessity not merely for a few women, but, much more importantly, for an entire social class. Where the Third Estate only mentioned the principle of women's equality in periods of acute struggle for power, in our time, this demand, without reservations or disclaimers, has been indelibly written upon the flag of the working class. The bourgeois proclamation of women's equality was purely theoretical: The bourgeoisie could derive no class benefit from giving women access to political

---

* Opening quotation mark here in original, apparent typo —Trans.

power. For the proletariat, on the other hand, the expansion of the franchise to women has countless benefits that lead them to hold high the banner of political equality for women and struggle for the realisation of this demand with a persistence of which only people led by the invincible instinct of class interest are capable.

But the moment the demand for the equalisation of women's political rights with those of men goes from being an abstract principle to being one of the factors of a class moment, this principle no longer needs to rely on ideological and sentimental arguments as it once did. Women's equality has left the realm of theoretical discussion to be debated in the realm of live political struggle.

The broader the segments of society involved in political life, the fuller the looming triumph of democracy, the more powerful its means of struggle with capital; the greater the number of members of the working class who have the possibility of actively intervening in the political life of their country, the greater the benefit for the entire working class.

As women join the ranks of independent sellers of labour power in ever-greater numbers, the demand ceases to be a *women's* demand and becomes a purely *proletarian* demand: 'Political rights for all adult citizens without distinction as to sex' becomes ever firmer and more persistent. All the sentimental cries of the feminists, all the 'idealistic' arguments taken from the arsenal of liberal ideology, pale in the face of that living, driving force that is class interest.

'But,' the feminists reply to us, 'even if our argument for women's political rights seems mistaken to you, does that reduce the significance of the demand for women's political equality itself, a demand that is equally urgent both for feminists and for the women of the working class? Surely, women of the two social camps can cross the barriers of class antagonism that separate them in the interests of their shared political aspirations. Surely they can join together in struggle against the hostile forces surrounding them!' Even if divergences of opinion between bourgeois and proletarian women may be inevitable on other issues, on this point, as the feminists see it, there is no discord between the women of the different social classes.

The feminists return to this issue with bitterness and incomprehension, seeing partisan bias in the resolute refusals of the representatives of the women of the working class to join forces with those of the feminists in order to win political rights for women.

But is this really so? Is there true identity of political aspirations amongst women, or does class antagonism prevent women joining forces to form an unbreakable cross-class army in this case, as it does in all others?

Only by answering this question can we determine the tactics of proletarian women in the struggle for political rights for women going forward.

What do the women of the bourgeoisie mean by political equality? Political equality is a means of sharing with the men of their class the class privileges and benefits of life that currently are exclusively enjoyed by the latter; more accurately, it is a way to consolidate the advantages that currently are the exclusive province of the men of the bourgeoisie. Where, for proletarian women, political rights are merely a tool in the struggle with the existing capitalist system, for bourgeois women, on the other hand, they are a new way of affirming their class dominance.

The women of the bourgeoisie do not intend to abolish contemporary class society with the aid of the rights they expect to win, but to further strengthen it. Indeed, the bourgeois champions of women's equality, no matter how radical their outlook, have ever stated that they need political rights for the same objective as proletarian women; never and nowhere have the feminists stated that they intend to use the rights they win as weapons in the struggle for a more perfect social structure, for the fundamental restructuring of economic relations. For them, class society is a phenomenon that is inviolate, sustainable, and permanent. Obtaining a more congenial position within the confines of the class world, availing themselves of all the advantages provided by class – those are the fundamental aspirations of the bourgeois feminists. To be sure, occasionally, bourgeois women, under the pressure of the labour movement, wrap themselves in the banner of social reformism, and sometimes even express sympathies with the ultimate goals of the proletariat. However, this lip service so diametrically contradicts the entire spirit of the feminist movement, its demands, aspirations, and method of struggle, that it can only confuse very naïve souls indeed. Whilst declaring themselves supporters of social reforms and even of socialism – in an immeasurably distant future, of course – the feminists do not intend to fight in the ranks of the working class in order to realise this coveted objective of the proletariat. With naïve sincerity, the best of them believe that, once they have attained seats in parliament, they will treat the social wounds that their current occupants, men, in their characteristic selfishness, not only allow to exist, but even to expand. However, no matter how benevolent the attitudes of some individual groups of feminists may be towards the proletariat, every time the matter of class struggle is raised, they fearfully depart from the battlefield, not wishing to mix with the ranks of the proletariat, so different in spirit to them, and hurry to take cover under the shade of bourgeois liberalism, whose attitudes are so familiar and understandable to them.

No, no matter how much the bourgeois feminists seek to obscure the actual goal of their political desires, no matter how much they reassure their little sisters that their entry into political life also promises immeasurable benefits for women of the working class, the class spirit of the bourgeoisie, which permeates the entire feminist movement, paints their class colours even on such an apparently universal demand of women as equality in political rights with men. Differences in their understanding of the *objective*, differences in the use to which bourgeois women can put the political rights once they have won them, create an insurmountable abyss between them and proletarian women. This is no way contradicted by the fact that the immediate tasks of bourgeois and proletarian women coincide to a certain extent, that, having gained access to political power, women of all classes above all seek to revise the civil code, which disenfranchises women to a greater or lesser extent in all countries, that they are trying to create more favourable working conditions for women by means of legislation, that they oppose regulations legalising prostitution, etc. However, these commonalities in the most immediate objectives are a *purely formal similarity*. Right now, class interests dictate diametrically opposing attitudes towards these ordinary reforms. We need not look long for examples. Look what stance the women deputies of the bourgeois parties of Finland took on such an apparently universal female demand as maternity insurance: Whilst acknowledging in principle that the reform was desirable, they nonetheless did not agree to a formulation of it that was consistent with the interests of the working class. In their view, a guarantee for every woman who becomes a mother, even if her marital union is not sanctioned by the church, would merely lead to the promotion of 'debauchery' and an increase in illegitimate births. The strict guardians of bourgeois morality deem it impermissible to vote for a law so 'dangerous' from the moral standpoint.

These sorts of collisions of the two worlds are just as inevitable amongst women as they are amongst men. We must not be deceived by the superficial similarities between the demands: Every matter that comes on the agenda will inevitably be coloured by the social group of women raising it.

The class antagonism that divides bourgeois and proletarian women will become particularly pronounced when women win the right to vote. Even now, it appears there is no longer a single significant question in the field of social policy that would not be capable of provoking a fierce dispute between women of the two fundamental economic classes. No wonder even political equality for women is interpreted differently in accordance with the class interests of the one or other social group of women.

What bourgeois women understand political equality to mean, and what their actual demands are in this area, can best be seen by the performance in the struggle of international feminism, that typical expression of the bourgeois feminist movement. International feminism offers something like the distilled essence of the clearest and most advanced demands of bourgeois women, and defines their true relation to the various sides of the female question.

When the central organ of international feminism was the International Council of Women (ICW), founded on the initative of American women in Washington in 1888, which had united under its banner women's organisations differing widely in terms of type and activities, the impossibility of cooperation between proletarian women and the feminists was too obvious and not particularly subject to doubt. The ICW was primarily meant to serve as a link between the most diverse women's societies and organisations, independently of their goals and orientations; it also served as a source of information and handled the convocation of international congresses of women. The tasks of the ICW include: 'to win equal voting rights with men in all countries where a representative form of government exists, promote international peace and the resolution of political conflicts between nations by means of arbitration.'[3]

However, despite the breadth of this programme, which even goes beyond specifically female tasks, the constitution of the Council wastes not a single word on the economic position of women wage labourers, the struggle against the exploitation of women's wage labour, or the legislative protection of women. Of course, for the members of the ICW, these respectable 'ladies', who had never known the horror of having to sell their labour power, the economic side of the female question could not be particularly significant. However, independently of this omission, which nonetheless does quite clearly paint the true face of international feminism, the position of equality campaigners abroad on the matter of women's political rights even more clearly delineated the sharp corners of bourgeois feminism.

Note the broad, nebulous wording of the demand for political equality for women in the ICW constitution; of course, in so doing, the International Council intended to facilitate the broadest possible segment of the female population joining the international feminist organisation, to win the greatest possible number of women's hearts regardless of their political and social views. However, the international feminists lost sight of one circumstance: The caution with which they approached one of the most essential demands of women, their hesitance to take on an obligation vis-à-vis female democracy clearly showed what an unreliable ally the ICW was in the struggle for full political rights for women, and how little they had to offer women of the working class.

The primary formation of international feminism, up until the more 'radical' elements split off in 1902, bore such a clear 'ladylike' imprint that there was no question of proletarian women joining in the first place. To be sure, even then, the feminists spoke often and passionately about their 'forgotten' and 'oppressed' sisters, and promised that, by strugging for their rights and privileges, they would pave the way to political rights for all women; however, at the same time, they themselves were so careful to shun representatives of the working class, these women whose spirit was so alien to them and who constantly spoke of the need to restructure the contemporary – 'civilised', 'enlightened', and pleasant – world that it was completely impossible to reach an agreement.

At the very first international women's congress in Chicago in 1893,[4] called by the ICW, the absence of any commonality in the interests of women of the bourgeoisie and the working class could be clearly felt. To be sure, the feminists did dedicate time to the 'problem of poverty', but this fundamental social problem of our day, refracted through the prism of the bourgeois worldview, lost all of its truly tragic character. 'The problem of poverty' was entirely positioned within the framework of ladies' philanthropy.

At the next international congress, in 1896 in Berlin, the well-meaning feminists even more meticulously sought to circumvent any thorny questions that might touch on class antagonism, and avoided anything that might indicate the demoralising and harmful influence of the capitalist structure of society. When Social Democrat Lily Braun dared to disrupt the 'harmonious' mood of the ladylike gathering by touching on the class antagonism existing within the world of women, the participants in the congress exacted their own style of revenge on this disruptor of 'lady-like' joy: They did not include her 'harmful' speech in the proceedings of the congress.[5] This fear of class hatred stirred up by the 'party goals' of social democracy was so potent in the bourgeois women that, when the feminists met the next year in Brussels, the organisers of the congress, in their official message to the delegates, stated that they warmly welcomed all participants 'with the exception of those who advocate class struggle.'

No less 'ladylike' was the character of the following two international congresses: in London in 1899 and in Paris in 1900.[6] At least as much time was dedicated to philanthropy, art, and housekeeping as to the matter of women's civil and political equality.[7] All five sections of the London congress were dedicated to ladylike interests: the difficulties of making a career in the arts; discussions of teaching and child-rearing methods, particularly sex education, suitable only for 'respectable' families. Much was said about 'the spirit of purity' that should permeate women's art, and the influence of this 'spirit' on 'the well-being of nations'. The matter of patronage for 'young female travellers' was hotly debated, etc. Only in passing, in the section on industry, was the position of women workers in industry touched on. Of course, at the same time, in the same section, 'another groundbreaking question was discussed: that of the unpaid work of housewives' and the need for bourgeois matrons to have their own 'pocket money'. It is entirely typical that debates on the position of female wage labour in industry, the appointment of women factory inspectors, and the organisation of female workers attracted the least attention of all. Feminist correspondents have sought to explain this fact by noting that the sessions of the industrial and arts sections coincided; the participants of the congress with 'refined' artistic tastes preferred to take part in the latter. However, this excuse shows us the true character of the congress, and allows us to judge the actual demands of these bourgeois fighters for women's equality. The characteristic attributed to the participants in the congress by these feminist correspondents is entirely confirmed by the work of the congress itself. Just listen to the good advice the respected participants gave each other, eloquently demonstrating the utility of the applied and decorative arts that offered salvation from idleness and boredom, recommending 'artistic enamelling', porcelain and glass painting, photography, artistic printing, etc. There was even a prescription for nerves frayed by a life of idleness and satiety: Aviculture, farming, and, particularly, horticulture were listed as occupations 'entirely beneficial to the body, pleasing to the eye, and refreshing to the soul' and even 'awakening an inclination to contemplation and higher thoughts.' What else could the heart desire? The more 'mercantile souls' were advised to breed . . . ostriches, given that the sale of ostrich feathers is quite a profitable endeavour these days. All these examples smack of caricature, but they are indeed listed in the proceedings of the congress . . . [8]

Particularly enlightening is the performance of our Russian women's equality trailblazers at the London congress. Two women physicians reported, with amazing naivety, on their attractive position in Russia: Women physicians are not only allowed in the civil service; they even receive a pension in the event of marriage, and, after death, even if their father is still alive, the children are not deprived of this pension until they reach the age of majority. Such 'idyllic' conditions in Russia, nothing like the 'decadent West'! The third Russian representative – a delegate of the Russian Women's Mutual Philanthropic Society – painted a similarly rosy picture of the position of Russian women from the standpoint of civil law; she was able to show the representatives of other countries how much they were 'lagging behind' Russia and how much better off Russian women were, in terms of property and marital relations, than even the female citizens of 'free republics' . . . All the bitterness of 'women's fate', all the horrors of the household oppression of Russian peasant women, women workers, saleswomen, and even 'noblewomen', all the disenfranchisement and oppression of the people were somehow obscured, just beyond the horizons of the feminists, who were breathless from joy at the thought of these 'advantages' enjoyed by bourgeois women in Russia.

Of course, the participants of the London congress did not miss the opportunity to visit Windsor Castle, that favoured residence of the queen, where they were 'served', by the special order of the 'highest person of *female sex*', a 'luxurious breakfast' that the participants mentioned with affection even long thereafter.

The London congress played a major role in the bourgeois women's movement; it not only distinguished itself by the unusually large number of participants (more than two thousand were counted), but also attracted particular attention from society and the press.

Though the London congress dedicated only minimum attention to the matters of female labour, the economic position of women, sexual morality, and prostitution, this omission was made up for by the Paris congress that took place in 1900. Socio-economic matters were given priority in Paris. We have already mentioned, in the chapter on the economic position of women, the conclusions that were reached by the Paris feminist congress of 1900 on the matter of protections for women workers. In Paris, the hostile overtones that could already be heard in London transformed into a proper chorus of hostile voices; the matter of legal standards for female wage labour was barely raised.[9] In the name of the 'principle of equality of rights', the bourgeois women denied the need for specific protection for female labourers; the Frenchwomen and Englishwomen defended this view with particular verve. The complete incomprehension of the interests of working-class women, the complete ignorance of their economic demands, are characteristic of the work of the Paris congress. The Paris congress eloquently showed that the feminist movement by no means includes the entire women's movement. The great masses of women remained on the margins; it was unable to understand their essential, vital interests. Even women employed in intellectual labour found no satisfaction. Feminism remained, as ever, primarily a representative of women of the bourgeois class.'[10] This testimony must be taken even more seriously, coming, as it does, from a person not infected by the deleterious influence of the 'one-sided' social democrats. Indeed, women of the working class were given neither space nor attention in Paris. To be sure, they were frequently mentioned, mainly in order to express parental concern about these 'unfortunate creatures', who were chosen as objects for the dissemination of bourgeois morality or for insulting charity 'from above'.

As the bourgeois women's movement has grown, as more and more women intellectuals have joined the ranks of independently employed women, the feminist movement has grown out of the nappies of 'ladies' philanthropy', 'decorative arts', and 'exemplary housekeeping'. The chaotic bloc of the IWC has ceased to satisfy the left wing of feminism, which has grown beyond the 'charitable' phase. Political disenfranchisement weighs heavily on independent bourgeois women, who have felt on their own backs the many dark sides of modern exploitative labour relations. Ever more persistently, bourgeois women have felt the need for socio-economic reforms that promise to lighten the load of female intellectual workers by fundamentally revising the civil code, repealing the disgrace to women that are the prostitution regulations, etc. Women have felt the need to join the life of the state; they have become aware that, without their direct involvement, these reforms will not happen. Political equality acquired primary significance in the eyes of bourgeois women.

Meanwhile, the IWC continued to speak complacently of 'sex education', the charms of horticulture for bored ladies, and to praise the fruits of the work of the societies for the rescue of damsels in distress, etc. The left-wing feminists found this atmosphere claustrophobic and suffocating. Thus, in 1902, the American national alliance organised something like an international meeting of women in Washington, at which the

---

*   Closing quotation mark in original; however, no opening quotation mark is present, so it is not entirely clear which words are being quoted. —Trans.

more democratically minded feminists decided to found the International Woman Suffrage Alliance (IWSA). The objective of this new organisation was to be the vigorous defence of women's political equality.[11]

The young IWSA differed fundamentally from the IWC in that it brought together feminists who were more united in their attitudes and views. The declaration adopted by the Alliance at the feminist congress in Berlin in 1904 was a testament to the fact that this organisation had set itself a specific, defined goal, dismissing all of the Council's sentimental attempts to renew the world with the aid of 'ladies' societies'. Where the previous type of feminism had nothing in common with working-class women, now, on the contrary, the objective put forward by the IWSA coincided with a purely proletarian demand: political rights for adult female citizens. This shared objective seemed naturally to raise the issue of cooperation between worlds of women that, until then, had been alien to one another. What, indeed, prevented women of different classes joining forces, when differences in nationality had been no barrier to unification? After all, it was merely a matter of cooperation to attain a clear, specific goal that was equally desirable to all women.

But do women of such different social classes really have the same understanding of this 'desirable goal' for women? The declaration of the IWSA states:

(1) Men and women are born equally free and independent, equally endowed with intelligence and ability and equally entitled to develop freely.

(2) The natural relationship between the sexes is inter-dependence and cooperation, and the restriction of the rights and liberties of one sex inevitably harms the other, and, with it, all humanity.

(3) In all countries, laws, customs, and beliefs that have promoted women's bondage, erected barriers to their education and obstacles for the development of their innate abilities have been based on false understandings and resulted in artificial and incorrect relations between the sexes in contemporary society.

(4) Autonomy in the family and the state is the inalienable right of all normally developed adult persons, and its denial to women has

resulted for them in social, legal, and economic injustice and caused the existing economic disarray throughout the world.

(5) A government that imposes laws on women citizens and collects taxes from them without giving them the right to consent or withhold consent that is granted to male citizens does violence to them that is not acceptable in a state based on just laws.

(6) Universal suffrage is the only legal and reliable means of defending the rights to 'life, liberty, and happiness' acknowledged by the American Declaration of Independence and, thereafter, by all civilised nations, the inalienable right of the human personality. Therefore, in all representative states, women must be granted all political rights and privileges of electors.'[12]

This exquisite 'declaration of rights' of women of the twentieth century arrived at the fundamental point of their demands with great caution: Women were to be granted all rights and privileges of electors. What

---

*   In the original, the declaration reads:
    '1. Men and women are born equally free and independent members of the human race, equally endowed with intelligence and ability and equally entitled to the free exercise of their individual rights and liberty.
    2. The natural relation of the sexes is that of inter-dependence and cooperation and the repression of the rights and liberty of one sex inevitably works injury to the other and hence to the whole race.
    3. In all lands those laws, creeds and customs which have tended to restrict women to a position of dependence, to discourage their education, to impede the development of their natural gifts and to subordinate their individuality have been based upon false theories and have produced an artificial and unjust relation of the sexes in modern society.
    4. Self-government in the home and the State is the inalienable right of every normal adult and the refusal of this right to women has resulted in social, legal and economic injustice to them and has also intensified the existing economic disturbances throughout the world.
    5. Governments which impose taxes and laws upon their women citizens without giving them the right of consent or dissent which is granted to men citizens exercise a tyranny inconsistent with just government.
    6. The ballot is the only legal and permanent means of defending the right to 'life, liberty and the pursuit of happiness' pronounced inalienable by the American Declaration of Independence and accepted as inalienable by all civilized nations. In any representative form of government, therefore, women should be vested with all the political rights and privileges of electors.'
    The full declaration can be found at https://www.gutenberg.org/files/30051/30051-h/30051-h.htm —Trans.

are these 'rights and privileges'; what hides behind this nebulous, utterly non-binding language? Are these rights linked to a property or other qualification? Are they only privileges of the 'ladylike' strata, or are they extended to all women, even those who do not meet any property qualification?

The fact that the IWC expressed its views on women's political rights only in the most general way can be explained by this all-encompassing organisation's efforts to include under its maternal wing women of every imaginable social stratum and political stripe. However, it should be recalled that the IWC did not set itself any specific goals; its role was and remains even now primarily an organisational one. On the other hand, the IWSA had an entirely specific political goal from the first moment of its existence; as such, we would be entitled to expect greater clarity and specificity in the formulation of their programme. However, the big-tent principle the Alliance inherited from the Council hindered this 'radical' feminist organisation's efforts at self-definition to a great degree.

It must indeed be taken into account that bringing together the most widely varied female elements, from women of the haute bourgeoisie to the women in the 'liberal professions' and even semi-proletarian women, made it extremely difficult to offer any further specificity on this fundamental point in the programme of the Alliance. It would seem as if merely asking what the foundations of women's political rights were meant to be is enough to put an end to the all the vaunted strength and unity of the Alliance. The matter of the property qualification, and that of direct and equal suffrage, would inevitably drive a wedge into the closed ranks of the feminists and sow dissension and discord where 'harmony' and 'unity' now hold sway thanks to the broad, nebulous language of the demands.[13]

In itself, the declaration of the Alliance arguably fails to offer a sufficient basis to suspect the organisation of being purely bourgeois in its inclinations; however, there are other objective indications of its true face. Observe the composition of the Alliance; its core consists of the same well-known representatives of bourgeois feminism who had just recently been united under the banner of the well-meaning Council. Of course, they include quite respected feminist campaigners, whose contributions to the bourgeois feminist movement are undeniably great; however, giving them their due and even admiring their individual qualities does not mean deluding oneself into believing that these women could rise above their class interests to realise the idea of cross-class unity for the first time in history within their own organisation. The bourgeois class spirit that invisibly hovers above the drafters of the declaration can already be seen from the fact that point 6 specifically states: women should be vested with the same political rights as men where a representative form of government exists. Why do the 'radical' feminists not say that, where the people do not yet have any representation, or where they are represented on an undemocratic basis, the members of the Alliance will fight to democratise the structure of the state in order to attain the greatest possible political rights for women, as well? Surely, the democratisation of the state is one of the main conditions for the expansion of political equality to broader segments of the female population. The question of the form of the representative system loses its primary significance only if the members of the Alliance approach the matter of women's equality from their narrow class standpoint, if they are on about bringing not all women, as they say, but only representatives of a certain privileged social stratum, into political life.

Can posing the question in this way inspire confidence in the women of the proletariat? Perhaps it is useful, in the interest of preserving the Alliance, to phrase fundamental principles cautiously in the feminists' declaration, but it is utterly worthless for attracting working-class women to the ranks of the Alliance. If the 'radical' feminists dared to pronounce themselves in favour of a complete, detailed electoral formula, an additional question would also arise, not that of uniting proletarian women with them, but of optionally collaborating with them. At the moment, given the deliberately nebulous phrasing of the demands, this question completely and irrevocably disappears.

The attitude of the left wing of feminism towards the matter of universal suffrage is instructive. When language on the foundations of political equality for women was discussed at the IWSA conference in Berlin in 1904, only a few individual voices were raised in defence of universal suffrage, but these voices were immediately drowned out by the chorus of opposition to any detailed formula. 'Is it not poignant that the represent-ative of the recognised General Alliance of German Women has taken a more radical stance this time than the left wing of the equality cam-paigners who had defended the principle of political equality for women at the international congress?'[14]

However, the radical feminists also did not return to the matter of universal suffrage at their next congress, in Copenhagen. The congress took place at a time of heightened interest worldwide in matters of pop-ular representation; the revolutionary storm in Russia had not yet died down, and, by disturbing the equilibrium of European social life, placed a number of mass political demands on the agenda. It would seem that this was a particularly opportune moment for a careful review of this fundamental point in the programme of the IWSA. The demand for a unlimited, universal right to participate in elections and legislative in-stitutions, as well as local government, practically wrote itself. However, the congress remained deaf to the effects of major political events outside its walls, and, with amazing persistence, avoided this nettlesome point in its programme once again. To be sure, individual voices were raised once again in defence of the principle of universal suffrage, and even the secretary—now president—of the IWSA, the American Chapman Catt, acknowledged that, going forward, the battle cry of the feminists should be 'One person, one vote', but these statements by the 'democrats' broke apart on the wall of the tenacious resistance of the whole mass of par-ticipants. Nor did the speech of the Finnish delegate, who emphasised that the greatest results in terms of political equality for women would be obtained where the struggle for women's political rights was intimately and inextricably connected to the general struggle of the proletariat for the democratisation of the state, prompt the congress to review the fun-damental points of the Alliance's declaration.[15] The congress participants had their reasons not to debate all these nettlesome matters or to adopt any 'imprudent' resolutions that might—God forbid!—require them to take 'revolutionary' positions.

Interesting, and entirely typical, is the conduct of our Russian dele-gates, the representatives of the Alliance for Women's Equality, at the Copenhagen congress. No tendency of international feminism has more than secondary significance for us; they all, at best, indirectly facilitate the clarification of the relationships between the feminist movement and the proletarian women's movement. To the contrary, the position of our Russian equality campaigners on this matter is highly essential, and has great, direct significance for women's cause in Russia as a whole. Where did our feminists, who were participating in the congress of the Alliance as official Russian delegates for the first time, stand on the demand for political equality? As it happens, the representatives of Russia, who had just left the political battlefield, in whose ears the powerful roar of popular excitement surely still echoed, from whose eyes the images of the people's struggle for political liberation, overwhelming in its grandeur, had surely not yet faded, were unable to 'match their tone' to the peacefully inclined feminists from politically 'favourable' countries. One would think that the Russian delegates at the Copenhagen congress could not help but bring with them echoes of the revolutionary storm they had experienced, and express a particularly democratic attitude capable of bringing along the rest of the congress participants, if only on the matter of the foundation of political equality.

In point of fact, however, nothing of the sort happened. Mrs Mirovich gave a very detailed account of the fruitful activities of the Alliance for Women's Equality, commended the first State Duma for its sympathetic attitude towards matters of women's equality, and painted a sunny picture of the touching sympathy for the female question with which all opposition elements of Russian society were brimming; however, by some strange 'oversight', she did not mention the greatest phenomena of the revolutionary period the country had just experienced; she did not display for the delegates of the entire 'civilised world' the imposing picture of the mass participation of working-class and peasant women in the strike and agrarian movements, nor did she mention the enormous, thankless labour women and men had shouldered equally in the struggle not just for the rights of women, but for those of the people as a whole. Proletarian women, their living and working conditions, their objectives, aspirations, their constant participation in the liberation struggle somehow escaped the attention of the Russian representatives. This at a time when the eyes of the entire proletarian world were on Russia, when democrats in all countries rejoiced in every victory of the Russian proletariat, sympathetically following all the vicissitudes of the political drama playing out on Russian soil . . . One got the impression that the only people fighting for women's political rights were the members of the Alliance for Women's Equality, and that it was only thanks to this 'active and energetic organisation' that Russian society had at last turned its attention to women's demands. The members of the Alliance for Women's Equality did not tarry at all on the basis of the political rights of women; at this critical moment, they could not bring themselves to stand in defence of unlimited suffrage and make clear to their 'sisters' abroad that this demand is the *conditio sine qua non* of their participation in the international feminist movement. It would have been particularly easy to raise this demand given that the principle of universal suffrage is included in the platform of our Alliance for Women's Equality! However, this aspiration must be one of those goods 'for display' that decorate the windows of cheap shops in order to deceive the naïve and inexperienced shopper.

Mrs Volkenshtein spoke in general terms of the need and utility of 'democratising' the women's movement, but neither she nor any of the other Russian delegates felt it necessary to introduce a proposal at the congress to state the demands of the IWSA in greater detail and specificity. The point concerning political equality for women remained as is in the declaration of the IWSA, in all its murky inviolacy.

Nor did the third congress of the IWSA, which took place in that year in Amsterdam, make any further strides in this regard. In vain, Mrs Mirovich speaks in lofty tones in her correspondence 'in the speech' on radicalism at this congress, stating that

> the Amsterdam congress was another step forward in the history of civilisation; all governments that recognise the principle of universal suffrage without distinction as to sex bear witness to the results of this reform for the entire world; and all experience speaks in favour of extending political rights to women.

Of course, if we count as a 'great victory' the fact that bourgeois governments sent official delegates (Norway, Australia, and three US states sent representatives to the congress), then Mrs Mirovich is quite right.

However, from the standpoint of the political interests of women, it would be a significantly greater 'step forward' for the IWSA to take a clearly defined position on the matter of women's political equality.

However, the well-attended Amsterdam congress (in which some three hundred delegates from twenty countries participated) was perhaps even more circumspect than the Copenhagen congress. It began on a remarkably poignant and instructive note: At one of the Protestant churches, a *woman minister* said mass. Then, during the grand opening of the congress, a cantata, specially composed for the occasion, in praise of the sovereign of the Netherlands, Queen Wilhelmina (after all, she is a woman!) was sung, and the chorus was also conducted by a woman. Not one of the democratically minded feminists raised her voice in protest at this manner of opening the congress, the stated objective of which was 'persistent and firm' struggle for women's democratic rights. Also typical was the following incident that took place at the congress: In her speech, the representative of Finland, Mrs Furuhjelm, again emphasised the intimate connection between the liberatory current in Finland and the struggle for women's political equality. Her presentation aroused the interest of some individual congress participants, and threatened to move the debates in a dangerous direction. The congress hastily ended the debates on the grounds that Finland is a 'revolutionary country'. Note that it was not police repression that forced the congress participants to issue this verdict, but the feminists' own rampant aversion to anything smacking of struggle.

The central question, that of women's suffrage, was postponed to the last day by the congress. This was likely not unintentional: Efforts to define the basis of women's political rights always threaten to yield conflict and discord. The following resolution was submitted for discussion:

> The Congress resolves that the immediate duty of women in the present moment is to ensure the support and cooperation of all social forces that sympathise with women's suffrage, regardless of their political and religious views; to avoid the diversion of forces to extraneous questions; to demand suffrage for women on the same basis on which they are enjoyed, or can be enjoyed, by men, and that any further expansion of the electoral system is decided jointly by men and women when both

sexes have equal voting and representation rights and equal political influence.[16]

Thus, the matter of universal suffrage for women was postponed until such time as those feminists who are included in the legislature, together with their bourgeois comrades, see fit to democratise the electoral system. It would seem that bourgeois women have inherited from the men of their class the technique of 'kicking things into the long grass'.

The third secretary of the IWSA, Mrs Kramer, decided to insert into the proposed resolution an amendment stating as follows: 'The International Woman Suffrage Alliance, acknowledging the existence of class struggle, firmly states its desire to unite women of all the world in order to attain political equality of the sexes by demanding the suffrage for women and equality with men as regards all other rights.'[17]

However, this amendment was met with such protest that Mrs Kramer had no choice but to withdraw it from the agenda. Particular concern and protest came from the representatives of England, the United States, and the Netherlands; they convinced their 'sisters' to be circumspect and not make demands that could harm the cause of including women in the class-based right to suffrage. In England, a reform in favour of political equality for women meeting the property qualification is entirely possible; it could ruin the entire thing to come out with new slogans in this critical moment. The proposed resolution was adopted with no amendments by twenty-eight votes to eleven.

Thus, the Amsterdam congress once again confirmed that, on the question of political equality for women, proletarian women can expect nothing from working together even with the left wing of the feminists. It is not by the struggle of one sex against another, but by defending their class interests against the other antagonistic classes, that women workers can attain full political rights. Unity of interests is a magnificent phrase; class struggle is a hard reality.[18]

Over the last years, the feminist movement in England has distinguished itself by its intensity and vitality. Here, women are displaying remarkable energy in the struggle for political equality; with their self-sacrifice and enthusiasm, the British feminists are attracting the attention of the whole world. Street demonstrations, a number of loud meetings, the 'attack' on Parliament, delegations that besiege ministers, and other 'militant' methods of awakening British society from its complacency have doubtlessly helped draw attention to matters of political equality for women.

Two massive demonstrations, one after another, in June of this year (one on 13 June, the other on 21 June by the Gregorian Calendar) had the same purpose: arousing interest in the demand for an electoral reform for the benefit of women.[19] However, the sympathy engendered by the energy of the British women in their struggle for women's cause cannot help but be cooled when one takes into account the goal pursued by the British suffragists and 'suffragettes'.

The rallying cry of the British feminists is currently: extension to women of the same voting rights enjoyed by men under British election law. In this regard, we must not forget that, in Britain, to this day, there are *restricted* voting rights even for men, that the right to vote is enjoyed only by a man (a specification introduced by the 1832 Reform Act in lieu of the term 'person' that had been used previously), who is an independent householder paying no less than 4 shillings (approximately 2 rubles) a week in rent. In demanding equal political rights with men whilst preserving the existing electoral system, the British feminists are advocating a property-based system of representation. Indeed, they do not even dispute this; the British suffragists base their demands on the old British formula: *No taxation without representation.*

This slogan is shared by both of the main feminist organisations in Britain that are fighting for women's political rights: Both the moderate wing of the suffragists around the National Union of Women's Suffrage Societies (NUWSS), a solid and already old organisation that brings together women of the upper strata of the bourgeoisie, and the new Women's Social and Political Union (today, the Women's Freedom League [WFL]), founded in 1905 and comprising more democratic elements.[20] Until recently, the NUWSS shunned all 'unconstitutional' methods of struggle, limiting themselves to the constant submission of petitions to Parliament and exercising 'indirect' influence on members of Parliament, in private meetings, mediation by respected ladies, etc.

The League, on the other hand, adopted 'militant tactics' from its very foundation, taking the view that the noisier they were, the more attention they would direct to women's demands, both from society and the government. The League preaches 'active influence' on the government by means of non-payment of tax,[21] organises demonstrations in front of, or even in, Parliament, discredits political parties hostile to the issue of women's political equality, disrupts their meetings, and agitates against them during election campaigns.[22] After Prime Minister Asquith stated to a delegation of suffragettes (as these 'militant' feminists call themselves, unlike the constitutionally minded 'suffragists') that the government could not currently take the initiative to carry out such a fundamental reform as including women in the political life of the country, the League decided to register their protest through 'action'. They conducted energetic agitation against the candidates of the Liberal Party during the parliamentary by-elections, and, to a certain extent, facilitated the victory of the Conservatives, to spite the Liberal government. Of course, the prison terms, fines, and government persecution to which the suffragettes are subjected merely increase their popularity and are the best possible propaganda for the idea of political equality for women. However, these militant tactics are met with harsh disapproval by the right-wing feminists; the hostility of the suffragettes to the Liberal cabinet is particularly disliked by the NUWSS.

However, the discord between both wings of British feminism does not go beyond matters of tactics and methods of struggle. The tasks and objectives of the two wings are entirely coextensive. In the united movement organ *Women's Franchise*, the suffragettes, that 'revolutionary and democratic' segment of the feminists, to quote the IWSA, *indignantly* denied the false accusation that they wish to link the matter of women's equality with that of universal suffrage.[23] The members of the WFL do not admit to this 'sin'; they by no means wish the opponents of universal suffrage, i.e., the bourgeoisie, to confuse the interests of women with those of 'the rabble'. To the contrary, it is useful for the bourgeoisie to learn to strictly distinguish between feminist demands and proletarian demands. This will allow the cause of bourgeois women to be all the more successful.

The unwavering position of the WFL on the matter of property-based suffrage allows the moderate suffragists to make their peace with the 'anti-constitutional' and 'unfeminine' methods of struggle of the suffragettes, to such an extent that, in the words of Mrs Mirovich, a sort of 'tacit agreement' has been reached between the two feminist organisations. This touching unity of the suffragists and the suffragettes confirmed that, no matter how 'revolutionary' and 'militant' the methods of struggle of the left wing of the feminists may be, they are fundamentally just as much a bourgeois class organisation as the NUWSS.[24] The class position of the feminists can be particularly acutely felt when their demands come into direct conflict with those of the proletariat. Of two bills seeking to expand voting rights to the female population that were introduced in Parliament in 1907, one came from the ranks of the bourgeoisie and was introduced by Liberal MP Dickinson, whilst the other was introduced by Sir Charles Dilke, and responded to the demands of the working class. Dickinson's bill merely modified the existing electoral system in Britain, without touching its foundations, by calling for the franchise to be extended not only to male ratepayers, but to female ratepayers as well. Dilke's bill, on the other hand, called for a fundamental change in the electoral system, granting every adult citizen, male and female, both active and passive suffrage. It was something to behold: the noise made by all British suffragists and suffragettes in defence of Dickinson's bill, and the passion with which they defended it against Dilke's bill. Their rationale for this approach was that it is always easier to make 'amendments' to an existing system than to replace the system itself, and they promised that linking the matter of political equality for women with that of universal suffrage would surely scupper the former, easier, reform. In support of their arguments, the feminists always offer highly problematic figures that supposedly show that, by expanding the franchise in Britain to women, even on the basis of the existing property qualification, 80 percent of women voters would belong to the working class. They constantly talk about how the most important thing is the victory of the 'principle', how it is merely necessary to open a breach in the wall 'separating one sex from the other', that as soon as property-qualified women have entered Parliament, they will carry out further reforms in the interests of their 'little sisters' . . .

Our Russian equal-rights campaigners completely sympathise with the British women's struggle for property-qualified rights. They report the 'victory' in the second reading in the British Parliament of Stanger's bill, which proposed to expand the existing electoral system to women, as cause for celebration.[25] The same women who today still experience all the hardships and adversity of political disenfranchisement, the same women who would presumably know from experience what it means to have no possibility of defending their most essential interests, lightheartedly throw themselves into the defence of an electoral system that leaves the most exploited and deprived segment of the female population as disenfranchised and overlooked as before . . .

By the suffragists' own estimates (and their calculations, of course, are biased in favour of an increase in the number of voters), the 'limited bill' will grant voting rights to no more than 1.5 million women. In other words, of 13 million adult female citizens of Britain, 11.5 million will be as disenfranchised as they are now. But, given that voting rights can only be exercised by women meeting property qualifications, even these 1.5 million voters will, of course, overwhelmingly belong to the bourgeoisie. And our equal-rights campaigners admire and applaud their 'magnanimous' British sisters. Of course, they are not guided by class interest; for them, like their British counterparts, what matters is the victory of the principle!

In vain, British social democrats observe that extending the franchise to women whilst preserving the existing system threatens to significantly increase the number of voters hostile to the interests of the working class, that this reform merely increases class inequality by introducing a sort of 'multiplication of votes': Every bourgeois man will have the opportunity to add those of his wife, daughter, and female relatives who take the opportunity to pay for their separate rooms to his own. Meanwhile, how many proletarians are able to rent independent rooms for their daughters and wives, rooms costing no less than 4 shillings a week, unfurnished? To the contrary, we know that even most well-paid female workers are living two or three to a room, that a proletarian's wife will never be able to afford the luxury of separate accommodations, and that, ultimately, the proposed reform will not offer any of the servants, pieceworkers, and craft workers, the whole enormous army of women living in boarding houses, the opportunity to be included on the electoral rolls. 'Thus,' as Clara Zetkin correctly notes,

> if limited voting rights were extended to women, only a small segment of the proletariat would be able to meet the requirements of the 17 property, educational, professional, housing, and employment qualifications set forth in the British Representation of the People Act, and attain political equality. The number of women denied the right to vote would likely be greater than the number of working-class men denied the right to participate in elections by the requirements of election law. Because female workers are generally paid less than male workers. A cursory glance at property qualifications suffices to show that women, given their worse economic position than better-paid male workers, will also be less able to avail themselves of the ballot. And from this standpoint, there is no doubt that what is characteristic of limited voting rights for women is not the principle of equality of rights between the sexes, but the recognition of the power and significance of property and income.*[26]

---

* The original reads: *Alles in Allem: sollte das beschränkte Frauenstimmrecht zur Einführung gelangen, so würde nur ein bescheidener Teil der Proletarierinnen den 17 verschiedenen Vorschriften des englischen legislativen Wahlgesetztes über Eigentum, Bildungsgrad, Beschäftigung, Wohnung und Dienst entsprechen und politisch emanzipiert werden können. Ja, die Zahl der nicht stimmberechtigten Frauen würde sicher im Verhältnis noch größer sein, als die Zahl der Arbeiter, die infolge der Vorschrift vom Wahlrecht ausgeschlossen sind. Denn die Arbeiterinnen werden im allgemeinen von den Kapitalisten noch härter ausgebeutet und schlechter bezahlt als die Arbeiter. Nach dem Grundsatz des beschränkten Frauenstimmrechts sind sie, als ökonomisch schlechter gestellt, auch weniger befähigt wie die besser gelohnten Arbeiter, den Stimmzettel zu gebrauchen! Und in diesem Zuge offenbart sich deutlich, daß für das beschränkte Frauenstimmrecht in Wirklichkeit nicht das Prinzip der Gleichberechtigung der Geschlechter ausschlaggebend ist, sondern das Prinzip von der Macht und Würde des Besitzes und Einkommens.*

(All in all, if limited voting rights for women were to be introduced, only a modest portion of proletarian women would meet the 17 different requirements of the English legislative election statute concerning property, educational level, employment, housing, and service and be able to be politically emancipated. Indeed, the number of women without voting rights would surely be proportionally even greater than the number of male workers who are excluded from voting rights by law, for female workers are generally more cruelly exploited and worse paid than male workers. Based on the principle of limited voting rights for women, they, being economically worse off, are also less able to make use of the ballot than better paid male workers! And, in

In any case, however, a property qualification, in whatever form, is an institution that protects the interests of the representatives of property and capital. It deprives women of the working class of political rights by no means because they belong to the 'fair sex' but because they belong to the class of the 'have-nots'. The disenfranchisement of proletarian women is as similar to the disenfranchisement of proletarian men as the brimming lady's *porte-monnaie* is to the full wallet of the respected bourgeois. What 'equality' are the feminists on about? . . .

Alas, quite a significant number of representatives of the working class, who support a property-qualified reform, can be found in the ranks of the left wing of the suffragist movement. Despite the fact that the Women's Freedom League is a typical bourgeois organisation, that it has more than once declared itself entirely alien to the fundamental aspirations of the proletariat, emphasising its 'single and exclusive goal' – the struggle for women's equality – the fundamental need for political rights leads proletarian women on the garden path of unity with bourgeois women. Of course, such a dimming of class consciousness is extremely harmful to the success of the proletarian women's movement, and not infrequently put outstanding activists in this area into an extremely difficult position. There have been cases in which such experienced campaigners for the cause of the working class as Miss Pankhurst and Miss Billington, distracted by the idea of women's equality, dedicated themselves entirely to purely feminist agitation during election campaigns, completely leaving the field of working-class politics.[27]

The defence of property-qualified voting rights for women in Britain was also taken up by the representative of the Independent Labour Party, Keir Hardie, MP.[28] At the seventh conference of the Labour Party in Belfast, Keir Hardie warmly supported a resolution in the sense of property-qualified representation for women: 'The Conference expresses its support for suffrage for all adults and for the recognition of equal rights for the sexes: It calls for the existing electoral system to be extended to women on the same basis as men.' This formula was opposed by a resolution of

---

this manner, it is clearly revealed that, for limited voting rights for women, what is decisive is not the principle of equal rights for the sexes, but the principle of the power and dignity of property and income.') —Trans.

Quelch, a member of the Social Democratic Federation: 'The Conference recognises: First, that the time has come to extend the suffrage to all adult men and women; second, that any bill on the subject of voting rights that rests on a property qualification, and thus includes only a limited part of the population, must be viewed as a reactionary measure.'

This second resolution was also warmly supported by the representatives of the trade unions. 'A bill in the sense of the first resolution would not serve the interests of working-class women,' declared Mabel Hoope, the delegate of the Postal and Telegraph Clerks' Association. Quelch's resolution was adopted by a majority of 605,000 votes to 268,000. At the next annual conference of the Labour Party, in Hull, this resolution received 784,000 votes in favour versus 257,000 against.[29] Is this not a clear indication that the workers themselves understand the danger of a property-qualified reform, and that only a lack of political self-awareness leads a minority to defend the 'limited suffrage bill'?

A tenacious struggle for the political enfranchisement of all women is being led by the Adult Suffrage Society, which was founded in 1905 at the initiative of social-democratic women (members of the SDF). This organisation gains more and more supporters every year; thanks to it, working-class women have begun to take a more conscious stance on their disenfranchised position and matters associated with the idea of women's equality. It was under its influence that the Belfast resolution was passed at the Labour Party conference last year; thanks to its propaganda, British trade-unionists are also beginning to speak in favour of universal suffrage, opposing property-qualified representation for women.

We need not discuss the SDF in this case – their position is clear, and only the Independent Labour Party continue to defend the 'limited suffrage bill'. The Independent Labour Party emphasised their position at the last conference by adopting the following resolution: 'The Conference is in favour of the equalisation of political rights for both sexes, and calls for the suffrage to be immediately extended to women on the same basis as men.'[30]

It is necessary to dedicate somewhat more time to the women's movement in Britain, because it is in that country, with the energetic struggle of the feminists for the suffrage, and, particularly with the opening of the possibility of the practical realisation of this desirable demand, that the line separating the women of the two different social groups is rather blurred, making it possible for proletarian and bourgeois women to act jointly. One must have a great deal of consciousness, a deeply rooted understanding of class interest, in order not to be distracted by victories 'in principle' that are dear to women's hearts. In this moment, it is necessary for the Labour Party to speak out, fully armed with its pronounced class position, and be particularly vigilant in relation to the escalating issues of proletarian women and capable of linking these demands to the overall liberation struggle of the working class. The social-democratic opposition to property-qualified suffrage for women has elicited fierce attacks from the feminists, leading them to count social democrats practically as opponents of women's equality.[31] But rather than getting angry for no reason, let them answer sincerely: Is there not an unconscious calculation of class interest lurking behind their defence of property-qualified suffrage?[32] 'Whoever is not with us, is against us.'

In disowning the defence of political rights for the most deprived and exploited stratum of the female population, the British feminists themselves are departing the field of struggle for the principle of full political equality for women, and openly joining the ranks of the defenders of the interests of property and capital. Indeed, the feminists themselves do not deny this. In her letter to the editor of the *Times*, well-known feminist Mrs Fawcett states that those gentlemen who imagine that the feminists are linking their demand for women's suffrage to a reform of the entire British electoral system are sorely mistaken. 'Many of us by no means want universal suffrage,' the esteemed lady naively exclaims. Another feminist, Lady Balfour, writes to *World's Work:* 'Women's suffrage doubtlessly limits the excessive demands that the ultra-radicals seek to implement, e.g., the demand for universal suffrage. Amongst us, there are many who oppose universal suffrage.' And even Miss Pankhurst, the socialist, one of the leaders of the 'combat division' of the suffragists, did not fail to inform the *Daily Mail* of the following: 'Many think that we are seeking suffrage for *all* women; *this is completely untrue.* To the contrary, our exceedingly moderate demands do not go beyond calling for women in secure positions and the same responsibilities as male voters to be included on the electoral rolls.'[33] 'The extension of the franchise to women who pay rates and taxes,' Lady Knightley openly acknowledged, 'would eliminate the need for universal suffrage, which is a great peril for modern society.'

Of course, men of the bourgeois class willingly support the feminists on this. Dr Stanton Coit, at a meeting in the Queen's Hall, in a paean to the principle of property-qualified representation for women, noted: 'Limited suffrage eliminates the danger connected to the extension of the franchise to ignorant persons of the female sex.'[34] Property-qualified representation, extended to women, is viewed by many known parliamentary identities as a means to consolidate the class power of the bourgeoisie. 'Limited suffrage for women is an example of a purely class-based electoral system; whilst it doubles the votes of the representatives of the propertied class, this reform only increases the number of working-class votes by one-tenth,'[35] states Arthur Henderson, MP, whose knowledge of British law is outstanding.

Despite all the feminists' efforts to unite the entire British women's movement, to channel it all into a single direction, the basis for an agreement between women of the two fundamental social groups constantly eludes them. The suffragists are fighting for their own class privileges and power; proletarian women, together with the men of their class, are demanding the elimination of all privileges and the triumph of truly democratic principles. As the class consciousness of proletarian women grows, such an agreement becomes less and less possible. And though there remain no small number of working-class women in the ranks of the British feminists, there can be no doubt that, as the movement of the whole proletariat in support of universal suffrage grows, the ranks of the feminists will thin out significantly.

The socio-political conditions in Britain, and, above all, the existence of the principle of property-qualified representation, allow for a clear differentiation of the objectives pursued by bourgeois and proletarian women. In other countries, such as France, the United States, and Switzerland, the external signs dividing the two paths of the feminist movement in support of political equality are considerably more faint and elusive.

Let us examine France. The position of the campaigners for women's political rights is incommensurably more complex and confused than in Britain. The principle of property qualifications defended by the British feminists immediately defines their face and their class aspirations. By defending the 'principle' of women's equality and, at the same time, supporting the interests of the propertied classes against encroachment by the 'impudent and ignorant rabble', they have the opportunity to attract the sympathies of the bourgeoisie, to position themselves as defenders of 'property', and, in this way, ensure the support of their class comrades for their demands. In France, where all adult men are enfranchised, the feminists, in struggling for their own political equality, have no other choice but to proclaim this democratic principle for themselves, as well. In this way, independently of their will, their demands are more democratically minded than those of their British comrades. In France, the defence of property-qualified suffrage for women lacks any foundation, and does not currently promise any direct benefits for the success of the cause of women.

The position of working-class women in France is also more difficult than in Britain. There, the struggle for women's suffrage necessarily merges with the proletariat's struggle for the further democratisation of the electoral system; in France, proletarian women must struggle independently, because the rights for which women of the working class are fighting have long since been won by all adult men. One must have a great deal of class consciousness and be deeply permeated by class interest in order to be aware of the intimate connection between the efforts of proletarian women for full political rights and the democratic demands of the working class as a whole. Though the most advanced champions of the proletariat are permeated by this consciousness, it, of course, is yet to develop in the broad masses. French social democracy has a great deal of work before it before the broad masses of the working class can be convinced of the existence of an unbreakable link between the general democratic aspirations of the proletariat and the demand for women's political equality, before the proletariat becomes aware that, in fighting for voting rights for women, they are simultaneously defending the interests of their class as a whole.

The fact that the female proletariat in France must share the same political slogan with bourgeois feminists harms the liberation movement of proletarian women. Distrust in the 'ladylike' endeavour that is bourgeois feminism casts a shadow on the independent actions of proletarian women. This results in a complex position that is considerably more difficult than that obtaining in Britain. However, greater attention should be paid to the bourgeois feminist movement in France in order to discern a number of contradictions that draw a marked line between them despite the shared political slogan of two social groups of women in struggle. It can be said with certainty that the feminist movement in France, even by the feminists' own account, is typically bourgeois in character. French feminism is one of the most moderate and retrograde feminist movements in Europe. Charity is its principal arena; to this day, most French women's societies and unions have limited their activities to educational and philanthropic activities.[36] In the area of social policy, the French feminists are concerned only with reforming the civil code, which, as is known, is extremely unfavourable to women, particularly married women.

Bourgeois women have also struggled for access to the liberal professions and the right to attain academic degrees, but the matter of political equality has only come on the agenda with particular persistence for French women in recent years. The demand for political equality has escalated as an ever-greater number of women of the middle and petite bourgeoisie in France have joined the ranks of the independently employed. The impetus for bourgeois women to organise around this demand was, of course, given by the international feminist movement. In 1900, the first organisation in France to have the stated goal of winning political rights for women appeared. This is the left wing of the French feminists, the heart and soul of which is the energetic and talented Hubertine Auclert. The right wing, which is grouped around the National Union of French Women led by the cautious and moderate Sarah Monod, only has the stated goal of fundamentally reforming the civil code. This division of tasks amongst feminist organisations is entirely natural, if one recalls that the right-wing organisation primarily unites under its banner women of the haute bourgeoisie, 'ladies' in the fullest sense of the word, for whom the reform of the civil code is their boldest wish, whilst the left-wing group, which makes elements of bourgeois democracy the cornerstone of their demands, naturally calls for political equality for women. The Women's Suffrage League, however, are barely distinguishable from the right-wing feminists in terms of their composition and tactics. For a long time, nothing of rallies, noisy meetings, street demonstrations, and other 'unfeminine' actions could be heard in France, despite the existence of a special 'militant' union of feminists struggling for equal rights. Genteel meetings, presentations with 'courteous' exchanges of views, refined and entirely 'decent' feminist congresses, banquets, or, at best, press organs and petitions to the Chamber of Deputies – that was the method of struggle adopted by French feminists. However, despite all the exquisite morality of the French women, women's cause moved with fits and starts; the demand for political equality remained 'two birds in the bush', without even the compensation of one in the hand. It seemed that the ladylike method of struggle did not promise any heartening results. Proletarian women shunned the feminists, and bourgeois women themselves made a wide berth around their 'little sisters' with their alien souls.

It is in this sad manner that the bourgeois women's movement in France has eked out its humble, inconspicuous existence. However, efforts to gain political rights have not only grown amongst independent bourgeois women; the need to defend their own interests as women and as a class has also grown amongst the more democratic part of the female population of France. Without a doubt, the attempts of Dr Madeleine Pelletier,* a socialist, to rally democratic women – primarily of the proletariat – around the slogan 'suffrage for all adult female citizens of France' have met with success. The new organisation, *Solidarité des Femmes*, decided to employ 'militant tactics' and contrast their revolutionary method of struggle with the 'salon' tactics of the bourgeois feminists. The demonstration organised in front of the National Assembly in 1906 was the work of *Solidarité des Femmes*, the direct engagement with the socialist caucus in the parliament to support women's equality,[37] the demonstration organised by women for 14 July 1907 – these were all new methods of struggle brought into being by the young organisation in order to draw the attention of society to the demands of women. Of course, the French suffragists borrowed these 'militant tactics' from their British counterparts; however, the organisation *Solidarité des Femmes* differs significantly from the British League (WSPU). Socialists are at the core of this organisation; the initiator of the *Solidarité* club, Madeleine Pelletier,

---

* Erroneously phonetically rendered in the original as *Пеллутье* (Pelloutier) —Trans.

seeks to maintain close links to the workers' party. Under the influence of this new women's organisation, the French socialists came out in favour of the need for *practical struggle* for women's suffrage in France at their 1907 congress in Nancy. This unanimously adopted resolution is of great significance for female workers in France, who have thus far only been involved in the overall labour movement to a very insignificant extent; no more than fifty thousand female workers are organised in the French unions, a negligible percentage of the women employed as industrial workers. Women workers in France, perhaps to an even greater degree than proletarian women in other civilised countries, have generally remained indifferent 'to politics', due on the one hand to the influence of syndicalism, which belittles the significance of 'politics and parliamentarianism', and, on the other hand, to the inadequate development of specific propaganda for the female proletariat by the socialists.[38]

Solidarité des Femmes has shaken proletarian women out of their indifference; their 'militant tactics', carried out in the special organ *La Suffragiste*, has won over the hearts of democratic women. Of course, right-wing feminists, led by the National Union, shun this 'revolutionary' organisation, which shocks them with its 'behaviour', but the Suffrage League, on the other hand, has been completely won over by the efficacy of these public appearances, and willingly supports the young democratic organisation. The political instincts of the leader of the left wing of bourgeois feminism, Hubertine Auclert, tell her that the 'new method' promises greater results than the 'old' peaceful one. At the suffragist demonstration in May that caused such a stir in Paris, where the candidacy of the independent socialist Jeanne Laloë for the Paris municipal elections was announced,[39] both women's organisations—the feminist League and the proletarian *Solidarité*—worked together hand in hand. Although this demonstration did not yield any practical results, it was nonetheless extremely significant from the propaganda standpoint.

Without a doubt, the existence of the women's proletarian organisation, with its decisive and energetic tactics, has had the effect of moving the entire French feminist movement to the left. At the very least, the tone of the resolution on women's political equality that was adopted at the congress of the French feminists, the *Congrès national des droits civils et du suffrage des femmes*, in the summer of 1908, is decisive for women of the French bourgeoisie.[40]

Below is the text of the resolution, which was adopted unanimously:[*]

Whereas,

- in the *ancien régime* in France, women who owned fiefs had always had the same voting rights in communal and provincial councils as men, women who independently owned assets also had the right to vote for deputies to the *États-Généraux* from 1302 to 1789, in accordance with the customs and statutes of the provinces,
- these rights were taken from women at the time of the revolution and not subsequently returned to them,
- in 1848, when so-called universal suffrage was given to men, women advocated in vain against this law, which deprived more than half the nation of any participation in social activity and voting on taxes,

the Congress resolves that the suffrage, which is described as universal, shall be enjoyed by all French citizens without distinction as to sex.[†]

---

[*]   The report of proceedings of the congress states that the resolution was in fact two votes short of unanimity ('Adopté à l'unanimité moins deux voix'). See *Congrès national des droits civils et du suffrage des femmes, tenu en l'Hôtel des Sociétés Savantes à Paris les 26, 27 et 28 juin 1908*, p. 196. Full text available in French at https://gallica.bnf.fr/ark:/12148/bpt6k1127818/f6.item.zoom —Trans.

† The original reads:

Le Congrès considérant qu'en France, les femmes ont toujours eu, sous l'ancien régime, les mêmes droits que les hommes, en tant que propriétaires de fiefs; qu'elles ont eu dans les mêmes conditions le vote pour les assemblées communales, provinciales; que les femmes possédant divisément en nom ont été en possession du vote pour les députés aux Etats-Généraux depuis l'origine, 1302, jusqu'en 1789, suivant les coutumes et règlements des provinces;

Qu'à la Révolution, les femmes ont été dépouillées de droits dont elles avaient la jouissance et l'exercice, sans que, depuis, elles aient été remises en possession de ces droits;

Qu'en 1848, lorsque le suffrage dit universel fut accordé aux hommes, les femmes ont vainement réclamé contre cette loi, qui met en dehors de tout participation aux affaires publiques, au vote de l'impôt, plus de la moitié de la nation:

Emet le vœu que le suffrage dit universel soit exercé par tous les Français sans distinction de sexe.

(Whereas: in France, during the ancien régime, women always had the same rights as men as owners of fiefs; they had the right to vote for communal and provincial

However, leaving aside the achievements of the young democratic wom-en's organisation in relation to agitation and propaganda in the interest of women's political rights, can we say with any certainty that *Solidarité* is a reliable bastion of the female proletariat? To be sure, its core membership is made up of socialist women; likewise, it has not broken off ties with the socialist party, and employs combative tactics that have led bourgeois suffragists to act more decisively in defence of political rights for women. However, there are circumstances that should give us pause and lead us to approach this organisation, which is yet to fully define its position, with a certain degree of caution. On the one hand, there is too strict a *separation* of women's demands from the struggle of the proletariat for general democratic ideals, too clear a detachment of the activities of *Solidarité* from the general struggle of the proletariat as a class; on the other, *Solidarité* works much too closely with typically bourgeois organisations like the League.

Distinguishing the liberation struggle of the female proletariat as a spe-cific, to a certain extent independent, branch of the general class struggle of the proletariat not only does not conflict with the interests of the cause of the workers but, as can be seen from practice in those countries where this separation has already taken place (Britain, the United States, Ger-many, Austria, Sweden, Norway, the Netherlands, Belgium, Finland), it offers invaluable benefits to the general struggle of the proletariat. It can be said with conviction that, only when the workers' party dedicates specific efforts and specific concern to the practical struggle for voting rights for the female half of the working class, will this demand have any chance of being satisfied. Until then, the principle of women's equality will remain a dead letter, preserved in the papers of the party. However,

---

assemblies under the same conditions; women holding assets in their own name had been in possession of the vote for deputies to the États-Généraux from its inception in 1302 until 1789, in accordance with the laws and customs of the provinces;

At the time of the Revolution, women were stripped of rights they had enjoyed and exercised, and have not since had these rights restored;

In 1848, when so-called universal suffrage was granted to men, women vainly pro-tested against this law, which excludes more than half of the nation from any partic-ipation in public affairs and voting on taxes:

The Congress resolves that so-called universal suffrage shall be exercised by all French citizens without distinction as to sex.) —Trans.

distinguishing any part of the workers' programme in the context of general class politics in order to wage a more successful struggle for its realisation is quite far from the *division* and *complete separation* of work related to that demand.

Having technically emphasised work related to the struggle for women's suffrage, *Solidarité* must be all the more explicit in their propaganda about the intimate link between the general democratic demands of the socialists and the matter of political rights for proletarian women. These questions should not be separated, but united; efforts should be made to merge the struggle for women's suffrage with demands for the further democratisation of the state structure in France: with fairer allocation of electoral districts, the abolition of the requirement to register one's residence at least six months before the elections, the introduction of referenda, etc. Meanwhile, by concentrating all their activities, all their forces, on the matter of political equality for women, *Solidarité* themselves narrow their objective and, like the feminists, necessarily convert the demand for women's suffrage from a *tool*, *a means* of class struggle, into an *end in itself.* Given that state of things, there is the risk that this young French democratic organisation may follow in the footsteps of working-class suffragettes in England, and, as a result of their close collaboration with bourgeois women, begin to engage in feminist politics rather than working-class politics. If this risk should become a reality, proletarian women will no longer have any place in the ranks of *Solidarité*, and the workers' party will then be obliged to make a clean break with this women's organisation and take the struggle for the political interests of working-class women into their own hands.

Our Russian equal-rights campaigners, of course, explode with indignation at this opinion of the council. 'Even' Bebel acknowledges that, although the bourgeois and proletarian women's movements must each follow their own line, it is highly useful to join forces in order to 'attack the enemy': *'getrennt marschieren, zusammen schlagen!'* ('March separately, strike together!'). And only his 'intolerant' Russian 'pupils' do not wish to acknowledge this rule and constantly put forward their 'intransigent' convictions.

But is it true that 'even Bebel' recommends this collaboration between women of the bourgeoisie and the working class for which our feminists so long? Joint 'attacks on the enemy' are not only permissible, but even quite desirable – under one condition: that joining forces does not require proletarian women to 'soften' their demands or modify their class politics in any way. If proletarian women's organisations are marching under the unfurled banner of their working-class programme, if they are engaging in class politics not sporadically, but in a sustained manner, and nonetheless do not scare off the feminists, that would be a welcome development indeed! In that case, joint actions by both social groups of women can only be beneficial to the cause. But is this fundamental condition feasible? Will the feminist organisations agree to walk side by side with the proletariat? When collaboration, 'unification', etc. are under discussion, the feminists usually mean that the conductor's baton will remain in their hands, that the tone of women's actions will not be set by the 'semi-literate', 'ignorant' little sisters, but by themselves, the *fines-fleurs* of the female bourgeois intelligentsia.

If we are unsettled by the close collaboration of *Solidarité* with the feminists, it is because this organisation, in itself, is still too weak to impress bourgeois women and force them to come to terms with the class demands of women workers. Even if we allow that *Solidarité* will help to move the suffragists to the left, that, in certain cases, they push them to take a more active role, we cannot help but notice that, on the other hand, the feminists also have an influence on the proletarian organisation, gradually, inconspicuously painting it in blander tones. To avoid this danger, which arises wherever the attempt is made to make peace and blur the existing, irreconcilable class antagonism by means of compromises, the matter of agreements must be approached with great caution. Of course, it is always the feminists who benefit from this 'agreement', but since it does not concern them, 'wariness' on the matter of agreements does not particularly bother proletarian women.

Whilst in Britain, the two fundamental currents in the women's liberation movement – the bourgeois and proletarian currents – can compete head to head, and in France, the feminist movement, quite weak in and of itself, nonetheless prevails over the first, modest attempts of proletarian female elements to stand in defence of their rights, in Germany, on the other hand, the proletarian women's movement, with their excellent organisation and the clarity of their objectives, is leaving behind the relatively backward feminist movement.

The German feminists are no less dedicated to the interests of their class than their French or British counterparts; the 'respected ladies' are not inclined to fall for the charms of 'socialist teachings'; they harbour no affection for social democracy, and, indeed, express their hostility to it quite clearly and vividly. Nonetheless, in Germany, more than in other countries, the feminists are under its 'secret spell'. The strength of the powerful, cohesive organisation with its clear class programme is already such that it forces even those who hate it from the bottom of their hearts to come to terms with it.

The 'leftward drift' of the politics of the German feminists is happening before our very eyes. Just five to six years ago, even the radical wing of the German feminists approached the question of women's political equality with great apprehension and caution. At their congress in Wiesbaden, the *Bund deutscher Frauenvereine* (BDF, Federation of German Women's Associations) formulated the following demand: 'It is entirely desirable for the associations to use all means to facilitate the dissemination of the idea of women's suffrage.'*[41] Although this organisation already joined the International Alliance at the Berlin congress and even raised its voice in defence of universal suffrage, its programme does not actually state its political demands in any detail. Judging from the articles that appear in the central organ of the BDF in opposition to universal suffrage, the BDF still has yet to take a firm position. But this is the 'right flank' of German feminism! This is where old campaigners for women's equality come together, those who just recently did not dare to dream of political rights and merely wished to gain access to higher education, the liberal professions, and the civil and social service for women. Even now, the correct Helene Lange and the solid Maria Stritt like to direct the movement towards peaceful 'kitchen table' tasks, educational

---

* The original, as quoted by Zetkin, reads: *dringend zu wünschen, daß die Bundesvereine das Verständnis für den Gedanken des Frauenstimmrechts nach Kräften fördern* (urgently desirable for the associations of the federation to promote understanding for the idea of women's suffrage to the extent of their abilities) —Trans.

problems, and soul-saving philanthropic undertakings. In the words of *Soyuz Zhenshchin*, even at the Hamburg congress of this right wing, i.e., in September of 1907, 'questions of voting rights for the industrial relations and commercial courts, the repeal of the ban on women participating in unions and meetings, and women's suffrage were relegated to the background.'*[42]

As for the young, 'left' wing of the feminists, which formed in 1904, and is headed by such strident champions of women's political equality as Minna Cauer, Anita Augspurg, and Käthe Schirmacher, they vacillated for a long time on the question of the foundations of women's political equality. The growing power of the proletarian women's movement, which took a firm stance in favour of unrestricted suffrage, had its effect: At the Frankfurt congress of the 'progressive' feminists in 1907, they at last came out in favour of universal suffrage without distinction as to sex in elections for all legislative and local government bodies. For all their political 'radicalism', the German feminists had an extremely hard time deciding to take this step. Without a doubt, if the proletarian women's movement had been less significant, if its influence on the masses had not increased with every passing year, if, finally, their devastating critique of restricted suffrage had not discredited the defenders of property qualifications in the eyes of the broad masses of women, the 'left' feminists would never have dared to proclaim this radical demand. But now they had no choice: Their desire to be popular amongst democratic women, their fear of remaining 'in the narrow circle of ladies' forced them to put on the mask of political radicalism.

No matter how democratic the demands of the progressive German feminists are, this does not change the bourgeois essence of their organisation and efforts. Daily life constantly contradicts their high-minded 'declarations of principle'. Despite all their efforts, the class sympathies even of leftist German feminists always will out. In talking about granting women the right to vote for the Prussian Landtag, the 'progressive' women did not forget to make their demands subject to the matter of

---

* In original: *на на второй планъ отошли вопросы объ избирательныхъ правахъ въ промышленные и коммерческіе суды, отмѣна запрещенія женщинамъ участвовать въ союзахъ и собраніяхъ, избирательныя права женщинъ.*

'a small property qualification': Only those who had lived in the same place for more than a year and paid the applicable direct taxes would be granted the right to vote.

During the 1903 election campaign, the radical wing of the feminists declared that, this time, they intended to agitate not only in support of those candidates who promised to defend women's political interests, but also those who stood for 'freedom, justice, and progress', in other words – bourgeois liberals. The feminists even took care to put out a circular on the subject to related organisations. Their class interests proved stronger than their 'sex' interests.

Whatever happened to all those beautiful words about how feminists are 'cross-class' defenders of the principle of women's equality? The 'apostasy' of the feminists was brought into even sharper focus by the fact that most of the candidates of the liberal bourgeoisie were either hostile or indifferent to women's political demands. But these men were 'class comrades'; their slogans were easily understood by and dear to the hearts of bourgeois women, and they defended the interests of property and capital against the 'unprincipled' inroads made by the social democrats. This was enough for feminists to back liberals who opposed women's emancipation against social-democratic candidates who supported it. There are data showing that the feminists (who deny this) supported the liberal candidate even against Bebel himself. In Hamburg, the feminists openly campaigned in support of the liberal, even though he had no chance of succeeding, given that the main struggle was between the social-democratic and conservative candidates: But the bourgeois women preferred to 'spoil their vote' rather than to allow a social democrat to win.[43]

Before the last Prussian Landtag elections, the Breslau* local committee of the Woman Suffrage Alliance (*Deutscher Verband für Frauenstimmrecht*) asked the three prospective candidates of the Conservative Party (*Deutschkonservative Partei*, DKP) and three candidates of the Free-Minded People's Party (*Freisinnige Volkspartei*, FVP) whether they intended to stand in defence of passive and active suffrage for women in all legislative bodies. The response of the conservative candidates was, of course, completely negative: In their view, the matter was not even up

---

* Now Wrocław —Trans.

for discussion. All three FVP candidates, after their customary bowing and scraping before the principle of women's equality, emphasised
that, in their view, the time had not yet come to raise the question given
that it was not yet sufficiently 'ripe'. Embittered by these responses, the
representative of the local women's committee asked whether, in that
case, it would not follow that women should completely refrain from
participating in the election campaign and influence their husbands to
do the same. 'For us women, which of the candidates is elected is now a
matter of total indifference, given that not one of them intends to fight
for women's just demands.' It did not even occur to the radical *Verein* to
remember the three Social-Democratic candidates, candidates who, at
that very moment, were carrying out an energetic struggle in Prussia for
the full democratisation of the electoral system, including women's rights.
However, class interest constantly overshadows the feminist objectives of
the German equality campaigners, and they would rather make their
peace with their disenfranchisement than facilitate the political liberation of the unpropertied class and the consolidation of the influence of
social democracy. After hesitating briefly, the Breslau alliance came out
in support of the FVP candidates. The committee's stated reason for this
decision was that the Free-Minded candidates were generally in favour of
the four-member electoral system and were defenders of 'justice', and any
aficionado of just systems and laws could not be an opponent of women's
equality![44] This is the sort of infantile blather one hears from the German
equality campaigners. But even this baseless argument disappears when
one recalls that the FVP are calling for the introduction in Prussia not of
equal voting rights, but of plural suffrage.

No matter how much the equality campaigners try to mask the nature
of their activities, here, as ever, they are in fact guided by a specific calculation based on class interest.

The class sympathies in the world of German bourgeois women are
ever more clearly defined, despite the leftward movement of the equality
campaigners. Some bourgeois women find it pointless to conceal their
class character any longer and openly stand with the bourgeois parties.
One such example is the newly founded women's equality organisation
known as the German Women's Liberal Party (*Liberale Frauenpartei*

Deutschlands, LFPD), who are adjacent to the FVP. This party, led by Mrs Lischnewska and famous equality campaigner Else Lüders, decided to support electoral reform in Prussia on the basis of the five-member electoral system and only agitate in support of candidates who have committed to act in this spirit. But this was, of course, merely a 'theoretical' decision. The FVP's negative attitude towards the equality campaigners' demands did not push the Women's Liberal Party away from them.

After directing a few reproaches at the FVP at the last FVP congress, the women nonetheless remained in the ranks of the party. On the contrary, the German liberals were so attentive to the 'ladies' that they dedicated one session of their congress specifically to the discussion of the question of political rights for women. Else Lüders, who spoke on the issue, introduced the following resolution on the occasion:

> Liberalism believes that the good of the nation lies in the development and elevation of the individual; it goes without saying that German women, too, must share in this development of the individual. The tasks of liberalism on the field of the female question are to make women equal to man in rights, as a human being and a citizen, in educational, social, professional, and political activity. Accordingly, we call for: (1) Full participation of women in local institutions, school boards, committees for the poor and orphans, and factory and housing inspectorates, (2) the same unrestricted and equal participation for women in all institutions having the objective of protecting economic interests: Health insurance funds, industrial relations courts, labour and trade governance bodies, (3) unhindered access for women to all professions, (4) access in principle for women to representation at the imperial, state, and local levels.[45]

The FVP did not currently feel the weakness of their political position, and, not being forced, like clerics, to grasp at the last resort, women's suffrage, showed no particular sympathy for these demands. Else Lüders's co-presenter, Dr Lehmann, hurried to note that, although he supported women's equality in principle, 'politics must nonetheless remain a matter for men.' 'Furthermore,' he went on,

> there are more women on Earth than men; if we give them the suffrage, they will be the majority in parliament. That cannot be permitted!

Without seeking to offer a practical solution for this issue, the present-
er thinks that, over time, it would be possible to divide Germany into
400 male and 100 female electoral districts, such that, for 400 male
deputies in the Reichstag, there would be 100 female deputies. We
might further provide that women lose the right to vote upon marrying, just as men lose it upon joining the military.[46]

Of course, the conference could not take Dr Lehmann's proposal seriously; however, Pastor Naumann's speech, which took an even more
negative stance on the matter of political equality for women, doubtlessly
resonated with the hearts of those present. Naumann argued that the
most suitable solution would be to divide the programme of the FVP
into two parts, like the programme of the social democrats: The first
part would contain all the *desiderata* that do not commit the party to
take practical action, and the second would contain the most immediate
tasks and demands. Women's political equality should, of course, be included in the first part. God forbid the party should now join the struggle to change the Prussian system of representation with a demand for
political equality for women; that would be an enormous mistake on the
part of the FVP. The liberal feminists were extremely disappointed and
outraged: They did not expect to meet with such resistance from their
'chosen' comrades, their 'favourite allies'.

One could not help but be reminded of an example of another party – a working-class party, to be sure – that took an entirely different
approach to women's demands. 'Why', the equality campaigners complained at the conference, 'do women hold a totally different position in
the Social-Democratic Party than in the FVP? Because that is where
they can mount a joint struggle with men. We should learn from their
example.' The outraged equality campaigners even threatened to leave
the FVP if they insisted on ignoring the demand for women's suffrage,
and go 'if not to the Centre, then to the Social Democrats.' Of course,
this threat, too, will remain a threat 'in principle'.

It was unthinkable to reach an agreement on one – single – joint demand with the Social Democrats, if for no other reason than that the
Women's Liberal Party, despite its brief existence, had succeeded in
showing the public its true face without any radical mask. We need only

remember that, at one of the meetings of the Women's Liberal Party, during a debate on the expropriation of Polish landholdings and the strengthening of German culture in Posen,* it became clear that the sympathies of the liberal equality campaigners were with the propagators of 'Prussian culture'.[47]

No matter what dulcet tones the Women's Liberal Party might sing, no matter how much they emphasise their sympathy with unrestricted political equality for women, there is not, and never can be, any basis for an agreement between them and a workers' party.

Looking at the three countries with the most typical forms of women's movements, we find that feminism everywhere maintains its narrow-class imprint, and even the most radical wing of the bourgeois women's movement is never able to rise above unconscious class calculations. If women of the working class actually wished to join international feminism, the first thing they would have to do is to hide their own programmes in their pockets. The history of the feminist movement in the West teaches us that, even in such an apparently shared point as the demand for political equality for women, the interests of the representatives of the various classes do not coincide. For proletarian women, political equality is merely the first step on the way to further gains; its goal is not rights and privileges for women, but the liberation of the working class from capitalist oppression. In raising the banner of women's equality, proletarian women do not intend to bring 'harmony and justice' to the existing 'old world', but, to the contrary, to hasten its fall.

It is hard not to recall the words of Clara Zetkin in a polemic with the feminists: 'It is not *us* who do not want what *little* you, the women of the bourgeois class, attain, but rather *you* who do not want the *greater* attainments for which proletarian women strive!'

However, it may be that all of our conclusions on the impossibility of close collaboration between the bourgeois women's movement and the proletarian movement are based on an erroneous analogy with western feminism. Unlike most feminists abroad, the banners of our equal-rights campaigners bear entirely democratic demands, up to and including the five-member electoral formula. The smaller degree of differentiation

---

*   Now Poznań —Trans.

between the social strata of the population, the need for the entire political opposition to coordinate their activities in the struggle against hostile
forces that are nowhere near defeated – perhaps all this, taken together,
creates a more favourable basis for agreements and collaboration between
all social elements struggling for political equality for women?

Let us begin with a look at the Alliance for Women's Equality. Indisputably, this is the most influential of the feminist organisations in
existence here in Russia. It has the most 'ideological' influence on the
orientation and character of Russian feminism, and, at the same time,
is the left, democratic wing of the movement. When you look through
their programme, their 'platform', at first, you are overcome by affection
for the 'radicalism' of the demands of Russia's leftist feminists. They hit
every note: from a Constituent Assembly up to and including amnesty! To say nothing universal, equal suffrage in direct, secret elections
without distinction as to sex, nationality, and religion. But before we are
fully overcome by affection and welcome this fact as a 'pleasant phenomenon', a testament to the extremely democratic character of our feminist
movement, it is useful to take account of the political and social atmosphere surrounding the first forays of these equal-rights campaigners into
the arena of political struggle. The programmatic demands of a political
organisation cannot be examined without simultaneously taking into
account the societal mood of the moment that dictates the positions it
takes. The Alliance for Women's Equality came into being during a fever pitch of social activity in Russia. The oppositional elements of the
population, awakened by the first thunderclaps of a revolutionary storm,
hurried to lean on one another, to rally together, in order to resist the
declining hostile forces that appeared to be retreating more reliably. That
was the spring of the unforgettable, turbulent magnificent year of 1905.

In the early days of its existence, the AWE brought together the most
diverse female elements, from solid bourgeois women up to and including 'socialists'; but such was the gravitational force of the organisation in
Russian society that no one was scared off or intimidated by the principle
of forming blocs.

Society, which had not yet managed to awaken from the long slumber
imposed upon it by the *ancien régime*, felt blinded by the red dawn that

had just barely begun to glimmer on the horizon, and eagerly grasped at every opportunity to show their 'community spirit,' their 'autonomy'. It was the dawn of the 'alliances'. 'Political slogans' hovered in the air, overshadowing all other demands, and the more 'radical', 'extreme', 'revolutionary' they were, the more they resonated in people's hearts. Class antagonism, which was ever more acutely felt, seemed to be overshadowed by the passionate thirst of the entire opposition to 'act in friendship, as one' as the liberation movement grew ever more vast. When social democracy made its existence felt and pointed out the natural boundaries that divided even the opposition into two antagonistic camps, 'society', i.e., the liberal democratic bourgeoisie, indignantly brushed aside the 'narrow doctrinaires'.

At the very first meeting of women in Saint Petersburg on 10 April 1905, organised by the initiators of the Alliance for Women's Equality, individual incisive voices of dissonance were heard from the ranks of the social democrats, warning proletarian women against being distracted by bourgeois feminism and countering the resolutions of the feminists with another resolution that came from the ranks of working-class women. The feminists, who, in their peaceful, benevolent disposition, had naively imagined themselves called upon to unite at last 'all' women under a single banner were genuinely disappointed and saddened. Despite all their 'democratism' and 'radicalism', they voted down the working women's resolution, and the assembly of – mostly bourgeois – women, of course, adopted 'their' own resolution.[48] Such collisions of the two worlds ended up repeating themselves at nearly every major assembly of women. Nonetheless, the Alliance for Women's Equality, who were meant to serve women of all strata and classes, was organised at that same time, in April of 1905. The Alliance drafted their programme amidst the incessant noise of societal forces coming to life. Life moved at an accelerated pace: The entire atmosphere seemed suffused with the revolutionary electricity that had built up over the years. The sea of women simmered uneasily, yet joyously. It is worth remembering the exhilaration that held sway amongst women over that entire year of 1905. 'Until last year (i.e., 1905),' *Zhenskiy Kalendar* reports, the matter of suffrage was of quite little interest to women; in any case, that interest was not expressed in any way. Whilst, in 1903, a number of *zemstva,* from the liberal ones to the most conservative, raised the issue of suffrage, some supporting active and passive suffrage, others supporting the expansion of existing redelegated rights of women, the latter never stated their position on the matter, as if it did not affect their essential, vested interests. Yet, last year, 1905, all of a sudden, there appeared not only interest in the issue, but uncommon upheaval and enthusiasm, which, without any propaganda, any general plan or organisation, and with remarkable unanimity, made their appearance in the most diverse and opposite corners of our fatherland.*[49]

Women were indeed not slumbering. Petitions, resolutions, declarations, and proclamations flew through the air from one end of Russia to the other. There was no one to whom women did address an appeal! There was no issue in which these fresh-baked feminists did not intervene! There were demands for the review of the civil code in the interest of women, requests to the home secretary to admit women to the office of township clerk,[50] appeals to the *zemstva* in hopes of gaining access to local government, and a 'motion' to admit women to the treasury chambers, treasuries, state bank, etc. But, of course, the fundamental demand was political equality. Without even mentioning the declarations, motions, etc. of other women's organisations, the Russian Women's Mutual Philanthropy Society alone managed to submit 398 petitions to *zemstvo* authorities and 108 petitions to city authorities seeking support for the demand for women's equality, to send 37 requests to local authorities seeking them to adopt resolutions

---

*   In original: *До прошлаго (т. е. 1905 г.).— сообщаетъ „Женскій Календарь",— вопросъ объ избирательныхъ правахъ весьма мало интересовалъ женщинъ; по крайней мѣрѣ, этотъ интересъ рѣшительно ничѣмъ не выразился. Въ то время какъ въ 1903 году цѣлый рядъ земствъ, начиная съ либеральныхъ и кончая самыми консервативными, поднималъ вопросъ объ избирательныхъ правахъ, одни за активное и пассивное избирательное право, другія за расширеніе существующихъ по передовѣрію правъ женщинъ, послѣднія ничѣмъ не проявили своего отношенія къ этому дѣлу, какъ будто оно не касалось ихъ насущныхъ, кровныхъ интересовъ. Но вотъ въ прошломъ, 1905 году, сразу проявился не только интересъ къ этому вопросу, но необыкновенный подъемъ и воодушевленіе, которые, безъ всякой пропаганды, безъ всякаго общаго плана и организаціи, съ замѣчательнымъ единодушіемъ стали обнаруживаться въ разныхъ самыхъ, противоположныхъ, углахъ нашего отечества.*

on women's equality, to send 6,000 submissions to various social and state institutions, to submit motions requesting support for the demands for women's equality to 5 governors-general, 80 governors, and 46 aristocratic leaders, not to mention the special submissions to ministers and even to the 'council of ministers'.[51] For the extremely cautious, moderate, and politically indifferent Women's Society, even these displays of political naivety represented a sort of civic action. Most importantly, however, they were a testament to the fact that even such an arch-bourgeois women's organisation did not withstand the emancipatory current, and dared to agree to such extreme measures as demands for amnesty and the abolition of the death penalty.[52]

From one end of Russia to the other, women stirred, thrilled, and made their presence felt. Just have a look at newspapers from 1905, and, in practically every issue, you will run across reports of women's mass meetings, assemblies, resolutions, petitions, declarations, etc. On one day, women in Saint Petersburg send a resolution on full political rights, covered with 1,208 signatures from women, to a meeting of *zemstvo* officials in Moscow;[53] on the next, a group of women from Moscow, mostly teaching staff, submit to the Moscow provincial assembly an address asking the assembly to 'raise their voices for women's rights' (*возвысить голос за право женщин*), and not to forget them when carrying out state reforms. Polish women submit a petition to the commission for the drafting of provisions on local institutions of the Kingdom of Poland, demanding *active* suffrage for themselves in the future local institutions. In spring 1905, women in Saratov organise a well-attended, noisy mass meeting, after which they submit to the provincial assembly a declaration on the necessity of granting women active and passive suffrage in local government institutions. A similar statement is submitted to the provincial assembly by female residents of the city of Atkarsk. Female residents of Chernigov (Chernihiv) add their signatures. Another group of women in Saratov submit the same demands to the city government of Saratov.[54] Female residents in Kishinev place an open letter in the newspaper, with 102 signatures, announcing their adherence to the demands of the women in Moscow and Saratov. In the summer of 1905, a statement from 955 is sent to the deputy mayor of Moscow, demanding that the commission elected by the city Duma to develop the basis for the new city by-laws recognise the principle of universal suffrage, extended to include women. Women in Voronezh submit a statement on the need to grant women the right to participate in *zemstvo* government to the provincial assembly of *zemstva*. The Women's Mutual Philanthropic Society sends a congratulatory telegram to the members of the congress of *zemstvo* and city officials in Moscow who speak in favour of extending the franchise to women. Female residents of Minsk organise a well-attended assembly of women, at which they issue a resolution on the need to improve the position of women and grant them equal civil and political rights to men.

Mass meetings of women take place in Saint Petersburg, Moscow, Odessa, Saratov, Yalta, and other cities. Wherever these meetings take place, the voices of women representing the extreme political parties are heard. The moderate voices are covered up by a chorus of rallying cries and militant slogans, expressions of enthusiasm and faith that victory is near. A close linkage is made between the matter of women's political equality and the liberation struggle of the people as a whole.

Such was the political atmosphere in which the AWE was born; nor did the other liberal bourgeois and bourgeois democratic organisations of the time make more moderate demands. In the bloom of the 'alliance of alliances', the bourgeois opposition did not want to hear of property-qualified representation. Is it any wonder that the AWE, which sought to unite the broadest possible circle of the female population under a single banner, bowed to the demanding voice of democracy in formulating their fundamental slogans?

In the first paragraph of their constitution, the stated goal of the AWE is to 'support general political liberation and attain equality of rights for women and men." This is a broadly phrased objective, going well beyond the boundaries of the usual feminist organisations. But it is precisely because the stated goal of the AWE was to 'support the general political liberation of the country' that they needed to reckon with the requests and demands brought forth by the political moment. In examining these ageing documents of the AWE, their platform and constitution, we must

---

* In original: *содѣйствовать общему политическому освобожденію и добиваться уравненія правъ женщинъ съ мужчинами*

not lose sight of the fact that many points that included in them under the influence of totally one-off historical events have now lost their significance for the members of the AWE, and, if they are not deleted, then only because there is a tacit understanding that they are not essential.

But let us treat the programme of the AWE as if it had not already lost its actual force, and see whether women of the working class would have been able to rally round the 'radical' banner of the AWE back when its colours had not yet begun to fade, without harming their own class interests.

The platform of the Alliance is prefaced with the following 'recitals':

> Whereas: 1) in the present regime, women are politically completely disenfranchised; the struggle for women's rights is inextricably connected with the political struggle for the liberation of Russia; 2) The disenfranchisement of women, who constitute more than half of the population, under conditions of political liberation of only men, hinders both the economic development of the country and the growth of political consciousness amongst the people, we . . . ' etc.

This is followed by a series of fundamental demands. Look carefully at this document. Is there even the slightest indication that the Alliance intends to struggle for the liberation of women of the working class not only from civil or political disenfranchisement, but from the worst evil of the present social structure – the chains and oppression of capitalism? From its very first steps, the Alliance limited their activities to political tasks. This is confirmed by the equality campaigners themselves: The Alliance do not at all seek to fight for the economic liberation of women; their task is much more modest: 'Attain equality of rights for women in elections to all legislative bodies and in the revision of the civil code.'* The Alliance demands nothing more.

But how is a woman of the working class to separate the struggle for political equality from the struggle for economic emancipation if both forms of struggle constantly intersect, adding to one another, merging into a single struggle? When a working-class woman defends her political demands, she simultaneously hastens the time of her economic

---

*　In　original:　*добиться уравненія правъ женщинъ при выборахъ во всѣ законодательныя учрежденія и при пересмотрѣ гражданскаго кодекса*

emancipation, and vice versa: by defending her economic interests against exploitation by capital, she clears the path to her political emancipation at the same time. The feminists propose that she should leave the previous path of general class struggle and strictly separate economic and political interests from one another, defending the former, if at all, in the ranks of her own class, and the latter under the banner of the feminist societies.[55] But why should proletarian women throw themselves into the embrace of the equality campaigners in order to defend their political interests? Has the AWE actually promised any extraordinary benefits for women in this regard? What was called for in the first point of the AWE's platform, which defined their political demands?

Immediate convocation of a constituent assembly on the basis of universal suffrage in direct, secret elections without distinction as to sex, nationality, and religion, having first established the inviolacy of the person and residence, freedom of speech, the press, assembly, and association, and restored the rights of all persons deprived thereof for their political and religious convictions.*

We speak of the AWE in the past tense because, in the present, their decisive *desiderata* have, for all practical purposes, been eliminated and replaced with more modest aspirations. What exactly remains of the previous demands of the AWE?

The political face of the AWE, as with that of all bourgeois liberal organisations, has changed together with the social atmosphere. The louder the reactionaries growled, the more moderate our 'leftist' equality campaigners became. The fact that the Alliance's previous programme has not been amended is meaningless; the character of an organisation must be determined based not only on its programmatic statements, but, to an even greater extent, on its practical activities, the sympathies it expresses. And the Alliance have made it ever more unmistakably clear where their sympathies lie.

---

* In original: *Немедленный созывъ учредительнаго собранія на основѣ всеобщаго, прямого, тайнаго избирательнаго права, безъ различія пола, національности и вѣроисповѣданія, съ предварительнымъ установленіемъ неприкосновенности личности, жилища, свободы слова, печати, собраній и союзовъ, возстановленіе въ правахъ всѣхъ пострадавшихъ за политическія и религіозныя убѣжденія*

Whilst, in their early days, the Alliance still expressed some affinity for the workers' party and flirted with 'socialism', as the 'self-definition' of the Alliance has progressed, their sympathy for the proletariat has faded, and their affinity for bourgeois liberalism has grown stronger. The Alliance boasted of being an organisation 'beyond class' and 'beyond parties', as feminists everywhere and always boast; they boasted that, in the days of the revolutionary storms, they 'impartially' supported all types of opposition, be it bourgeois liberals, bourgeois democrats, or finally, proletarians; in a word, whatever they considered more 'important' in a given time and place.[56] Nonetheless, in the first months of the Alliance's existence, they made undeniable advances towards the socialist parties, though, to be sure, they did not exactly know which one they preferred. At the congress of delegates in October, the AWE came out in favour of 'the desirability of unification with the socialists, given that the interests of the working-class parties relative to the current economic structure coincide with the interests of women.'*[57] This statement is quite decisive: It allows us to assume an understanding on the part of the equality campaigners of the link existing between the proletariat's liberation struggle and women's struggle for their rights. But we should never jump to conclusions. Under what circumstances did the second congress of delegates of the AWE take place? It coincided with turbulent days in the life of Moscow, when the wave of the great October strike was rising. 'The tempo of life was accelerated,' the equality campaigners themselves note in their third bulletin, 'a storm could be felt in the air; nerves were extremely tense; this mood could not but influence the work of the congress, but it also brought the beating pulse of life into it.'† Who was setting the tone at the time? On whose forces did society rest its hopes? Whose power was first deployed before the amazed, and even overjoyed, eyes of the bourgeois opposition, who had not yet managed to grasp the 'shadow side' of the proletarian movement? Failing to reckon with the popular masses meant losing the

---

* In original: *желательность единенія съ соціалистами, такъ какъ интересы рабочихъ партій по отношенію къ современному экономическому строю совпадаютъ съ интересами женщинъ.*

† In original: *Жизнь шла ускореннымъ темпомъ, въ воздухѣ чувствовалась гроза; нервы были напряжены до крайности; это настроеніе не могло не отразиться на работахъ съѣзда, но оно-же внесло въ него и біеніе пульса жизни.*

battle, renouncing any chance of success ab initio. What is surprising here is not the fact that the equality campaigners struck ingratiating notes, acknowledging the proletariat as an 'ally' with a friendly nod, at their October congress; what is much more characteristic is the fact that, despite this flirtation with the 'socialist' parties, the congress decided to support *other democratic* organisations as well, whose platforms included the demand for political equality for women and to 'refrain from joining only those parties' (*воздерживаться от вступления лишь в те партии*) whose programmes did not include this point.[58]

If the AWE had seriously gravitated towards the 'socialist' parties in those days, if their statements had indeed been sincere, such an 'addendum' to the resolution they adopted, an addendum that nullified that very decision, would, of course, have been impossible. What ultimately prevented the Alliance moving closer to the workers' party, seriously offering to collaborate with it, forming some sort of special department to serve the interests of women's democracy? Were the equality campaigners perhaps scared off by the tactics of the social democrats? Nothing of the sort! Oh, how the equality campaigners loved to flaunt their 'revolutionary' attitude in those days! From calling for a constituent assembly, boycotting the Duma, up to *'the most active interventions'* (*самых активных выступлений*) – *they did not shy away from anything*. What, then, prevented them converging with the workers' party? The instinctive consciousness of class antagonism, discord, fundamental economic interests. As the Alliance gradually but inexorably moved right, their aversion to the workers' party grew. The Alliance were already making 'rightward' steps in the first year of their existence, in 1905, of all times!

Already in May 1906, a revision of the platform of the Alliance for Women's Equality, primarily the entire first point concerning the constituent assembly, was proposed at their congress. Voices were raised in support of eliminating the political programme of the Alliance in general; this view was justified by the fact that the emancipatory tendencies of the Alliance 'are a burden to its right-wing, undeveloped, frightened members, having a depressing effect on them' (*висят гирей на его правых членах, неразвитых, запуганных, действуют на них удручающе*). Mrs L. Gurevich found that the main obstacle to joining the Alliance for many members was indeed the first point; Mrs Klirikova and Mrs Konstantseva insisted on shifting the centre of gravity of the programme from the liberation movement to women's suffrage, preserving only minimum political demands.[59]

When the extreme political radicalism of the Alliance was under discussion, did the esteemed delegates take into account whom exactly their political programme was scaring away from the Alliance – bourgeois 'ladies' or women of the working class? Not the latter, of course . . . And nonetheless, despite their constant sighing about how few proletarian women are in the Alliance, the need to 'democratise' it and attract their 'little sisters', they once again forgot all about them even when reviewing the purely political demands. Such is the logic of the liberal bourgeoisie!

Most of those at the congress voted, however, to keep the programme as is. However, we must not overestimate the significance of this fact. It is once again worth remembering the political circumstances under which the May congress of delegates took place.

The First Duma was in its honeymoon period: The mood amongst opposition elements was cheerful, full of hope and illusions; the reactionaries hid their claws. The mood amongst the feminists was particularly triumphant and proud: They carried out their first 'civic act', submitting two petitions to the State Duma, one from the WMPS, the other from the AWE. Distancing themselves from their previous programme was a political impossibility. It is all the more characteristic that, despite the triumphant mood of the moment, the political slogans of the AWE provoked attacks and doubts.

It is quite instructive that, at this very congress, along with debates on the issue of revising the programme, the AWE was peppered with accusations of being too active in the general liberation struggle. Members of the AWE had apparently completely forgotten the first section of their constitution, forgotten that the AWE's objective was not merely the struggle for women's equality, but also 'support for general political liberation'. Mrs Chekhova, who today edits *Soyuz Zhenshchin*, was forced to ward off these attacks and prove that the AWE's participation in the general political struggle did not do any harm to women's cause.[60] It was palpable that the Alliance was beginning to take on an increasingly narrow feminist hue. The delegates of the congress blasted the Alliance for their 'ambiguous' activities and their inability to steadfastly defend and carry out their fundamental task: struggle for women's rights. 'In the activities of other allied organisations,' one male attendee said, 'you can feel their character, but the Alliance for Women's Equality does not have one; nothing can be found in their reports about the struggle for women's equality. Meanwhile, this issue should be resolved straight away; otherwise, it threatens to be postponed for a long time."*

Mrs Volkenshtein considered it superfluous to dedicate forces to 'organising soup kitchens, helping the hungry, prisoners, unemployed, and the like, and proposes preserving forces and using them exclusively on agitation for women's rights given the importance of the current moment.'†

Mrs L. Gurevich spoke in the same spirit. She reproached the members of the Alliance for being afraid to be openly feminist. 'What is at fault for this, other than purely psychological causes, is the insufficient development of logic and argumentation in women. The Russian social democrats, too, are at fault: Bebel himself does not fear the female question, whilst the Russian social democrats respond to it with inappropriate half-smiles and chuckles.'‡

(When and where?)

We need to be clearly aware of the profound link between the female question and the revolutionary movement; by leaving the female question unresolved, we leave a gap for reactionaries to slip through. The

---

* In original: *Въ дѣятельности другихъ союзныхъ организацій чувствуется своя особая характерная физіономія, а у „Союза Равноправности" этого нѣтъ, въ его отчетахъ ничего не слышно о борьбѣ за женское равноправіе. Между тѣмъ, вопросъ, этотъ долженъ быть рѣшенъ теперь-же; иначе онъ грозитъ быть отложеннымъ на долгое время.*

† In original: *на организацію столовыхъ, помощь голодающимъ, заключеннымъ, безработнымъ и т. п. и предлагаетъ беречь силы и тратить ихъ лишь на агитацію за женскія права, ввиду важности текущаго момента.*

‡ In original: *Виновато въ этомъ недостаточное развитіе логики и аргументаціи у женщинъ, кромѣ причинъ чистопсихологическихъ. Виноваты въ этомъ и русскіе соціал-демократы: самъ Бебель не боится женскаго вопроса, тогда какъ русскіе соціал-демократы ставятъ его съ неумѣстными полуулыбками и усмѣшками*

Alliance for Women's Equality must defend not only their own rights, but the rights of all the people, as well.[61]*

The latter statement by Mrs Gurevich is entirely correct; one can only be amazed at the political short-sightedness of those members of the AWE who, in such a revolutionary moment, proposed to abstain from any participation in the general movement and concentrate their activities on the exclusive defence of narrow female demands. In that turbulent, revolutionary year of 1905, the AWE did indeed depart the shores of the purely female movement; a powerful wave of popular ferment carried off our equality campaigners along with the other opposition organisations. But can we hold it against the AWE that they deviated from the immediate objectives of feminism? Do avid feminists imagine that the AWE would have been more useful to the cause of women's political liberation if they had walled themselves off from the general liberation struggle of the people and simply gone on and on about the interests of women's equality like the proverbial magpie?

The proceedings of the Alliance for Women's Equality from May 1905 to May 1906 are full of references to their supportive role in the general movement and struggle for the reform of the structure of the state. Subdivisions of the Alliance organised aid for the unemployed and striking workers in various places, opened soup kitchens, organised health brigades and clinics (which proved indispensable in confrontations with the Black Hundreds), aided political exiles and prisoners, participated in demonstrations (e.g., in Moscow at Baumann's funeral, when the equality campaigners carried their own banner, with the slogan 'Universal suffrage without distinction as to sex'), and raised funds to support the movement. Particularly active was the Moscow division of the AWE; more than ten thousand rubles passed through their hands over the year. Similarly lively was the work of the Tver division, which concentrated primarily on aid to the unemployed. Most of the divisions, captivated by the importance of the political events of the moment, in the face of which purely female interests receded to the background, dedicated themselves

---

*   In original: *Нужно Нужно ясно сознавать глубокую связь, существующую между женскимъ вопросомъ и революціоннымъ движеніемъ; оставивъ нерѣшеннымъ женскій вопросъ, мы оставляемъ лазейку реакціи. „Союзъ Равноправія" долженъ защищать не только свои права, но и права всего народа.*

to working in support of the liberation movement, instinctively recognising that the victory of 'women's cause depends entirely on the outcome of
the people's struggle as a whole.'

Nor did the bureau of the AWE remain inactive; in addition to sending congratulations to the Finnish senate and Finnish women (after the
Senate included the words 'without distinction as to sex' in the bill for
the new electoral system), to Bebel on the occasion of the introduction
of a proposal for electoral reform that included women in the Prussian
Landtag, we also find the Alliance actively participating in the general political arena. There was practically not a single major phenomenon
of socio-political life in Russia, not a single major act of the liberation
movement, with which the bureau of the AWE did not resonate in one
way or another.[62]

Surely the political activities of the AWE merited censure from some
of its members? Were they not, in fact, a testament to the political instinct present to a certain degree even in narrow champions of 'women's
equality only'? The AWE's deviation from their immediate task, the fact
that they constantly left the prescribed framework of feminism, paying
tribute to general political aspirations, is merely a testament to the fact
that the struggle for political rights for women is so intimately connected with the general struggle for democracy that separating, dissociating
one from the other is simply impossible. The equality campaigners rose
up at their May congress against the 'ancillary activities' of subdivisions
of the Alliance in the general liberation struggle because it supposedly
diverted the forces of the feminists from their immediate task, but because the 'revolutionism' of which they boasted when the revolution was
breaking out detracted in their eyes from their previous attractiveness,
and prevented more 'solid' and peaceable female bourgeois elements
from joining the Alliance.

Not long before the May congress in Saint Petersburg, this progressive
rightward drift led the left wing of the AWE, which gravitated towards
the 'socialist parties', to split off. The AWE did not mourn this loss. At
the congress, to be sure, there were attempts on this occasion to revisit
the relationship of the equality campaigners to the socialist parties, but
the assembly was afraid to delve into this nettlesome question. It sufficed

for the AWE to give the social democrats their due for their 'idealistic (?) preaching' of women's equality. To the contrary, Mrs Chekhova counted amongst the achievements of the Alliance the fact that, under *its influence*, the social democrats 'changed their attitude towards the female question: They no longer claim that equality for women can only be achieved under a socialist system; at mass meetings and rallies, they now always speak of women's equality'.[63]*

What is this – conscious distortion of the facts or naïve ignorance? Neither is acceptable in a person who is one of the leaders of a given social movement.

Although the AWE still reckoned with social democracy to some extent up to the end of 1905, after a series of events that drew a clear demarcation line between the aspirations of the bourgeoisie and the working class, fear of a possible 'dictatorship of the proletariat' led the equality campaigners to recoil in fear from all dangerous allies. Already during the elections to the first State Duma, many subdivisions of the AWE openly supported the People's Freedom candidates.[64] When, at the May assembly of delegates, the correct relationship with deputies of the State Duma, i.e., with which fraction to ally themselves, was up for discussion, the members of the Alliance raised various proposals: 'to turn to the Cadet party, the labour group, to establish relations with all opposition parties,' but the representatives of the workers were not even mentioned, even though they had already organised their own caucus by the time the petition was submitted to the Duma. The equality campaigners ultimately submitted the petition directly to the equality commission; obviously, the Alliance did not want to link their activities to a party that was alien in spirit and inclinations.

That the Women's Mutual Philanthropic Society selected the Cadets as the expression of women's demands, that a petition from the Society was submitted to Prof. Petrazhitskiy – that is entirely natural; the political sympathies of the Society lean too clearly to the right, and, perhaps, if the

---

* In original: *измѣнили свое отношеніе къ женскому вопросу: они уже болѣе не утверждаютъ, что равноправіе женщинъ возможно осуществить лишь при соціалистическомъ строѣ; на митингахъ и массовкахъ они теперь повсемѣстно говорятъ о равноправіи женщинъ*

Octobrists had promised their support to women, the Society would have turned to them even more enthusiastically. However, the fact that the Alliance for Women's Equality, which claims to be politically radical, carefully avoided the extreme parties is a characteristic fact that we must not lose sight of when evaluating the nature of this women's political organisation.

In May 1907, the Alliance once again submitted a petition, this time to the second State Duma, and despite the fact that, according to the equality campaigners themselves, the majority of the twenty thousand signatures on the petition came from proletarian women, the petition was addressed to the Trudovik faction. This time, even the previous justification was absent: The social-democratic faction not only was present in the Duma, but had both influence and prestige. So great was the equality campaigners' hostility to the representatives of the working class, however, that they preferred to link their actions even to the less influential Trudoviks of the second Duma in order to avoid open relations with the representatives of the workers.

The appeal to the Trudoviks was the AWE's last tribute to democratic traditions. As the self-definition of the equality campaigners of the Alliance grew, their Cadetist leanings became ever clearer, at the same time as their hostility to the 'extreme parties' grew. In March 1907, a sort of 'spiritual union' was officially proclaimed between the AWE and the Cadets. At a well-attended mass meeting organised by the AWE in Salt Town, Saint Petersburg, only female members of the Cadets appeared. The members of the State Duma invited as speakers belonged overwhelmingly to the Cadet party; of course, no deputies from the workers' party were present. Both the speeches of the speakers and the entire appearance of the audience were totally 'decent' and 'ladylike'. The organisers of the meeting were concerned with ensuring that the 'strident' extremists did not introduce dissonance into the harmonious assembly, and they were quite irritated by the performance of some of the members of the party.

In early 1908, members of the selfsame AWE founded the Women's Political Club with clearly expressed Cadetist sympathies. The political propaganda in the Club exclusively supports the Cadets; the most visible figures of the Cadet party speak there. The link between the Club and the Cadets is obvious. To be sure, the Club does not operate under the banner of the Alliance for Women's Equality, and the more left-leaning elements of the AWE emphasise this fact, noting that they are innocent of Cadetism. However, not only the structure of the Club, but, to an even greater degree, all of the Club's activities, the entire spirit of the Alliance are a testament to their touching unity with bourgeois liberalism.

In order to ascertain the extent of the evolution that has taken place within the Alliance from the day of its foundation up to the appearance of their own house organ, it suffices to peruse the first bulletins of the Alliance and look at the articles in its freshly baked organ. Although, in the first months of its existence, the Alliance tried to assure people that even representatives of the most extreme political tendencies could walk under its banner, by 1907, the Alliance dissociated itself from them and made clear that it does not share their extremism or narrowness. Of course, the Alliance also adapted their tactics to their more moderate stance: 'We are far from the naive, short-sighted feminism,' says the lead article of *Soyuz Zhenshchin*,

> that dreams of solving the female question without any linkage to general political and social issues, to gain equality of rights with men independently of general legal and social equality. The tactics of our struggle for women's equality must certainly change in many particular aspects, depending, e.g., on the conditions of popular struggle in general. Thus, the wide range of ideas represented in the work of the first State Duma compelled us to review all Russian laws related to the matter of women's equality and submit to the corresponding commission of the Duma the draft bill for the legal equalisation of women that we had written. From the first State Duma, which had raised the issue of general equality of rights, it was possible to expect a radical solution to the female question, as well. The work of the second State Duma was no longer as broad or ideological in nature as that of the first.'[65]

---

*   In original: *Мы далеки отъ наивнаго и близорукаго феминизма, который мечтаетъ разрѣшить женскій вопросъ внѣ связи съ общими политическими и соціальными вопросами, уравнять права съ мужскими независимо отъ общаго правового и соціальнаго равенства. Тактика нашей борьбы за равноправіе женщины неизбѣжно должна мѣняться во многихъ своихъ частностяхъ— въ зависимости, напр., отъ условій общенародной борьбы. Такъ, широкій идейный размахъ въ работахъ 1-й Государственной Думы заставилъ насъ взяться за пересмотръ всѣхъ русскихъ законовъ, связанныхъ съ вопросомъ о*

At one time, the AWE sought to play an active role. At one time, it did not limit its tasks to propagandising in favour of the idea of equal rights. At one time, did not insist that political rights for women could only be won with the active participation of the AWE. However, 'tactics must change depending on the conditions of popular struggle in general'; the equality campaigners understood this proposition in their own way, and shifted their 'tactics' almost entirely in the form of changing the Alliance's relations to the workers' party. The intensity of these efforts to distance themselves from the workers' party varied along with the prevalence of the desire at any given time to blur the differences between the demands of bourgeois and proletarian women. There was a time that the AWE responded with hurt and indignation when that party stated that socialist women could not and should not struggle under the flag of the Alliance inasmuch as they had demands that differed from those of bourgeois women. Now, the equality campaigners of the Alliance themselves emphasise their 'ideological' divergence from social democracy, criticising and diligently seeking out its mistakes – in a word, making clear that the Alliance does not and cannot have anything in common with it.

However, their hostility to that party in no way prevents the AWE continuing to proclaim themselves an organisation that is beyond class or party and serves the interests of all 'women', including the most disenfranchised and deprived amongst them. 'Before us', says *Soyuz Zhenshchin*,

> stands the woman of the countryside, that sphinx of the intelligentsia, a powerful slave with the eyes of a queen, who is obliged to 'submit to a slave', to be the slave of a slave, till the day she dies . . . We must deal with this complex position of the country woman who, at the same time, gives us an example of a self-sufficiency and an independence that we do not always have, and of profound mental and physical

---

женскомъ равноправіи, и предложить соотвѣтственной думской коммиссіи выработанный нами законопроектъ правового уравненія женщины. Отъ Первой Государственной Думы, поставившей вопросъ о всеобщемъ уравненіи въ правахъ, можно было ждать и радикальнаго разрѣшенія женскаго вопроса. Работы Второй Государственной Думы уже не носили того широкаго и идейнаго характера, какъ работы Первой.

enslavement, upon close acquaintance with whom the blood stops flowing and the heart stops beating.*

And then, apparently bowing to the inevitable, *Soyuz* adds: 'Let the proletarian woman struggle on her own for her rights in the ranks of the conscious proletariat, but we, the intelligentsia, raised at the expense of her blood and sweat, we must help her with all the riches of our knowledge.'[†66] But do not think that the AWE, in an outbreak of 'magnanimity' actually renounce the desire to lead proletarian women, that they seriously wish to let them 'struggle for their own rights in the ranks of the conscious proletariat'. And there's the rub: The equality campaigners of the AWE know perfectly well, understand perfectly well, that, if they wish to be a *force* that society, the political parties, and the government must reckon with, then they must, above all, recruit a sufficient number of 'little sisters' to their feminist banner, and then, relying on them, in a compelling tone, demand the satisfaction of their female demands. Hence the duplicity of their attitude towards the female proletariat, to its tasks, aspirations, and its struggle, a duplicity that is also characteristic of feminist movements abroad. On the one hand, there is a frank hostility to social democracy, its tasks and objectives, a seething bitterness towards everything to do with the workers' party; on the other, they borrow a number of demands from it, constantly 'playing' with concepts and demands that are dear to the hearts of proletarian women. Listen to how the equality campaigners of the Alliance for Women's Equality speak of their tasks, and you will understand that, like sirens, they seek with their dulcet tones to catch politically inexperienced and naïve women of the working class in their net.

---

* In original: *Передъ нами стоитъ деревенская женщина,—этотъ сфинксъ для интеллигенціи, мощная рабыня со взглядомъ и походкой царицы, которая обязана до гроба „рабу покоряться", быть рабыней раба... Мы должны разобраться въ этомъ сложномъ положеніи деревенской бабы, которая, въ одно и тоже время, даетъ намъ примѣръ самодѣятельности и самостоятельности, не всегда намъ свойственной, и глубокаго порабощенія души и тѣла, отъ ближайшаго знакомства съ которой стынетъ кровь въ жилахъ и останавливается сердце.*

† In original: *Пусть пролетарка сама борется за свои права въ рядахъ сознательнаго пролетаріата, но мы, интеллигенція, воспитанная за счетъ ея крови и пота, мы обязаны помочь ей въ этомъ всѣми богатствами своихъ знаній.*

Foremost amongst all of the tasks we have set out to accomplish must be that of popularising the idea of women's participation in universal suffrage. Only a representative body in which women legislators stand side by side with male legislators can throw off the yoke of social enslavement and liberate humanity from it. Only with the participation of women in conditions of political equality can the ideal of socialism be realised.[*67]

In her speech at the Amsterdam congress, the representative of the Alliance made the 'socialist' tasks of the AWE even clearer:

Too often, we have had to hear from the social democrats that the women's movement is a purely bourgeois movement, that it only serves the interests of bourgeois women, that it only struggles for political rights, and that, as soon as that goal has been attained, proletarian women will be oppressed by politically emancipated bourgeois women just as politically emancipated proletarian men are oppressed by politically emancipated bourgeois men. I do not know whether they are genuinely convinced of this, or whether this is, tactic – in any case, an ill-considered one – on their part. We, for our part, must clarify this matter in the interests of unity. Without this unity, the great goal of the women's movement – equality and justice in human relations – will not be attained for quite some time yet. We must publish a sort of manifesto so that it will be impossible to divide the women's movement and obstruct its work.[†]

---

* In original: *Впереди всѣхъ намѣченныхъ нами задачъ передъ нами должна стать задача популяризировать идею участія женщинъ во всеобщемъ избирательномъ правѣ. Только такое народное представительство, при которомъ женщина-законодательница станетъ рядомъ съ законодателемъ-мужчиной, можетъ сбросить ярмо соціальнаго рабства и освободить отъ него человѣчество. Только при участіи политически - равноправной женщины можетъ быть осуществленъ идеалъ соціализма.*

† In original: *Намъ слишкомъ часто приходилось слышать отъ соціал-демократовъ, что женское движеніе есть чисто-буржуазное движеніе, что оно служитъ интересамъ только буржуазныхъ женщинъ, что оно добивается только политическихъ правъ и что, какъ только эта задача будетъ достигнута, женщина-пролетарка будетъ угнетаться политически-свободной буржуазной женщиной такъ-же, какъ теперь угнетается политически-свободный пролетарій политически-свободнымъ буржуа. Не знаю, искренно-ли они убѣждены въ этомъ или-же это у нихъ, во всякомъ случаѣ, мало продуманная тактика. Мы-же должны въ интересахъ единенія*

Suffrage is not the final objective of the women's movement. It is merely the *immediate* objective, the *means*, the *lever* with which to attain the main goal. The main goal, of course, is, with women's participation in the life of society and the state, to bring justice into human relations, to put an end to the division of human beings, as animals, into classes; to bring about brotherhood amongst peoples and forever to abolish the mailed fist and mutual extermination.'[68]

It really does seem as if the AWE is a supporter of the realisation of the ideals of socialism, does it not? For all their hatred of social democracy, the equality campaigners nonetheless cling to the edges of the socialist banner. Renouncing socialism would mean openly acknowledging that they belong to the bourgeois world and truly alienating from themselves the element of the female population whom they must make special efforts to attract. After all, the Alliance never lose hope of rallying all democratically minded women under their banner.[69] The position of the equality campaigners under these conditions is quite difficult, but there is a way out: Give up their hatred for *orthodox* Marxism and proclaim themselves supporters of *'revisionism'*; the benefit of this vague concept is that the most eclectic theories can be included within it, and, most importantly, it allows for the possibility of rejecting the principle of class struggle:

> Where orthodox Marxism sees only the irreversible current of a latent process guided by economic movements, critical socialism sees a broad arena of struggle not only of overriding economic drives, but also of self-sufficient psychic impulses . . .
>
> Contrary to orthodox Marxism, which calls for a break, at least in the remote future, that is created by means of a long historical process

---

выяснить этотъ вопросъ. Безъ этого единенiя великая цѣль женскаго движенiя—равенство и справедливость въ человѣческихъ отношенiяхъ—долго еще не будетъ достигнута. Мы должны обнародовать своего рода манифестъ, дабы невозможно было расколоть женское движенiе и помѣшать его работѣ.

* In original: *Избирательное право не есть конечная цѣль женскаго движенiя. Оно — только ближайшая цѣль, средство, рычагъ къ достиженiю главной цѣли. Главная-же цѣль заключается въ томъ, чтобы, при участiи женщинъ въ общественной и государственной жизни, внести справедливость въ человѣческiя отношенiя, положить конецъ дѣленiю людей, какъ животныхъ, на классы; внести братство между народами и упразднить навсегда вооруженный кулакъ и взаимное истребленiе.*

of social foundations, critical socialism seeks to *recreate*; the tool that critical socialism has selected, the means of attaining its goal is a cultural and legal struggle, broad *democratism*. Not only by means of economic struggle, not only by means of sharpening class instinct, not by cries of hostility and preaching of a takeover, but by means of long, insistent cultural and educational work, by awakening legal awareness, by means of broad socio-economic reform efforts will that high degree of *culture and power*, holding within itself the basis of new creation, which, at the same time, is the transitional phase from democracy to socialism, be attained.'[70]

Thus, 'broad democratism' is the slogan that inconspicuously replaces 'socialism'; 'cultural and educational work' and a peaceful path of 'broad social reformism' are the substitute for 'cries of hostility and preaching of a takeover.' In a word, the unpleasant fact of class struggle is omitted and replaced by peaceful, amicable cooperation of all women, which better suits the goals of the Alliance. The path to socialism, cleared of all the sharp-edged stones deliberately placed upon it by social democracy, becomes a pleasant, entirely safe trail that gradually, imperceptibly leads humanity to a goal that is remote, but, to be fair, not bad – a socialist system . . . Socialist ideals in themselves are not frightening; it is just social democrats, that restless, impatient party brimming with hatred for all things bourgeois, that make them 'dangerous'. And the AWE shares their

---

* In original: 'Тамъ, гдѣ ортодоксальный марксизмъ усматриваетъ только безповоротное теченіе стихійнаго процесса, направляемаго экономическимъ движеніемъ, критическій соціализмъ видитъ широкую арену борьбы не только всеподчи-няющихъ экономическихъ двигателей, но и самодовлѣющихъ психическихъ импульсовъ . . .', 'Въ противоположность ортодоксальному марксизму, призывающему къ разрушенію, хотя-бы и въ отдаленномъ будущемъ, создавшихся путемъ долгаго историческаго процесса общественныхъ устоевъ, критическій соціализмъ стремится къ ихъ пересозданію; орудіе, которое избралъ критическій соціализмъ, средство, которымъ онъ надѣется достичь своей цѣли,—это культурно-правовая борьба, это широкій демократизмъ. Не только путемъ экономической борьбы, не только путемъ обостренія классоваго инстинкта,—не криками вражды и проповѣдью захвата но путемъ долгой и упорной культурно-просвѣтительной работы, путемъ пробужденія правосознанія, путемъ широкаго соціально-экономическаго реформаторства будетъ достигнута та высокая степень культуры и. власти, таящая въ себѣ залогъ новаго творчества, которая вмѣстѣ съ тѣмъ явится переходной ступенью отъ демократіи къ соціализму.'

frank hostility; blinded by class interest, they are willing to heap upon it every imaginable fabrication and libel, claiming, for example, that

> very many, entirely sincere supporters of the idea of equal rights . . . take a totally negative stance towards the so-called women's move-ment, to women's efforts towards the partial satisfaction of their de-mands and the creation of a political organisation of women. They link the solution of the female question with the moment of the liquida-tion of the current political system and its replacement with a socialist system, and call upon women to struggle together with them for the economic emancipation of all the working masses.[71*]

Incidentally, let us also recall here how the representative of the Alli-ance for Women's Equality observed at the Amsterdam congress that 'the social democrats prefer, with women's help, to make themselves lords over the situation, and only then grace us . . . ' and also that 'with the exception of Bebel and a number of other distinguished people who un-derstand the true interests of humanity and have the courage to fight for them, the party, as a whole, was indecisive, and their attitude towards us was rather more hostile than favourable.'[72†]

It would just be interesting to know where *Soyuz Zhenshchin* came up with the idea that the party 'takes a totally negative stance towards the so-called women's movement' and links the solution of the female question 'with the moment of the liquidation of the current political (?) system and its replacement with a socialist system', that the party is

---

* In original: *оченьмногіеипритомъвесьмаискреннiе сторонники идеиравноправiя. . . относятся вполнѣ отрицательно къ такъ называемому женскому движенiю, къ стремленiю женщинъ къ частичному удовлетворенiю своихъ требованiй и созданiю—женской политической организацiи. Они связываютъ разрѣшенiе женскаго вопроса съ моментомъ ликвидацiи современнаго политическаго строя и замѣной его строемъ соцiалистическимъ и призываютъ женщинъ къ совмѣстной съ ними борьбѣ за экономическое освобожденiе всѣхъ трудящихся массъ.*

† In original: „*соцiал-демократы предпочитаютъ сдѣлаться, при содѣйствiи женщинъ, господами положенiя и тогда только помиловать насъ . . . ', „за исключенiемъ Бебеля и нѣкоторыхъ другихъ выдающихся людей, понявшихъ истинные интересы человѣчества и имѣющихъ мужество боротьсяза нихъ, партiя, въ общемъ, была нерѣшительной и скорѣе враждебной, чѣмъ благосклонной къ намъ.*"

rather 'hostile' towards women, etc. Without actual facts supporting the hostility of this party to the women's liberation movement, the equality campaigners of the AWE are forced to resort to convoluted logical constructs that allegedly lead to the conclusion that orthodox Marxism

> offers no justification for agitation in the interest of women's equality, or any other agitation based on legalism, or any other movement diverging from them in its understanding of historical and economic development and the evaluation of the factors on which it is based. This dismissive, and occasionally hostile attitude towards the women's movement flows *quite naturally and even logically* from its fundamental *dogma* and *theoretical constructs.*[73]*

The equality campaigners deliberately conflate bourgeois women's struggle for their narrow-class rights and privileges with working-class women's struggles for truly universal emancipation of women, and, having made this substitution, lightly reproach the workers' party for not wishing to applaud their efforts to bring about the rule of bourgeois women together with bourgeois men . . .

Our equality campaigners, however, follow the recipe of their comrades abroad. The most radical wing of feminism abroad, too, is not averse to dreaming of a future socialist system; there, too, cooperation amongst women takes the place of class struggle; there, too, the feminists turn against the workers' party and cooperate ever more closely with the liberal bourgeoisie, whilst continuing to try to win over proletarian women and convince them that the theory of class struggle is an 'outdated and unscientific doctrine'. This duplicity of feminist organisations is their most dangerous property, dangerous for the less conscious strata of the female proletarian population. If the AWE had the courage to admit that they are an organisation that exclusively serves bourgeois women, an organisation that pursues *democratic* goals and does not seek to act as leaders of the

---

* In original: *агитація въ пользу женскаго равноправія не оправдывается, какъ и всякая другая агитація, въ основѣ которой лежитъ правовая идея, какъ всякое другое движеніе, расходящееся съ нимъ въ пониманіи историкоэкономическаго развитія и въ оцѣнкѣ основныхъ его факторовъ. Это пренебрежительное и подъ-часъ враждебное отношеніе къ женскому движенію вытекаетъ изъ основной его догмы и теоретическихъ построеній вполнѣ естественно и даже логически.*

female proletariat, it could only be welcomed as one more organisation in the opposition. But, although the AWE has in fact long since cut off the few threads that had linked it to the people's parties in the first days of its existence, although, in practice, they adhere to the declaration of one of the prominent German feminists that 'we, the women of the bourgeois class, cannot support the class politics of social democracy,' the Alliance does not yet wish to throw off the socialist cloak it donned back in 1905. And this fact must be taken into account: The equality campaigners' deliberate blurring of their class character can do great harm to the proletarian women's movement. As such, we must undertake all efforts to strip the left-wing feminists of the socialist cover they wrap themselves in and reveal the true *bourgeois face* of this women's organisation that claims to be 'cross-class' and 'nonpartisan'. Women of the working class will derive the greatest benefit not from blurring the class aspirations of the various social groups of women fighting for their emancipation, but from clearly delineating these aspirations and objectives.

If there is no place for proletarian women in an organisation that tears up the banner of the workers' party whilst continuing to wave a few scraps of these banners to attract gullible and naïve women's hearts, then working-class women have even less in common with another political organisation of women: the Women's Progressive Party. As has already been noticed, this party is politically to the right of the Alliance and even more prominently bears the imprint of bourgeois feminism. The political desires of the Progressives, of course, are more modest than those of the Alliance. The Progressive programme omits the question of struggling for general political liberation and forthrightly states that its task is struggling for the political equality of women. Based on the proposition that 'political equality is one of the main causes of women's enslavement' (*политическое равноправие является одной из главных причин порабощения женщины*), there is not a peep from the Progressives about struggling with the existing socio-economic conditions that burden and oppress women to an even greater extent than political disenfranchisement. Political and civil equality – that is the slogan of the Progressive Party.

And how exactly does the Women's Progressive Party define political equality for women? What are their demands?

'Election of legislators by all citizens having reached the age of 25 without distinction as to sex; active and passive suffrage for all citizens without regard to sex; organisation of local authorities based on the same principles as the legislature.'*

Thus, we see that the Progressive programme includes a demand for *universal* suffrage for citizens at least 25 years of age. But why do the Progressives not discuss their demands in detail? Why are they silent on the question of whether 'active and passive suffrage for all citizens' means *direct and equal* voting rights?

Judging from the face of the Party and the spirit that permeates it, the Progressives, if they were sincere, would need to take a position in their programme either in favour of indirect elections or in favour of unequal property-qualified representation. Indirect elections are an excellent filter for elements of society that are detrimental to 'high politics' and the most reliable way to guarantee 'the light of modern culture' – the bourgeois intelligentsia – a place in the legislature. In increasing the voting age from 21 to 25, the Women's Party shows a doubtless tendency to introduce a restrictive principle into the determination of the legal capacity of citizens at least in this regard. No matter how much the Progressives seek to assure us that they would never dream of limiting anyone's rights,[74] increasing the voting age shows their sympathy for property qualifications; after all, this age restriction is a sort of property qualification in itself, the full weight of which falls upon the working class, where a person's conscious life begins significantly earlier, and where political self-definition develops with greater intensity at a younger age. The cautious formulation of the fundamental demand of the programme of the WPP is even more characteristic in that it was drafted at a heightened period in the political life of Russia, the spring of 1906, when no dissonance could yet

---

* In original: *Избраніе народныхъ представителей всѣми гражданами, достигшими 25-лѣтняго возраста, безъ различія пола; предоставленіе всѣмъ гражданамъ, независимо отъ пола; активныхъ и пассивныхъ избирательныхъ правъ; организація мѣстнаго самоуправленія на тѣхъ-же началахъ, на какихъ покоится народное представительство.*

be heard between the radicalism of the political slogans and the dying down of that radicalism in reality.

Also striking is the extremely nebulous phrasing of another essential demand: Civil equality for women. The relevant point in the programme reads: 'The existing criminal and civil laws must be revised with the participation of women.' (*Существующие законы уголовные и гражданские должны быть пересмотрены при участии женщин.*) Not a word about the basis of this revision; meanwhile, this demand would most immediately serve the interests specifically of women of the *haute bourgeoisie*, members of the WPP. The Alliance for Women's Equality not only took a more definite position, but also did more in practice on this matter: With the aid of a special commission of jurists, the Alliance reviewed a number of Russian civil laws, making amendments in the appropriate places in the interests of equalising the civil rights of the sexes.[75] This work was submitted to the equality subcommittee of the first State Duma; in this sense, the Alliance proved more active in this regard than the Progressives. Meanwhile, *Zhenskiy Vyestnik* paid particular attention to the civil equality of women, and it could be expected that, at least this time, the Progressives would throw off their customary inertia and seek to 'defend' the principles of civil equality for women not just in words, but in deeds. The Women's Progressive Party is, as yet, a weak and passive political organisation, lacking the power to defend any desires or demands of women. Perhaps this is why it did not go through the same political evolution as the Alliance.

Even before the Party was officially formed, some moderate feminists came together around the magazine *Zhenskiy Vyestnik*, run by Dr Pokrovskaya. *Zhenskiy Vyestnik* never distinguished itself by political radicalism, and even in those days of October, it was at pains to maintain its 'objective' tone and its 'critical' attitude towards the movement of the popular masses; in the days of the hottest revolutionary battles, it managed to keep its narrow bourgeois feminist outlook intact, and none of the 'political storms' of 1905–1906 caused it to respond more hotly to the events of the world around it. In a year as rich in societal sensations as 1905, even the Chronicle of *Zhenskiy Vyestnik* maintained its entirely specific 'ladylike' character as always. As if the entire world were making purely ladylike requests; as if the great liberation struggle of the people, a struggle that, incidentally, involved thousands, indeed tens of thousands of women, did not concern the representatives of feminism. Questions relevant to the lives of working-class women, of course, received minimal space. However, at that time, it seemed as if *Zhenskiy Vyestnik* had no interest in allying itself or collaborating with proletarian women.

To the extent that *Zhenskiy Vyestnik* reacted at all to what was going on all around, it did so from an entirely distinctive perspective: Even then, this class organ of the bourgeoisie not only opposed those fighting for the political restructuring of the country, but even those who sought to improve their lot by taking strike action. 'We bow,' *Zhenskiy Vyestnik* says,

> before the heroism of husbands and fathers, but, at the same time, we note that their heroics are not primarily at their own expense, but at that of wives and mothers. In point of fact, working-class men are running away from the groans of their hungry families at home. They find comfort in aggrandising themselves by struggle, amongst their friends and comrades, and then they nip down the pub, get drunk, and go home to beat up their groaning wives and their children who cry from hunger. Wives and mothers do not have the heart to do such things. From day to day, from morning to night, they remain with their starving children, their souls tormented by their cries. We ask: Who really bears the greatest burden from strikes? Wives and mothers. And under such circumstances, men dare to reproach the conservatism of women when the latter stop their husbands participating in strikes! Let husbands take upon themselves the work of sitting for half a day with their children through the hunger caused by strikes, and free their wives from their hungry cries for that time! Maybe then they will not so lightly accuse women of conservatism. Some will, of course, object that men are currently waging a struggle for freedom, for the sake of which all must make sacrifices. Though I agree that freedom is precious, I cannot agree that one must throw oneself headlong into the struggle for it, sparing nothing. I insist that, in any struggle, the number of innocent victims must be kept to a minimum. And now men, impatiently chasing the spectre of freedom that has made its

appearance in Russia, act as if they are fighting on an uninhabited island where no women or children will have to pay for it.[76]*

Need I say more? Is it not clear that right-wing feminists themselves close the door to working-class women, declaring for all to hear that they neither comprehend nor sympathise with the workers' movement? But *Zhenskiy Vyestnik* only expressed itself this openly before it became the organ of a nascent feminist organisation with a defined political programme. The formation of the Women's Progressive Party forced even *Zhenskiy Vyestnik* and individual members of the party to speak another language. In her Presentations on the Female Question (*Рефераты но женскому вопросу*), Mrs Vakhtina declares: 'From all the above, it is clear that we narrow feminists, as Mrs Kollontai likes to call us, do not fight at all for class interests or for the bourgeoisie, as Mrs Kollontai says, and not even specifically for women; no, we, members of the Women's Progressive Party, fight for all humanity.'[†77] And Dr Pokrovskaya

---

* In original: *Мы преклоняемся передъ геройствомъ отцовъ и мужей, но вмѣстѣ съ тѣмъ утверждаемъ, что они геройствуютъ главнымъ образомъ не за свой счетъ, а за счетъ матерей и женъ. Въ самомъ дѣлѣ, рабочій бѣжитъ отъ стоновъ своей голодной семьи изъ дома. Онъ находитъ себѣ утѣшеніе въ своемъ увлеченіи борьбой, въ кругу товарищей и друзей, а то пойдетъ въ кабакъ, напьется и, вернувшись домой, изобьетъ стонущую жену и плачущихъ отъ голода дѣтей. У матери и жены не хватитъ духа поступить такъ. Изо дня въ день, съ утра до ночи она остается съ своими голодными дѣтьми, и ея душу терзаетъ ихъ плачъ. Мы спрашиваемъ: на кого-же упала тутъ главная тяжесть забастовокъ? На жену и мать. И при подобныхъ условіяхъ мужчины осмѣливаются укорять женщинъ въ консерватизмѣ, когда послѣднія удерживаютъ мужей отъ участія въ стачкахъ! Пусть мужья во время стачечныхъ голодовокъ возьмутъ на себя трудъ каждый день полъ дня просидѣть съ дѣтьми, а женамъ предоставятъ на это время свободу отъ ихъ голоднаго плача! Можетъ быть, тогда они не будутъ такъ легко обвинять женщинъ въ консерватизмѣ. Мнѣ, конечно, возразятъ, что въ настоящее время мужчины ведутъ борьбу за свободу, ради которой надо жертвовать всѣмъ. Соглашаясь, что свобода драгоцѣнна, я не могу согласиться съ тѣмъ, что борьбу за нее надо вести очертя голову и не щадя ничего. Я настаиваю, что въ какой-бы то ни было борьбѣ должно быть какъ можно меньше невинныхъ жертвъ. А теперь мужчины, нетерпѣливо стремясь къ призраку свободы, появившемуся въ Россіи, поступаютъ такъ, какъ будто они борются на необитаемомъ островѣ, гдѣ за это не расплачиваются женщины и дѣти.*

† In original: *Из всего сказанного видно, что мы, узкия феминистки, как угодно было г-же Коллонтай назвать нас, боремся вовсе не за классовые интересы и*

even tries to provide something like a socio-political programme in order to show her sympathy for the workers and her paternalistic concern for them. This programme comes down to a recital of cooperativist ideals from a distinctive point of view. In convincing workers to abandon the harmful method of struggle by strike action, which only worsens the position of the working class, because it 'leads to increased prices for goods' (*ведет к повышению цен на продукты*), as entrepreneurs and workers take losses from strikes, and then pass them on to the entire population, 'Pokrovskaya proposes that workers should form cooperatives, the only thing capable of saving humanity from the current "economic chaos".'[78] *Zhenskiy Vyestnik* does not expect much of trade unions:

> Trade unions facilitate the development of solidarity amongst the workers, but it must at the same time be acknowledged that they contribute their part to the abundant economic chaos, given that each trade union often acts to the detriment of others. The shoemakers, for example, increased their wages by striking. The bosses passed this pay rise onto their products, meaning that workers in other trades have to pay more for shoes. They then begin demanding pay rises of their own, which affects the shoemakers, whose living conditions worsen, and the latter then have to go on strike again to increase their wages, thus increasing the cost of living accordingly. In this way, the working population runs around in a vicious circle, forever agitated and finding no way out.*

не за буржуазию, как говорит г-жа Коллонтай, и даже не лично за женщину; нет, мы, члены женской прогрессивной партии, боремся за все человечество.

* In original: *Профессіональные союзы содѣйствуютъ развитію солидарности среди рабочихъ, но вмѣстѣ съ тѣмъ приходится признать, что они вносятъ свою долю участія въ обилій экономическій хаосъ, такъ какъ каждый профессіональный союзъ часто дѣйствуетъ во вредъ другимъ. Сапожники, напр., при помощи забастовки увеличили свою заработную плату. Хозяева переложили это увеличеніе на свой товаръ, и потому другимъ профессіямъ рабочихъ приходится платить дороже за обувь. Они тогда въ свою очередь начинаютъ требовать повышенія заработной платы, что отражается на сапожникахъ, жизнь которыхъ ухудшается, и послѣднимъ опять приходится прибѣгать къ стачкѣ, чтобы увеличить свою заработную плату соотвѣтственно увеличившейся дороговизнѣ жизни. Такимъ образомъ, рабочее населеніе вращается въ заколдованномъ кругу и вѣчно волнуется, не находя изъ него выхода.*

She goes on:

> Struggling against capitalism by means of strikes creates conflicts of
> interests between workers in different industries. A pay rise for bakers
> actually reduces the wages of workers of other trades. The only pana-
> cea for all these evils is cooperation, which will perhaps 'lead sooner
> to liberty, equality, and fraternity and the economic liberation of the
> masses than capitalism, which has grown to monstrous proportions',*

Pokrovskaya prescribes.

Thus, *Zhenskiy Vyestnik* is willing to depart from the usual framework
of narrow feminist objectives and deal with socio-political questions, if
for no other purpose than to show working-class women that even the
Progressives are 'pained' by the needs of their poor little sisters, and to
show their comprehension of the immediate demands of proletarian
women. To be sure, this understanding bears a clear bourgeois imprint;
the panacea that the feminists have so laboriously found is scarcely capable of inspiring enthusiasm even amongst the less conscious proletarian
women, but what matters is not results, but the motives guiding the feminists. And the motives are all the same: Attract working-class women to
their ranks by all means necessary.

In spring 1907, the Women's Progressive Party founded their own
club, the purpose of which was meant to be:

> To achieve equality of rights between women and men. Mutual moral
> and material support. Educating women: Presentations, lectures for
> popular education, etc.; providing entertainment. Bringing members
> closer to one another to discuss and examine various questions related
> to their activities.†

---

* In original: *Борьба съ капитализмомъ при помощи стачекъ создаетъ
противоположность интересовъ рабочихъ въ разныхъ производствахъ.
Повышеніе заработной платы пекарей, въ сущности, понижаетъ таковую
рабочихъ другихъ профессій. Единственной панацеей отъ всѣхъ этихъ золъ
является кооперація, которая, быть можетъ„ [sic] скорѣе приведетъ къ
свободѣ, равенству, братству и экономическому освобожденію массъ, нежели
капитализмъ, выросшій до чудовищныхъ размѣровъ.*
It appears a closing quotation mark was omitted in the original. —Trans.

† In original: *Достиженіе равноправности женщинъ съ мужчинами. Взаимная
нравственная и матеріальная поддержка. Просвѣщеніе женщинъ: чтеніе*

However, despite their desire to recruit democratic elements amongst women, the Progressive Party itself is very selective when it comes to admitting new members to the club. To an even greater extent than the Alliance, this feminist organisation views the proletariat as alien, and feels a sort of respectful fear of women of the working class. Of course, the Women's Party would like to count in its ranks those broad, agitated masses of women factory workers, but not to grant them admission to the Progressives' club, let them sit amongst the 'respectable' champions of equality in their silk and lace, let them debate with educated women; no, our right-wing feminists could never permit such a thing. 'Political calculation' bows before ladylike prejudice. Can we expect much of such a 'political' organisation?

From the moment their party appeared on the scene, the Progressives decided to remain on strictly legal ground. Even in a period of relative freedom, when assemblies were being organised clandestinely all over the place, the Progressives ran to get permission from city hall and insisted on police officers being present during their meetings. 'We insisted on this to set a precedent of women's political organisations being sanctioned by the administration.'[*][79] This method was strongly condemned by the Alliance at the time; however, if this had been the only 'faux pas' on the Progressives' part, it might have been possible to accept it. The much bigger obstacle to attracting democratic female elements to the Party is their moderate political sympathies and their clearly expressed bourgeois class spirit.

Where the socio-political face of the Alliance for Women's Equality places them closer to the Cadets, the Progressives can be likened, if not to the Octobrists, then at least to the Peaceful Renovationists. To be sure, the Progressives take a clearly negative stance towards the activities of the Union of the Russian People, and even discuss measures and methods of struggle with the 'true Russian women' who are struggling in the countryside not only against 'sedition', but against women's

---

рефератовъ, популярно - образовательныхъ лекцій и т. д.; устройство развлеченій. Сближеніе членовъ между собою для обсужденія и разработки различныхъ вопросовъ. касающихся ихъ дѣятельности.

* In original: *На этомъ настаивалось, чтобы былъ прецедентъ санкціонированія администраціей женскихъ политическихъ организацій.*

equality.[80] However, in entering the struggle against the Black Hundreds, the Progressives doubtlessly simultaneously gravitate towards the Octobrists. When, at one meeting of the Party, the question of which faction of the Third Duma a petition on equal rights should be submitted to was under discussion, Guchkov's name was bandied about together with the candidacy of Milyukov and the other Cadets. Upon realising in time that the Octobrists had in no way expressed sympathy for women's equality and never presented themselves as supporters of it, however, the Progressives gave up the idea of acting through Guchkov and opted for Milyukov. This meeting took place before the Octobrists had introduced a bill on *zemstvo* self-government that also granted property-qualified voting rights to women in the Duma. One wonders how the Progressives would now feel about Guchkov's candidacy. There are many reasons to think that they would have preferred to join their activities with the Octobrists; Cadetism, in the eyes of many Progressives, is too 'radical' politically.

And, despite the narrow bourgeois spirit, despite the moderation of the political face of the Women's Party, this organisation does not lose hope of 'uniting all women who sympathise with the cause of women's emancipation under its banner' (*объединить под своим знаменемъ всех сочувствующих делу женского освобождения женщин*). In their defence of the idea of 'uniting' women, *Zhenskiy Vyestnik* gives the palm of primacy in the struggle for equality to representatives of the bourgeois class.

> It is only natural that feminism first arose amongst women of the intelligentsia. A simple, ignorant woman who leads a life full of great deprivations, humiliations, abuses, insults, and all manner of outrages is not capable of considering why her life is this way. As a result, she either obeys slavishly, or, in some individual cases, commits crimes to protest against her position. But a woman of the intelligentsia, whose relationship with life is more conscious, seeks to clarify the reasons of women's cruel fate.[*][81]

---

* In original: *Совершенно естественно, что феминизмъ возникъ сначала среди интеллигентныхъ женщинъ. Простая невѣжественная женщина, ведущая жизнь, полную тяжелыхъ лишенiй, униженiй, оскорбленiй, обидъ и всяческихъ надругательствъ, не въ силахъ отдать себѣ отчета, почему ея жизнь такова. Вслѣдствiе этого, она или рабски покоряется ей, или въ единичныхъ случаяхъ*

Do the Progressives really imagine that working-class women are just 'simple, ignorant women', for whose rights the 'braver' bourgeois feminists must go to bat? Do they really believe that they are doing working-class women a favour by bringing them into the bourgeois feminist movement? Fortunately, there is no need to worry about the corrupting influence of the Progressives on women workers: As much as they talk about the benefits of uniting all women, the Progressives take no practical steps towards proletarian women. To date, the Women's Progressive Party has not made a single attempt to disseminate feminist ideas amongst working-class or peasant women as the Alliance has done. Whether the Progressives feel that it will be difficult to win over the hearts of women workers with the modest aspirations of their programme, or their overly pronounced class spirit prevents them accepting 'plebeian' women into their ranks as equals, the fact is in any case that the Progressives only stand for organising all women on paper; in practice, they are at great pains to defend their party against intrusion by overly democratic female elements. It is their loss, and working class women's gain.

There is one more feminist organisation that, despite lacking a defined political programme, has in fact been participating actively in the struggle for women's political equality in recent years. That organisation is the Russian Women's Mutual Philanthropic Society (WMPS). Despite the fact that this organisation, which is ladylike through and through, with its select, well-meaning membership, is at great pains to maintain its previous 'politically neutral' position, that it continues to carry out its usual cultural and philanthropic work and turns away from broad social objectives, the awakening of political life continuously pulls even this purely feminist society into its orbit and, one way or another, requires it to react to the political events that are taking place. The WMPS has had occasion to submit petitions, distribute appeals and greetings, express disapproval, and gather information. And, here, too, this has led the more lively and active elements of the Society to come together around a women's suffrage department, where, no longer dismissing political and

---

протестуетъ противъ своего положенія преступленіемъ. Но интеллигентная женщина, болѣе сознательно относящаяся къ жизни, пытается выяснить причины тяжелой женской доли.

social life, they carry out the usual feminist work around the slogan of political equality for women. The convocation of the All-Russia Women's Congress is as much the work of the WMPS, or, more accurately, their suffrage department, as it is that of the Alliance for Women's Equality.

But where do the political sympathies of this first purely feminist organisation in Russia lie? Is there any doubt that the Society's political convictions side with moderate liberalism, and that they, like the Progressives, find the Cadets occasionally far too 'red'? Although the Society submitted their petition to the First State Duma through the Cadet faction, this was, of course, not due to any particular sympathy towards the party of 'people's freedom', but merely because, of all the parties whose programmes mentioned women's equality, they were the most *right-wing*. The Society's petition was, of course, phrased in the vaguest, most general terms possible: Deploring the fact that, amongst 'the first representatives of the Russian people', 'there is not a single woman, nor a single representative elected directly by women', the petition proposes to 'submit for decision by the State Duma the question of political equality for women in Russia' and 'bring renewal to the lives of women by granting them equal rights to participate in serving their country'. In this way, the WMPS evaded every pitfall in defining their political demands. There was no concern of a split within the harmonious Society with their clearly defined bourgeois character: The vague phrasing of their aspirations was necessary for the benefit of women outside the Society, for those who signed the petition. The more general and unspecified the aspirations of the Society, the more reliably the names of women of different political stripes could be collected on the petition.

In the same way, the WMPS took care not to make their demands clear or emphasise their political sympathies in the declaration submitted to the Second State Duma through speaker F. Golovin on the need to grant women equal political rights with men.[82] Only in the 1907 report of the Suffrage Department of the WMPS do we manage to find a clear, unambiguous definition of the Society's fundamental political objectives and demands: 'The objective of the Department must be to unite women in (?) one platform: "equal voting rights to men".' (*Цель отдела должна состоять в объединении женщин в (?) одной платформе:*

„*равные избирательные права с мужчинами"*). This permits only one conclusion: In any case, the Women's Society's political demands are on the same level as those of international feminism. Could one expect any more from an organisation with such a pronounced 'ladylike' character?

If there could remain any doubt at all about the political radicalism of the Women's Society, the attitude of this 'first' Russian feminist organisation towards the Octobrist bill on *zemstvo* self-government should have dispelled all remaining illusions. The principle of property qualifications does not perturb our 'women's equality pioneers'; they appear to have arrived at the idea of property-qualified representation of the female element in local self-government on their own; at least, the declaration 'on the need for equal participation for women in *zemstvo* and city government' that they submitted to the Second State Duma says nothing about the principles on which this equality is to be based, nor is any mention made of the desirability of simultaneously democratising the *zemstva* themselves. To the contrary, we reiterate that the semi-philanthropic Society makes no claim to be politically radical, and shows even less concern about attracting working-class women to their ranks than the Progressive Party.

Under the influence of political events and the pressure of the changing societal atmosphere, the character and appearance of our feminist organisations in Russia are also changing. The 'radical' Alliance for Women's Equality, which had gravitated towards socialism and the revolutionary parties in its younger days, is rapidly fading and moving right, whilst the virtuous WMPS, which had long shied away from all things 'political', is gradually developing a 'taste' for political actions and beginning to show a previously uncharacteristic degree of activity. And only the Women's Progressive Party, which continues to vacillate between Cadetism and Octobrism, continues to lead a quite pitiful and inconspicuous existence.

Which of these organisations can proletarian women rely on? In which of them will they find actual supporters and defenders of their interests? Is it not obvious that none of the aforementioned bourgeois women's organisations is capable of responding to the essential demands of women workers, that proletarian women can expect nothing from the bourgeois champions of equality, no matter how radical their political demands may be? Working together with them promises women of the working class nothing but bitterness and disappointment.

* * *

The feminist movement in Russia is taking on more and more bourgeois colouration. Not only is it not connected to the broader labour movement, but it takes a more and more diametrically antagonistic stance towards it. Although the left wing of feminism, the Alliance for Women's Equality, does continue to champion democratic demands, their diligent dissociation from the class party of the workers is a testament to the fact that the spring of feminism is past, that the romantic illusions have died out, that the bourgeois women's movement no longer even finds it necessary to hide its true class nature.

But, since the feminists themselves no longer wish to 'cooperate' with the workers' party, they must naturally seek support elsewhere. In itself, the feminist movement is still too weak to rely exclusively on its own forces. It is entirely normal and logical to seek this support from their kindred spirits in the bourgeois parties. The only question is: How reliable are the representatives of bourgeois liberalism as allies to women? To what extent can their mediation promise real political benefits?

How proudly the feminists list even the slightest symptoms of sympathy with women's cause on the part of the bourgeois opposition! What outsized significance they assign to the declarations of principle that the liberal bourgeoisie gave out so generously during the revolutionary period! Of course, the greatest number of these declarations that, in one way or another, proclaim the principle of equality for women, date back to the 'mutinous' year of 1905. In this period of heightened political activity, under the pressure of the waves of the people's movement that inexorably moved towards them, the bourgeois opposition learned to speak the people's language. Were there any democratic principles they would have refused to write on their banners? Was there any political demand taken up by the masses that they would have decided to reject? In that memorable year, women were part of the aroused popular masses; they were ubiquitous in the ranks of the workers' and peasants' movements; their voices were constantly heard in nearly all opposition organisations. Failing to take women's demands into account meant going halfway, risking the loss of what was the most essential thing in that critical moment: popularity and the trust of the masses.

Over the entire length of 1905, the organs of local government, those 'nests of opposition', sometimes on their own initiative, other times in response to demands submitted to them by women's groups, adopted resolutions in which they pronounced themselves in favour of equal rights for women and men, some in all areas of state and social life, others only in the organs of local government. A number of provincial and district *zemstva* that had spoken out in favour of fundamental reforms in the area of the organisation of the state and local government at their meetings also proclaimed their support for the principle of women's equality: The *zemstvo* assemblies of the provinces of Tavriisk, Simbirsk, and Kostromsk came out in favour of full equality of rights for the sexes; the Nizhny Novgorod provincial *zemstvo* supported equal participation for women and men in small local government units. The district *zemstva* of Saint Petersburg, Yuryevets, Temnikovsk, and Balakhinsk spoke in favour of granting women passive and active suffrage in reformed city and *zemstvo* governments; those of Vyatka (Kirov), Kremenchuk, Gorodnensk, Elizavetgrad,* Simferopol, Ardatov, Dmitrovsk, Kologriv, and Staritsk favoured granting equal voting rights with men to the female population in all legislative and local government institutions. The city councils of Kronstadt, Voronezh, Kovno, Libava (Liepāja), Vyatka, Kutaisi, Kursk, Stavropol, Tbilisi, Yerevan, Novgorod, and Kostroma called for the extension of the franchise in local government to women. City representatives spoke in the same spirit at the district congresses of Tver and Kostroma.

As comforting as these facts may be, we should recall that, even in that heated political moment, resolutions favourable to women were usually only adopted after passionate debates, that proposals to grant suffrage to women always met with outraged objections, and, in many cases, passed by only one or two votes, and that, ultimately, a number of cities and *zemstva* (Saint Petersburg and Moscow councils, Nolinsk and Makaryev

---

* Now Kropyvnytskyi —Trans.

district *zemstva*, the extraordinary provincial *zemstvo* assembly in Saratov, Oryol *zemstvo*, the assembly on the introduction of *zemstvo* institutions in Vilensk, etc.), categorically refused to accept political equality for
women. There are individual cases in which equal rights for women and
men were recognised, based on property qualifications; thus, for example,
the Novorossiysk provincial assembly on reforming *zemstvo* institutions
resolved to grant suffrage in local *zemstva* for all payers of *zemstvo* taxes,
for all persons of both sexes who had completed higher or secondary
education, and for representatives of the professions, to the exclusion of
'labourers', a term that is notoriously elastic. The Chernihivsk council
recognised that all inhabitants of the city who had reached the age of 25
and been registered there continuously for two years should be granted
the right to participate in local government.

Nor should we forget that all of these resolutions were, more than anything, purely 'Platonic' in character: Those who drafted them knew perfectly well that they were nowhere near being implemented; the demands
raised were phrased in the broadest possible terms, as 'extreme' as possible,
so as to have 'room for negotiation'. And, if the representatives of local
government, despite this, were so reluctant to proclaim the as-yet abstract
principle of women's equality as one of their *desiderata* even in the revolutionary year of 1905, what would have happened had this democratic demand actually been practically implemented? Surely, the feminists do not
seriously believe that the representatives of the liberal bourgeoisie would
actually have defended this 'aspiration in principle' in practice.

The attitude of the congresses of city and *zemstvo* figures on the subject of women's equality is characteristic. Despite the fact that women's
organisations submitted seventeen declarations demanding the recognition of women's suffrage to the Polish congress of city and *zemstvo*
figures, the local government representatives refused to consider the matter. This was repeated at the next congress of city and *zemstvo* figures
in September 1905. This time, too, motions were submitted by women
proposing that the congress speak out in favour of full rights for women.
F. A. Golovin explained that the congress did not wish to consider this
matter because at the previous, Polish, congress, it had been decided to
discuss it preliminarily at the local level; at the same time, no responses

had yet been received from local government institutions. V. D. Nabokov offered a different reason for the congress's refusal to examine the matter of women's political rights: In his view, this important matter could only be decided by a future legislature elected on the basis of universal suffrage. By a majority of 72 votes to 63, the congress declined to discuss the motions of the women's organisations.

However, in November, when the wave of revolution had carried off even the most cautious and conservative elements of the opposition, the congress office adopted the following resolution whilst drafting the basis for the convocation of the constituent assembly: 'Russian citizens of both sexes having attained the age of 21 shall have the right to participate in elected representation.'[83]*

In just the same way, the inclusion of political equality for women in the draft plan of organisation of the legislature drawn up at a private meeting of city government figures in Moscow can hardly be considered the 'enormous triumphant step' our equality campaigners present it as. It suffices to recall the vacillations and energetic protests occasioned by the adoption of this point.[84] Characteristic is the survey conducted by the Alliance for Women's Equality not long before the September congress of *zemstvo* and municipal figures on the question of women's suffrage: 35 of them responded more or less sympathetically; 22 were not opposed in principle to equality, but found it 'untimely', 'inapposite', etc. to address the issue; and 4 categorically rejected the need for women's equality. This survey, which painted a picture that was by no means comforting (most of those surveyed did not answer at all, thus showing their indifference to the question posed), is nonetheless counted by the equality campaigners amongst the indicators that Russian liberalism is sympathetic to the cause of political emancipation for women. In their desire to find something that confirms this sympathy on the part of bourgeois liberals, the equality campaigners are even willing to distort the recent past: 'The answers were written,' the pamphlet *Zhenskoye Dvizheniye* states,

> at a very turbulent moment of our troubled time: The crushing misery
> of the people and the cruel oppression of the social movement led to

---

* In original: *Право участія въ выборномъ представительствѣ принадлежитъ россійскимъ гражданамъ обоего пола, достигшимъ 21 года.*

the manifesto of 6 August 1905 on the State Duma, an advisory body with no legislative significance, maintaining in their previous force all bans and restrictions imposed by the police, the censors, and others on meetings, individual liberties, and freedom of expression. The manifesto encountered dismal indifference across the country. It was as if the population had conspired not to implement its provisions, but to go forward on their own path, though it was not clear what path that might be. The Alliance's questions propose a fundamental rupture in the state and social order; it was not easy for people of moderate views to give reasoned answers, nor could figures of more radical tendencies answer with their previous courage; the parliament was forming one way or another, and the attitudes and speeches of visible figures were becoming more responsible. Perhaps this is why many declined to respond to the survey.[85*]

Do our feminists seriously believe that the period of 6 August to 17 October 1905 was a period of 'reduced demands', in which people of moderate views were afraid to break with the foundations of the state, and the radicals were no longer (?) able to answer the questions posed with their former (?) courage?

Fortunately, the days of September and October 1905 are still well remembered by all, and there is no chance of finding witnesses willing to testify that that was a time of *reduced* intensity in society. Of course not. It was not fear of breaking with the very foundations of the state that led the liberal bourgeoisie to view the matter of women's political

---

*   In original: „*Отвѣты писались*" въ „*очень смутный моментъ нашего бурнаго времени: сокрушительныя народныя бѣдствія и мучительно-подавленное общественное движеніе привело къ манифесту 6-го авг. 1905 г. о Государственной Думѣ совѣщательной, безъ всякаго законодательнаго значенія, съ сохраненіемъ въ прежней силѣ всѣхъ полицейскихъ, цензурныхъ и прочихъ запретовъ и пересѣченій относительно собраній, свободы личности и слова. Манифестъ былъ встрѣченъ мрачнымъ равнодушіемъ во всей странѣ; какъ будто населеніе сговорилось не вводить въ жизнь его положенія, а итти впередъ своимъ путемъ, но какимъ именно, было неясно. Вопросы союза женщинъ предполагаютъ коренную ломку государственныхъ и общественныхъ порядковъ; людямъ умѣренныхъ взглядовъ было нелегко давать мотивированные отвѣты; не съ прежней смѣлостью могли отвѣчать и дѣятели болѣе радикальнаго направленія; парламентъ все-таки зарождался, отношенія и рѣчи видныхъ дѣятелей становились отвѣтственнѣе. Можетъ быть, въ силу этого многіе и воздерживались отъ отвѣтовъ на анкету.*"

equality with indifference, but the hostility inherent in that class, which only disappeared when, with the aid of 'precautionary measures' in the form of the requirement of a property qualification, it became possible to transform the demanded reform into a means of tightening the bourgeoisie's grip on power.

The supposed gravitation of bourgeois liberals to the practical defence of women's equality, even in the revolutionary year of 1905, is dubious in the extreme. Of course, in the bourgeois democratic organisations, in all the unions of the intelligentsia that rapidly multiplied in 1905, political equality for women met with much greater sympathy, and found its way into programmes with much less friction. The union of engineers, teachers, the union of physicians, and other organisations that brought together the members of the liberal professions, not to mention those that were proletarian in character, unions like those of the railway and postal and telegraph workers, adopted this demand together with other democratic points in their programmes. However, it must be noted that, at the congress of writers and journalists in March 1905, when adopting a detailed electoral formula, the words 'without distinction as to sex' were not included without struggle, and that only at the insistence of the socialist parties. Nor did this demand make it into the platforms of the academics' union or that of the constitutionalist *zemstvo* members. The 'Alliance of Alliances' itself initially took an utterly ambiguous position on this matter. 'Despite the fact that women closely followed the appearance of every new political alliance and, every time political equality for women was not included in the draft platform of an alliance, they went to the alliance to call for the insertion of the words "of both sexes" in the four-member formula of the Constituent Assembly, orally or in writing, stating the reasons for the demands, despite this, at the organising assembly of the Alliance of Alliances, these words were by no means included in all platforms of the alliances.'[*][86]

---

*   In original: *Несмотря на то, что женщины зорко слѣдили за возникновеніемъ каждаго новаго политическаго союза и каждый разъ, какъ въ проектъ платформы союза не вносилось политическое равноправіе женщинъ, входили въ такой союзъ съ заявленіемъ о внесеніи словъ „обоего пола"- въ 4-хъ-членную формулу Учредительнаго Собранія —устно или письменно, съ мотивировкой*

The very fact that women showed up in the office of the congress of the Alliance of Alliances in spring 1905 was met with frank astonishment: 'Why are there women here? There must be some sort of misunderstanding.' 'But the women calmly and firmly took their positions, and people quickly got accustomed to their presence,' the equality campaigners themselves report.

> Of fourteen alliances that came together, barely four included the seven-member formula with equal rights for both sexes in their platforms. However, women's participation in congresses of delegates had a positive influence on the other alliances. Representatives of the extreme parties, who supported agitation for women's equality, were active within each of them in order to give the platform a clearly democratic character. Relying on the extreme parties, women were able to introduce amendments into all platforms.[87*]
>
> However, initially, 'women's[†] chances were so poor that it was not even decided to bring a detailed formula for the constituent assembly in the platform of the Alliance of Alliances to a vote; instead, they agitated against it, wishing to silence the female question and have time to agitate in the interests of their own rights amongst the intelligentsia. This was entirely successful. Every time a resolution of the A of A was drafted, even allies inevitably forgot about women, and the women persistently demanded to be mentioned in the appropriate part of the resolution. The very first time, two months after the organising assembly, the majority came out 'in favour' of including women. With every resolution, this majority grew, and, at the Saint Petersburg congress in July, women achieved a total victory in the A of A; when it came to a vote, mentions of women were included in the resolution with only

---

требованій, —несмотря на это, на организаціонномъ собраніи Союза-союзовъ слова эти были включены далеко не во всѣ платформы союзовъ.

* In original: *Среди 14-ти объединившихся союзовъ едва четыре ввели въ свою платформу семичленную формулу, уравнивавшую права обоихъ половъ. Но участіе женщинъ на делегатскихъ съѣздахъ хорошо повліяло на прочіе союзы. Внутри каждаго изъ нихъ дѣйствовали представители крайнихъ партій, которые поддерживали агитацію за равноправность женщинъ, чтобы придать платформѣ ярко-демократическій характеръ. Опираясь на крайнихъ, женщинамъ удалось внести поправки во всѣ платформы.*

† Closing quotation marks for nested quote absent in original —Trans.

one vote against, that of P. N. Milyukov. Subsequently, we demanded detailed specification of the formula for the constituent assembly in the A of A platform, and that was done.*[88]

If including a demand for equal political rights for women and men in the programmes of even democratic organisations met with such difficulties in that revolutionary period, what could women expect from bourgeois democrats in a period of political calm and reduced intensity in society?

Not much need be said of the Cadets' attitude towards the question of political equality for women: The facts are all too well known.[89] At the October congress, this question was met with an extremely unfriendly reception; the visible Cadet leaders, chief amongst them Milyukov and Struve, expressed their totally negative view of this 'utopian' demand. For lack of arguments, Struve tried to rely on Muslim women and the danger of 'complications' that might arise from this. Judge for yourself whether it would be just for Russian women to gain access to the ballot box at the same time as a Muslim woman living on the same land, governed by the same laws, remains disenfranchised because Sharia prohibits them dealing with public affairs!

After turbulent debates, the majority of the congress accepted the demand for political equality for women, but 'out of respect for the prominent members of the party who were in the minority' (*из уважения к видным членам своей партии, оставшимся в меньшинстве*), the congress permitted a footnote on the party programme declaring that

---

* In original: *Но въ началѣ „шансы женщинъ были настолько слабы, что не рѣшались вотировать за детализацію формулы учредительнаго собранія въ платформѣ Союза Союзовъ, а напротивъ агитировали противъ этого, желая замолчать женскій вопросъ и имѣть время для агитаціи въ пользу своихъ правъ среди интеллигенціи. Это вполнѣ удалось. Каждый разъ при составленіи резолюціи С. С. о женщинахъ неизбѣжно забывали даже сторонники, и женщины незклонно требовали вставленія упоминанія о нихъ въ соотвѣтственномъ мѣстѣ въ резолюціи. Въ первый-же разъ, мѣсяца черезъ два послѣ организаціоннаго собранія, большинство высказалось „за“ включеніе женщинъ. Съ каждой резолюціей это большинство увеличивалось, и на Петербургскомъ съѣздѣ въ іюлѣ мѣсяцѣ женщины достигли полной побѣды въ С. С.—при личной баллотировкѣ упоминанія о нихъ были включены въ резолюцію противъ одного голоса—П. Н. Милюкова. Вслѣдъ за этимъ мы потребовали детализаціи формулы учредительнаго собранія въ платформѣ С. С., что и было исполнено.*

the point concerning political equality for women was not binding on party members. Keep in mind that these debates took place in *October 1905*. To be sure, at the next Cadet congress, this footnote was removed; but we must remember under what circumstances this second congress took place. That was on the eve of the First Duma, the heated pre-election period, a time when the Cadet party was at the apex of its popularity and political influence. If the Cadets had left that footnote in effect at that decisive political moment, they would have shown themselves simply to be bad 'politicians' . . . However, our equality campaigners object, the defence of women's equality was by no means bait put out by the Cadets to win the hearts of naïve democratic voters, a decorative principle that they would lightly forget when standing at the lectern in front of the people's representatives. When it came to the actual defence of women's interests in the First Duma, the Cadets beautifully fulfilled the obligations they had assumed.

Let us tarry a bit more on this important event in the history of the women's movement, the recognition of political equality for women by the first elected Russian popular representatives.

When the feminists speak with affection and joy of the sessions of 2 and 4 May and 5, 6, and 8 June 1906, they normally highlight the 'chivalrous behaviour' of Prof. Petrazhitsky, Karyeyev, Lomshakov, and the other Cadets, only mentioning the defence of women's equality from a more democratic group of representatives, i.e., the Trudoviks, in passing. Surely it was they who first raised their voice in favour of including the words 'without distinction as to sex' in the formula for electoral law in the address in response to the speech from the throne. 'We are saying that electoral law must be reformed on the basis of a four-member formula. We are forgetting in this first Russian parliament about Russian women, who, side by side with the others, fought for freedom. (Extended applause) We are forgetting that the son of a slave woman cannot be a citizen . . . ' (Raucous applause) 'Thus spoke the Trudovik Ryzhkov. He was supported by Trudoviks Bondarev, Buslov, Onipko, and Zabolotny . . . "

---

* In original: *"Мы говоримъ о томъ, что избирательное право должно быть реформировано на основаніи 4-хъ-членной формулы." Мы забываемъ въ этомъ первомъ русскомъ парламентѣ о русской женщинѣ, которая, на-ряду съ другими, боролась за свободу (продолжительные аплодисменты). Мы забываемъ, что*

Following the Trudoviks, the floor was granted to the cadet Lomsha-kov: 'The emancipation of the peasants,' he said,

> the emancipation of the working class, the emancipation of all citizens, the emancipation of women – that is the first objective of our work. And here, as in all other matters, for us, there can and will be no retreat. An accidental slip of the tongue by one of our comrades here – for I believe it to be a slip of the tongue – directed not to us, but to those present who do not agree with our programme on the matter of women's equality. For us, women are equal in rights to men, equal not only in political rights, but in civil rights, completely equal with no exceptions. . . .*

However, the speech did not meet with any enthusiasm on the part of his party comrades. A typical representative of the Cadets, the slim, cautious Nabokov, explained to the Duma that the commission that had drafted the reply address had decided not to go into detail on the electoral formula for the very reason that this issue had given rise to disagreements within the commission itself and that it would be more 'cautious' to keep it to general terms.

> On the matter of universal suffrage, we had a majority and a minority. The minority were in favour of disclosing this formula, and for introducing universal suffrage as it is understood by those who stand for universal, direct, secret, and equal voting rights without distinction of sex, nationality, and religion. The majority believed that 'we would be acting with greater circumspection and caution if we were to leave the formula we have introduced, which best reflects the actually expressed

---

сынъ рабыни не можетъ быть гражданиномъ..." (Бурные аплодисменты). Такъ говорилъ трудовикъ Рыжковъ. Его поддерживали трудовики Бондаревъ, Бусловъ, Онипко, Заболотный . . .

* In original: *Раскрѣпощеніе крестьянъ, раскрѣпощеніе рабочаго класса, раскрѣпощеніе всѣхъ гражданъ, раскрѣпощеніе женщинъ"—вотъ первая задача нашей работы. И здѣсь отступленія, какъ и во всѣхъ другихъ вопросахъ, для насъ быть не можетъ и не будетъ. Случайная обмолвка одного изъ нашихъ товарищей здѣсь,—я это считаю именно обмолвкой,—направлена къ намъ не по адресу, она направлена по адресу тѣхъ изъ присутствующихъ, которые не раздѣляютъ нашей программы по вопросу о женскомъ равноправіи. Для насъ женщина равноправна съ мужчиной, равноправна не только политически, но и граждански, равноправна вполнѣ и безъ исключеній . . .*

will of the people; but, if we introduce any sort of additional specifica-
tions, we not only cannot state with certainty that it is the one will of
the entire people, but even risk failing to achieve unanimity within the
Duma as such, the majority kept the term 'universal suffrage'.*

On the matter of sex, the commission believed that, at the point in the
address that concerns equality of nationalities and religions, the word
'sex', which had been omitted by accident, should of course be added.

This somewhat belated correction concerns another part of the reply
address, concerning the drafting of a law granting equality of rights to
all citizens, with the abolition of all restrictions and privileges based on
class, nationality, and religion. The failure to include the words 'and sex'
in this section is, in any case, entirely typical; it shows that women can
hardly feel reassured about their fate upon placing the defence of their
interests in the hands of enlightened liberals . . .

However, it is not one of the Cadet representatives, but once again the
Trudovik Anikin who objects to Nabokov's statement on the first point
concerning political rights for women.

Likewise, they say that it would not be a unanimous expression of the
will of the people if we grant equal rights to women, fully one-half of
our country, fully one-half of suffering mothers who carried us in arms
as children. As if women cannot submit their ballot or their electoral
note, as if they for some reason were incapable of that! In a free country,
all are free, and even the rapporteur on the draft said that, in the part
of the address concerning civil rights, women were omitted by accident. Where they were omitted accidentally there, here, they are being

---

*   In original: *По вопросу о всеобщемъ избирательномъ правѣ у насъ образовалось
     большинство и меньшинство. Меньшинство стояло за раскрытіе этой
     формулы, и за внесеніе всеобщаго избирательнаго права такъ, какъ понимаютъ
     его тѣ. которыя стоятъ за всеобщее, прямое, тайное и равное голосованіе,
     безъ различія пола, національностей и вѣроисповѣданій. Большинство полагало,
     что „мы поступимъ болѣе осмотрительно и болѣе осторожно, если оставимъ
     внесенную нами формулу, которая всего болѣе подойдетъ къ дѣйствительно-
     выраженной волѣ народа; но, если мы внесемъ сюда какіе-либо дополнительные
     признаки, то мы не только не сможемъ съ увѣренностью сказать, что это есть
     единственная воля всего народа, но даже рискуемъ не получить единогласія
     въ Думѣ"; и поэтому, большинство осталось при терминѣ „всеобщаго
     избирательнаго права"*

omitted deliberately, and that deliberate omission is criminal. I think that their civil rights must be confirmed.*

By this, Nabokov is already moved to make a more definite statement of the actual stance, if not of all Cadets, then of an influential segment of the party, on the matter of political equality for women:

> I must emphasise that which I already had the honour to discuss; on this matter, we, for example, who belong to the People's Freedom Party, did not bargain off our convictions, and spoke of the formula that, in our view, unites the whole people and can be adopted. The previous speaker may be correct; for us, i.e., the majority, we are not fully and definitely convinced of it. We would not dare to state that the unanimous will of the people demands political equality for women, and we did not speak of any such unanimous popular will. If we are wrong about that, then that is the only thing we are wrong about.†

He is supported by Prince Shakovskoy. Shakovskoy, too, defends the commission's draft, deeming it necessary to postpone a decision on the matter of direct elections and women's rights until such time as the corresponding law is being drafted. The Duma, in his view, only had to

---

* In original: *Точно также говорятъ, не будетъ единодушнымъ выраженіе воли народа, если мы уравняемъ въ правахъ женщинъ, цѣлую половину нашей страны, цѣлую половину страдающихъ матерей, выносившихъ насъ на рукахъ, какъ дѣтей. Какъ будто женщина не можетъ, положить свой избирательный шаръ или подать свою избирательную записку, какъ будто-бы она почему-то этого не можетъ сдѣлать! Въ свободной странѣ всѣ свободны, и самъ докладчикъ проекта, сказалъ, что въ части адреса, гдѣ говорится о гражданскихъ правахъ, по недосмотру пропущены женщины. Если онѣ тамъ пропущены по недосмотру, то здѣсь онѣ пропущены по досмотру, и этотъ досмотръ преступенъ. Я думаю, что онѣ должны быть утверждены въ гражданскихъ правахъ.*

† In original: *Я долженъ подчеркнуть то, о чемъ я имѣлъ уже честь говорить; въ данномъ вопросѣ мы, напримѣръ, принадлежащіе къ партіи народной свободы, не поступаясь нашими убѣжденіями, говорили о формулѣ, которая съ нашей точки зрѣнія, объединяя весь народъ, можетъ быть принята. Предшествующій ораторъ, можетъ быть, и правъ; для насъ, т. е. для большинства, полнаго и опредѣленнаго убѣжденія въ этомъ нѣтъ. Мы не беремъ на себя смѣлости утверждать, что единодушная воля народа требуетъ политическаго равноправія для женщины, и мы не говорили о такой единодушной волѣ народа. Если мы ошибаемся въ этомъ, то именно только въ этомъ.*

adopt a resolution on these two matters after they had been fully and robustly clarified.

Frenkel took the side of the 'cautious' Cadets, against Lomshakov and Protopopov, and spoke in favour of extending the franchise to the female portion of the population, and denied that it was necessary to disclose an electoral formula. He based his view on the fact that

> within the confines of this very commission, a sufficient number of persons on the right, albeit the minority, took the view that it was not necessary to grant suffrage to women at this particular moment, and that, in order for us to be entitled to speak of the unanimous demands of the country, we needed to find complete unanimity in the ranks of our commission; after all, we cannot judge these matters as lightly as they are being judged here.*

Thus, even on the very first day of the existence of the representative body, with its unparalleled significance, in that triumphant moment full of expectations and hope, our esteemed Cadets still could not make up their minds to stand openly on the side of democratic demands. They did not have enough 'courage to claim' that the people wish to send their directly elected representatives to the Duma in order to double the number of their voters in the interests of a democratic Russia by extending the franchise to women.

In a touching show of unity, the independent peasant Kruglikov and the Octobrist Count Heyden stood with the 'cautious' Cadets. 'Honourable representatives,' said Kruglikov, 'when they sent us here, quite a few peasants did not even know about universal suffrage without distinction as to sex. Our women are not interested in universal suffrage; our women are there to look after the household, to look after the children

---

* In original: *въ предѣлахъ той-же комиссіи было достаточное число лицъ справа, хотя и меньшинство, которое стоитъ на точкѣ зрѣнія ненужности предоставить теперь - же избирательное право женщинамъ, и для того, чтобы мы имѣли право говорить объ единодушномъ требованіи страны, намъ нужно было констатировать полное единодушіе въ рядахъ нашей комиссіи— мы, вѣдь не можемъ судить такъ легко, какъ здѣсь судятъ.*

and the hearth."* Count Heyden, of course, argued in more refined terms, but, in essence, totally agreed with the view of the peasant Kruglikov:

> I have a mandate from my countrymen to state that they do not share the opinion of Mr Zabolotny that they cannot live without universal suffrage in direct, equal, and secret elections; they find that they can live with universal suffrage, and life experience shows that it is not absolutely necessary to extend equal rights to women as well. Initially, we must first get accustomed to parliamentary activity in the composition to which we are already accustomed, i.e., with an assembly consisting only of men.†

As is known, when the amendment calling for the disclosure of the electoral formula came to a vote, it was rejected by the majority; the same fate was met by the amendment calling for the inclusion of the words 'without distinction as to sex'.

As for another point of the reply address that called for all citizens to be equal before the law, the amendment introduced into the text by the commission themselves, including the words 'without distinction as to sex', was adopted following minor debates. However, this time, too, it was not a representative of the People's Freedom Party, but the worker Mikhailichenko, who stood in defence of this amendment during the plenary session.

A careful examination of the course of the debates in the Duma during the drafting of the reply address shows that, contrary to the assertions of the feminists, the impression left by the defence of women's equality by the Cadets is by no means favourable. No, in those first days of the First

---

*   In original: *Господа представители, когда насъ провожали сюда, то весьма многіе крестьяне и не знали объ общемъ избирательномъ правѣ безъ различія пола. Женщинамъ у насъ не до общаго избирательнаго права; женщины у насъ для того, чтобы смотрѣть за хозяйствомъ, чтобы смотрѣть за дѣтьми и за печкой.*

†   In original: *Я уполномоченъ отъ своихъ товарищей по губерніи заявить, что они не раздѣляютъ мнѣнія г. Заболотнаго, что безъ прямой, равной, тайной и всеобщей подачи голосовъ нельзя жить; они находятъ, что можно жить и при всеобщей подачѣ голосовъ, и житейскій опытъ находитъ, что не нужно еще непремѣнно распространять равныя права и на женщинъ. Намъ первое время нужно еще самимъ привыкнуть къ парламентской дѣятельности, въ томъ составѣ, къ которому мы уже привыкли, т. е., чтобы собраніе было только изъ мужчинъ.*

Duma, the Cadets did not show themselves to be reliable defenders of women's interests.

But nonetheless, the feminists will object, rushing to the defence of the Cadets, the party of 'people's freedom' did an excellent job justifying women's hopes during the memorable 'women's days' on 5, 6, and 8 June.

A proposed constitution establishing civil equality was introduced by members of the Duma; the fourth series of laws included the principle that 'restrictions provided for persons of the female sex by the civil laws, restrictions on receiving education at all levels, restrictions on active and passive suffrage, and, in general, restrictions on public rights, to the extent not impeded by the essence of the duties associated with those rights, shall be abolished.'[*]

This time, the Cadet party presented a series of orators who defended the principle of equal rights for the female population: Kokoshin, Prof. Kiryeyev, Prof. Petrazhitsky – all impressive names. In a detailed speech, Professor Petrazhitsky, to whom the women's petition drafted by the Women's Society had been submitted, demanded equality of rights for women in all areas of social and political life: 'I have been given a mandate addressed to the State Duma,' the professor said,

> in relation to our memorandum. I am in receipt of a petition seeking equal rights for women from the Russian Women's Mutual Philanthropic Society addressed to Deputy Kendrin and myself, bearing more than four thousand signatures, and I have been given the mandate to make this known to the Duma. Alas, the right of petition is not yet recognised in our country, and under the rules currently in force, I am deprived of the possibility of carrying out the mandate given to me by the Women's Society. However, I consider it my duty to provide at least some small support to the satisfaction of the just desires of thousands of petitioners and say a few words from this platform in the interest of abolishing the disenfranchisement of women. This is all the more a

---

[*] In original: *ограниченія, установленныя для лицъ женскаго пола гражданскими законами, ограниченія получать образованіе во всѣхъ ступеняхъ, ограниченія въ активномъ и пассивномъ избирательномъ правѣ и всѣ вообще ограниченія въ публичныхъ правахъ, поскольку этому не препятствуетъ существо обязанностей, связанныхъ съ этими правами, подлежатъ отмѣнѣ.*

duty of conscience given that, unfortunately, the female question arouses nowhere near as much interest and sympathy as it deserves.*

In demanding equal rights for women in the area of civil legal relations, mainly in inheritance rights, demanding access for women to all levels of education, all occupations and professions, a defender of women's equality must naturally also address the question of women's participation in the legislature and local government institutions. Here, however, the esteemed professor with his Cadet spirit involuntarily lost his nerve and hastened to justify himself to his party comrades, who did not share his passion for women's rights.

> The main, and apparently most radical, point of our programme, is that of granting women suffrage in the area of local government and the legislature. This point is such that, given how widespread prejudices are, defending it means sacrificing one's reputation as a serious politician and even subjecting oneself to ridicule. As such, I consider it all the more a duty of conscience to say here that the interests of the state, society, and culture demand that we take this last, greatest step – granting suffrage to women.†

---

* In original: *На меня возложено порученіе по адресу Государственной Думы, находящееся въ связи съ нашею запискою. На мое имя и на имя депутата Кедрина поступило отъ „Русскаго женскаго взаимноблаготворительнаго общества" петиція о женскомъ равноправіи, скрѣпленная болѣе чѣмъ 4.000 подписей, и мнѣ поручено доложить ее Думѣ. Къ сожалѣнію, у насъ право петицій еще не признано, и по существующимъ у насъ правиламъ я лишенъ возможности исполнить возложенное на меня женскимъ обществомъ порученіе. Но я считаю долгомъ хоть косвенно и въ слабой степени оказать содѣйствіе удовлетворенію справедливыхъ желаній тысячъ просительницъ и сказать съ этой трибуны нѣсколько словъ въ пользу устраненія безправія женщинъ. Это—тѣмъ болѣе долгъ совѣсти, что. къ сожалѣнію, женскій вопросъ далеко не возбуждаетъ того интереса и сочувствія, котораго онъ заслуживаетъ.*

† In original: *Главный и кажущійся наиболѣе-радикальнымъ пунктъ нашей программы—предоставленіе женщинамъ избирательныхъ правъ въ области мѣстнаго самоуправленія и народнаго представительства. Это такой пунктъ, что защищать его, ввиду распространенности предразсудковъ,— значитъ жертвовать репутаціей серьезнаго политика и даже подвергаться насмѣшкамъ. Тѣмъ болѣе долгомъ совѣсти считаю здѣсь сказать, что интересы государства, общества и культуры требуютъ сдѣлать этотъ послѣдній крупнѣйшій шагъ—признать за женщинами избирательныя права.*

The poor deputies of the socialist parties! How many times have they had occasion, in such cases, to 'risk their reputation as serious politicians' by standing in defence of women's interests!

But Prof. Petrazhitsky, of course, mostly had other members of his party in mind; it is in their eyes that he was risking his reputation as a 'serious politician'. In order to save himself from accusations of being 'utopian' and 'unserious', he even had to call upon the aid of John Stuart Mill: 'As a predecessor in the defence of this point, I am proud to be able to point to the great thinker John Stuart Mill, who, already in the middle of the last century, took the view that women should be granted suffrage.'* The representative of the party of 'people's freedom' took his self-sacrifice in defence of women's equality to such an extent that he decided to go farther than Mill himself:

> But I will go further than John Stuart Mill. I find it desirable for women to be involved in politics, and that, the greater their involvement, the better for the state, society, and progress. This proposition may seem strange and paradoxical to you; I note some ironic smiles, but I hope that, upon hearing my explanations, you will acknowledge that it is at least worthy of consideration. What is politics, and what does it mean to be engaged in politics? Engaging in politics means concerning oneself with the general welfare; taking an interest in politics means taking an interest not in one's own narrow, selfish interests, but the interests of the general welfare.†

---

* In original: *въ качествѣ предшественника по защитѣ этого пункта, я съ гордостью могу указать на великаго мыслителя Джона-Стюарта Милля, который уже въ половинѣ .прошлаго вѣка стоялъ на той точкѣ зрѣнія, что женщинамъ должны быть предоставлены избирательныя права.*

† In original: *Но я пойду дальше, чѣмъ Джонъ - Стюартъ Милль. Я нахожу, что желательно, чтобы женщины занимались политикой, и чѣмъ больше онѣ сю будутъ заниматься, тѣмъ лучше для государства, общества и прогресса. Вамъ это положеніе кажется страннымъ и парадоксальнымъ; я замѣчаю ироническія улыбки, но надѣюсь, что, выслушавъ мои объясненія, вы признаете, что объ этомъ, по крайней мѣрѣ, слѣдуетъ подумать. Что такое политика, и что значитъ заниматься политикой? Заниматься политикой—значитъ заботиться объ общемъ благѣ; интересоваться политикой — значитъ интересоваться не шкурными своими интересами, эгоистичными, а интересами общаго блага.*

Petrazhitsky concluded his speech with the words: 'The interests of the general welfare and the culture demand that we grant women political, i.e., social, rights and duties."

Despite the beautiful form of this speech, the esteemed professor's argument hardly sounded convincing; he built his case for recognising women's equality on the usual ideological foundation of bourgeois liberalism: 'elevating the culture', the principle of the 'general welfare', the principles of 'justice', 'humanity', etc. Not a word about the growing significance of women's labour in the economic lives of peoples; not a word about the political significance that the extension of the franchise to women would have for democracy. Most characteristic of all, however, is the fact that, in defending the *principle* of equality for women, the esteemed professor hastened first to calm public opinion with the caveat that the propositions he put forward were still far from establishing real equality of the sexes *in fact*.

> If our propositions on women's participation in administration, on the civil service, participation in the legislature, etc., become law, it would be naïve to think that such laws would result in actual equality for women in the area of administration, the legislature, etc. Old prejudices, the selfish interests of the representatives of the privileged sex, and other obstacles, particularly initially, will prevent not only actual equality and justice, but even any movement in that direction, for a long time yet. Only a relatively small number of women, only those who are especially and extremely sensible and outstanding, indeed, more sensible and outstanding than the men competing with them as candidates for the office of deputies, administrators, etc., will actually attain those rights.†

---

* In original: *Интересы общаго блага и культуры требуютъ отъ насъ, чтобы мы предоставили женщинамъ политическія, т. е. общественныя права и обязанности.*

† In original: *Если наши положенія относительно участія женщинъ въ управленіи, относительно государственной службы, участія въ народномъ представительствѣ и т. д., сдѣлаются закономъ, то наивно было-бы думать, будто на основаніи этихъ законовъ получится фактическое равенство женщинъ въ области администраціи, народнаго представительства и т. д. Старые предразсудки, эгоистическіе интересы представителей привиллегированнаго пола и другія препятствія будутъ еще долго, съ особенною силою въ началѣ,*

In other words: 'Don't be afraid to recognise women's equality *in principle*, dear comrades; in practical reality, this aspiration is still far from being realised.' Obviously, such a refrain was necessary in order to incline the Cadet majority of the First Duma in favour of women's equality.

The diplomatic note that was sounded each time by the Cadets' orators when the subject of women's equality came up showed that, although the overall mood of the country and the Cadets' efforts to maintain their popularity forced them to express sympathy to women's democratic demands, on the other hand, the 'responsible position' of the party, from which they conducted negotiations about establishing a Cadet ministry, required them to remain within the confines of 'caution' and 'Realpolitik'. This duplicitous situation also led to the ambiguous position adopted by the Cadets on the matter of women's equality.

The Cadets were unable to highlight their 'progressiveness' on this issue even at the expense of the 'right-wing' opponents of women's equality. The Right, in the person of Count Heyden, did not so much dispute the principle itself as raise the 'complexities' and 'difficulties' of putting it into practice. 'These rights (i.e., women's rights),' said Heyden,

> are also extremely complex given their attendant effects on family law.
>
> Currently, the wife follows the husband; consequently, if the wife leaves her husband, the family, under our laws, is grouped around the husband. If wives are given equality in rights to husbands, it will be necessarily immediately to draft a law on the dissolution of spousal cohabitation, to draft a law on the parent to whom the children of separated spouses will go. Nothing can be done about this with the stroke of a pen; it is necessary to delve into the most diffuse properties, the properties of peasant life, where, for example, in the area of land ownership, by custom, the daughter does not inherit from the father if there are living brothers. Consequently, the entire communal structure is built on units of the male sex. Once women have equality,

---

мѣшать не только достиженію полнаго равенства и справедливости, но даже нѣкоторому приближенію къ этому. Лишь сравнительно-немногія женщины, лишь особенно и чрезвычайно дѣльныя и выдающіяся, гораздо болѣе дѣльныя и выдающіяся, чѣмъ конкурирующіе съ ними въ качествѣ кандидатовъ въ депутаты, въ администраторы и т. д. мужчины, фактически достигаютъ соотвѣтственныхъ правъ.

of course, they must also have rights in the community and rights to peasant property. As such, this brings up truly expansive issues that are by no means so easy to address.*

Heyden was seconded by Prof. Kovalevsky:

Equal rights within the state also impose equal duties upon citizens. As such, discussing the matter of political equality for women immediately raises the issue of whether to extend to compulsory military service to women; shall we form a corps of Amazons, or not? In all probability, no one is planning to form a corps of Amazons. In this regard, it will be necessary to make the same amendment the English have made since the days of Elizabeth and the first codifiers of the common law, including Judge Coke. The English express this with the famous aphorism: Parliament can do anything, but it cannot turn a man into a woman and a woman into a man.†

---

* In original: *Эти права тоже чрезвычайно сложны, ибо попутно они затрагиваютъ семейное право.*

Въ настоящее время жена слѣдуетъ за мужемъ; слѣдовательно, если жена отъ мужа уйдетъ, семья, по нашему закону, группируется вокругъ мужа. Если дать женѣ равныя права съ мужемъ, надо немедленно выработать законъ о разлученіи совмѣстнаго жительства супруговъ, выработать законъ о томъ, къ кому переходятъ дѣти разлученныхъ супруговъ. Тутъ каранда-шемъ ничего не подѣлаешь; надо вникнуть въ весьма пространныя особенности, въ особенности въ крестьянскомъ быту́, гдѣ, напримѣръ, по обычаю, въ надѣльномъ имуществѣ дочь не является наслѣдницей послѣ отца при живыхъ братьяхъ. Слѣдовательно, весь укладъ общины складывается на единицахъ мужского пола. Разъ женщина будетъ равноправна, понятно, она должна имѣть права и въ общинѣ, и въ крестьянскомъ имуществѣ. Слѣдовательно, сюда входитъ весьма обширный матеріалъ, который далеко не такъ легко разработать. —Trans.

† In original: *равныя права въ государствѣ налагаютъ на гражданъ и равныя обязанности. Поэтому, при обсужденіи вопроса о женскомъ политическомъ равноправіи сейчасъ-же возникаетъ вопросъ о томъ, распространимъ-ли мы на женщинъ и воинскую повинность, образуемъ ли мы корпусъ амазонокъ или нѣтъ? По всей вѣроятности, никто не собирается образовывать корпуса амазонокъ. Придется на этотъ счетъ сдѣлать ту-же поправку, которую англичане сдѣлали со-временъ Елизаветы и первыхъ коди-кифаторовъ [sic] общаго земскаго права, въ томъ числѣ— судьи Кока. Англичане выражаютъ это извѣстнымъ афоризмомъ: парламентъ все можетъ сдѣлать, но не можетъ обратить мужчину въ женщину и женщину въ мужчину.*

Lastly, the third to stand in opposition to women's equality was the peasant Kruglikov. However, his argument mostly amounted to sayings taken from the holy scriptures: 'Wives submit to their husbands' (*жена да заботится мужа*), 'Eve was made by the Lord as a helper for Adam, but not with equal rights' (*Ева сотворена Господом помощницей Адама, но не на равных правах*), etc. 'If we give equal rights to peasant women, what will come of it? What are peasant men to do then? Are women to be sent to town meetings? Are they also meant to be sent to the fields? And conscripted as soldiers? And the men are meant to stay home?' asked Kruglikov.* However, Kruglikov was such a nothing opponent and expressed so little of the actual mood amongst the peasantry at that historic moment that he was completely unable to get the Cadets to engage with him.

It is in general noteworthy that not a single clear defender or spokesman for women's disenfranchisement could be found at the First Duma. The same societal mood that took shape beyond the walls of the Duma and forced the majority of the Duma, to their own surprise, to propose and defend radical, almost 'socialist' reforms, also pushed the Duma farther to the left than they themselves wanted to go on the matter of women's equality. In this case, the Cadets merely swam with the overall current; instead of finding themselves in the role of glorious, but solitary, fighters for democratic principles, including women's equality, they merely had to second the voices raised from the leftist benches.

The liberal bourgeoisie waited in vain for the demand for women's equality to meet with opposition from the peasantry, whose inertia, ignorance, and conservatism would have seemed to guarantee it. These unfounded expectations were dashed by reality. The most passionate, energetic, and – above all – sincere defenders of women's equality in the Duma turned out to be none other than the representatives of the peasantry, the Trudoviks. Though the arguments of these defenders of women's equality, too, occasionally stumbled, though the Trudoviks, following in the footsteps of bourgeois liberalism, bolstered their conclusions with references to 'natural law', 'justice', and 'the people's welfare'

---

*   In original: *Если и бабамъ равныя права дать, что-же тогда выйдетъ? Чѣмъ-же мужики должны заниматься тогда? Бабъ, стало быть, на сходку посылать? И въ поле, стало быть, ихъ посылать? И въ солдаты отдавать? А мужикамъ дома быть?*

(see Zabolotny's speech), a great force made its presence felt behind these external deficiencies: the unvarnished voice of life itself was speaking with the voices of the Trudoviks. For the Trudoviks, the defence of women's equality was not merely a duty imposed by a political petition, but a direct, living demand of an entire stratum of the population, a demand to which the latter's class interests were most intimately linked. The total victory of democratic principles over the old feudal system was the *conditio sine qua non* of the continued existence of the peasantry. As long as class privilege remained in force, as long as even one part of the peasantry remained burdened by any legal restrictions, the people cannot breathe truly freely and stand up straight after becoming accustomed to hunch over to carry 'gentlemen' on their backs. The 'nobility', that part of humanity that is provided with full rights and holds all privileges, was completely opposed by the peasantry, including peasant women. Even allowing that the political consciousness of the peasantry had only just formed, and that the words 'class struggle' had reached the ears of their representatives for the first time in the halls of the State Duma, in some subconscious region, the idea took shape that a peasant woman might be just a *baba*, but she was nonetheless closer to a peasant man than those alien, and even hostile, representatives of the bourgeoisie and the aristocracy. Class instinct quite correctly caused them to see the extension of 'rights' even to peasant women a sort of safeguard against the hegemony of the other estates. It was necessary to insist on 'rights' not passing by 'their siblings – peasant women'.

This view of the peasantry was expressed in particular detail at the congresses of the peasant unions. As early as the founding congress in July 1905, peasant deputies stated that 'given that we peasants, upon acquiring land, do not exclude women from its use, it would be inconsistent of us to deprive them of political rights. This is particularly important in those areas where the male population engages in seasonal work out of town and only the women remain at home.'*[90] In support of his views, one

---

*   In original: *что, разъ мы, крестьяне, добиваясь земли, не исключаемъ изъ пользованія ею и женщинъ, то было-бы непослѣдовательно лишать ихъ политическихъ правъ. Это особенно важно въ тѣхъ мѣстностяхъ, гдѣ мужское населеніе занимается отхожими промыслами и дома остаются однѣ женщины.*

of the peasants present stated that, having attained suffrage for women, as well, the peasantry can rely on this to create a 'second army' in defence of peasant interests [*sic*]. At the same time, the congress adopted a unanimous resolution in favour of granting women *active* suffrage in all representative institutions, and the majority of votes (with three opposed) were case in favour of *passive* suffrage. A number of resolutions adopted at peasant meetings (in the provinces of Penza, Kharkiv, Kovno, Poltava, etc.) confirms that, for peasant men, the matter of political equality for women was closely merged with the expansion of their own rights and was treated by them not from the point of view of 'abstract justice' and other lofty ideological categories but was prompted by the practical considerations of life.

This explains why the peasant representatives' speeches in the First Duma were also more sincere and convincing than all the superficial eloquence of the Cadets' performances. However, do the conduct of the Trudovik group in the First Duma and the peasantry's defence of women's rights during 1905 give us cause to count the peasantry amongst the constant, consistent defenders of women's equality? In highlighting the Trudoviks' contributions to the cause of women, we must once again take into account the societal atmosphere that dictated the political positions of the first people's representatives. To reiterate, in calling for the civil and political emancipation of women, the peasant representatives merely sought to bring about the most complete and irreversible solution to their own disenfranchisement. That was a moment in which the interests of the old and new Russia clashed acutely, a moment in which it seemed that only a fundamental break with the previous foundations would be able to put an end to the hated remnants of the feudal bureaucratic system; and the more fundamental this break, the more reliable the victory of the new Russia would be. Since then, much has changed, not only in the societal atmosphere surrounding us, but in the psychology of the peasantry themselves. The questions are no longer posed as barely and acutely; though democratic demands have not lost their force and urgency, they are losing the heightened idealistic character they had been given by the revolutionary mood of the masses. Doubtlessly, a certain 'sobriety' has taken hold amongst the peasantry. The face of the

Trudoviks of the Second Duma was already totally different to those of the First, and it was totally in vain that the equality campaigners submitted their petition to the Duma through them. Women cannot count on the peasants to be reliable allies. Is it not typical that the peasantry defended women's rights and interests even in the revolutionary period only inasmuch as these rights and interests were contrary to the rights of the privileged classes of Russia? The peasantry demanded equal political rights for women, equal land rights for peasant women, but, when the matter of equality for women within the confines of mutual relations amongst peasants was raised, equality rarely found sympathy; this was the case in peasant discussions of the matter of equal inheritance rights, voting rights for women at town meetings, etc. When a new societal wave once again brings matters of democratic representation to the political foreground, the peasantry may raise their voices in defence of '*baba* interests', but it is also possible that they will decline to do so. The moment in which the interests of a democratic Russia that had taken its first steps on the path of open political struggle openly and acutely conflicted with the old class system, feudalism, and the gentry cannot be repeated, because, despite all the celebrations amongst reactionaries, the old, pre-revolutionary Russia no longer exists . . . When political life flows by 'peacefully', without any dramatic, open collisions between 'old' and 'new' Russia, the matter of women's equality naturally takes on the appearance of an abstract principle that is not directly connected to the immediate objectives of the peasantry, and, as such, is not capable of eliciting any particular sympathy or enthusiasm amongst them.

To the contrary, the equality campaigners themselves are also rather cooling off towards the peasantry. They are now transferring all their hopes over to the Cadet party, whose spirit is much more familiar to them. And though, in the past, this party had more than once given cause to doubt their dedication to the cause of women, shared class interests naturally pushed our equality campaigners into the Cadets' embrace. Perhaps the example of their Western European comrades has convinced them that the bourgeois prejudice against women's emancipation falls away as feminists turn away from the 'nets of the socialists' and work together increasingly closely with the liberals. Bourgeois women, like

proletarian women, are inevitably winning access to one occupation after another, taking their places side by side with the men of their class,
and, having become a social force, they must be reckoned with one way
or another based on pure class considerations. To ignore their demands
and aspirations would mean harming their own class interests, pushing
one of their own into the ranks of the opposition, thus weakening and
splitting the bourgeoisie's own forces.

Under the onslaught of democratic demands from the working class,
on the one hand, and under pressure from the bourgeois women's movement, on the other, the bourgeoisie are forced to give serious consideration to the question of what role in politics women can be given so as to
ensure that they close ranks with their fellow members of the bourgeoisie
and defend their shared class interests together with them. One such
means of *rendering harmless* the women's movement is that of including
women in political life, but with a specified *property qualification*. By this
means, it is possible, contrary to the proverb, to kill two hares at once: In
the first place, increasing the representation of the propertied classes; in
the second, to return oppositionally inclined female elements to the bosom of their own, bourgeois, class. If bourgeois women are granted the
opportunity to freely cast their own votes, they will of course use them
to increase the political power of their own class, and, of course, cease
to support even occasionally the 'enemies of property and order' in the
interests of their female ideals. 'Property-qualified suffrage for women,'
Clara Zetkin notes in this regard,

> absolutely does not eliminate the political disenfranchisement of the
> entire female sex, but is instead a means to increase the power of
> the propertied classes, protecting the totality of the political and so-
> cial enslavement of the exploited masses. It comes as no surprise that,
> reactionaries of various stripes are glowing with sympathy for proper-
> ty-qualified women's suffrage in all countries. Their reliable instincts tell
> them that, given its significance in the class struggle of labour against
> capital, this is not a progressive measure, but a reactionary one.*[91]

---

* The original reads: *Weit davon entfernt, auch nur die politische Unfreiheit des gesamten
weiblichen Geschlechts zu beseitigen, ist das beschränkte Frauenstimmrecht ein Mittel, durch
die Befestigung der Macht der besitzenden Klassen die politische und soziale Knechtschaft*

Zetkin's accurate view of the significance and role of property-qualified representation for women is constantly confirmed by everyday life. One need not go far to find examples: On 28 January 1908, none other than the Octobrists, those principled opponents of women's equality, introduced in the State Duma a *zemstvo* electoral law reform bill that would extend active suffrage to property-qualified members of the female population (meeting residency and rate payment requirements).

Section 10 of the bill 'Rules for the Selection of District and Provincial Electors' (*Правила об избрании уездных и губернских гласных*) states:

> The right to participate in electoral assemblies and select electors shall be enjoyed as appropriate (§ 4) by persons who are Russian subjects . . . if such persons . . . have for no less than one year owned real property within the limits of the district on which, during the three years prior to the election, district and provincial *zemstvo* rates have been paid in an average amount not less than four rubles per annum.*

Further on, § 11 of the Rules provides that 'persons of *male* and *female* sex enjoy the right to participate in *zemstvo* electoral assemblies, but those less than 25 years of age may not participate personally in said assemblies.'† These sections provide *active* suffrage for property-qualified

---

der gesamten ausgebeuteten Masse aufrecht zu erhalten. Kein Wunder daher, daß in allen Ländern die Reaktionäre jeglicher Schattierung beginnen, für das beschränkte Frauenstimmrecht zu schwärmen. Sie erkennen mit sicherem Instinkt, daß es nach seiner Wirkung in dem Klassenkampf zwischen Kapital und Arbeit eine weit mehr reaktionäre als fortschrittliche Maßregel ist. (Far from eliminating even the political unfreedom of the entire female sex, limited suffrage for women is a means to preserve the social serfdom of all the exploited masses by consolidating the power of the propertied classes. Thus, it is no wonder that reactionaries of all stripes in all countries have begun gushing over limited suffrage for women. With their reliable instincts, they recognise that, given its effect in the class struggle between capital and labour, it is a much more reactionary measure than a progressive one.) —Trans.

* In original: *правомъ участія въ избирательныхъ собраніяхъ для выбора гласныхъ пользуются по принадлежности (ст. 4) лица, состоящія въ русскомъ подданствѣ... если эти лица... владѣютъ въ предѣлахъ уѣзда не менѣе одного года недвижимымъ имуществомъ, обложеннымъ за предшествующее выборамъ трехлѣтіе уѣзднымъ и губернскимъ земскими сборами, въ среднемъ, ежегодно не ниже четырехъ рублей*

† In original: *лица мужского и женского пола пользуются правом участия в земских избирательных собраниях, но не достигшие 25 лет не могут участвовать в*

women; however, the Octobrist bill does not grant women *passive* suf-frage. § 13 provides that 'persons of female sex meeting the requirements set forth in §§ 4 and 10 shall be entitled to participate personally in *zemstvo* electoral assemblies, but may not be elected as *zemstvo* electors.'* As if to compensate for this restriction, persons of female sex who, for some reason, are not permitted to participate personally in *zemstvo* elec-toral assemblies are granted the right to grant their male relatives who do not meet the property qualification a proxy to participate in elections, if those persons meet the other requirements set forth for personal par-ticipation in *zemstvo* elections. 'Such persons may be elected as zemstvo electors.'† Adult electors of both sexes who have not reached the age of 25 are granted the right to delegate their vote to a person meeting the re-quirements set forth in the rules; minors are represented by their guard-ians and trustees. Moreover, female electors who are minors are granted the right (§ 12, para. 2) to delegate their right to male relatives who do not meet the property qualification.

The entire bill is permeated with a clear class spirit; its objective is to solidify the domination of *zemstva* governments by the representatives of the propertied class.

Of course, what is proposed is not representation for people, but for property. Both the property qualification provided pursuant to the bill and the preservation of the class-based electoral system based on the amount of property tax paid are a testament to the blatant desire of the Octobrists to concentrate local government in the hands of the represent-atives of property and, moreover, of large property holdings. Of course, the extension of active suffrage to women does not result from principled considerations, but the totally understandable concern for consolidating representation for the propertied strata of the population. Women are permitted to participate in the election of electors in order to safeguard the homogeneous class interests of a sufficient number of electors who

---

этих собраниях лично.

* In original: *женскаго пола, удовлетворяющія условіямъ, изложеннымъ въ ст. 4 и 10, имѣютъ право личнаго участія въ земскихъ избирательныхъ собраніяхъ, но не могутъ быть избираемы въ земскіе гласные*

† In original: *Лица эти могутъ быть избираемы въ земскіе гласные.*

are homogeneous in terms of their property status. Compared to the ordinance of 1864, the 1890 ordinance on *zemstvo* institutions narrowed the group of people to whom women could delegate their votes. The percentage of proxies issued by women proved quite small, and that, given the large number of individual female property owners, quite often resulted in the number of *zemstvo* electors appearing at assemblies being smaller than the number of electors to be elected.[92]

There are two ways to do away with this abnormal situation: Either broaden the framework that determines the capacity to participate in *zemstvo* government, i.e., grant access to local government institutions to the democratic strata of the population, or keep the property qualification completely intact and grant the previously disenfranchised female element of the propertied classes access to elections. For the Octobrists, it was entirely logical and natural to opt for the latter solution.

If the Octobrists had actually intended to allow women to participate in local government, if they had unexpectedly become inflamed with sympathy for the cause of women's equality, they would, of course, not limit themselves to granting active suffrage to women. However, in this case, it was only important to ensure an adequate number of electors of their own class, and that objective was totally met by allowing property-qualified women to participate in elections. The supplementary provision of § 12 of the bill, according to which minor female electors may *delegate* their rights to male relatives who do not meet the property qualification, serves to confirm that the living person, the woman, is a mere smokescreen, a means to create an additional property-qualified elector.

What view do our equality campaigners take on the bill proposed by the Octobrists? Does it meet with sympathy amongst bourgeois women, or does the property qualification it provides, which clearly defends the interests of only the propertied classes, lead at least the radical left wing of the equality campaigners to condemn it?

When, already in autumn of 1907, the issue of reforming local government on principles that would grant active suffrage to women who pay *zemstvo* rates came up, some members of the Alliance for Women's Equality were entirely sympathetic to the proposal, and, though they

complained that such a reform would be incomplete, they did so exclusively on account of the denial of passive suffrage to the female population.[93]

However, it turned out that the publishers of *Soyuz Zhenshchin* did not
stand in solidarity with that segment of the equality movement, and even
added a footnote to an article expressing sympathy with the proposed
reform in which they expressed the opinion that the reform of local government 'must not be carried out otherwise than on the basis of universal suffrage, both for men and for men' (*должна быть произведена
не иначе, как на основе всеобщего избирательного права, как для
мужчин, так и для женщин*). With this footnote, the *Soyuz Zhenshchin*
publishers appeared to confirm that they had not changed their prior
political foundations and remained true to their democratic banner. The
same issue of *Soyuz Zhenshchin* includes an editorial containing a harsh
response to the Octobrists who, before the elections to the Third Duma,
had called upon Moscow women – 'property-qualified female citizens' –
to delegate their votes only in the interests of candidates of the Octobrist
Party. At the time, although the equality campaigners felt flattered to
a certain extent by the Octobrist appeal, they nonetheless resolutely refused to collaborate with them.[94]

The equality campaigners also showed no particular sympathy for the
small *zemstvo* unit reform bill proposed at the congress of *zemstvo* figures in August 1907. The proposed reform called for passive suffrage for
women, but the equality campaigners grouped around *Soyuz Zhenshchin*
were not impressed. Of course, the origins of the magnanimity of these
defenders of women's political rights are understandable. The entire local
reform bill is based on a narrow property qualification, and its drafters ev-
idently were acting out of a desire to swell the ranks of the electors of their
class and, perhaps also, to rely on the female conservatism that opponents
of equality are wont to bring up. In any case, on the occasion of the congress of landlords, where any somewhat sensible idea got caught up in the
impassable thicket of prejudices and caste appetites, even this spark of in-
novation was, if not a step, then at least a slight movement forward [*sic*].'[95]

Expressing certainty that women's interests would meet with little
sympathy in the Third Duma, where 'the friends of Dubrovin and Pur-
ishkevich are given more space than the Octobrists themselves' (*друзьям*

Дубровина и Пуришкевича отведено больше места, чем самим октябристам), the equality campaigners once again mention the intimate link between the fate of the opposition and that of women's cause in Russia. 'Every defeat of the opposition deals a heavy blow to women's interests, whilst every victory hastens the hour of women's victory' (*Каждое поражение оппозиции наносит тяжелый удар женским интересам; зато, и каждая победа приближает час женской победы*). As such, it is obvious that, already in November 1907, the Alliance for Women's Equality held fast to the democratic demands that formed the basis of their programme and condemned property-qualified representation, and even the inclusion of women in the ranks of property-qualified electors did not soften their hearts or incline them favourably towards the proposed *zemstvo* reforms.

But more than six months have gone by, and what grey, dismal, and dire months they have been! Reactionaries are holding their heads high in victory; the Third Duma unequivocally and systematically supports reactionaries in their struggle against the reforms that life has brought about. The demands of one opposition group after another are dropped. Is it any surprise that even our equality campaigners have not maintained their previous position on local government reform and the fundamental principles for elections contained therein? However, one caveat is needed: We have seen no direct statements from the left wing of our feminists in the Alliance for Women's Equality indicating a change in their view on property qualifications. We will carefully peruse the literature of the Alliance in an attempt to find a direct answer on their view of the Octobrist bill. *Soyuz Zhenshchin* dedicates a significant amount of space to critiquing and parsing this bill, but all notes and objections are directed not against the main content of the law – *the principle of property qualifications* – but against the restrictive provisions of the law that deprive women who are *zemstvo* ratepayers of passive suffrage. *Soyuz Zhenshchin* also published an entirely well-founded critique of the bill by the Women's Mutual Philanthropic Society, but, here, too, not a single word indicates the publication's own stance. To what extent do *Soyuz Zhenshchin* themselves stand in solidarity with the considerations expressed therein? Do they have no other, weightier arguments against the Octobrist bill?

Meanwhile, the Women's Society parses the bill from a purely bourgeois feminist point of view. They reproach the Octobrists for the fact
that the new bill restricts women's rights even compared to the 1864
Ordinance on *Zemstvo* Institutions, under which women, until the 1890
reform, were able to delegate their property qualification not only to relatives, but to any man who was property-qualified in the respective lo-
cality. In the present time, i.e., forty-four years after the *zemstvo* reform,
according to the text of the motion of thirty members of the State Duma,
the right of landholding women to delegate their votes remains limited to
close relatives.*[96] However, the Women's Society opposes § 13 of the bill,
which denies property-qualified women the right to be elected, more
vigorously than anything else. The feminists make an unexpected discov-
ery: 'One cannot but assume that the extension of women's voting rights
is being carried out for purposes that have nothing in common with the
interests of women themselves' (*Невольно является предположение,
что расширение избирательных прав женщин практикуется с
целями, ничего общего с интересами самих женщин не имеющими*).
And, in an effort to accuse the drafters of the bill of 'insincerity' and lack
of dedication to women's interests, they state:

> Both the ordinance on *zemstvo* institutions and the bill proposed by
> thirty members of the State Duma define women's voting rights in a
> manner that blatantly contracts the fundamental principles on which
> the right to vote is based. They take the foundational principle of elec-
> tions to be property, not persons; and that point of view fundamentally
> changes as soon as the subject of women comes up. Then, legislatures
> are no longer guided by property as the condition for the right to vote,
> but the person. Many *zemstvo* figures had already pointed out this con-
> tradiction in the *Zemstvo* Institutions Ordinance, which violates the
> idea of justice, back in 1903, when changes to property qualifications
> were under examination.†[97]

---

*   In original: *В настоящее-же время, т. е. через 44 года со времени введения
      земской реформы, согласно тексту заявления 30 членов Государственной Думы,
      права женщин- землевладелиц по передоверию ограничиваются по-прежнему
      кругом ближайших родственников.*

†   In original: *как положение о земских учреждениях, так и законопроект 30
      членов Государственной Думы, при определении избирательных прав женщин,*

Obviously, if the Octobrists had granted passive suffrage to women, whilst preserving the property qualification on which the bill was based, the feminists would have considered the matter quite justly resolved, and would have rejoiced at the proposed reforms. This assumption is confirmed by the feminists themselves in the opinion expressed by the board of the Women's Society on the bill in question. They merely call for the elimination of the 'restrictions to the rights of women set forth in § 13 of the motion by thirty members of the State Duma' (*правоограничений женщин, изложенных в статье 13-ой заявления 30 членов Государственной Думы*), whilst completely avoiding the issue of fundamentally changing this bill in relation to women's rights. The feminists do not protest against the property qualification on which *zemstvo* election law is based, nor do they mention the undeniable injustice of allocating voices based on class, nor do they even demand a reduction or modification of the property qualification . . . [98]

Does it really come as a surprise to see the right-wing feminists grouped around the WMPS take such a stance on property qualifications? We have already mentioned their prominently expressed 'ladylike' character more than once. But does the radical Alliance for Women's Equality share this view? What is the meaning of the Alliance's steadfast reluctance to state *their* view of the Octobrist bill? Does it mean that the footnote added by the Alliance nearly a year ago to Mrs Bezobrazova's article remains in effect, and that 'the Alliance remains opposed in principle to property qualifications'? Or, on the other hand, does it mean that 'without changing their principles', the Alliance have managed to change their 'tactics' so radically that they consider it entirely permissible for themselves not only not to struggle actively against a proposal based on property qualifications, but even to decline to criticise the basis of it on the pages of their house organ? By all appearances, even the left wing of our feminists have

---

вступают в явное противоречие с основным принципом, обусловливающим право на избрание. Основным принципом для выборов признается ими имущество, а не лицо; и эта точка зрения коренным образом изменяется, как только дело доходит до женщин, и законодатели руководствуются уже не имуществом, обусловливающим право на избрание, а лицом. На это противоречие в „Положении о земских учреждениях", нарушающее идею справедливости, указывали многие земские деятели еще в 1903 г., когда рассматривался вопрос об изменении цензовых норм.

decided to remain silent on the nettlesome question of property qualifications and wait 'in the wings' to see whether the Octobrists pass this law,
which is so favourable to bourgeois women, as the first step in a chain of
further victories 'in principle' for women. To the contrary, in this case,
the Octobrists are not alone, as *Soyuz Zhenshchin* itself reports; the Cadet
faction in the Duma, for their part, have decided to make only the following amendments on the subject of women's rights to the bill: To add the
words 'of both sexes' after the word 'persons' in § 10 and strike §§ 12 and
13 as irrelevant following the inclusion of those words.

> If the amendment granting passive suffrage to women is voted down
> in the commission or the Duma, the parliamentary commission of the
> People's Freedom Party deem it necessary to vote in favour of §§ 12
> and 13 in their current version given that the right of delegation pro-
> vided by those sections constitutes some completely inadequate com-
> pensation for the denial of passive suffrage.'[99]

All these indirect indications suggest that the left wing of the feminists
shares the position of the WMPS on this issue. But, *ce n'est que le premier
pas qui coûte* . . . Who can guarantee that, having accepted the principle
of property qualification in local government, our equality campaigners
will not find it permissible to adopt this principle for the national legislature as well? Of course, they will hasten to hide behind a whole arsenal
of 'tactical' considerations; they will assure us that, in penetrating the
walls of the legislature, property qualification advocates are also blazing
the trail to full political rights for all women, that they will also be able
to take women who do not meet the property qualification through the
breach they have opened up. However, no matter how tempting these
lovely fairy stories may sound, they remain nothing more than 'fairy
stories' intended for gullible souls. Their charms are mercilessly crushed
by the truth of life. Examples are easy enough to find: How touchingly

---

*   In original: *В случае- же отклонения в комиссии или в Думе поправки,
предоставляющей женщинам пассивное избирательное право, фракционная
комиссия партии народной свободы считает необходимым голосовать за
статьи 12 и 13 в их настоящей редакции, ввиду того, что предусматриваемое
означенными статьями право уполномочия является некоторой, хотя и
совершенно-ничтожной, компенсацией за лишение пассивного избирательного
права.*

the Norwegian feminists spoke in defence of property-qualified suffrage for women in local government elections! With what conviction they proved to proletarian women that, out of dedication to 'women's cause', they should be 'patient' and 'wait' until property-qualified women take their places on equal terms with men. Of course, having attained rights for themselves, the advocates of the property qualification will spare no efforts to reorganise local government on truly democratic foundations. And? Did the bourgeois women make even a single attempt to do so? To the contrary, they distanced themselves even more dramatically from proletarian women, who continued to wage a persistent struggle for universal suffrage. When, in 1907, the issue of extending suffrage to women meeting certain property qualifications came on the agenda in the Storting, the feminists, with all their class passion, held fast to property qualifications, distancing themselves from the workers, who demanded the complete abolition of property qualifications. They even refused to participate in the grand demonstration organised by the working class for the purpose of supporting a bill that would extend the suffrage to all adult citizens, male and female, of Norway. Only time will tell what position the Norwegian feminists will stake out in the upcoming, spring 1909 election campaign, in which they will be participating for the first time as fully fledged citizens. However, the intention of the workers' party to turn this election campaign into a campaign to win universal suffrage has thus far met with an icy reception from the feminists.

No matter what the feminists say, class instinct always proves more powerful than favourable impulses in the area of cross-class politics. For the moment, the feminists are united in their disenfranchisement with the 'little sisters', and the bourgeois women can, with complete sincerity, speak in favour of the general interests of women. But, once the distinction has been established, once bourgeois women have gained access to political activity, leaving their 'little sister' in her disenfranchised position, those who just recently had defended 'the rights of all women' turn into impassioned defenders of the privileges of their class. This is why, each time feminists start telling working-class women about the need to struggle together to realise some principle 'in the interest of all women', working-class women react to this demand with natural distrust, and, above all, try to make sure that there is not some new privilege exclusively for bourgeois women lurking in the wings.

'But,' the offended equality campaigners will object, 'even if a certain measure of unconscious class calculation hides within our activities and aspirations, surely that does not diminish our work, our struggle for the political liberation of women! You surely cannot deny that we have achieved a number of things in the service of the cause of equal rights for women! Even allowing that proletarian women have preceded us in the struggle for women's economic independence, even allowing that they are practically ahead of us in solving the family problem, in the struggle for women's political emancipation, we cannot concede our primacy. We are the vanguard of the struggle for women's political rights. Remember Olympe de Gouges, remember all the great, sacred names of women, on both sides of the ocean, who laid down their lives for the ideal of women's political equality, and you will have to acknowledge that these pioneers of "bourgeois feminism" cleared the path for all women. . . . '

Let us see whether this assertion is true.

When the feminists paint us a picture of women's heroic liberation struggle, when they proudly tell us of their victories in the area of political equality, they usually bring out their pantheon of women's names, in which Olympe de Gouges, Rose Lacombe, Abigail Smith Adams, et al., those first pioneers of feminism, take pride of place. It is from them that the feminists trace their lineage. And, considerably more importantly, it is to the images of these doubtlessly bright, charming, and heroic women that they attribute all achievements in the cause of raising the issue of political equality for women. The role played by the masses of women, the influence of the direct participation of the latter in the struggle for the political liberation of their countries, almost completely disappear from the field of view of these bourgeois equality campaigners. In evaluating, from their narrow feminist point of view, the public appearances of women in the period of the French Revolution, in the period of the struggle for the liberation of America, etc., they completely fail to take into account the enormous significance that women's participation in the general political struggle had for the cause of women's political emancipation, and they naively transfer all achievements in this area onto the shoulders of two or three heroic women who were able to bring about the feminist movement with their energy and dedication to 'the idea'. Surrounded on all sides with hostile camps of men, the pioneers of women's emancipation selflessly fought for the acknowledgement of the principle of women's equality. In their relentless struggle with the other sex, the first champions of women's equality laid the foundation of the future feminist movement; since then, women have walked on the true path, uniting with one another, and, in one century, achieved greater successes in the cause of their political liberation than women had managed in the entire prior history of humanity.

But were these victories actually achieved by women in struggle with the other sex?

Before us, there are two methods of struggle: One is general collaboration with those seeking to fundamentally change the structure of society; the other is unity amongst women in defence of their specifically female interests. Which of these two methods has actually influenced the fate of women's cause, and continues to do so now?

Let us return to the days of the great French Revolution. Here, beneath the surface, the feminists seek the beginnings of the contemporary bourgeois feminist movement. 'Women's position in the pre-revolutionary era was as sad and bad as that of men. In those days, there was true equality of the sexes, but it was equality of suffering, injustice, abuse, and oppression by feudalism and absolutism.'[100] Women did indeed groan under the yoke of the very same hostile social forces. Peasant women, women artisans and traders were plundered and destroyed as greedily by the royal treasury as their male counterparts; the biased, corrupt courts of the *ancien régime* persecuted its victims, male and female alike, with the same cruelty and injustice, sentencing them to the same cruel, ignominious punishments and tortures. And did hunger, that eternal, constant scourge of the French people in the pre-revolutionary period, spare women? To the contrary, they were doubly tortured by it, for themselves, and for their children. Bitterness, desperation, and hatred built up equally in the hearts of the men and women of 'old France'. Under such conditions, the great movement could not pass by Frenchwomen without leaving a trace; independently of their own will, the representatives of the 'fair sex' were drawn into the general movement of the people, into the great political struggle. Some went there to fight for 'freedom', 'equality', and the right 'to bread', and others in order to protect and defend their accustomed rights and privileges against the 'riotous rabble'. Women left behind the peace of the hearth, abandoned their gilded salons, and walked down the thorny path of general political struggle. When the first thunderous sounds of the people's uprising were heard, the 'daughters of the people' were on the front lines of the struggle for the liberation of their homeland.

Judge for yourselves: What was more significant for the cause of women's political emancipation, for the acknowledgement of the principle of women's equality: The women's societies, clubs, journals, pamphlets, special women's petitions and appeals, or the first sparks of revolution thrown by women in Dauphiné,[101] the revolutionary manifesto of the women of Angers, that first sign of protest against arbitrary feudal-monarchist rule, their participation in the storming of the Bastille, their courageous fighting in Versailles, their active collaboration with the federal movement in 1790, their selfless defence of the 'new' France, their dedication to the cause of liberty? If we were to list all the heroic acts of the masses of women during the French Revolution, it would require an entire book. The women of Dauphiné and Brittany were the first to challenge the government; they were followed by the female citizens of Angoulise [sic]* and Chevanceaux. At the elections for deputies to the Estates-General, 'peasant women and women of the petit bourgeoisie (in Angoulise and Chevanceaux), having gathered privately, cast their votes, and no protest ensued from the chamber.' On 2 May 1789, women fishmongers in Paris sent a delegation to the electoral assembly of the Third Estate in order to encourage the electors and remind the future deputies of their needs; on 19 May, other women market traders, in turn, greeted the electoral assembly, insistently repeating to the deputies: 'Do not forget the people, gentlemen!' The women celebrated the joyous event of 4 August with a grand demonstration. In order to cover the deficit looming over the

---

* *Ангулиз* (Anguliz) in original, a nonexistent place name, for which the only Google references are from the Swedish translation of this text. Possibly Angoulins or Angoulême is meant. —Trans.

state, a first delegation of women appeared in the National Assembly on 7 September, sacrificing their valuables on the altar of the country. On 5 October, women raised the banner of revolt, and, with their own forces, carried out one *of the largest* actions of the Revolution – the famous march to Versailles. After the king fled to Varennes, women expressed their indignation openly, and, following the installation of Louis XVI in Paris, they contested the honour of guarding the city gates with men. Women participated vigorously in the memorable petition on the Field of Mars, and were amongst the victims of the bloody massacre connected with that event. On 20 June 1792, a crowd of women could also be seen on the streets by the Tuileries, and in the legislative assembly, together with men.

On the decisive day of 10 August, when the last hour of the monarchy was struck, women fought in the front lines, and 'distinguished themselves with their fearlessness and courage.' When, like the eerie sound of a tocsin, the news that 'the country is in danger' spread across France, women abandoned their 'peaceful' feminine activities, armed themselves, and marched equally with male soldiers to the battlefields . . . Historians have found that they defended the cause of liberty no less passionately than men and defended democratic victories with their lives. At the same time, women raised their voices in defence of the deprived and needy segment of the population more often than men. Indeed, is it any wonder? The masses of women who joined the movement, after all, were themselves *deprived* and *needy*; all the oppression and injustice of the existing structure of society weighed even more heavily and palpably on them than on men. It was they, the *filles du peuple*, who organised 'women's riots' in order to lower the artificially inflated prices of provisions. It was they who, with their energy and their selfless struggle forced social assistance to be provided to the hungry and compelled a series of measures to be taken against bread resellers.

Did these, and a long list of other actions by the masses of women that are omitted here, not contribute to the recognition, at least in principle, of equal civil rights for women? Even the most ardent feminist agitation paled into insignificance compared to the facts of women's active participation in the cause of the people as a whole. What practical significance could even the most glorious, the most eloquent defence of the *principle* of women's equality have if the latter had not already succeeded in presenting themselves as inspired fighters for freedom, as politically conscious citizens? For the most recent successes of women's political emancipation, the names of such outstanding revolutionary figures as Madame Roland, Robert-Kéralio, Théroigne de Méricourt, Legros, and other 'nameless' female citizens who did not participate directly in the nascent feminist movement had the same significance as the names of Olympe de Gouges, Rose Lacombe, and Etta d'Aelders. To the contrary, these women's names, too, are intimately linked to the great events of the Revolution: The first feminists were, above all, champions of the people's freedom. Olympe de Gouges, to be sure, did not participate in street demonstrations – she could not be found in the ranks of the fighters on bloody, mutinous days – but reliable information indicates that her heart, no matter how ardently it burned with the desire for 'women's liberation', never ceased to beat in unison with those who fought for freedom and to ache with the suffering of the popular masses.

> Faced with the dominant hunger, she, by means of public appeals and her own example, succeeded in getting the entire mass of rich women to gift their valuables to the state with selfless willingness. She vividly described the shelters for the poor in Saint-Dénis, and attentively studied the burning question of growing poverty. To combat poverty, she initially called for the foundation of social assistance funds, but, after she became aware of the humiliation of receiving charity, she began to agitate in word and in print for the creation of exemplary state workshops for the unemployed, which was partially implemented.*[102]

---

*   The original reads: *Angesichts der Hungersnot veranlaßte sie durch einen öffentlichen Aufruf und durch ihr Beispiel, daß zahlreiche Frauen in wetteiferndem Opfermut ihren Schmuck dem Staate schenkten. Ergreifend schilderte sie das Elend im Armenhaus von St. Denis und beschäftigte sich mit der brennenden Frage der Zunahme der Bettelei. Zuerst verlangte sie Einrichtung öffentlicher Unterstützungskassen zu seiner Bekämpfung, dann aber, als ihr das Erniedrigende des Almosenempfanges zum Bewußtsein kam, agitierte sie in Wort und Schrift für die Errichtung staatlicher Musterwerkstätten für Arbeitslose, ein Gedanke, der teilweise zur Verwirklichung kam.* (Confronted with hunger, she caused numerous women to gift their jewellery to the state in a competitive spirit of sacrifice. She rivetingly described the misery in the poorhouse of St-Dénis and concerned herself with the burning question of the increase in begging. First, she demanded the creation of state support funds to combat it, but, when she became conscious of the humiliation involved in receiving alms, she agitated orally and in writing for the

For her, the cause of women's liberation was merely the logical consequence of the great cause of liberating 'the nation', the complete victory of the desired democracy over the hated feudal-monarchist regime.

Rose Lacombe gave herself to freedom's cause with perhaps even greater ardour than Olympe de Gouges. On 10 August, she earned the Civic Wreath for her bravery. She unfailingly stood watch for the interests of the convention, appearing constantly with reports and proposals on that day. She became an implacable leader of the republican and revolutionary women's societies, using her enchanting eloquence not only to propagandise in the cause of women, but, even more, to serve 'the cause of freedom'.

Etta Palm d'Aelders completely dedicated herself to organising 'fraternal societies', competing in this regard with Louise Robert-Kéralio. D'Aelders's feminist aspirations gave rise to distrust and condemnation on the part of Louise Robert, but, like an intelligent politician, once she understood the intimate link existing between general democratic aspirations and the movement for women's liberation, she gradually changed her attitude towards the feminists and even gave space to the female question in *Le Mercure National*, the organ she edited.

No matter how great the service of the first conscious feminists to the women's movement, however, in order for the question of women's equality to be posed practically to society, bare feminist principles were not enough – it was necessary for the masses of women to merge their forces with the general current of liberation in order to show themselves *in fact* as 'citizens', as interested as men in the victory of the 'new' France over the 'old'. Not by submitting their own separate petitions, appeals, creating their own separate clubs, speaking of their rights as women and agitating for their specific, female interests did women acquire the halo of actual 'citizens' in the eyes of their male contemporaries, but by standing in defence of their shared cause, side by side with men as equal comrades in the struggle. Distinguishing women's specific demands in the list of democratic demands was doubtlessly useful in the sense that it allowed special attention to be concentrated on them, helped awaken self-awareness amongst women themselves; but no matter how great the

---

creation of model state workshops for the unemployed, an idea that was partially implemented.) —Trans.

first feminists' achievements were, we must not forget that the very concept of equality of the sexes was born of women's struggle for the ideals of the people as a whole.

In overstating the services rendered to the women's liberation movement by the first fighters for women's equality and simultaneously understating the significance of the general movement for democracy, the feminists are willing to reproach the French Revolution itself for 'not giving anything to women'.

Is this reproach just, and, if it is just, to what extent is it so? The least 'antagonism' between the sexes was felt in the period preceding the French Revolution, and in the first years of the Revolution. When the people rose up in just outrage to break off their shackles, women entered the ranks of freedom fighters, and there met with a joyous reception from the men of their class. Not just the peasantry and the lowly urban masses, but the lights of the Third Estate, the middle and upper bourgeoisie, reacted with no hostility at all to women's emancipatory aspirations in their struggle for the 'natural rights of man'. To a certain extent, they even supported these aspirations, viewing them as the logical conclusion of the democratic movement. To be sure, the question of women's equality was primarily abstract, but even that was a favourable symptom for women. Recall the signs of attention and sympathy with which all three French provisional governments encouraged women's entry into the social arena. 'When the women's delegates,' Lasserre tells us,

> appeared face to face with the people's representatives with petitions or donations to the people's cause, with proposals for services for national defence and armament, when their voices were raised from the remote provinces in statements on the formation by then of squads of Amazons or auxiliary squads for the national guard, when they revealed abuses, injustices, dangers, and conspiracies with collective or individual petitions, or when they proposed a resolution on reforms, they were applauded and thanked. They were given accolades and mentioned in reports.[103]

The repeated attempts by revolutionary legislation to reorganise the rearing and education of the youth based on the principles of equality of the sexes and democracy are a testament to the same sympathy for women and their emancipatory objectives. Is it not characteristic that, not long before the beginning of the French Revolution, a *lycée,* something like a free university, was organised at the initiative of Montesquieu, Laharpe, Condorcet, and other encyclopaedists, that also opened its doors to women. Madame Roland, Tallien, and Sophie de Grouchy (later Condorcet) were regular visitors. In the very first year of the Revolution, one of the ideologues of the Third Estate, of democratic convictions, Condorcet, offered an enthusiastic defence of women's equality, basing his argument on demands for complete democratisation and the premise of 'natural rights', equal for representatives of both sexes.

A hostile attitude towards women's emancipatory aspirations, a loss of sympathy to them, could only be felt in the later period of the Revolution, only when the main enemy had already been defeated, the feudal-monarchist system had been broken, and the Third Estate began to feel that they stood on solid ground. Further support by the Third Estate for extreme democratic demands threatened merely to stand in the way of the establishment of their class rule. And the convention decided to put a stop to women's emancipatory aspirations. In their anti-feminist speeches, their attacks on 'women's mad desire to become men', Amar and Chaumette instinctively defended the privileges of the Third Estate against democratic inroads in the form of a hungry, exhausted, long-suffering 'female rabble' that besieged and threatened the convention. In rejecting the demand for women's equality, the Third Estate were not so much taking a hostile attitude towards women as such as they were opposing inroads by the democracy of the poor on the new rights and liberties. Whereas, in the initial period of the Revolution, women's demands were consonant with the revolutionary bourgeoisie, once the Third Estate had achieved dominance, these demands were merely a manifestation of the burdensome dissatisfaction of the restless 'rabble', that eternal threat to the prosperity of the friends of 'order and property'. During the Revolution, the women's movement had merged so completely with the struggle for general democratic principles that, with the victory of the friends of 'property', 'property qualifications', and 'order', it was inexorably doomed. Women, who had been caught up in and carried away by the wave of popular outrage, found themselves stranded when the declining waves of the revolutionary current once again returned to the shore, forced to passively look on as the boats of bourgeois prosperity passed them by.

However, despite this, when the feminists claim that the French Revolution 'gave women nothing', they are transgressing against historical truth. To be sure, the revolution did not yet bring about the liberation of *women* as such. But is it nonetheless possible to claim that women, as citizens, as human beings, won nothing from the fall of the old, pre-revolutionary regime? Surely the majority of the principles proclaimed by the Declarations of Rights of 1789 and 1798 applied equally to all French citizens without distinction as to sex. Surely the 'liberties' and benefits associated with them also became the patrimony of French women. Surely the inviolacy of the individual, protection from the oppression and arbitrariness of feudalism, and notorious guarantee of 'private property', surely all of these gains of the Revolution also concerned the most essential interests of the female part of the French population. Freedom of conscience, equality before the court, the right not to be detained or arrested other than in the cases provided by law – all of these new gains were enjoyed by women on equal terms with men. From then on, women could freely and openly defend their views. And surely the right of divorce, invaluable for women, that was recognised by the Revolution was not a trivial gain for them. Not to mention the establishment of freedom of occupation and the abolition of guild privileges.

To be sure, the 'new' regime did impose new fetters on women: It was the new regime that drafted the notorious Code Napoléon, which was so unfavourable to women; it was the new regime that legalised regulated prostitution and gave its imprimatur to humiliating regulations for women . . . The 'new regime' also banned women forming 'associations' and defending their interests as women by means of coalitions. However, in this case, the Third Estate was not so much attacking women, as it was attacking *those women* who could, in the ranks of the growing industrial proletariat, stand in defence of their class interests with the aid of 'associations'. Did this ban not do even greater harm to the interests of the proletariat than to those of the pioneers of women's emancipation? Did the restrictive laws of post-revolutionary France impose greater impediments on the labour movement than the feminist movement? Only one thing remained both for women and for workers: settling for the few democratic gains left by the bourgeoisie in power.

In an effort to remove all elements from their path that stood in the way of the definitive consolidation of their rule, the bourgeoisie took little notice of the demands of the working masses and completely ignored the requests of women. Indeed, that is quite natural. In those days, no specific class yet existed whose economic interests dictated the need for women's equality. Women's struggle for their political liberation only could, and only did, gain serious political significance in the context of the overall rise and development of the general labour movement, which sought to realise the ideal of true, full democracy.

In America, where women's voices were raised in defence of their rights and equality even earlier than in France, the same intimate, inextricable link existed between the general democratic movement and the political movement of women that we observe in France. American women enthusiastically supported the emancipatory aspirations of their country and vigorously participated in the struggle for American independence. Names like Mercy Otis Warren and Abigail Smith Adams are not only found in the lists of the first fighters for women's equality, but also have pride of place in America's struggle for liberation. Mercy Warren insisted on the need to separate from the metropolis even before Washington himself had decided to dream of such a thing; the Declaration of Independence was drafted with her direct participation. The demand for equal rights for women, those true comrades of the men who fought for freedom and democracy, was merely the logical conclusion of the general democratic aspirations of American citizens. This demand flowed so naturally from general democratic ideals, its realisation drew such a clear line between the 'old' and 'new' world that the very first two states of the young republic, New Jersey and Virginia, proclaimed equal voting rights for women and men.

However, as soon as the jubilation over the victory won against the old system had died down and the old foe no longer threatened the interests of the middle and upper bourgeoisie, who had established themselves in power, extreme democracy ceased to elicit the same enthusiasm and sympathy from them. In drafting the principles of the federal constitution, the young republic refused to grant political equality to its female comrades. Meanwhile, women themselves, who had joined shoulder to shoulder with men in the struggle and had never contemplated distinguishing their interests in front of the shared enemy, now appeared for the first time with purely feminist propaganda demanding the recognition of their political rights whilst awaiting the decision of the constitutional convention. However, the new republican government was deaf to their demands and did nothing more than to grant women access to education on the same terms as men. That was the only gain the women who had fought for America's independence could boast.

America and France can serve as illustrative examples of how negligible and weak feminists' efforts to realise their demands are in cases where they have no support from any social class that is fighting for its own interests. As long as it suited the bourgeoisie to support women's emancipatory aspirations, they supported their demands and even occasionally had the magnanimity to throw them a few crumbs; but as soon as they felt that they were on solid ground, all their efforts were directed at consolidating the newly won power for themselves alone. Then, they threw out women's demands together with the four-member electoral formula and other burdensome democratic demands as long as they did not meet with organised opposition from the broad, organised popular masses.

'But,' the feminists hasten to object, 'there is no point in taking examples from such a remote period and digging up "archaeological antiquities."' Of course, at the time of the American independence struggle or that of the French Revolution, the influence of feminism on the success of women's cause was utterly negligible; the feminist movement had only just come into being; those were the first, abortive sparks of the coming, brightly burning flame. The bourgeois women's movement has gained strength and significance over the past twenty to twenty-five years, and, in order to evaluate the results obtained by it, we must take examples from the recent past, weigh the achievements of feminism in those countries where women have actually won something, where women's political equality has been won in practice.

However, if we limit ourselves, for the sake of complete impartiality, to those countries where women have equal political rights to men, can we state with conviction that women do in fact owe the victory of their demands to the successes of bourgeois feminism? But do the efforts of the bourgeois women's movement not, always and everywhere, fall to pieces against the recalcitrant resistance of the bourgeoisie, and are the feminists not completely powerless to break this resistance as long as their demands do not coincide with those of a live democratic struggle in which they find active support?

Look how persistently the British feminists have, since 1867, besieged the Parliament with their petitions demanding equalisation of their rights with those of men. The British women's movement is one of the most influential in the world; its effect on public opinion is by no means negligible, and, nonetheless, Parliament persists in dismissing women's demands. If, in the most recent past, members of Parliament have begun to be more favourably inclined to the question of political equality for women, if society, too, is showing greater sympathy towards it, is that not because that demand of women is decisively defended by the working class?

Bourgeois feminists love to point with pride to their victories and refer to Australia, four states in North America, Norway, and Finland as countries where, thanks to the efforts of feminists, the principle of women's political equality has been realised in practice. However, do the feminists have sufficient grounds to attribute these undeniable victories of women's cause to their own efforts?

Let us take the example nearest to us – Finland, the first country in Europe to grant women equal political rights to men. Positively breathless from joy, the feminists praise the achievements of the bourgeois women's organisations, the Union and the Finnish Women's Alliance, and inform us of the extraordinary successes of the feminist movement in Finland. As an admonition to other countries, they note the 'close link' that supposedly existed between women of all social classes and caused proletarian and bourgeois women to fight closely together in defence of the general women's demand for political rights. The solution to the mystery of the rapid large-scale success of women's cause in Finland lies in this 'solidarity' of women. This is what feminists claim.

The reality was totally different. Finland is a country with clearly delineated class contradictions. The bourgeois and proletarian women's movements here were clearly delineated from one another from the very beginning. The working-class women's unions that came together in 1900 immediately joined the workers' party, forming a sort of subsidiary of it to serve the female proletariat. The Finnish feminist movement, on the other hand, bore a clear bourgeois imprint from the very moment it appeared on the scene, and exclusively served the interests of 'respectable society ladies'. It carefully avoided everything that smacked of 'radicalism', and approached even such a unifying demand as women's suffrage with great caution.

At the general women's congress in 1904, which was also attended by representatives of the workers' party, the bourgeois Union continued to insist on equal political rights for women on the existing foundations, i.e., preserving the property qualifications, the four-chamber system of representation, and the plurality vote.

The Finnish Women's Alliance went even further, insisting on granting women only active suffrage. The Union expended no small amount of strength and energy on counter-agitation with a view to counteracting the implementation of complete political equality for women. They explained their approach with concerns about the fate of women's cause: If you demand a lot at the start, you risk getting nothing. One must be 'prudent' and take a gradual approach, winning concessions step by step. However, in reality, the esteemed ladies were quite simply afraid that 'ignorant', dangerous proletarian women, with their 'red flags' and 'red ideas' might join the ranks of legislators. This can be seen from the position the bourgeois female deputies of Finland's Seim took on their current comrades, women of the working class. The well-known feminist, Baroness Gripenberg, a member of the International Women's Alliance, feels no compunction to state at women's meetings in Europe that the extension of the franchise to all male and female citizens of Finland is an 'enormous political mistake' . . . Only the bias of the feminists allows the achievement of political equality for women in Finland to be attributed to the bourgeois women's movement. This victory came as a complete surprise for the bourgeois champions of women's equality themselves. Even now, they are unable to comprehend the causes of it, and do not know whom to credit with this 'surprising' success.

Entire legends are made on this basis; at one meeting of equality cam-paigners in Saint Petersburg, one of the prominent activists of our fem-inist movement, based on the words of Finnish equality campaigners, reported that the demand for women's suffrage was only included in the bill under the threat that women of all social strata would leave the ranks of the political parties to which they belonged. The 'terrified men', of course, had no other choice but to give in to the onslaught of their de-manding, threatening female comrades . . . More thoughtful feminists have a different explanation for this victory: In Finland, the sexes have long been educated together, and that fact subtly prepared people's minds to recognise women's equality. Lastly, a third group believes that the main cause lies in the fact that women participated alongside men in the struggle to restore the overthrown constitution. In that difficult moment, women – chiefly 'educated' women, naturally – conducted themselves in such an exemplary fashion, showed such political tact, such an under-standing of the importance of the events, that men deemed it their duty to repay them, and 'rewarded' their exemplary conduct by extending the franchise to them.[104] The feminists look for all manner of explanations for their success; there is only one that they do not wish to acknowledge: that they owe their victory completely to the working class.

Without a doubt, there were entirely specific, objective conditions in Finland that facilitated the realisation of women's equality, but these objective conditions would not have sufficed had the working class not written the clearly formulated demand for universal suffrage without dis-tinction as to sex on their banner. In the struggle for the restoration of the constitution, the bourgeois classes of Finland were forced *nolens vo-lens* to seek support from the broad popular masses; only by establishing full democracy could the Finns gain support against the threat of hostile influences from without. However, the bourgeoisie vacillated for a long time before agreeing to make concessions and support the demands of the extreme parties. An enormous amount of energy, a major expenditure of force by the social democrats was necessary in order to win the inclusion of the five-member electoral formula in the new constitutional laws.

The female proletariat, in the ranks of their party, worked active-ly in that very direction. As early as the Tampere congress of 1905, working-class women introduced a resolution expressing the decision of proletarian women that they would no longer submit any petitions to the Seim, but would demand and, by all means necessary, obtain a fundamental reform of the representative system. In Finland, the events of October were preceded by a series of demonstrations by women of the working class, which did not cease even after the publication of the October manifesto. On 17 December 1905, working-class women organised meetings all over Finland that were attended by more than ten thousand women; on 30 December in Helsinki, another demonstration of women took place, in which peasant women from the surrounding areas participated actively. Social democracy stood at the head of the proletarian women's movement, fighting for the complete democratisation of representation. Any time the proletariat displayed a certain vacillation and uncertainty as to whether the matter of political equality for women should be removed from the agenda, the organised segment of the female proletariat were able to remind their male comrades with their tenacity and fortitude how harmful such an inappropriate concession would be to the interests of the class as a whole.

More than once, the feminists took advantage of this in order to jab the social democrats for their neglectful attitude towards women's political equality, and used it as proof of the need for a separate feminist movement. In so doing, however, they forgot to take note of one quite important fact, i.e., that the general feminist movement was completely superfluous here. It was not the bourgeois champions of women's rights, but working-class women themselves who reminded all concerned of women's democratic demands and forced the popular masses to take the growing demands of the female world into account. The events in Finland only illustrate the proposition that, where proletarian women themselves stand guard for their interests, where they insistently remind men of their most immediate demands, those demands will be realised the soonest.

It would be an enormous mistake to presume that the feminists in Finland actually played a decisive role in the victory of women's suffrage. It was during the hardest, most hotly contested battles, in times of acute struggle for the democratisation of the Finnish state, that the least was heard from the feminists. Had proletarian women ridden the coat-tails of the bourgeois feminists, had they indeed entrusted their fate to these 'cautious', 'prudent' bourgeois organisations, the question of political equality for women would have taken many years to resolve. However, class consciousness was the salvation of the women of the Finnish proletariat; they remained in the ranks of their party, and, struggling together for the interests of the class as a whole, they simultaneously also won the realisation of their specific demands as women.

No matter how much the feminists boast of the victory for women's cause in Finland, this victory was entirely the result of working-class struggle. That – the fact that it came from the ranks of a powerful political party and was supported by the organised forces of the proletariat – was the only reason that the Finnish Senate, the Finnish bourgeoisie, and Finnish society seriously took the demand for women's political equality into account. If it had only been the feminists going on about women's equality, Finnish society would hardly have found it necessary to take them into account, no matter how great their numbers.

Even smaller was the role of bourgeois feminism in winning women's suffrage in Australia. 'In South Australia,' reports W. Reeves, who is acquainted with the facts, 'the entire struggle for women's political rights was initiated, waged, and brought to an end almost exclusively by men. The role played in this by Miss Spence, Miss Nichols, and their allies was, of course, useful, but its significance was entirely secondary.'[105]

Even smaller was the influence of the bourgeois women's movement on the outcome of the struggle for political reform linked to the extension of suffrage to women in New Zealand and Western Australia. In South Australia, there was at least the Women's Suffrage League, which had been in operation since 1888; also active there was the Women's Christian Temperance Union, which was incomparably more popular than the WSL. Not even this existed in New Zealand. There were no feminist organisations here; no specifically female agitation or propaganda took place here. 'Even with the most generous exaggeration, one could not say that even a single female orator or women's movement leader in New Zealand had struggled in the front lines and had a significant influence on shifting public opinion.'[106] Nonetheless, a bill was passed there in 1893 that granted full political rights to women. Similar bills were passed: in

South Australia in 1895, in Western Australia in 1900, in New South Wales in 1902, in Tasmania in 1903, and, lastly, in Queensland in 1905. What forces, what factors, then, facilitated the realisation of the most deeply held goal of the feminists if, according to those familiar with the facts, their own efforts had nearly no influence on the realisation of the principle of political equality for women?

As the matter of political rights for women grows beyond the stage of being an abstract principle dear to the hearts of feminists alone, and transforms into a slogan of contemporary political struggle, it inevitably touches the interests of all existing political parties in one way or another. Of course, attitudes towards the matter will vary depending on what social group is proposing and supporting it; at the same time, the very principle of women's equality takes on quite different appearances depending on what party, to what end, puts this demand of women on the agenda. It goes without saying that, more often than not, this demand is made and supported by the working class, which has a direct interest in the further democratisation of the state. However, there are political situations in which it proves beneficial for other, purely bourgeois parties to support the principle of political equality for women, when the realisation of this women's slogan is capable of serving the interests of the bourgeois strata of the society. Normally in such cases, bourgeois parties will propose limited, property-qualified suffrage for women; however, it does happen that they find it useful to defend even full equality for women. This was the approach taken at times by Belgian clerics, who had insisted on property qualifications; this approach was taken more than once by bourgeois parties in America, Australia, France, Denmark, and other countries. Women's suffrage is proposed as a sort of antidote to universal suffrage for men. Thousands of hopes are rested on women as a less conscious and more conservative element.

When the conservative landowners' party in Western Australia needed to increase the number of their supporters in order to counteract the young party of the gold diggers that had started to win excellent political victories over the settled population of the territory, the conservatives turned to women's suffrage. The ground was shaking under the feet of the solid landowners; the old, accustomed structure threatened to collapse under the onslaught of newcomers – the party of the goldfield workers. It was necessary to take decisive measures. Granting women access to the ballot box promised to increase the number of voters of the conservative landholders' party, given that the majority of the female residents of Western Australia belonged to the class of farmers and stockmen; amongst the nomadic gold diggers, on the other hand, they were only found in insignificant numbers. In the hands of the conservatives, women's political equality was a trump card with which the 'old men' hoped to 'beat' the restless, homeless proletarian element of the 'young' party of the gold diggers. However, this calculation proved erroneous: 'In the very first elections to the federal parliament, the advocates of free trade and the interests of the working class emerged victorious, and Forrest's party, who had by then already lost their leader, lost their previous leading position.'[107]

In New Zealand and South Australia, the matter of political equality for women was also raised, depending on current conditions, either by progressives or by conservatives. However, credit for the final victory of the bill on women's rights is due exclusively to the working class. In 1891, the conservative Hall, then in opposition, hoping to undermine the prestige of a ministry composed of members of the progressive party, demanded that the government introduce a bill on extending political rights to women in Parliament. In hopes of saving the popularity of the party and the ministry, the prime minister not only did not dismiss the conservatives' demand, but introduced the bill in Parliament. However, the progressives, who had not committed to voters to support the principle of women's political equality and had not wished to stand in support of a bill that had been introduced at the insistence of a rival party, refused to support the government's proposal. The defeat of the bill appeared inevitable. 'But the new labour element,' Reeves says, 'spoke in favour of the reform and supported it on the strength of purely personal conviction without any connection to such circumstances. In this way, the reform easily passed the lower house.'[108]

In the upper house, it was passed by a majority of only two votes, exclusively thanks to the support of the Temperance party, which enjoyed the sympathy of the working class. Though conservatives and progressives in

Australia gave way to the slogan of political equality for women only as a means of struggling against one another, the workers' party fought for women's rights in all areas with the same tenacity and commitment to the cause. 'In New Zealand, as here in Australia, the members of Parliament belonging to the Labour Party, to a man, cast their vote in favour of granting suffrage to women.'[109]

The fact that women in Australia and New Zealand now enjoy political rights – unrestricted rights, at that – is entirely thanks to the active support of the working class, whose vital interests are most intimately and inextricably linked with this demand of women. Is it not typical that, whenever and wherever the question of granting women access to the political life of the country first arises, the bourgeois parties first seek to limit themselves to the introduction of a bill in Parliament that extends the franchise only to women meeting a property qualification? It took no small effort on the part of the democratic element in parliament to counteract these attempts by the bourgeoisie to even further consolidate their rule with the aid of female voters.

If the feminist movement hardly played any role in introducing women's suffrage in Australia, its influence on the realisation of this principle in four states of North America – Wyoming, Utah, Colorado, and Idaho – was hardly any greater. It should be noted that women were granted equal political rights to men in these states back when they were still merely 'territories' that did not enjoy the same rights as states. The population of the new territories was significantly more democratic in character than the thorough bourgeois spirit of the conservative element of the population of the 'old', 'long-serving' states. In the territory, every radical reform in favour of democracy did not meet the same resistance it elicited from the proprietary *haute bourgeoisie* of the states. The territory of Wyoming granted political rights to all of its relatively small number of inhabitants without distinction as to sex in 1869. Later, when the territory of Wyoming was transformed into a state, the federal Congress did not see any need to change the fundamental points of the constitution of the former territory, and thus, women's political rights were preserved.

In the territory – now a state – of Utah, political rights were already extended to women in 1870. This reform was passed by the established population, the Mormons, who intended to include their wives in political life, thus weakening the influence of the element of, overwhelmingly proletarian, newcomers. Here, too, women's suffrage was meant to act as an antidote against the 'machinations' of democratic elements that had begun to get a grip on power. In the struggle with the Mormons, the federal Congress initially disenfranchised all residents of Utah, both men and women, who advocated polygamy in 1882, and later, in 1887, politically disenfranchised women in Utah in general. Only thereafter, when Utah became a state, did the federal Congress restore women's previous political rights.

The power struggle between the various social strata and political parties constantly causes them to grasp at the demand for political equality for women and place it on the agenda at a time when this reform promises some benefit or other to one or another group or party. The American Republicans and Democrats, one or the other of whom have supported this demand, are of course quite unconcerned with the victory 'in principle' of women's cause; any expression by them of sympathy for women's political equality is based solely on the benefits the reform promises to offer them.

The demand for political equality for women is either placed on the agenda or returned to politicians' back pockets depending on the 'political situation'. For the majority of the bourgeois parties, this is a sort of chess move that allows them to pin their adversaries against the wall. However, it is this very attitude that makes the support of the bourgeois parties both weak and unreliable.

Though the working class played a less prominent role in the extension of the franchise to women than in Finland or Australia, though the reform there was, to a greater extent, the fruit of diplomatic manoeuvres by bourgeois parties struggling to gain power, we must at the same time take note of the characteristic fact that, in those North American states where women's suffrage has been introduced, the feminist movement was either completely absent (Utah, Wyoming) or not very well developed (Colorado and Idaho) at the time of the reform. To listen to the feminists, it would seem that the success of women's cause should depend on the degree of development of the feminist movement; however, in reality, we observe the exact opposite. In countries, like the territories of

North America, Australia, New Zealand, and even Finland, where the bourgeois women's movement is still poorly developed, where it is not yet firmly rooted, women are winning political rights, at the same time as in Britain, the older states of North America, Sweden, Germany, and other countries, with much broader and more influential feminist movements, women are still politically disenfranchised.[110] How can we explain this phenomenon? Are the facts discussed above not a testament, on the one hand, to the powerlessness of bourgeois feminism to emancipate women, and, on the other hand, to the fact that the matter of women's political equality has already grown beyond its initial stage, and transformed from a narrow female demand to one of the practical slogans of our day. For the success of women's cause, this is in any case a favourable indicator. If women's victories depended only on the degree of power and strength of the feminist movement, women would have to wait a long time before at last attaining the desired results.

The feminists boast of the successes in Norway and Denmark, successes attained in recent years with a relatively well-developed feminist movement. However, a closer look at exactly what took place in Norway suffices to show that there were socio-political factors completely unrelated to feminism that led to the realisation of the reform in the interest of women. When, in 1901, the question of granting all adult inhabitants of municipalities the right to vote was placed on the agenda, and the ruling bourgeoisie felt in that demand the power of the democratic elements asserting it, they quickly resorted to tried-and-true measures and countered the demand for universal suffrage in the municipalities by calling for suffrage for women meeting a specified property qualification. This reform saw off the danger of an undesired democratisation of local government that would grant 'harmful' and 'ignorant' proletarian elements access to it. The 'liberal' reform of 1901, which included women in local government, completely satisfied the reactionary bourgeoisie, and elicited cries of joy amongst the bourgeois feminists. This reform harmed only the interests of proletarians of both sexes. But what did that matter to the champions of the principle of women's equality?

The very same pure class calculation guided the Norwegian liberal party when, in 1907, they began to persistently advocate women's suffrage in the Storting against the conservatives and the social democrats. At the time, the conservatives were opposed to political equality for women in general; the social democrats were waging a persistent struggle for unrestricted suffrage, and only the liberals, who had weighed all the benefits promised to their party by *property-qualified* representation of women advocated a bill in the Storting that granted political rights only to women meeting a specified property qualification. The simple fact that the liberals refused to vote for another bill, introduced by the social democrats, that provided unrestricted suffrage for women, suffices to show that it was not love of abstract justice or the principle of women's equality that led the liberals to become such zealous defenders of women's interests. By 121 votes to 48, the social democrats' bill was voted down and the liberals' proposal adopted. However, women even owe the adoption of property-qualified voting rights for women to the support of the social democrats. The representatives of the working class exhausted every possibility in the struggle to pass actual democratic representation for women; but when they were faced with the question of whether to vote down the property-qualified bill by voting against it together with the conservatives, or defend at least restricted, diluted suffrage for women, they chose the latter as the lesser evil. As a result of the 1907 electoral reform, 300,000 women have now been added to the number of fully fledged citizens, but 250,000 of the most exploited, deprived, and oppressed even now remain deprived of the possibility of defending and asserting their interests . . .

What did the Norwegian feminists do in this doubtlessly critical moment? Where did their sympathies lie, and how were they manifested? We already noted their ambivalent behaviour above. The feminists, those passionate champions of the 'principle' of women's equality, not only did not support the demand for unrestricted suffrage, but pointedly distanced themselves from the representatives of the proletariat, expressing their clear sympathy to bourgeois liberalism and vesting in it all their hopes. In refusing to walk together with their 'little sisters', the women of the proletariat, in that critical moment, they forgot all the lofty promises that they had just recently made to the trusting women of the working class. At the upcoming 1909 Storting elections, in which Norwegian women will have access to the ballot box for the first time, bourgeois feminists will have occasion to show in practice whether they are indeed on the side of actual political equality for women, or whether, by the 'principle' of women's equality, they only mean the possibility of 'equally' sharing power with men in the existing class society. The Norwegian government, under pressure from the social democrats, intends to introduce a bill in the next Storting, i.e., in 1909, that extends the franchise to all citizens, male and female, aged twenty-five and older, without any property qualification. What stance will the bourgeois women deputies take on this? Will they support the widespread campaigning that the social democrats have decided to carry out around this issue?

It was the same naked class calculation that guided the Danish bourgeoisie in passing the electoral reform that also included women (those meeting the property qualification, of course) in local government. The feminists, who rejoice at this new 'victory', not only welcome it as a partial victory, but as a victory *in principle,* the consequence of which will be the extension of political rights to women in all areas of political life in the more or less near future. But this victory *in principle* is nothing more than a new weapon for the bourgeoisie to aim against the democratisation of local government.[111] The class parliament was faced with a dilemma: Whether to grant access to local government to all inhabitants or carry out a liberal reform entirely 'in principle' that extended the right to vote to women who meet the (quite high) property qualification in order to avoid inspiring distrust amongst the solid bourgeoisie. They opted for the latter reform; it did not harm the interests of the bourgeoisie, and was quite 'radical' . . . However, this time, too, the feminist movement had only indirect influence of the passage of this reform; the entire role of the bourgeois advocates of equality boiled down to taking a position in support of the interests of the propertied bourgeoisie at the time of the struggle for local government reform. Even when the feminists are *extreme* advocates of equality, their demands are by no means a threat to the rule of the bourgeoisie. The main concern of the Danish equality campaigners was dissociating themselves from the demands of the workers' party, showing their solidarity with the 'prudent' policy of the liberals and condemning the reckless extremism of working-class politics.

In May 1908, pacified by their first victory in Denmark, the feminists organised a brilliant, boisterous celebration of their purely 'ladylike' success in Copenhagen. They also invited proletarian women to celebrate this win 'in principle' for women together with them. The celebration was meant to show gratitude towards the government for taking such a 'highly humane' and 'radical' view. But proletarian women refused to join in celebrating a victory for the principle of women's equality that had been bought at such a high price: The new electoral law not only deprived the impoverished female population of representation in local government, but went so far as to reduce the rights of even the male proletariat compared to the previous law. For their part, the proletarian women organised a demonstration in protest against the law, but, of course, the bourgeoisie, pacified by their victory, had no desire to support their 'little sisters' this time.

In summing up the above examples, we cannot escape the conclusion that, in all countries, the feminist movement played a most insignificant role in the practical attainment of political rights. Only time will tell whether the future actions of the suffragists will be more successful in this regard, whether the new ascendancy of the feminist movement, concentrated particularly in Britain, will yield greater results. For now, we can only say that the demand for women's political equality has only been realised in two ways: Either under *direct* pressure from the proletariat, who demand the complete democratisation of the representative system, or under their indirect influence in cases where the bourgeois parties grasped at women's suffrage as a panacea for the looming 'proletarian peril'. But whilst, in the first case, the issue at hand was always *unrestricted* suffrage for women, in the second, the bourgeoisie sought to rely only on *property-qualified* representation. It is only possible to trust in the victory of complete political equality for women when the masses of the working class stand in defence of this demand.

Let us, lastly, look at what the bourgeois women's movement has done here in Russia in the interests of political equality for women.[112]

To listen to our equality campaigners, their contributions in this area have been invaluable. But was it under their influence that Russian society took an interest in women's demands? Was it pressure from feminist organisations that led political unions and parties to include demands for political equality for women in their programmes? What of the fact that feminists abroad have thus far only attained minor results in the struggle for women's liberation? Of course, our feminists, who managed to inspire sympathy for women's demands in Russian society, will be able to attain their coveted goal faster and more simply than their sisters abroad.

But did sympathy for women's equality honestly develop in Russian society as a result of the manifestations of bourgeois feminism? Had sight of the shining image of women fighters not long since accustomed Russian society to seeing women as conscious, active citizens? But can these 'selfless images' of women fighters really be attributed to the bourgeois feminist movement? There cannot be the slightest doubt that these thousands of women who lost their lives in anonymity had enormous significance for societal attitudes towards women's equality, a significance that is immeasurably greater than even the most heartfelt feminist appeals and the fieriest speeches of women's equality advocates. Remember how warmly these 'selfless images' were spoken of in the First Duma. Even the representatives of the bourgeois party appeared to feel indebted to them. The halo surrounding these women fighters also cast light on the whole female question in Russia . . .

'We are saying that electoral law must be reformed on the basis of a four-member formula,' exclaimed Deputy Ryzhkov to thunderous applause. 'We are forgetting in this first Russian parliament about Russian women, who, side by side with the others, fought for freedom.' (Extended applause) *'We are forgetting that the son of a slave woman cannot be a citizen . . .'* (Raucous applause)

But it is not these 'Russian women' that the feminists recall when they speak of the contributions of 'those who fight for women's emancipation'. In their blind self-aggrandisement, our feminists are not even able to take note of the socio-political motives that, over time, led Russian society to support the demand for political equality for women. It is as if they do not notice that the efforts of the opposition to support all democratic demands were a powerful factor in this case, that the living, driving force, women's mass participation in the general liberation movement, made women's aspirations for political equality a *real, live slogan;*

that the selfless commitment of a certain category of women to the cause of freedom did away with old prejudices about women's lack of political consciousness, their 'slavish' instincts and conservative inclinations . . .

Just as women's active participation in the liberation struggle served as the impetus to raise the question of women's equality in France in the days of the Great Revolution, here, too, it was not specifically feminist campaigning, but women's vibrant love for the cause of the social liberation of humanity, the organic merger of democratic men and women in the struggle for a new political system that, step by step, allowed the idea of women's political capacity to take root in social consciousness.

Is there even a single major event from the emancipatory period we just experienced in which the participation of working-class women, peasant women, and women of the intelligentsia was not indispensable?

The achievements of heroic individuals in the cause of the people's liberation are disputed, and not without success, by the grey masses of women in the latent impulse that broke their age-old shackles. Remember the procession of 'women's riots' that took place everywhere between 1904 and 1906. The impetus was the war with Japan. The burden of all the horrors, all the hardships, all the social and economic evil connected to that ill-fated war lay on the shoulders of peasant women, wives, and mothers. When the reserves were called up, their already burdened shoulders were burdened with double the work, double the concern, unexpectedly forced those dependent women who feared everything beyond their narrow domestic interests to face theretofore unknown hostile forces head-on and, for the first time, to palpably feel all the humiliations of disenfranchisement, to fully experience all the sorrow of undeserved affronts . . . Those grey, forgotten peasant women, who for the first time left the comfort of their nests, hastened to the cities, there to cross the thresholds of government institutions in search of news of their husbands, sons, fathers, to seek assistance, to defend their interests . . . All the disenfranchisement of the peasantry, all the falsity and injustice of the existing social structure in all its ugliness peasant women saw with their own astonished eyes. From the city, they returned, sobered and tempered, holding in their hearts an endless supply of sorrow, hate, and anger . . .

In the summer of 1905, a series of 'women's riots' erupted. With fierce hatred and astonishing daring for women, the women smashed the military and police administrations, repelled reservists . . . Arming themselves with rakes, pitchforks, and brooms, the peasant women evicted companies of guards out of their towns and villages. In their own way, they protested against the unbearable burden of the war. They were, of course, arrested, convicted, and sentenced to cruel punishments. But the 'women's riots' did not cease. And, in this protest, the defence of general peasant interests and 'women's' interests merged so closely that any attempt to separate the one from the other, to attribute the 'women's riots' to the 'feminist movement,' is utterly unfounded.

After the 'political' actions of the peasant women came a series of 'women's riots' that were economic in nature. This was the era of ubiquitous peasant agitation and agricultural strikes. The peasant women frequently were the instigators of this agitation, and led the men to join in. There were cases in which, having failed to gain the sympathy of the peasant men, the peasant women alone went to the manor houses with their demands and ultimatums. Arming themselves with whatever was to hand, they walked in front of the men to meet the forces sent to quell the uprisings . . . The '*baba*', who had for centuries been beaten down and oppressed, unexpectedly found herself as one of the indispensable actors in the unfolding political drama . . . Over the entire revolutionary period, in close, unbreakable unity with the men, she unwaveringly stood guard for the interests of the peasantry as a whole, reminding all of her own specific needs as a woman with remarkable internal timing only when it did not threaten to harm the cause of the peasantry as a whole.

This did not mean that peasant women remained indifferent to their demands as women, as if ignoring them. To the contrary, the mass appearance of peasant women on the general political arena, their mass participation in the general struggle, consolidated and developed women's self-awareness. As early as November 1905, peasant women in Voronezh province sent two delegates to the peasant congress with a mandate from the women's meeting to demand 'political rights' and 'freedom' for women on equal terms with men.[113] The enthusiasm with which women at the time grabbed hold of the idea of women's equality can be seen from a report from members of the Alliance for Women's Equality who had been working amongst peasant women and gathering signatures from them for a petition to the First Duma. 'The idea of equal rights', a member of the AWE who had been working in Tula province states,

> appealed to them, to say the least; for them, it was their 'long-awaited daily bread', as one married peasant woman put it. If you heard the stories, brought forth under the vivid impression of the petition, of women's sorrow, of the painful disenfranchisement of women, that I have heard whilst writing down illiterate women's names at their heartfelt request, you would have felt the warmest joy at having participated actively in such a truly great cause as women's liberation. The only things that compare to it are the liberation from serfdom and the emancipation of the Negroes. I had never heard such sorrow as poured out before me at that time. It all accumulated and surged forth throughout the land, so much so that, if equality does not take hold in the village, it would be possible, if one acted skilfully, to carry out a grand women's strike against all those who do not recognise women's rights.*

Signatures were added to the Alliance for Women's Equality petition to the Second Duma with even greater intensity; entire villages signed. Not satisfied with merely signing, the peasant women issued a sort of 'judgment' on the matter of women's rights then and there. The women who gathered signatures report that peasant women came from afar, not intimidated by the distance, just to 'subscribe' to the petition. Old women brought their underage granddaughters, asking that they, too, should not be 'overlooked'; adolescent girls, often enough 'independent'

---

* In original: *Идея равноправности мало сказать—понравилась имъ; она составила для нихъ давно жданный насущный хлѣбъ", по выраженію одной замужней бабенки. Если-бы вы слышали тѣ, вырвавшіеся подъ живымъ впечатлѣніемъ петиціи, рассказы о женскомъ горѣ, о мучительномъ женскомъ безправіи, что переслушала я, пока записывала имена неграмотныхъ по ихъ горячей просьбѣ, вы-бы почувствовали самую горячую радость за то, что приняли живое участіе въ такомъ по истинѣ великомъ дѣлѣ, какъ освобожденіе женщинъ. Съ нимъ на ряду только можно отмѣтить освобожденіе отъ крѣпостного права и освобожденіе негровъ. Столько горя, сколько вылилось передо мною сейчасъ, я еще не слышала. Точно все уже накипѣло и хлынуло черезъ край, хлынуло настолько, что, если не пройдетъ вопросъ равноправія въ деревнѣ, можно было-бы, умѣло дѣйствуя, провести грандіозную женскую забастовку противъ всѣхъ тѣхъ, кто не признаетъ правъ женщины..*

householders, protested if their signatures were rejected. 'How can this be? We're old enough to starve, old enough to feed and clothe orphans, but when it comes to our rights, we're not old enough?' they exclaimed with indignation.

> Peasant women not only expressed their demands as women through the AWE. They also acted completely independently. It suffices to recall the historic letters – mandates from peasant women of the provinces of Voronezh and Tver – sent to the first State Duma, or the telegram sent to Deputy Aladin by peasant women of the village of Nogatkino.
>
> In this great moment of right against power, we, peasant women of the village of Nogatkino, salute the elected representatives of the people who demanded the resignation of the ministry in an expression of distrust towards the government. We hope that the representatives supported by the people will give the people land and freedom, open the prison doors to those who fight for the freedom and happiness of the people and grant civil and political rights both to themselves and to us, Russian women, who are disenfranchised and deprived even in our own families. Remember that a slave woman cannot be the mother of a free citizen* (on behalf of 75 women from Nogatkino).

The female peasant population of the Caucasus defended their rights with particular vigour. Peasant women from Guria issued resolutions at peasant meetings in Kutais Governorate demanding equal political rights to men. At a meeting of rural and urban political actors that took place in the province of Tbilisi on the matter of the introduction of the *zemstvo* ordinance in the Caucasus, the delegates from the local population included Georgian women who insistently reminded those present of their rights as women.

---

*   In original: *Въ великій моментъ борьбы права съ силой, мы, крестьянки села Ногаткина, привѣтствуемъ избранниковъ народа, выразившихъ недовѣріе правительству требованіемъ отставки министерства. Мы надѣемся, что представители, поддержанные народомъ, дадутъ ему землю и волю, отворятъ двери тюремъ борцамъ за свободу и счастье народа и добьются гражданскихъ и политическихъ правъ, какъ для себя, такъ и для насъ, безправныхъ и обездоленныхъ, даже въ своей семьѣ, русскихъ женщинъ. Помните, что женщина-раба не можетъ быть матерью свободнаго гражданина.*

Of course, together with demands for political equality, peasant women everywhere also raised their voices in defence of their economic interests; the matter of 'shares', of land, was as great a concern for peasant women as for peasant men. In some places, peasant women, who had passionately supported the idea of expropriating privately held land, cooled to the measure when doubts arose about whether shares would also be distributed to women. 'If the land is taken from the landlords and just given to men,' the peasant women worried, 'then we, the women, will be in complete bondage. Now at least we are able to make a few kopecks of our own on the farm, but that way, we'd just have to work for the menfolk.'[114] Here, *Zhenskiy Vyestnik* hastens to draw the conclusion that the expropriation of land for the peasantry in general would be 'a great injustice towards women' (*великой несправедливостью по отношению к женщине*), finding that 'it is difficult to expect progress in such a civilisation, when even a liberal reform is a means of even greater enslavement and disenfranchisement of half the population' (*трудно ожидать прогресса при такой цивилизации, когда даже либеральная реформа является средством еще большого порабощения и бесправия половины населения*).

However, the distrust of *Zhenskiy Vyestnik* and the concerns of the peasant women were completely unfounded; simple economic calculations forced the peasantry to stand in favour of distributing land to 'the womenfolk' as well. The agrarian interests of the male and female parts of the peasant population are so tightly intertwined that, in fighting to eradicate the bondage of the existing landholding relations for themselves, male peasants naturally also defended the economic interests of their 'womenfolk'. The feminists look in vain for signs of 'the antagonism of the sexes' in the peasant milieu; their calculation that they could split the peasantry into two mutually hostile camps – men and women – by playing that note. Though the age-old struggle between 'the master' and his battered, obedient slave – woman – can still be felt when social life follows a more mundane, less intense course, in times of increased

---

*   In original: *Если землю отнимутъ у помѣщиковъ и отдадутъ ее однимъ мужчинамъ, то намъ, бабамъ, будетъ совсѣмъ кабала. Теперь мы хоть въ экономіи свои копѣйки зарабатываемъ, а тамъ придется работать все на мужиковъ.*

tension between social forces, in periods of acute struggle for the interests of the peasantry as a whole, this internal discord totally fades away. In the recent period of peasant activity, we have seen not only the economic, but also the legal interests of women defended by representatives of the peasantry with the same passion and selflessness with which they defended the shared demands of the peasantry as a whole. Although the tempo of social life has decreased, and the wave of popular ferment has died down, the demands and aspirations expressed by the peasantry so recently, demands that are far from having received the desired satisfaction, do not allow the internal domestic discord between '*muzhik*' and '*baba*' to overshadow the shared demands, which, in their entirety, continue to stand before the patiently waiting peasant masses.

If peasant women obtain improvements in terms of their domestic, economic, and legal situation in the near future, that will of course only be thanks to the shared, cohesive efforts of the democratic peasantry towards the realisation of the shared demands of the peasantry, which have not ceased to be heard in one form or another in the peasant milieu. The efforts of the feminists to 'make way for women' are surplus to requirements . . . If peasant women free themselves from the bondage of existing land relations, they will attain more than all feminist organisations together are capable of giving them.

If even half the fundamental demands of the conscious peasantry are satisfied, 'the tears of the womenfolk', too, will be cut in half . . .

In fighting for the shared economic and political interests of the peasantry as a whole during the period we experienced, peasant women were simultaneously fighting for their own specific demands and needs as women. The same applies to the women of the working class: Through their irreplaceable participation in the shared liberation movement, they, to an even greater extent than peasant women, prepared public opinion to recognise the principle of women's equality. Need we mention the role the masses of proletarian women played in the historical events we experienced just recently? Need we draw a picture of the irreplaceable collaboration of working-class women in all the decisive political actions? Those pictures are still too fresh in the mind, the pulse of the reality we only just experienced still beats within them . . . How vividly they stand before us, the images of the 'grey' women of the working class, their inquisitive, hopeful gaze directed at the orators in crowded meetings of the Gapon detachments, electrified, their hearts burning with enthusiasm . . . Concentrated, triumphant, full of irrevocable decision, women's faces shine in the tight ranks of the workers' procession on that memorable Sunday in January . . . The sun, unusually bright for Saint Petersburg, illuminates this concentrated, silently triumphant procession, playing on the women's faces, of which there are so many in the crowd. The reward for the women's naïve illusions and childlike credulity: the mothers, adolescent daughters, and wives of the working class are a common sight amongst the masses of the victims of that January day . . .

The slogan that jumped from shop to shop – general strike – is taken up by these women, who just yesterday had been unconscious, and, in some places, leads them to be the first to down tools.

In the provinces, too, working-class women do not lag behind their comrades in the capital: Exhausted by work and hard proletarian life, women down tools together in the days of October, and steadfastly deprive their little ones of a last crust of bread in the name of the common cause . . . In simple words that touch the soul, the orator, a working-class woman, calls upon her male comrades, supporting their vigour, breathing energy into them. She is everywhere. If we were to report the facts of women's mass participation in the movement in those days, enumerate the active manifestations of discontent and protest, recall the selfless acts of working-class women and their burning commitment to democratic ideals, we would have to reconstruct the history of the Russian liberation movement, picture by picture.[115]

Against the background of this social struggle, working-class women's needs as women gradually awakened, and their specific demands warmed up, within them. Working-class women fought tirelessly, protested daringly, bravely sacrificed themselves for the common cause; but the more active they became, the more the process of their intellectual awakening accelerated. Working-class women began to take stock of their environment, and, convinced of the injustices connected with contemporary social relations, began to feel all the sorrow of their specific suffering and misfortune as women all the more painfully and acutely.

Together with the shared demands of the proletariat as a whole, the voices of the women of the working class could be heard more and more clearly and distinctly, reminding all present of their needs. As early as the elections to the Shidlovsky commission, the refusal to admit women as delegates from the working class elicited a murmur of discontentment amongst the women: Through the shared suffering and sacrifice they had just experienced, women and men of the working class were, in practice, rendered equal in the arena of cruel lived reality. Women fighters and citizens found this emphasis on their age-old disenfranchisement particularly unjust in these moments. When a woman elected as one of seven delegates from the Samsonievskaya Manufactory was declared ineligible by the Shidlovsky commission, the agitated female workers of several manufactories decided to submit the following letter of protest to the Shidlovsky commission:

> Delegates representing working women are not permitted in the commission over which you preside. This decision is unjust. Women predominate amongst the workers at the factories and manufactories of Saint Petersburg. In the spinning and weaving shops, the number of women grows with every passing year, because men are moving over to factories where the pay is higher. We, working women, bear the heavier burden. Exploiting our helplessness and meekness, we are oppressed worse than our male comrades and paid less. When your commission was announced, our hearts beat with hope: 'At least, the time has come,' we thought, 'when the working women of Saint Petersburg may speak loudly, for all Russia to hear, in the name of our sister workers, of the oppression, affronts, and insults that no working man has ever experienced and of which no working man can know.' And now, when we have already elected our delegates, we are told that only men can be delegates. But we hope that this decision is not final. After all, the Sovereign's dictate does not separate working women from the working class as a whole.*

---

*   In original: *Депутатки отъ женщинъ-работницъ не допускаются въ комиссію подъ вашимъ предсѣдательствомъ. Такое рѣшеніе представляется несправедливымъ. На фабрикахъ и въ мануфактурахъ Петербурга работницы преобладаютъ. Въ прядильныхъ и ткацкихъ мастерскихъ число женщинъ съ каждымъ годомъ увеличивается, потому что мужчины переходятъ на заводы, гдѣ заработки выше. Мы, женщины-работницы, несемъ болѣе*

Depriving women of suffrage, removing them from political life in the very moment when the possibility of direct participation of the population in conducting the country's affairs had opened up for the first time, was seen as an outrageous injustice by the part of the female population that had borne all the burdens of the liberation struggle on their shoulders. More than once, working-class women appeared at election campaign meetings of workers for the First and Second Duma, making their disapproval of the law depriving them of a voice in such an important matter as the election of representatives to the State Duma known with noisy protests. In some cases (e.g., in Moscow), working-class women showed up at electors' assemblies to break up the meetings and prevent elections being conducted. The enormous number of signatures from working women gathered on women's petitions is a testament to the fact that proletarian women had ceased to be indifferent to their disenfranchisement, that the impossibility of asserting and defending their interests by open, legal means was distressing to them. According to the feminists themselves, of forty thousand signatures gathered for women's petitions to the first and second State Dumas, the overwhelming majority came from proletarian women.

Working-class women were irreplaceable participants in all women's meetings in the period of 1905 to 1906, listening, trustingly, to the voice of our equality campaigners, the champions of 'the cause of women'. But the feminists' proposals did not meet their awakening needs and did not resonate with their pained souls. In response to a meeting organised in spring 1907 by equality campaigners who sympathised with the Cadets, three meetings were organised, at the initiative of working-class women,

тяжелое бремя. Пользуясь нашей безпомощностью и безотвѣтностью, насъ больше притѣсняютъ наши-же товарищи, и намъ меньше платятъ. Когда было объявлено о вашей комиссіи, наши сердца забились надеждою: наконецъ, наступаетъ время,—думали мы,—когда петербургская работница можетъ громко, на всю Россію и отъ имени всѣхъ своихъ сестеръ-работницъ, заявить о тѣхъ притѣсненіяхъ, обидахъ и оскорбленіяхъ, которыхъ никогда не испытывалъ и которыхъ не можетъ знать ни одинъ работникъ-мужчина. И вотъ, когда мы уже выбрали своихъ депутатокъ, намъ объявили, что депутатами могутъ быть только мужчины. Но мы надѣемся, что это рѣшеніе неокончательное. Вѣдь указъ Государя не выдѣляетъ женщинъ-работницъ изъ всего рабочаго класса.

in the Nobel House, two in the spring, and one in the autumn of 1907. The attendees were overwhelmingly women of the proletariat, and even the working-class women who spoke from the platform of their specific needs as women (maternity protection, restrictions on child labour, political rights for women, etc.) called upon their class comrades to support and fight for the interests of women of the working class.

The convening of the first 'women's congress' led working-class women to take a lively interest in the upcoming 'event' in the feminist world. And even though working-class women have no illusions about the upcoming congress, although they expect no practical results from it, this bourgeois initiative, given the current mood amongst women workers, is still bound to play a certain role in the awakening self-awareness of proletarian women.

However, this awakening will, of course, be of a totally different character than the feminists expect. Women workers are drawn by their growing self-awareness to the side opposite that of feminism. Women workers are beginning to pay greater attention to their needs as women, beginning to demand protection for their health as mothers, to raise the issue of their rights in all areas of social and political life. But surely these demands do not contradict the programme of the working class? In defending their specific interests as women, women workers are at the same time defending the interests of their class. However intensive, however pressing women's most immediate demands may be, any gains made in this area can only be of real significance to women of the working class against the background of shared gains: improved working conditions, democratisation of the state, etc. The mere principle of equality remains – and, indeed, cannot but remain – empty noise for working-class women.

But the feminists cannot agree with this manner of posing the question. Blinded by their slogan – 'uniting all women to conquer the world' – they extend their hands to peasant women, proletarian women, warning them not to trust their class comrades. In an attempt to play 'purely female notes' and thus win women's hearts, they go into the proletarian and peasant milieu with naïve man-hating sermons. They seek to replace the concept of class struggle with the artificial idea of 'discord between the sexes', seeking to unload the guilt in the oppressed position of women workers and peasants from the shoulders of the propertied classes onto those of abstract men. 'Men,' they say, seeking to propagandise the feminist mindset amongst women workers and peasants, 'need women's enslavement.'[116] Carried away by their narrow feminist ideals, they even claim in their awkward language that 'the female question will inevitably be immeasurably broader and immeasurably more significant than the great worker question.'[117]

Do they not even understand that, by dissociating themselves from their male comrades, renouncing their tasks as a class for the sake of narrow female objectives, working-class women would cease to be the social force that they are now, and, in so doing, would not only not strengthen, but would, to the contrary, actually undermine the significance of women's cause? Women's demands, adapted to satisfy women of opposite poles of society, would lose all their specificity, even if the ranks of the army of women defending them were to grow by a factor of ten. Currently, the political demands now raised by women of the working class only enjoy the significance of a fact of enormous political importance because the vital interest of a specific social class stands behind them.

But in those cases where bourgeois equal-rights campaigners use democratic slogans, when they demand political rights for *all* adult citizens, they can be sure that that demand of theirs will always find lively resonance and active support in the working class . . .

In vain, the feminists feign disbelief at this; in vain, they list the socialists' 'insidious betrayals' of the cause of women's political liberation with spiteful smugness. This is not the place to discuss the tactics of the workers' party in the matter of winning women's suffrage; it suffices to note that although in some countries (Belgium, Sweden, and Austria), under highly specific political conditions, the position adopted on the subject by the socialists was not free of opportunism, this 'inconsistency' in their tactics was definitively rejected and condemned at the subsequent international congress in Stuttgart.[118]

The first issue of *Soyuz Zhenshchin* in 1908 features a specific list of the 'wrongs' of social democracy against the principle of women's political

---

*   In original: *женскій вопросъ неизмѣнно будетъ неизмѣримо-шире и неизмѣримо-значительнѣе великаго рабочаго вопроса*

equality. It would seem that, in Belgium, when even the clerics were willing to recognise the principle of women's equality, the socialists, for some reason, found it 'untimely to extend the franchise to women and convinced women in the party to abandon their efforts to include women's suffrage in the bill' (*несвоевременным распространение избирательных прав на женщин и уговорили партийных женщин отказаться от включения женских избирательных прав в законопроект*). In Sweden, the socialists proved even bigger 'traitors'. Branting, the long-serving leader of the party, spared no effort to beat the idea that they should have political rights out of the heads of 'the women of the party', consoling them with the hope that 'women will only get the vote when socialism arrives' (*женщины получат избирательные права, только когда наступит социалистический строй*). Poor Branting! If he only knew how he is being smeared by our equality campaigners.

The equality campaigners have even more to say about the Austrians. *Soyuz Zhenshchin* cites even the following sensational information: 'The social democrats even organised a meeting of women workers at which a resolution was adopted calling upon women who demanded the vote not to prevent a reform being carried out for men only.'* Thunderous was the indignation directed by the feminists at the Social-Democratic Federation (now: Party) in Britain for refusing to support the feminists' struggle for *property-qualified* suffrage for women; in so doing, they of course forget that it is this party that energetically defends the interests of the most deprived and disenfranchised segment of the British population, demanding the vote for *all* adult citizens, male and female. In their indignation at the socialists, our equality campaigners are even willing to resort to outright libel; thus, they level the following accusation at Quelch, a zealous campaigner for universal suffrage: This 'prominent member of the Social Democratic Party has spoken out many times against raising the demand for women's suffrage *for the time being*.'† (?) Meanwhile, they

---

* In original: *соціалъ-демократія организовала даже собранія работницъ, на которыхъ проводила резолюціи, чтобы женщины, требовавшія избирательныхъ правъ, не мѣшали ей провести реформу для однихъ мужчинъ.*

† In original: *видный членъ соціалъ-демократической партіи, много разъ высказывался противъ выставленія требованія женскихъ избирательныхъ правъ въ настоящее время.*

give out against the members of the social-democratic faction in the first and Third Duma for 'glossing over' (*замалчивание*) the demand 'without distinction as to sex' in a few cases. With regard to the 'deliberate' or 'accidental' omission by Deputy I. P. Pokrovsky of the fifth member in the electoral formula, the equality campaigners give a lesson in 'political wisdom', insisting that, particularly in the Third Duma, 'it was significant to give a detailed discussion of electoral law, without totally unnecessarily omitting the formula adopted by the popular masses.'* . . . The equality campaigners love to present themselves as 'democrats', particularly when it entails no obligations for them . . .

However, though the feminists have recorded all the 'slips' and 'mistakes' of the socialist parties in such detail, why are they incapable of also noting all the gains, the victories that women have made exclusively with the aid of the working class? Why do they not remember the successes of women's cause in Finland and Norway? Why do they not mention that it was only thanks to the efforts of the social democrats that the law, hated by women, banning their participation in political organisations fell at last in May 1908?

The contributions of social democracy to the cause of women's political liberation are so obvious and indisputable that there is hardly any need to list them. But why on earth is it that our 'socialist-minded' equality campaigners do not want to acknowledge these contributions? Surely, it is obvious even to them that it is *in the interests of women's cause itself* not to break up and split the forces of the proletariat by recruiting women of the working class to the ranks of bourgeois feminism? Of course, they know and understand that no less than we do; but, in this case, the feminists have less to say about the victory of women's cause than they do about their own class interests. The feminists only need proletarian women only as raw materials with which to build their stairway to the kingdom of their own bourgeois prosperity. And are not all means acceptable to that end? Even libelling socialists, seeking to split the forces of the proletariat by preaching 'discord between the sexes', and their fulsome praise for the 'peerlessly high mission' of the pioneers of women's emancipation. But

---

*   In original: *имѣло значеніе подробно детализировать избирательное право, не опуская, безъ всякой нужды, усвоенной народной массой формулы.*

the feminists overestimate their forces and boast of their 'great' contributions to no avail. Surely, we have seen that, in all areas of social life, whether in women's struggle for economic independence, the efforts to solve the complex family problem, or in the struggle for political equality for women, the contributions of bourgeois equality campaigners have been negligible.

Working-class women have no reason to expect any tangible results for themselves from the successes of the feminist movement. Bourgeois feminism is powerless to liberate them as individuals, to improve their lot as sellers of labour power, or make the burden of motherhood any lighter for them. Women workers can only forge their happiness, as human beings and as women, with their own hands. But that happiness forged by proletarian women will inevitably become the legacy of all other women. This is why feminists, were they to give more than mere lip service to looking with eyes undimmed by class hatred at the gravely difficult struggle of the proletariat to liberate humanity from capitalist slavery, would have to joyfully salute every new victory of the workers. Then, the latent anger and class hatred for 'utopias' living in the hearts of even left-wing 'champions of equal rights' would disappear. Following the rocky road that brings the proletariat slowly, but surely, nearer to their coveted goal and ideal, the feminists should, filled with hope, cry out: 'Your victory is our hope!'

TRANSLATOR'S ACKNOWLEDGEMENT

This translation is made possible by the generous support of the contributors to the ongoing (as of 20 February 2023) Crowdfunded Translation Project, which seeks to secure funding to translate the entire work. The translator thanks all who have contributed and will contribute to this project for making the translation of this important work possible.

APPENDIX

Original German text of 'Schwangeren- und Wöchnerinnenschutz' (Protection of Women in Pregnancy and after Childbirth)

The following German text appears in the 1909 Znanie edition of *The Social Basis of the Female Question*; it is also available at: https://library.fes.de/parteitage/pdf/pt-jahr/pt-1906.pdf).

Je mehr die Teilnahme der Frau am Berufsleben wächst, desto dringender wird die Frage: Wie vereinigt sich die Frauenerwerbsarbeit mit der Mutterschaft? Besonders die proletarische Frau und ihre Kinder leiden schwer durch diese Doppelbelastung; Unterleibserkrankungen, Erschwerung der Schwangerschaften und Entbindungen, Fehl- und Frühgeburten, frühe Sterblichkeit und Siechtum der Kinder haben häufig ihre Ursache in den ungünstigen Einflüssen der Frauenarbeit.

Der Weg einer Einschränkung (Halbtagsschicht) oder gar eines Verbots der Arbeit verheirateter Frauen ist für uns nicht gangbar. Die Arbeiterfrauen greifen nicht zum Vernügen zur Lohnarbeit, sondern aus wirtschaftlicher Not, und eine Erschwerung oder ein Verbot der Arbeit außer dem Hause würde die Frau nur noch viel mehr in die ungeschützten Gebiete der Heimarbeit treiben.

Ferner aber würden die unehelichen Mütter und Kinder, die den genannten Gefahren ohnehin schon in erhöhtem Grade ausgesetzt sind, ohne Schutz bleiben. Und schließlich sind wir überhaupt nicht für eine solche Einschränkung der Frauenarbeit, weil wir in der letzteren den einzigen Weg zur Frauenbefreiung sehen.

Für uns kommt nur in Frage:

1. Die Frauenarbeit so zu gestalten, daß sie die Frauen nicht daran hindert, gesunde Mütter gesunder Kinder zu werden, und

2. Einrichtungen zu schaffen, die den Frauen die Last der Mutterschaft erleichtern.

Zu 1 fordern wir:

I. Einführung des Achtstundentages für alle Arbeiterinnen über achtzehn Jahre (des Sechsstundentages für die 14 bis 18jährigen), der durch eine stufenweise Herabsetzung der täglichen Arbeitszeit auf 10 bezw. 9 Stunden für eine kurze, gesetzlich bestimmte Übergangszeit vorbereitet werden kann. Denn jede einseitige Arbeit ist gesundheitsschädlich, wenn sie zu lange dauert.

II. Verbot der Beschäftigung von Frauen mit solchen Arbeiten, die ihrer ganzen Beschaffenheit nach die Gesundheit von Mutter und Kind ganz besonders schädigen.

Wir denken hier vor allem an Arbeiten, die Vergiftungsgefahren mit sich bringen, an Industriezweige, in denen Blei, Quecksilber, Phosphor, Schwefelkohlenstoff und sonstige Gifte verwendet werden; ferner an Heben und Tragen schwerer Gegenstände und andere speziell den weiblichen Organismus und die Gesundheit der Nachkommenschaft gefährdenden Arbeiten.

III. Verbot solcher Arbeitsmethoden, die den weiblichen Organismus gefährden, vor allem Ersetzung der Maschinen mit Fußbetrieb (Pressen, Heftmaschinen, Näh- und Stickmaschinen) durch solche mit mechanischer Kraft. Wo diese Forderung zu einer Begünstigung der Heimarbeit führen könnte, wie z.B. in der Konfektionsindustrie, muß dem durch Einrichtung von Betriebswerkstätten vorgebeugt werden.

Zu 2 fordern wir:

Von der Arbeiterschutzgesetzgebung:

I. Das Recht der kündigungslosen Einstellung der Arbeit 8 Wochen vor der Niederkunft.

II. Ausdehnung des Arbeitsverbots für Wöchnerinnen auf 8 Wochen, wenn das Kind lebt, - auf 6 Wochen nach Fehl- und Totgeburten, oder falls das Kind innerhalb dieser Frist stirbt.

Von der Krankenversicherung:

I. Obligatorische Gewährung einer Schwangerenunterstützung (die das KVG bis jetzt in das freie Ermessen der Kasse stellt) im Fall der durch die Schwangerschaft verursachten Erwerbslosigkeit auf die Dauer von 8 Wochen.

II. Freie Gewährung der Hebammendienste und freie ärztliche Behandlung der Schwangerschaftsbeschwerden.

III. Ausdehnung der Wöchnerinnenunterstützung von 6 auf 8 Wochen, falls das Kind lebt, und, wenn die Mutter fähig und willens ist, ihr Kind selbst zu stillen, auf die Dauer von mindestens 13 Wochen; Ausdehnung der Krankenkontrolle auf die Zeit von der 8. Woche ab.

IV. Erhöhung des Pflegegeldes an Schwangere, Wöchnerinnen und Stillende für die Dauer der Schutzfrist auf die volle Höhe des durchschnittlichen Tagesverdienstes.

V. Obligatorische Ausdehnung der unter I – III angeführten Bestimmungen auf die Frauen der Kassenmitglieder.

VI. Ausdehnung der Krankenversicherungspflicht auf alle lohnarbeitenden Frauen, auch die landwirtschaftlichen Arbeiterinnen, Heimarbeiterinnen und Dienstboten, sowie überhaupt auf alle Frauen, deren jährliches Familieneinkommen 3000 Mark nicht übersteigt.

Von der Gemeinde:

Errichtung von Entbindungsanstalten, Schwangeren-, Wöchnerinnen- und Säuglingsheimen, Organisation der Wöchnerinnenhauspflege, Beschaffung guter keimfreier Kindermilch, sowie Gewährung von Stillprämien, so lange diese Periode nicht in die Unterstützungsfrist einbezogen ist.

Vom Staate:

> Gewährung von Zuschüssen sowohl an die Krankenkassen als auch an die Gemeinden, damit diese den genannten Mutterschutzforderungen gerecht werden können.
>
> Aufklärung der Frauen über die richtige Erfüllung ihrer Mutterpflichten durch Aufnahme der Säuglingspflege in den Schulplan der obligatorischen Fortbildungsschulen. Verteilung von Merkblättern mit Regeln für die Pflege und Ernährung des Säuglings und die Pflege der Wöchnerinnen seitens der Standesbeamten.

NOTES

Introduction

1   Schlesinger-Eckstein, *Женщина къ началу XX вѣка* (Women at the beginning of the twentieth century).

2   Prof. Pierstorff, *Женскій трудъ и женскій вопросъ* [1902 Russian edition available at https://dspace.spbu.ru/handle/11701/36532—Trans.], p. 27. [Original: *Frauenarbeit und Frauenfrage* (Women's labour and the female question), full text available at https://books.google.com/books?id=CA8-AQAAMAAJ&printsec=-frontcover&source=gbs_ge_summary_r&cad=0#v=onepage&q&f=false—Trans.]

3   Compilation *Правовое Государство* (*Pravovoye gosudarstvo*, The rule of law), article by Chernyshev.

4   *Статистическій Справочникъ* (*Statisticheskiy spravochnik*, Statistical handbook), Issue III, 1908.

5   For 100 men living from their labour in St. Petersburg, there were 27 women in 1881, 34 women in 1890, and already 40 women in 1906 (Levinson-Lessing, pp. 141–47).

6   Levinson-Lessing, *О занятіяхъ женск. насел. С.-Петербурга по переписямъ 1881, 1890 и 1900 г.г.* (*O zanyatiyakh zhensk. nasel. S-Peterburga po perepisyam 1881, 1890 I 1900 g.g.,* Employment in the female population of St. Petersburg according to the 1881, 1890, and 1900 census) pp. 141–47. (The independently employed population of St. Petersburg is taken together with the suburbs).

7   L. Braun, *Женскій вопр.* (*Zhenskiy vopros, The female question*), pp. 157, 224. [Original – *Die Frauenfrage*, available in full text at https://www.gutenberg.org/files/14075/14075-h/14075-h.htm —Trans.]

8   The growth of female labour is even more appreciable when longer periods are compared; thus, for example, in the US, over 26 years (from 1870 to 1896), the number of women wage earners increased from 1.836 million to 3.914 million, i.e., an increase of 117 percent, whilst the number of male wage earners increased from 10.7 million to 18.8 million, i.e., by only 76 percent. In England, over twenty years (1871 to 1891), the number of women wage earners increased by 21 percent, whilst that of male wage earners increased by only 8 percent, etc.

9   Cf. Sobolyov, *Женскій трудъ* (*Zhenskiy trud,* Female labour), p. 73.

10 Despite the rapid growth in female labour, there is not a single branch of industrial activity, with the exception of domestic service, where female labour grew at the expense of male labour not only relatively, but in absolute terms as well.

11 Prof. Khvostov wrote his work *Женщина наканунѣ новой эпохи* (*Zhenshchina nakanune novoy epokhi,* Woman on the eve of a new era) in the summer of 1905,

when the Alliance for Women's Equality (*Союз равноправности женщин*) had only just formed. [Kollontai is referring here to Prof. Veniamin Mikhailovich Khvostov. The full text of the work cited can be found at https://rusneb.ru/catalog/000199_000009_008887813/ —Trans.]

12   Before this, in 1898, only the annual *Zhenskiy Kalyendar (Женскій календарь,* Women's calendar) existed. *Zhenskoye Dyelo (Женское дѣло)* existed for only two years, but, starting in 1904, a new feminist journal, *Zhenskiy Vyestnik (Женскій Вѣстникъ,* Women's bulletin) appeared. It was replaced by *Soyuz Zhenshchin (Союзъ женщинъ,* Women's alliance).

13   Under Russian law, women have full civil capacity upon reaching the age of majority: They can independently carry out civil transactions, become the guardians even of unrelated persons, give evidence as witnesses, etc. Women independently control their own assets, even after marriage, because the law recognises the spouses' assets as separate. In Russia, husbands are not the legal guardians of their wives, as is the case even in France. Only in the field of inheritance rights are women worse off than men: Female descendants inherit only one-fourteenth of real property and one-seventh of personal property, and women in the collateral line inherit even less.

14   Cf. The chapter *Women's Societies and their Tasks (Zhenskiye obshchestva i ikh zadachi, Женскія общества и ихъ задачи)* in the book *Женское движеніе* (The women's movement) by Kechedzhi-Shapovalov. [Refers to *Женское движеніе въ Россіи и заграницей.* [*Zhenskoye dvizhenie v Rossii i zagranitsei,* The women's movement in Russia and abroad] by Mikhail Vasilyevich Kechedzhi-Shapovalov, full text at https://rusneb.ru/catalog/000199_000009_003705171/ —Trans.]

15   'The tasks of the first congress of Russian women comprise philanthropy and education. Russian women have long actively participated in both fields, and thus have much to say about these matters' (*Задачи перваго съѣзда русскихъ женщинъ обнимаютъ благотворительность и просвѣщеніе. Въ той и другой области русскія женщины давно принимаютъ дѣятельное участіе и потому онѣ могутъ многое сказать по даннымъ вопросамъ.) (Женск. Вѣстникъ,* 1905, no. 1).

16   Kechedzhi-Shapovalov, *Къ свободѣ (K svobode,* To freedom), p. 39. [Full text at https://db.rgub.ru/youthlib/3/Kechedzhi-Shapovalov_M.V._K_svobode.pdf —Trans.]

17   See *Равноправіе Женщинъ—Отчеты и Протоколы (Ravnopravie zhenshchin, Otchyoty i protokoly,* Women's equality – reports and proceedings) 1906. [These are the proceedings of the 3rd conference of the All-Russia Alliance for Women's Equality —Trans.]

18   The organ of this party was the *Zhenskiy Vyestnik,* edited by female physician Mariya Ivanovna Pokrovskaya.

19   'The distinctive characteristic of the women's political club is its profoundly democratic organisational structure, which was achieved firstly by broadly granting all interested parties access to all meetings, charging a nominal admission fee of 2 kopeks, and, secondly, by allowing that every group of 25 club members who were members of *political parties* or trade unions could have a representative on the board to protect their interests.' (*Отличительной чертой женскаго политическаго клуба является его глубоко-демократическая организація, которая достигалась: во-первыхъ— тѣмъ, что доступъ на всѣ собранія былъ широко открытъ всѣмъ желающимъ, причемъ за входъ взималась минимальная плата въ 2*

коп., во-вторыхъ—тѣмъ, что каждые 25 членовъ клуба, организованныхъ партійно или профессіонально, могли имѣть въ правленіи представителя для защиты своихъ интересовъ.) [See *Женскій политическій клубъ* (*Zhenskiy politicheskiy klub,* The Women's Political Club) , by M. Margulies [likely Margarita Nikolayevna Margulies-Aitova—Trans.] in *Женскій календарь* (Women's calendar), 1907.]

20 It must, however, be noted that one of the achievements of the Women's Political Club was the organisation's attempt to form the first political clubs for proletarian women in St. Petersburg. In spring 1906, there were four such clubs, of which the activities of the Vasileostrovsky club were particularly lively; here, lectures and discussions were held in an effort to awaken working women's interest in the political life around them. After existing for a month and a half, they were shut down by the police following the dissolution of the first Duma. This also marked the end of the Women's Political Club.

21 'If we were to record every separate demand of the Social-Democratic Party and every position they have taken relative to the positions of the other parties,' says Lily Braun, 'it would require an entire book. Every time the issue of rights specific to women has come up, our party has stood in defence of them.' These words only concern Germany, but they apply equally to all other civilised countries.

22 Of course, the esteemed bourgeois investigators of the female question do not agree with this. Prof. Khvostov, in his book on 'Woman', notes that, 'for working women, the female question increasingly converges with the overall labour question, and that ultimately divides the women of both classes . . . However, this discord is not such a great problem as to make it impossible to reach agreement at least on momentary interests. Both classes of women have shared interests, e.g., the demand for political equality with men and equal education . . . In most civilised countries, this discord is not particularly acute, and women of different classes find it possible to work together closely on the basis of their shared interests. But where there are conscious efforts to heighten hostility between classes, unity becomes difficult. This is the case in Germany, where the socialist party's programme calls for the abolition of the existing social structure and supports class struggle' (*для женщинъ-работницъ женскій вопросъ все болѣе сливается съ общимъ рабочимъ вопросомъ, а это въ концѣ концовъ разобщаетъ женщинъ двухъ классовъ... Рознь эта однако по существу дѣла не столь велика, чтобы не было возможности соглашенія на почвѣ, по крайней мѣрѣ—интересовъ момента. У того и другого класса женщинъ есть общіе интересы, какъ напр. требованіе политическаго равноправія съ мужчинами и равнаго образованія... Въ большинствѣ культурныхъ странъ рознь эта особенно рѣзко не проявляется, и женщины разныхъ классовъ находятъ возможнымъ дружно работать на почвѣ общихъ интересовъ. Но тамъ, гдѣ примѣшивается сознательная политика обостренія классовой вражды, тамъ объединеніе становится затруднительнымъ. Такъ обстоитъ дѣло въ Германіи, гдѣ соціалистическая партія вводитъ въ свою программу разрушеніе существующаго общественнаго строя и поддержаніе классовой борьбы*) (p. 48). It follows from the esteemed professor's argument that, were it not for the malicious plots of the social democrats, who 'support class struggle', it would have been entirely possible for women to come together in a party of all women.

23   The very principle of equal rights is seen by each group of women in accordance with the social stratum to which they belong. Women of the upper bourgeoisie, who suffer from inequality above all in property rights, e.g., inheritance rights in Russia, most enthusiastically struggle for the repeal of the sections of the civil code that are harmful to women's interests. For women of the middle bourgeoisie, equality comes down to the matter of 'freedom to work'. However, both groups are aware of the need to have a voice in the governing of the country, given that, without it, no victory or reform can last. Hence the shift of the core of the issue to the struggle for full political rights.

Chapter 1. Women's Struggle for Economic Independence

1   'The statistical data related to the three most significant medieval cities unanimously show such a substantial predominance of the female population over the male population at a given age that we can only presume that the female question was a more acute, burning issue in the cities of the late Middle Ages than it is today. From a sufficiently reliable census of the population of Nuremberg conducted in late 1449, we see that, in the wealthy class, there were 1,000 adult men for 1,168 adult women. However, the predominance of the female population was not observed only in the wealthy class, but also amongst those in service (labourers, journeymen, and servants). If we take all of these classes of the population together, we find 1,207 women for every 1,000 men. In Basel, the sex ratio in 1454 was apparently the same. In the parish of St. Alban and St. Leonard, for every 1,000 men over the age of 14, there were 1,246 women of the same age. Lastly, the 1385 census that covered most of the adult population of Frankfurt-am-Main yielded 1,536 men and 1,089 women, i.e., roughly 1,100 men for every 1,000 women. The latter figure is lower than the actual figure; there is reason to believe that the predominance of the female population in Frankfurt-am-Main in 1385 was significantly greater' (Bücher, *Женскій вопросъ въ средніе вѣка* (The female question in the Middle Ages), p. 8 [Karl Bücher's *Die Frauenfrage im Mittelalter*] can be found in full text in the original German at: https://www.gutenberg.org/ebooks/60062 —Trans.]

2   Bücher, *Женскій вопросъ въ средніе вѣка* (*Zhenskiy vopros v srednie vyeka*, The female question in the Middle Ages), p. 16.

3   'Above all, women could be found in the textile industry and weavers' workshops. In Silesia, the number of female spinners already exceeded that of male spinners in the fourteenth century; many home-based wool and linen weaving workshops existed in Bremen, Cologne, Dortmund, Danzig, Speyer, Ulm, and Munich. The 1455 Basel tax register mentions workshop-based female carpet weavers; however, women were also employed as skinners, bakers, belt makers, heraldry knitters, cloth shearers, strap makers, tanners, and gold-beaters. Particularly in France, where the collection of trade guild statutes compiled by Étienne Boileau in 1254 allows for an exacting overview of all areas of female labour, women were employed in the most varied branches of craft production. We find a large number of female apprentices and journeymen working for gem cutters, silk spinners, and needlers. In some branches of industry, such as the weaving and fringe-making industries, women could become masters and take on apprentices; meanwhile, when women were first allowed access to the trades, only servants and masters' daughters were taken on as apprentices. As a result, the number of women without such

connections apprenticed to learn a trade grew more and more' [L. Braun, *Женскій вопросъ* (*Die Frauenfrage* [The female question], available in full text at https://www.gutenberg.org/files/14075/14075-h/14075-h.htm —Trans.], pp. 37–38).

4   With the inclusion of women in manual labour, the intellectual professions also had to be opened to them, which we do in fact observe: Thus, in fourteenth-century Frankfurt, we find female doctors, teachers, scribes, etc.

5   Bücher, *Женскій вопросъ въ средніе вѣка*, p. 41.

6   'Thus, when one master beltmaker in the mid-sixteenth century in Strasbourg trained his own two stepdaughters in the trade, he incurred the wrath of the journeymen's guild in his workshop to such an extent that they went on a strike that lasted two years and ended in defeat for the master and for female workers. In another case, another means of struggle – the boycott – was successfully employed. Rope makers in Strasbourg complained that the masters in Nuremberg harmed the trade by employing girls in it; they threatened to declare all rope makers who had completed their apprenticeship in Nuremberg unfit and dishonest unless an end was put to this evil . . . Men considered working together with women beneath their dignity. The statutes of the organisations of tailors, belt makers, and pursemakers categorically prohibited journeymen from doing so. Journeyman bookbinders in Nuremberg declared anyone who worked with female servants dishonest, and that which was initially prescribed only by journeymen's organisations and workshops was subsequently incorporated into city and state ordinances. The latter not only banned women working in workshops, but went so far as to declare every man working together with women a disgrace.' (Lily Braun, *Женскій вопросъ*, pp. 41–42)

7   Lily Braun, *Женскій вопросъ*, p. 189.

8   In Lyon in 1787, 30,000 poor people were counted; in Paris, with a population of 680,000, there were 116,000 poor people (see K. Kautsky, *Классов. против. во франц. в 1789 г.* (Class contradictions in France in 1789). [Full text in German at https://play.google.com/books/reader?id=0Ik4AAAAYAAJ&pg=GBS.PA3&hl=en_GB —Trans.]

9   Lefaure, *Le socialisme pendant la révolution* (Socialism during the revolution). [Full text at https://gallica.bnf.fr/ark:/12148/bd6t5368061p —Trans.]

10 Webb, *Истор. анг. тредъ-юніоновъ* (*Istor. ang. Tred-yunionov*, The history of trade unionism), p. 124. [1920 edition available in full text at https://archive.org/details/historyoftradeun00webbuoft —Trans.]

11 M. Kechedzhi-Shapovalov, *Женское движеніе* (The women's movement), p. 29. [Full text at https://rusneb.ru/catalog/000199_000009_003705171/ —Trans.]

12 In the period of 1830–1845, the lot of female factory workers was particularly sad: In Lyon, for a 14-hour work day, the annual income of female silk weavers rarely exceeded 300 francs.

13 For example, at the large Yaroslavl Manufactory, there were 2,250 women for 1,625 men; female labour was distributed over all crafts, and only the stationery and glass workshops employed almost exclusively men. See M. Tugan-Baranovskiy, *Русская фабрика* (*Russkaya fabrika*, The Russian factory). [Full text of republished edition at http://www.library.fa.ru/files/tugan_baranovskiy.pdf —Trans.]

14 V. Kilchevskiy, *Необходим. свѣдѣнія женщинамъ* (Necessary information for women), p. 20. [Refers to *Необходимыя свѣдѣнія женщинамъ о нихъ*

самихъ (*Neobkhodimye svyedyenia zhenshchinam o nikh samikh*, Necessary information for women about themselves), full text available at https://rusneb.ru/catalog/000199_000009_003988411/ —Trans.]

15 Chernyshev, *О всеобщем избират. правѣ* (On universal suffrage), pp. 311, 314. [Refers to I. Chernyshev, *О всеобщем избирательном праве и его применении в России* (*O vsyeobshchem izbiratel'nom pravye i yego primyenyenii v Rossii*, On universal suffrage and its application in Russia), available in full text at https://www.litres.ru/i-chernyshev/o-vseobschem-izbiratelnom-prave-i-ego-primenenii-v-rossii/ —Trans.]

16 Chernyshev, *О всеобщем избир. правѣ*, p. 314.

17 Levinson-Lessing, *О занятіяхъ женскаго насел. С.-Петерб. и т. д.* (Employment in the female population of St. Petersburg, etc.), p. 119.

18 'Both in literature and in life, we often hear that there is inadequate employment for women, that the areas in which their labour can be applied are limited. How can we reconcile this complaint with the fact that millions of women are employed?' asks Prof. Sobolyov. 'The fact is that these complaints are not at all heard in those areas of the economy where female labour is widespread, but in the sphere of the intellectual, so-called "liberal professions" . . .' This also explains the one-sided understanding of the female question as a question of expanding the sphere of women's labour. This expansion occurred long ago, and continues to occur to the greatest extent. The core of the question does not lie there, but in improving women's labour and income' (Sobolyov, *Женскій трудъ* [Female labour], p. 80). (In original: *Въ литературѣ и въ жизни часто приходится слышать о недостаткѣ занятій для женщинъ, объ ограниченности для нихъ сферы приложенія труда. Какъ совмѣстить такую жалобу съ фактомъ хозяйственнаго труда многихъ милліоновъ женщинъ?... Дѣло въ томъ, что жалобы раздаются вовсе не въ тѣхъ областяхъ народнаго хозяйства, гдѣ женскій трудъ широко примѣняется, а въ сферѣ интеллигентныхъ, такъ называемыхъ „либеральныхъ профессій"... Этимъ и объясняется одностороннее освѣщеніе женскаго вопроса, какъ вопроса о расширеніи сферы труда женщинъ. Это расширеніе давнымъ давно совершилось и продолжаетъ совершаться въ самыхъ широкихъ размѣрахъ. Главный центръ вопроса не въ этомъ, а въ улучшеніи труда и заработка женщинъ.* —Trans.)

19 H. von Nostitz, *Рабочій классъ Англіи* (*Rabochiy klass Anglii*, The working class of England), pp. 422. [Hans von Nostitz, *Das Aufsteigen des Arbeiterstandes in England* – full text in German at https://babel.hathitrust.org/cgi/pt?id=hvd.hnhsne&view=1up&seq=7 —Trans.]

20 Kechedzhi-Shapovalov, *Женское движеніе*, pp. 19, 20.

21 Lily Braun, *Женскій вопросъ*, p. 265.

22 F. & M. Pelloutier, *Жизнь рабочихъ во Франціи (Zhizn' rabochikh vo Frantsii, La vie ouvrière en France)*, p. 75. [Full text available at https://funambule.org/lectures/divers-docs-historiques/F.Pelloutier_la-vie-ouvriere-en-france_1901.pdf —Trans.]

23 Gertsenshtein, *Дѣтскій и женскій трудъ* (*Dyetskiy i zhenskiy trud*, Children's and women's labour), pp. 38–39.

24 E. Wurm, *Жизнь нѣмецкихъ рабочихъ* (*Zhizn' nyemyetskikh rabochikh*, Lives of German workers), chapter *Доходы рабочихъ* (Workers' income).

25 Lily Braun, *Женскій вопросъ*, p. 265.

26 *Женское движеніе за 50 лѣтъ* (*Zhenskoye dvizhenie za 50 let*, 50 Years of the wom-
    en's movement), *Міръ Божій* (Mir Bozhiy*)*, 1903.

27 A. Kollontai, *Жизнь финл. рабочихъ* (*Zhizn' finl. rabochikh*, The lives of Finnish
    workers), pp. 81–83.

28 Pazhitnov, *Положеніе рабочаго класса въ Россіи* (*Polozhenie rabochego klassa v
    Rossii*, Position of the working class in Russia), p. 75. [Available in full text at
    https://archive.org/details/polozhenie_rabochego_klassa_v_rossii —Trans.]

29 Dementyev, *Фабрика и т. д.* (*The Factory etc.*) p. 137. [Likely refers to *Фабрика,
    что она дает населению и что она у него берет* (*Fabrika, chto ona dayot nasele-
    niyu i chto ona u nego beryot*, The factory: What it gives the population and what it
    takes from the population) – full text at http://www.hist.msu.ru/Labour/Dement-
    ev/index.html —Trans.]

30 'Compared to products mass-produced by mechanical means, products produced
    at home by women represent only a small amount of socially necessary labour; this
    leads to the erroneous conclusion that women's labour capability is insignificant.' –
    Clara Zetkin, *Женщина и т. д.* (*Woman etc.*), p. 11. [Likely refers to Zetkin's 1889
    essay *Die Arbeiterinnen- und Frauenfrage der Gegenwart* (The question of women
    workers and women in the present day), available in full text at https://library.
    fes.de/pdf-files/netzquelle/01720.pdf. In the original, the quote reads: *Doppelt
    und dreifach mußten dieselben aber in Folge der weiblichen Konkurrenz sinken, da die
    weibliche Arbeitskraft meist von vornherein zu bedeutend niedrigeren Preisen feil war.
    Ursache davon war das geringe Ansehen, in welchem die bisherige nichtverdienende
    Tätigkeit der Frau stand und stehen mußte, seitdem deren Produkte im Verhältnis zu
    den mechanisch produzierten Erzeugnissen der Großindustrie nur ein geringes Quantum
    gesellschaftlicher Durchschnittsarbeit repräsentierten und damit den Trugschluß auf die
    geringere Leistungsfähigkeit der weiblichen Arbeitskraft zuließen.* (However, they [i.e.,
    wages] had to go down to one-half or one-third as a result of female competition.
    The cause of this was the low regard in which women's previous unwaged work had
    been held and had to be held since their products represented only a small amount
    of socially necessary labour compared to the mechanically produced products of
    large-scale industry, thus permitting the erroneous conclusion that female labour
    power was less efficient.) —Trans.]

31 M. Kechedzhi-Shapovalov, *Женское движеніе* (The women's movement), p. 122.

32 Only in England are there still trade unions in which established prejudices still
    keep the doors shut to women despite the fact that the trades union conference
    already resolved in 1889 to accept women as members of professional organisations.

33 Pelloutier, *Жизнь рабочихъ во Франціи*, p. 73.

34 A female inspector in the Duchy of Baden noted an increase in premature births in
    the female workers: From 1882 to 1886, an average of 1,039 such births a year were
    counted; 1,244 were counted already in the period of 1887 to 1891. An increase in
    the number of surgical births (from 1,118 to 1,385 a year) was also noted.

35 'It might be thought that banning adolescents and women of all ages from working
    more than ten hours a day would not affect the labour of adult men. But this is
    not true. A rule that neither adolescents nor women of any age may be required
    to work more than ten hours a day is in point of fact the same thing as a rule that
    the machines will not work more than ten hours a day in any factory.' Speech of

Gibson, 1884, quoted in E. Kuvshinskaya, *Борьба рабочихъ за политическую свободу въ Англіи* (*Bor'ba rabochikh za politicheskuyu svobodu v Anglii*, Workers' struggle for political freedom in England), p. 193. [The speech in question is by Thomas Milner-Gibson, vice president of the Board of Trade and an opponent of legislative limits on working hours; he is quoted in Hansard as follows: 'It might be thought that by preventing young persons, and women of all ages, from working more than ten hours, the labour of male adults was not interfered with. But that was not so. To enact that no young persons or women of any age should work more than ten hours was, in point of fact, to enact that no factory engines should be kept in operation more than ten hours.' – https://api.parliament.uk/historic-hansard/commons/1844/mar/15/hours-of-labour-in-factories —Trans.]

36   Lily Braun, *Женскій вопросъ*, p. 406. [*Die Weberinnen von Lancashire waren vor dem Schutzgesetz ebenso ausgebeutet und organisationsunfähig, wie heute die Mehrzahl der Arbeiterinnen. Erst nachdem ihnen durch das Gesetz untersagt wurde, auf schlechte Arbeitsbedingungen einzugehen, begannen sie, den Gewerkschaften und Genossenschaften beizutreten.* —Trans.]

37   This law, the stated rationale of which was that 'an excessive working day not only ruins the health of the worker, but impedes the development of his intellectual capabilities, and thus violates his human dignity' was enacted pursuant to the proposal of the Luxembourg Commission on 2 March 1848 [*Considérant 1. Qu'un travail trop prolongé non seulement ruine la santé du travailleur, mais encore, en l'empêchant de cultiver son intelligence, porte atteinte à la dignité de l'homme* – https://www.herve-guichaoua.fr/IMG/pdf/d_cret_loi_du_2_mars_1848.pdf —Trans.]

38   Paul Louis, *Женскій трудъ во Франціи* (Female labour in France), pp. 7–10.

39   Lily Braun, *Женщина и политика* (*Zhenshchina i politika*, Women and politics), p. 53. [p. 39 of the original, *Die Frauen und die Politik*, which reads: *Selbst Bismarck, der grimmigste Feind der Sozialdemokratie, mußte öffentlich anerkennen, dass ohne ihr Vorgehen von Sozialreform in Deutschland noch keine Rede sein würde* (Even Bismarck, the fiercest enemy of social democracy, was forced to admit publicly that, without its actions, social reform in Germany would not even be a topic of discussion.), full text at https://library.fes.de/pdf-files/netzquelle/01765.pdf —Trans.]

40   Posse, *Исторія рабочаго законодательства въ Россіи* (*Istoriya rabochego zakonodatel'stvo v Rossii*, A history of labour laws in Russia), p. 54. [The original reads: 'къ сокращенію производства, которое достигло въ послѣднее время столь значительныхъ размѣровъ, что товаромъ переполнились всѣ рынки'; full text at http://elib.shpl.ru/ru/nodes/57601-posse-v-a-istoriya-rabochego-zakonodatel-stva-v-rossii-ocherk-spb-1906 —Trans.]

41   M. Lunts, *Фабричное законодательство въ Россіи* (*Fabrichnoye zakonodatel'stvo v Rossii*, Factory legislation in Russia), *Рабочій Ежегодникъ* (*Rabochiy Yezhegodnik*), 1906.

42   'At the insistence of Home Affairs Minister Plehve dated 30 May 1903, on a temporary basis, in derogation and supplementation of applicable statutory provisions, it was ordered that local factory inspectorate officials were subordinated to the governor (mayor, chief of police)'. Posse, *Исторія рабочаго законодательства въ Россіи*, p. 65.

43   Lily Braun, *Женскій вопросъ*, p. 413. [Original: *1) Absolutes Verbot der Nachtarbeit für Frauen. 2) Verbot der Verwendung von Frauen bei allen Beschäftigungsarten, welche*

dem weiblichen Organismus besonders schädlich sind. 3) Einführung des gesetzlichen Achtstundentages für die Arbeiterinnen. 4) Freigabe des Sonnabendnachmittags für die Arbeiterinnen. 5) Ausdehnung der Schutzbestimmungen für Schwangere und Wöchnerinnen auf mindestens einen Monat vor und zwei Monate nach der Entbindung; Beseitigung der Ausnahmebewilligungen von diesen Bestimmungen auf Grund eines ärztlichen Zeugnisses. 6) Ausdehnung der gesetzlichen Schutzbestimmungen auf die Hausindustrie. 7) Anstellung weiblicher Fabrikinspektoren. 8) Sicherung völliger Koalitionsfreiheit für die Arbeiterinnen. 9) Aktives und passives Wahlrecht der Arbeiterinnen zu den Gewerbegerichten. —Trans.]

44   T. Bogdanovich, *Женское движеніе за 50 лѣтъ*, Mir Bozhiy, 1903.

45   B. Webb, *Women and the Factory Acts*, 1898. [In original: But it is curious that we seldom find these objectors to unequal laws coming forward to support even those regulations which apply equally to men and to women. —Trans.]

46   *Отчеты и протоколы*, 1906, p. 3.

47   *Женскій Вѣстникъ*, 1905, issue 12.

48   Bücher, *Женскій вопросъ въ среднie вѣка*, p. 41.

Chapter 2. Marriage and the Family Problem

1   'The less developed human labour is, the more limited the quantity of its product, and thus the extent of societal wealth, the greater is the significance of family bonds in the social structure' [Original: *Je weniger die Arbeit noch entwickelt ist, je beschränkter die Menge ihrer Erzeugnisse, also auch der Reichtum der Gesellschaft, desto überwiegender erscheint die Gesellschaftsordnung beherrscht durch Geschlechtsbande;* English version available at marxists.org: 'The lower the development of labor and the more limited the amount of its products, and consequently, the more limited also the wealth of the society, the more the social order is found to be dominated by kinship groups.' https://www.marxists.org/archive/marx/works/1884/origin-family/preface.htm —Trans.] (Engels, *Origins of the Family, Private Property, and the State*, p. 1).

2   Here, in Russia, where large-scale capitalist production has not attained primacy, an incomparably greater number of productive functions fall within the domestic sphere than in the West; a number of branches of the economy, which have already passed into the hands of capitalist production abroad, continue to constitute a customary aspect of housekeeping.

3   August Bebel, *Woman and Socialism*, pp. 113 and 114. [Full text of original at https://www.projekt-gutenberg.org/bebel/frausoz/frausoz.html, English translation available at https://www.marxists.org/archive/bebel/1879/woman-socialism/index.htm —Trans.]

4   Aleksandra Yefimenko, *Изслѣдованія народной жизни* (*Isslyedovaniya narodnoy zhizni*, Studies of folk life), p. 92. [Full text available in Russian at http://publ.lib.ru/ARCHIVES/E/EFIMENKO_Aleksandra_Yakovlevna/%c5%f4%e8%ec%e5%ed%ea%ee%20%c0.%df._%20%c8%f1%f1%eb%e5%e4%ee%e2%e0%ed%e8%ff%20%ed%e0%f0%ee%e4%ed%ee%e9%20%e6%e8%e7%ed%e8.%20%ce%e1%fb%f7%ed%ee%e5%20%e-f%f0%e0%e2%ee.%20%c2%fb%ef%f3%f1%ea%201.(1884).pdf —Trans.]

5   The number of women participating in seasonal work outside of their places of residence can be seen from the fact that, in the 1880s, in eleven counties in Tver Province alone, 20,929 women left every year.

6   *Капиталистическій способъ производства, въ большинствѣ случаевъ, не устраняетъ для рабочаго необходимости жить своимъ отдѣльнымъ хозяйствомъ; но онъ отнимаетъ всѣ свѣтлыя стороны этой жизни, оставляя лишь ея темныя стороны, главнымъ образомъ изнуреніе женщины, ея оторванность отъ общественной жизни. 'In most cases, capitalist mode of production does not eliminate the worker's need to live in his own separate household; it does, however, eliminate all the bright sides of this life, leaving only the dark ones, chief amongst them the overwork of women and their isolation from social life.' Промышленный трудъ женщины означаетъ въ настоящее время нс освобожденіе ея отъ домашней работы по хозяйству, а прибавленіе къ старому бремени еще новаго.* 'Women's industrial labour does not at present mean their liberation from domestic labour, but the addition of a new burden to the old one' (*Коммент. къ Эрфурт. программѣ, стр. 31*). (*Коммент. къ Эрфурт. программѣ [Komment. k Erfurt. programmye]*) [*Das Erfurter Programm / The class struggle*], p. 31).
     [In the original, this passage reads: *Die kapitalistische Produktionsweise löst den Einzelhaushalt des Arbeiters in den meisten Fällen nicht auf, aber sie raubt ihm alle seine Lichtseiten und läßt nur seine Schattenseiten fortbestehen, vor allem die Kraftvergeudung und die Abschließung der Frau vom öffentlichen Leben. Die industrielle Arbeit der Frau bedeutet heute nicht ihre Entlastung von der Haushaltungsarbeit, sondern die Vermehrung ihrer bisherigen Lasten um eine neue.* – https://www.marxists. org/deutsch/archiv/kautsky/1892/erfurter/2-proletariat.htm#t3; in the English translation found at marxists.org, we find the following translation: 'The capitalist system of production does not in most cases destroy the single household of the working-man, but robs it of all but its unpleasant features. The activity of woman today in industrial pursuits does not mean to her freedom from household duties; it means an increase of her former burdens by a new one.' https://www.marxists.org/ archive/kautsky/1892/erfurt/ch02.htm; —Trans.]

7   Lead, mercury, iodine, phosphorus, nicotine, and other poisons are not infrequently found in the premature foetuses of proletarian posterity.

8   'In England, infanticide is not committed merely by unwed mothers seeking by this means to save their honour, but also by married women forced by heinous calculation or poverty to exterminate the fruit of their wombs' (Shashkov, p. 380).
     'One January midnight in London, a woman approaches a constable and asks:
     "Where is the police station?"
     "What business have you there?" the constable asks her.
     "I need to turn myself in because I killed my baby."
     "Why did you do that?"
     "Out of necessity: I couldn't go on watching him suffer from hunger."
     Does this tragic dialogue require any commentary?
     In 1862, England recorded 5,709 violent deaths of children by asphyxiation, burning, beating, drowning, poison, hanging, decapitation, and even being buried alive; these cases were primarily explained by the fact that "the parents were living in extreme poverty".'

9   Lily Braun, *Профессія и матер. (Professiya i matyer.)*, pp. 9–10. [Braun does not appear to have published a separate work with this title in German. The work cited

here appears to be a translated excerpt of Braun's *Die Frauenfrage,* in which we find the following in chapter 6, *Die Lage der Arbeiterinnen in der Gegenwart* (The contemporary situation of working women): *Im wohlhabenden Viertel der Berliner Friedrichstadt starben von 1000 Säuglingen 148, im armen des Wedding 346* [148 out of every thousand infants died in the wealthy neighbourhood of Berlin-Friedrichstadt, as against 346 in the poor neighbourhood of Berlin-Wedding.]

10   '. . .In the past, some slavemasters tore husbands and wives apart, and took children from their parents as soon as they became able to work; but capitalists have gone beyond these horrors of slavery: They are tearing *infants* away from their mothers, requiring them to be handed over to strangers; thousands of children are subjected to this fate every day. They are cared for by charitable institutions charged with making it easier for mothers to be separated from their children.' Kautsky, *Комментарiи къ Эрфуртской программѣ, Разрушенiе семьи въ раб. классѣ* (*Kommentarii k Erfurtskoy programmye, Razrushenie sem'i v rab. klassye*). Commentary on the Erfurt Programme, The Dissolution of the Working-class Family.

[In the original, the passage quoted reads:

Manche Sklavenhalter rissen ehedem den Mann vom Weib, die Eltern von den arbeitsfähigen Kindern; aber die Kapitalisten übertrumpfen noch die Scheußlichkeiten der Sklaverei; sie reißen den Säugling von der Mutter und zwingen diese, ihn fremden Händen anzuvertrauen. Und eine Gesellschaft, in der das täglich in Hunderten und Tausenden Fällen sich ereignet, eine Gesellschaft, die eigene, von ihren „Spitzen" begünstigte „wohltätige" Anstalten geschaffen hat, welche es der Mutter erleichtern sollen, sich von ihrem Kind zu trennen – eine solche Gesellschaft hat die Stirn, uns vorzuwerfen, wir wollten die Familie auflösen, weil wir der Überzeugung sind, daß die Arbeiten des Haushalts immer mehr, wie bisher, so auch weiterhin, sich zu besonderen Berufsarbeiten entwickeln und damit das Haushaltungswesen und das Familienleben umgestalten werden!

The English translation published on Marxists.org reads:

Many a slave-holder has in former times torn husband from wife and parents from children, but the capitalists have improved upon the abominations of slavery; they tear the infant from the breast of its mother and compel her to entrust it to strangers' hands. And yet a society in which hundreds of thousands of such Instances are a daily occurrence, a society whose upper classes promote 'benevolent' institutions for the purpose of making easy the separation of the mothers from their babies, such a society has the effrontery to accuse the Socialists of trying to abolish the family, because they, basing their opinion on the fact that the family has ever been one of the reflexes of the system of production, foresee that further changes in that system must also result in a more perfect family relationship.

(Marxists.org URLs provided in previous footnotes)

It should be noted that the English translation mistranslates the final part of the passage, which, in the original, actually reads: '. . . because we take the view that household work will carry on as it has thus far, increasingly developing into particular professional occupations, thus reconfiguring housekeeping and family life!' —Trans.]

11   Hirsch, *Verbrechen und Prostitution.*

12   A. Bebel, *Женщ. и соцiал. (Zhenshchina i sotsializm, Die Frau und der Sozialismus),* p. 154. [In the original, the quoted passage reads: *Für die freiwillig oder gezwungen in Ehelosigkeit lebenden Männer, wie für jene, denen die Ehe das Erwartete nicht*

bietet, liegen also die Verhältnisse für Befriedigung des Geschlechtstriebs ungleich günstiger als für die Frauen (https://www.projekt-gutenberg.org/bebel/frausoz/frau1211. html), translated in the English edition on marxists.org (https://www.marxists. org/archive/bebel/1879/woman-socialism/ch12.htm#s1) as: *To those men then, who voluntarily or involuntarily lead an unmarried life, and to those who do not find their expectations realized in marriage, opportunities for satisfaction of the sexual impulse are far more favourable than to women.* —Trans.]

13   Woman doctor Elizaveta Drenteln, *О проституцiи* (*O prostitutsii*, On prostitution).

14   Dr Ryan says that at least 400,000 people live from prostitution in London.

15   Hirsch, *Verbrechen und Prostitution als soziale Krankheitserscheinungen*, p. 10 [full text at https://upload.wikimedia.org/wikipedia/commons/b/b1/Verbrechen_und_ prostitution_als_soziale_krankheitserscheinungen_%281A_verbrechenundpro-00hirsiala%29.pdf – the quote is found on p. 11 of this edition. —Trans.].

16   See M. Pokrovskaya's article *Ярмарочная проституцiя* (*Yarmarochnaya prostitutsiya*, Fair Prostitution).

17   Dr Blashko, *Проституцiя начала XIX в.* (*Prostitutsiya nachala XIX v.*, Prostitution in the early 19th century), p. 16.

18   Ibid.

19   Drenteln, *О проституцiи* (On prostitution), p. 5. The peasantry accounts for 74% of the women engaged in prostitution at the Nizhny Novgorod fair. Drenteln, *O проституцiи*, p. 18.

20   *Verbrechen und Prostitution*, p. 14.

21   Sabinin, *Проституцiя*, p. 79. [most likely refers to A. Kh. Sabinin, *Проституцiя, Сифилис и венерические болезни* (*Prostitutsiya, sifilis i venericheskiye bolyezni*, Prostitution, syphilis, and venereal diseases) (1906) —Trans.]

22   Prof. Elistratov, *Бѣдн. и простит.* no. 3, *Союзъ Женщ*, 1907.

23   Sabinin, *Проституцiя*, ch. IX.

24   In Tula, according to Dr Arkhangelsky, mothers themselves bring their innocent sixteen-year-old daughters to the bawdy house, because 'no good for their daughters will come of marrying a drunk, violent muzhik. Better they sow their wild oats from age 16 to 18', and then work at a factory, etc. The madams of the bawdy houses are happy to take the girls, and instruct the mothers to take their daughters' innocence first . . . 'In such flourishing years,' the prostituted daughter has 'many customers, she is chic, earns well, and occasionally gives her mother money to alleviate her poverty' (Sabinin, *Проституцiя*, p. 89).

25   In St. Petersburg, 65 percent of prostitutes come from the peasantry.

26   Elistratov, *Бѣдн. и прост.*, issue no. 3, *Союзъ Женщинъ*.

27   Shashkov, *Историч. судьбы женщины*, p. 509. [Likely refers to Shashkov's 1871 *Исторические судьбы женщины, детоубийство и Проституцiя* (*Istoricheskiye sud'by zhenshchiny, dyetoubiystvo I prostitutsiya*, Infanticide and prostitution: The historical fates of women), https://rusneb.ru/local/tools/exalead/getFiles. php?book_id=000199_000009_003584504&name=%D0%98%D1%81%D1% 82%D0%BE%D1%80%D0%B8%D1%87%D0%B5%D1%81%D0%BA%D0% B8%D0%B5%20%D1%81%D1%83%D0%B4%D1%8C%D0%B1%D1%8B%2-0%D0%B6%D0%B5%D0%BD%D1%89%D0%B8%D0%BD%D1%8B,%20 %D0%B4%D0%B5%D1%82%D0%BE%D1%83%D0%B1%D0%B8%D

0%B9%D1%81%D1%82%D0%B2%D0%BE%20%D0%B8%20%D0%B-
F%D1%80%D0%BE%D1%81%D1%82%D0%B8%D1%82%D1%83%D1%86%
D0%B8%D1%8F&doc_type=pdf—Trans.]

28   Shashkov, *Историч. судьбы женщины*, p. 509.

29   Sabinin, *Проституція*, p. 79.

30   Dr Blaschko, *Проституція* (Prostitution), p. 20.

31   Hirsch, ch. 1, p. 97.

32   Sabinin, *Проституція*, p. 80.

33   Sabinin, *Проституція*, p. 84.

34   Elistratov, *Бѣдн. и прост.*, issue no. 4, *Союзъ Женщинъ*, 1907.

35   According to research from Berlin that is in our possession, fully one-third of the
     prostitutes covered by the survey huddled in corners, and approximately 6% had
     no shelter at all. More specifically, the figures on the housing of girls up to age
     20 are even more eloquent: Only some 3.5% have their own flat; 40% only use a
     'corner' to sleep in, and 9.5% lack even such a corner (*Бѣдность и прост* [Poverty
     and prostitution], Prof. Elistratov). A dismal picture of the living conditions of
     female workers, saleswomen, and waitresses is provided by Prof. Herkner in his
     work *Рабочій трудъ на Западѣ (Rabochiy trud na Zapadye, Labour in the West)* [A
     Russian translation of Herkner's 1894 work *Die Arbeiterfrage* (The question of la-
     bour), which can be found in full text in the original at https://ia800704.us.archive.
     org/8/items/diearbeiterfrage00herkuoft/diearbeiterfrage00herkuoft.pdf —Trans.].

36   A. Bebel, *Женщина и соціализмъ (Die Frau und der Sozialismus)*, p. 154. [In
     the original, the quoted passage reads: *Die Zahl der Prostituierten wächst in dem
     Maße, wie die Zahl der Frauen wächst, die in den verschiedensten Industrie- und
     Gewerbezweigen als Arbeiterinnen beschäftigt und oft mit Löhnen abgefunden werden,
     die zum Sterben zu hoch, zum Leben zu niedrig sind. Die Prostitution wird gefördert
     durch die in der bürgerlichen Welt zur Notwendigkeit gewordenen industriellen Kris-
     en, die Not und Elend in Hunderttausende von Familien tragen.* (https://www.pro-
     jekt-gutenberg.org/bebel/frausoz/frau1241.html), translated in the English edition
     on marxists.org (https://www.marxists.org/archive/bebel/1879/woman-socialism/
     ch12.htm#s1) as: 'The number of prostitutes increases at the same rate at which
     the number of working women increases, who find employment in various lines of
     trade at starvation wages [more accurate would be: and are often paid wages that
     are too high to die, but too low to live]. Prostitution is fostered by the industrial cri-
     ses that have become inevitable in bourgeois society, and to hundreds of thousands
     of families mean bitter need and desperate poverty.' —Trans.]

37   'The influence of the poor compensation of servants,' Dr Blaschko says in relation
     to 'temptation', 'can be seen from the fact that, according to the statistical data
     collected by Berendt, of 78 servants, 58, i.e., nearly half, received some 120 marks
     (less than 60 rubles) a year' (Blaschko, *Проституція*, p. 22).

38   'The writer Charles Benoît researched a series of specific budgets of Parisian nee-
     dle trade workers. He found that, no matter how many savings were made in the
     outgoings, these budgets usually ended up with a more or less significant deficit;
     and if they did manage to make ends meet, this was only possible by means of such
     deprivations as not heating their homes, a primarily potato-based diet, constant
     malnutrition, etc. During the dead season, during which there was a systematic
     interruption in the professional work of these unfortunate workers, their budgets

could only conceivably be balanced by a lifestyle that bordered on literal starvation.' (*Публицистъ Шарль Бенуа обслѣдовалъ рядъ конкретныхъ бюджетовъ
парижскихъ работницъ иглы. Оказалось, что, при всей экономіи расходныхъ
статей, эти бюджеты обычно заключались болѣе или менѣе крупнымъ
дефицитомъ; а если удавалось сводить концы съ концами, то лишь съ такими
лишеніями, какъ отказъ отъ отопленія, перенесеніе центра тяжести
питанія на картофель, постояннымъ недоѣданіемъ и т. д. Въ періодъ-же
мертваго сезона, систематически - прерывающаго профессіональную
работу несчастныхъ труженницъ иглы на цѣлые мѣсяцы, равновѣсіе
бюджета, если и мыслимо, то развѣ только при жизни, граничащей съ
настоящимъ голоданіемъ.*) (*Союз женщ.*, № 4, 1907, p. 4).

39 1903 edition of *Женскій календарь* (Women's calendar), pp. 483 et seq.

40 At the time of printing, I suddenly became aware that, in the textile industry, there
is a not-insignificant contingent of female workers whose annual wage does not
even rise to the level of 150 rubles (approx. 12 rubles a month). Is it possible to
live on that wage? Let us take for example the approximate budget of the relatively
highly paid weavers, who are paid about 22 rubles a month (270 rubles a year). For a
corner with no place for washing or cooking, she has to pay 3 to 3.5 rubles a month.
Quite modest food – mostly bread, sausage, herring, tea, and, once in a while, hot
food – will cost her 10 to 12 rubles a month. Clothing, linens, and shoes swallow
up an average of 3 to 4 rubles a month; meanwhile, there remain such necessary
expenditures as bathing, laundry (roughly 70 kopecks a week), lighting, post, etc.
In order to meet the most basic cultural needs - buying newspapers, books, paying union dues or affording even the most modest entertainment – it is necessary
to forego necessities, cut expenditures on food and clothing (buying worn, often
torn clothes from rag traders), deprive oneself of lighting in the evenings, etc. If a
single, relatively 'highly' paid female worker can barely make ends meet, what can
be said about the women who make 9 to 12 rubles a month, especially if they must
additionally care for an elderly mother, little brothers and sisters, or an 'illegitimate'
child . . .?

41 'Meanwhile, neither illness, nor serious family circumstances are taken into account as justifications for absences or lateness. In the summertime at one St. Petersburg factory, female workers who had dropped their children off at a crèche asked
to be dismissed 10 minutes early so that they would be able to take their children
home on time. However, the manager did not find this reason worthy of consideration. And the women were forced to accept a daily fine and the risk of job loss, or
leave their children at the mercy of fate at home. The factory management do not
take the personal circumstances of workers into account; after all, they use these
fines to recover part of the production expenses, or, often enough, the total amount
of the fines constitutes a substantial part of their salaries.' *Женск. вопр. и проф.
Союзы* (The female question and trade unions), article by S. D., *Союзъ Женщинъ*
(Women's Alliance), no. 4, 1907, p. 9).

42 *Женскій календарь* (Women's calendar), 1903. An entire category of female pieceworkers in the confections industry make 9 to 12 rubles a month; 15 rubles is
already considered 'good' pay.

43 Not to mention the wages of female artisans; female burlap makers barely make 5
rubles a month. There are trades in which the normal income does not exceed 10
kopecks a day.

44 Pazhitnov *Положеніе рабочаго класса въ Россіи* (Position of the working class in Russia), p. 149. [Available in full text at https://archive.org/details/polozhenie_rabochego_klassa_v_rossii —Trans.]

45 *Матеріалы къ выясненію вопроса объ обезпеченіи горнорабочихъ (Materialy k vyyasneniyu voprosa ob obespechenii gornorabochikh,* Materials on the maintenance of mine workers).

46 Permits to open brothels were issued in London (in 1180), in Hamburg (in 1292), in Regensburg (in 1506), in Zürich (in 1314), in Basel (in 1556), in Vienna (in 1384), and in Ulm (in 1440). Brothels flourished particularly in the fifteenth century; at that time, they became known as 'tolerance houses' (Sabinin, *Проституція*, p. 59).

47 Prostitutes are subjected to torment and inhumane punishment nearly everywhere: Cutting of hair, noses, ears, branding, punishment with whips and lashes, incarceration, exile. In many places they were under the supervision of the executioner and had no right to cross the boundaries of their neighbourhood (Sabinin, *Проституція*, p. 56).

In Germany, a girl denounced for debauchery was publicly whipped, paraded through the city streets to a drumbeat, and forever exiled from the city; they did not realise that, by depriving her of food and shelter, they were condemning her forever to the trade of debauchery. In France, such women were fined, incarcerated, scourged, and exiled, and the administration acted with the most outrageous arbitrariness. In Spain, prostitutes were placed on a donkey, mercilessly whipped, and then cast out of the city as the bells tolled; if they returned, they were cast out again after removing one of their arms. Sometimes, they were branded with a glowing iron, or tied to the tails of wild horses and thrown to the ground. Often enough, all this barbaric cruelty was carried out for amusement or the desire to rob public houses and profit at the expense of wealthy prostitutes (Shashkov, *Историч. судьбы женщины*, p. 500).

48 Sometimes, hundreds of 'public women' were murdered at a time. Thus, under Henri III, Marshall Strozzi 'ordered 800 public girls following his camp into the Loire'. In 1560, under the influence of Protestant rigour, a crusade against prostitution was launched in Paris; the police, together with a mob, smashed public houses, confiscated the property found therein, cast prostitutes out of the city, whipped them, and branded them; in a word, they enacted every possible cruelty in order to wipe them from the face of Parisian soil (Shashkov, *Историч. судьбы женщины*, p. 500).

49 Special regulations decisively determine the entire lives of women subject to supervision and make their existence only slightly less burdensome than the incarceration of convicted criminals. Here is an example from the Berlin regulation on officially regulated prostitutes:

'A woman trading in her body and subject to police supervision for this reason shall comply with the following provisions:

She shall submit to medical examination and, to this end, present herself to the police at specified intervals.

If she takes ill with one of the specific diseases or any other, she shall make herself available for admission to the hospital specified by the police and remain there until she is cured.

She must wear simple and decent clothing.

5. She may not: walk on certain streets (specified by the police), stand near churches, schools, universities, social monuments, military posts, visit theatres and gardens belonging to them, concerts, circuses, zoological and botanical gardens, or travel on prohibited streets in an open carriage.

11. She shall not live near churches, schools, universities, social institutions, military posts, and any place set forth in § 5, nor may she live on the ground or basement floor of houses with exits to the outside. She is also forbidden from living in hotels, guesthouses, and furnished rooms and from entering them. She is forbidden from living with or visiting persons found to be engaged in procurement (Bogdanovich, *Женское движеніе* [The women's movement], pp. 212–213).

50 Interesting in these last lines is the concern that the state might be suspected of intending to provide patronage to debauchery. Apparently, this fear prevents the issuance of a law creating standing committees of physicians and police. Despite the fact that the latter have existed in Russia for more than half a century, they remain temporary measures, and are established not by primary legislation, but by administrative action' (M. Pokrovskaya, *Ярмарочная проституцiя*, p. 12).

51 Bebel, *Женщина и соцiализмъ* (Women and socialism), p. 158.

52 Prof. Elistratov, *О прикрѣпл. женщины к простит.* (*O prikrepl. zhenshchiny k prostit.*, On women's affinity for prostitution), p. 27. [Full text available at https://library6.com/books/432025.pdf —Trans.]

53 One example of a regulation on the basis of which the measures taken by the vice police are totally limited, without any exceptions, to the unpropertied strata of the population are the rules of the medical-police committee of Riga. 'Pursuant to § 158 of these rules – concerning the disclosure of sources of syphilis infections – the committee, upon receiving information on the source of the infection, shall review the circumstances of the case and, if there are sufficient grounds, summon the person named to appear before it' only 'where said person belongs to the *lower classes* of the population, i.e., craftworkers, servants, male and female labourers, etc.' (Elistratov, *О прикрѣпленіи женщины къ проституцiи (O prikreplenii zhenshchiny k prostitutsii*, pp. 3–24. Emphasis supplied).

54 *Прост. въ гор.* (*Prost. v gor.*, Prostitution in the cities[? —Trans.]), p. 36, quoted by Prof. Elistratov.

55 *Поднадзорныя прост.* (*Podnadzornye prost.*, Regulated prostitutes), pp. 32–33, quoted by Prof. Elistratov.

56 Blaschko, *Проституцiя*, p. 36.

57 Prof. Elistratov, *Прикрѣпленіи женщины къ проституцiи*, p. 230.

58 These shelters are unsatisfactory in all regards, and, moreover, are only present in the capital cities.

59 'The overwhelming majority of the members of the Society', the Society's report for 1906 notes, 'are more or less affluent persons' (*Отчет Вз.-благ. Об-ва за 1906 г.* [*Otchyot Vz.-blag. Ob-va za 1906 g.*, Report of the mutual philanthropic society for 1906], p. 147).

60 According to the 1906 report, the number of women spending time in all nine departments was 2,808 people, of which 1,985 were permanent.

61 In the same 1906 reporting period, the Society had four such hostels, in which 566 people lived, overwhelmingly dressmakers and craftswomen, governesses and servants, factory workers, etc.

62 *Союзъ Женщинъ*, no. 5, 1907.

63 'But there is another question: Who is responsible for providing social and material support to mother and child? "The husband," say the advocates of marriage. To be sure, that is far from the ideal answer, but it is nonetheless the answer. In most cases, the husband plays his role as protector of mother and child quite satisfactorily, and thus makes the further multiplication of posterity possible. The husband plays this role as well as the male chimpanzee who remains awake through the night and protects his female and his young, who slumber on tree branches and soft leaves, from attacks by bloodthirsty panthers. This defence of beings who are physiologically weak, but necessary for the continuation of the species has existed since time immemorial. To destroy it without any replacement, to take a pregnant or nursing woman or a helpless mother with her infant child and force her to face all the horrors of the struggle for existence would be a step not only in comparison with the barbarism of the Black tribes of Africa; it would be a regression even in comparison with gorillas and chimpanzees' (Gumplovich, *Бракъ и свободная любовь* [*Brak I svobodnaya lyubov'*, Marriage and free love], p. 6). [Full text available at https://db.rgub.ru/youthlib/3/Gumplovich_V._Brak.pdf —Trans.]

64 Bebel, *Положение женщины* (The position of women), p. 3.

65 R. Bré, *Право на материнство* (*Pravo na materinstvo, Das Recht auf die Mutterschaft*), p. 81.

66 R. Bré, *Право на материнство* (*Das Recht auf die Mutterschaft*), p. 77.

67 R. Bré, *Право на материнство* (*Das Recht auf die Mutterschaft*), p. 82.

68 R. Bré, *Право на материнство* (*Das Recht auf die Mutterschaft*),, p. 79.

69 R. Bré, *Право на материнство* (*Das Recht auf die Mutterschaft*), p. 76.

70 Ellen Key cites a saying on marriage in which her own view on the subject is given the fullest expression: 'Marriage is what I call of the will of two to create a third that is greater than those who created it. Marriage is what I call the mutual respect of a man and woman whose will is one and the same.' (*Бракъ,—такъ называю я волю двухъ создать третьяго, который больше тѣхъ, что создали его. Бракомъ называю я взаимное уваженіе мужчины и женшины, какъ желающихъ одной и той же воли.* —Trans.)

71 E. Key, *Любовь и бракъ* (*Lyubov' i brak, Kärleken och äktenskapet*), p. 230. [English translation available in full text at - https://www.gutenberg.org/files/57592/57592-h/57592-h.htm —Trans.]

72 Ibid, p. 231.

73 'If we are of the view that children should appear on the world, and that the family generally provides the best conditions for their education in the first years of life, then we must seriously consider the consequences of women working outside the home in the present time, and having done so, we must say to ourselves that, at that time, there is no greater need than to create the conditions within civilisation, come up with a plan of social organisation, that would return mothers to children and the home' (Ellen Key, *Вѣкъ ребенка* [*Vyek rebyonka*, The century of the child], p. 72). [Full text in English available at http://www.gutenberg.org/ebooks/57283 —Trans.]

74 E. Key, *Любовь и бракъ* (*Kärleken och äktenskapet*), p. 183. [English translation available in full text at https://www.gutenberg.org/files/57592/57592-h/57592-h. htm —Trans.]

75 'Motherhood is the natural balance between the happiness of a separate personality and the happiness of society, between self-assertion and self-sacrifice, between emotional and intellectual principles.' (E. Key, ibid., p. 197).

76 E. Key, *Любовь и бракъ* (*Kärleken och äktenskapet*), p. 8. [English translation available in full text at https://www.gutenberg.org/files/57592/57592-h/57592-h.htm —Trans.]

77 Children, church, clothing, and kitchen.

78 Clara Zetkin, *Женщина и ее экономическое положение* (*Zhenshchina i yeyo ekonomicheskoye polozhenie*, Woman and her economic position), p. 81.

79 E. Key, *Любовь и бракъ* (*Kärleken och äktenskapet*), p. 371. [English translation available in full text at https://www.gutenberg.org/files/57592/57592-h/57592-h. htm —Trans.]

80 Hearing the feminists preach about how motherhood 'itself' is a goal in life, it is hard not to remember the acute words of the Zürich doctor Brubpbacher on the professions of 'motherhood' and 'fatherhood': 'Imagine a man,' the doctor says, 'who sees his purpose in life as the uninterrupted production of posterity and gives his all to this end; what would you say about him?' (E. Iher, *Die proletarische Frau und die Berufsstatistik* [Proletarian women and occupational statistics]). [It appears that this actually refers to Emma Ihrer's work *Die proletarische Frau und die Berufstätigkeit* (Proletarian women and professional activity), in which we find the quote: *Der Züricher Arzt Brubpacher meint mit Recht: Stelle man sich einen Mann vor, stündlich dem Fortpflanzungsgeschäft sich widmend, in seiner Gesamtheit in ihm aufgebend! Unnatürlich und lächerlich zugleich.* (The Zürich doctor Brubpacher is right to say: 'Imagine a man who dedicates every hour of his life, gives every fibre of his being to the business of procreation!' Unnatural and ridiculous at the same time. Available in the original in full text at https://library.fes.de/cgi-bin/digisomo.pl?id =03653&dok=1905/1905_05&f=1905_0443&l=1905_0449 —Trans.]

81 E. Key, *Любовь и бракъ* (*Kärleken och äktenskapet*), p. 373. [English translation available in full text at https://www.gutenberg.org/files/57592/57592-h/57592-h. htm —Trans.]

82 Ibid, p. 373.

83 Ibid, p. 377.

84 E. Key, *Бракъ и любовь*, p. 373. [This footnote is present at the bottom of the corresponding page of the original, p. 208, but is nowhere marked in the text. The original also lacks closing quotation marks for this quote from Key. —Trans.]

85 G. Yekk, *Интернаціоналъ* (*Internatsional*, The international), p. 39.

86 *Bericht über die vierte sozialdemokratische Frauenkonferenz in Mannheim* [Report on the Fourth Social Democratic Women's Conference in Mannheim], 1906, p. 467. [Available in full text in the original at https://ia802700.us.archive.org/31/items/ die-frauenkonferenzen-der-spd-1900-1911/4.%20Bericht%20%C3%BCber%20 die%20vierte%20sozialdemokratische%20Frauenkonferenz%20in%20Mannheim%2C%20abgehalten%20am%2022.%20und%2023.%20September%20 1906.pdf —Trans.] This year, A. P. Omelchenko, who shares the Marxist worldview, nonetheless tried to prove, against all appearances, that social democracy

had always and everywhere been a defender of family principles, and that, in the collectivist structure, the family would find its fullest expression. 'The family,' Omelchenko says, 'is a bilateral union between a man and a woman, bound to one another by the fact of a freely born child, and parents and children who, by the right of blood relations, require care in the pre-school age; this not only does not contradict the collectivist structure, but logically flows from it, if we recall that free sexual love is the basis of the family. (Omelchenko, *Свободная любовь и семья* [Free love and the family], p. 22). And further: 'The socialist system, in addition to creating the conditions for fully human life, is also dear by virtue of the fact that it opens up the objective possibility for the implementation of the family principle in all its powerful content' (p. 24). These statements Omelchenko seeks to support with excerpts taken from Bebel, but these excerpts only prove that, in the socialist system, love will be of primary significance in the conclusion of a marriage, that 'the false prejudices that currently poison the happiness of family life' will be absent. However, these excerpts by no means serve as a basis to claim that the contemporary form of the family will pass over into the socialist system; Bebel's knowledge of historical materialism is too profound to make such a careless prediction as Omelchenko seeks to pin on him.

87 P. Lafargue, *Женскій вопросъ*, p. 5. [*Les ouvriers, comme toujours, ont été les premiers à tirer les conséquences logiques de la participation de la femme à la production sociale, ils ont remplacé l'idéal de l'artisan, - la femme exclusivement ménagère, - par un nouvel idéal, - la femme, compagne de leurs luttes économiques et politiques pour le relèvement des salaires et l'émancipation du travail.*

La bourgeoisie n'est pas encore parvenue à comprendre, que depuis longtemps son idéal est démodé et qu'elle doit le remodeler pour le faire correspondre aux nouvelles conditions du milieu social.

See https://www.marxists.org/francais/lafargue/works/1904/pl19040000.htm —Trans.]

88 'We see that, in countries with more developed capitalist production, in Britain and the US, many families with modest means already prefer boarding houses to individual households. Here, we see movements in the direction of family cooperatives that seek to solve this issue on a larger scale.' (*Мы видимъ, что въ странахъ съ наиболѣе - развитымъ капиталистическимъ производствомъ— въ Англіи и Америкѣ— многія семьи со скромными средствами уже теперь предпочитаютъ Boarding house единичному хозяйству. Здѣсь-же мы встрѣчаемъ и зачатки движенія въ пользу семейныхъ кооперативовъ, которые стремятся разрѣшить этотъ вопросъ въ большихъ размѣрахъ.*) (Schlesinger-Eckstein, *Женщина къ началу XX вѣка*, pp. 75–74).

89 Blaschko, *Проституція начала XX вѣка* (Prostitution at the beginning of the 20th century), pp. 11–12.

90 Recently, in Russia, the first attempt was made to protect the interests of motherhood: The government bill for the protection of workers in case of illness submitted to the Duma mentions postnatal illness as one of the grounds on which insurance benefits are to be paid to members of health insurance funds. This is not the place for a detailed critique of the bill, the very foundations of which are most unsatisfactory. (The main burden of insurance is carried by the workers themselves; the state is not required to contribute materially to the funds: The administration of the

funds is, for all practical purposes, in the hands of the management of the companies; the contributions are large, whilst the support provided to insured is relatively small, etc.). It is necessary only to mention its fundamental inadequacies in relation to maternity insurance. Women in the postnatal period only get four weeks of leave following childbirth; no protections in pregnancy are provided; the benefits paid by the insurer are on the order of two-thirds of daily wages, which, given how little women workers are paid, of course, deprives them of the possibility of ensuring the necessary care for themselves and their children during the difficult perinatal period; moreover, even these modest provisions do not extend to all women, but only to a limited category of female workers.

Chapter 3. Women's Struggle for Political Rights

1   C. Zetkin, *Zur Frage des Frauenwahlrechts*, p. 4. [The original reads:

Wir sind der Überzeugung, daß die Forderung des Frauenstimmrechts ihre tiefste, ihre stärkste Begründung nicht findet in der Wohlhabenheit einer dünnen Schicht des weiblichen Geschlechts, nein: in der Armut, in der Not, in der Ausbeutung, der die große Masse des weiblichen Geschlechts preisgegeben ist. Mit aller Entschiedenheit weisen wir die angezogene frauenrechtlerische Begründung zurück. Sie ist nichts als eine Variation des alten liberalen Gemeinplatzes vom Nationalreichtum und dem Recht des Besitzes.

('It is our belief that the demand for women's suffrage finds its deepest, strongest justification not in the prosperity of a narrow stratum of the female sex, but in the poverty, need, and exploitation to which the great mass of the female sex is exposed. We most decidedly reject the justification offered by the feminists. It is nothing but a variation on the old liberal platitude of the wealth of nations and property rights.')

Full text available at https://play.google.com/books/reader?id=8Q8GaoxkB6c-C&pg=GBS.PA4&hl=en_GB —Trans.]

2   'In order for the slogan of women's suffrage to become a historically founded mass demand, it was necessary for the capitalist system of production to reach a significant degree of maturity. This fact is closely linked to the revolutionisation of the activity of women, and, with it, of household management. [In the original: *Die Vorbedingung dafür, daß der Ruf nach dem Frauenstimmrecht als eine historisch begründete Massenforderung erklingt, ist erst durch die größere Reife der kapitalistischen Produktion geschaffen worden. Sie steht im engsten Zusammenhang mit der Revolutionierung der wirtschaftlichen Tätigkeit der Frau und damit des Haushalts.* (The prerequisite for the call for women's suffrage to take on the character of a historically founded mass demand was only met by the greater maturity of capitalist production. It is intimately connected with the revolutionisation of women's economic activities, and, with them, of the household.) —Trans.], C. Zetkin, *Zur Frage des Frauenwahlrechts*, p. 8.

3   *Союзъ Женщинъ,* no. 2, 1907, p. 15. The preamble to the constitution of the ICW contained the following declaration: 'We, women of all nations, in the sincere conviction that unity of thoughts, sympathies, and goals will best facilitate the growth of human well-being, and that an organised women's movement will best preserve the supreme principles of the family and the state, unite in a federation of women workers in the name of the struggle against all forms of ignorance and injustice and to facilitate the application to life, custom, and law of the Golden Rule: *Do unto others as you would have them do unto you.*' (I. Poznanskaya, *Международный*

женский конгресс в Лондоне [The International Women's Congress in London], *Женское дѣло*, April 1899.)

4   At the Chicago congress, the constitution of the ICW that had been drafted in Washington was reviewed, and representatives of various nationalities were elected as officers of the Council. For further details, see: *Женское дѣло*, April 1899, and *Союзъ Женщинъ*, no. 2, 1907, p. 15.

5   This speech was separately printed by the German Social Democratic Party, and is available in Russian translation: *Положеніе женщины въ настоящемъ и будущемъ* (The position of women, present and future). Published by Demos. [Available in full text in German at https://books.google.com/books?id=iIakn-QEACAAJ&printsec=frontcover&source=gbs_ge_summary_r&cad=0#v=onepage&q&f=false —Trans.]

6   Details on the London congress (other than the record of proceedings in English) can be found in *Женское дѣло*, 1899, September and August, and 1900, April and July.

7   E. Ihrer, *Die Arbeiterinnen im Klassenkampf* (Female Workers in the Class Struggle), p. 44. [Full text available at https://library.fes.de/pdf-files/netzquelle/01719.pdf —Trans.]

8   These very facts can be found in M. Watson's article on the London congress, *Женское дѣло*, September 1899.

9   The feminists explained their fundamental hostility to factory legislation as follows: 'Other speakers (in London) spoke in favour of special laws for female labour that would limit working hours and protect women's health from the harmful conditions of various industries. However, the overwhelming majority fundamentally opposed this view: Laws should protect all workers, not only women. Limits on working hours should also include all; otherwise, they only harm women, who already had difficulty competing with men as it was; limiting women's working hours would only result in them being denied work, it being more profitable to replace them with men' (A. Carrick. *Иностранные отголоски,—Женское дѣло*, 1899, July, p. 105).

10   Details on the Paris congress can be found in the following articles: T. Bogdanovich, *Женское движеніе*, *Mir Bozhiy*, 1903, p. 236, and M. Watson, *Женское дѣло*, June–July 1900.

11   The organisational plan and programme of the IWSA were ratified at the following congress of women's equality campaigners in Berlin in 1904.

12   N. Mirovich, *Женское движеніе въ Европѣ и Америкѣ* (The women's movement in Europe and America), pp. 6–7.

13   Cf. Zetkin, Zur Frage des Frauenwahlrechts, p. 13.

14   C. Zetkin, *Die internationale Frauentagung zu Berlin*, *Neue Zeit*, 1904, no. 41.

15   For details on the Copenhagen congress, see Mirovich, *Женское движеніе—Союзъ Женщинъ*, 1907, no. 5, and *Женскій Вѣстникъ*, 1906, no. 11.

16   International Woman Suffrage Alliance, Report of Fourth Conference, p. 7.

17   *Die Gleichheit*, 1908, no. 16, p. 143.

18   *Die Gleichheit*, 1908, no. 16. For details on the Amsterdam congress, see *Союз Женщ.*, 1908, no. 7–8 and *Die Gleichheit*, 1908, no. 17.

19   Both the first demonstration, organised by the right wing of the feminists, and the second, which was arranged at the initiative of the 'democratic' wing of the suffragists, were carried out under the banner of property-based suffrage for women.

20   'Voting rights for women are understood in the same way by all participants in the movement. They have the same standpoint as the international alliance of women, i.e., to attain the same voting rights for women that are already enjoyed by the men of their country' (*Союзъ Женщинъ*, 1908, no. 2, p. 23).

21   'Women in the Union (or "League") take the position that submission to a country's laws is not compulsory for the part of the population that is deprived of the possibility of participating in their creation. The WFL do not require all their members to take action, but only accept those who agree with their views and sympathise with their tactics. According to the WFL, one of the means of struggle is discrediting the ruling Liberals to the extent possible. In so doing, they do not take into account any considerations other than women's suffrage.' (*Союзъ Женщинъ*, 1908, no. 1, *Хроника женскаго движенія за-границей, Англія* [*Khronika zhenskogo dvizheniya za-granitsei, Angliya*, Chronicle of the women's movement abroad, Britain])

22   'The members of the WFL were able to disrupt a number of meetings important to the government at which cabinet members appeared to explain their programme. Despite all the measures taken by the police, the suffragists were able to crash these meetings. They interrupted the minister's discussion on any matter (the navy, etc.), and asked whether the government intended to take a position in favour of voting rights for women; the police removed the women; there was commotion, and sometimes even fighting, given that some men, particularly members of the male Women's Suffrage League, interceded for the women; the mood was ruined, and the minister was not able to marshal his arguments in order to continue the speech. The significance of the meeting was undermined' (*Союзъ Женщинъ*, 1908, no. 1, *Хроника женскаго движенія за-границей, Англія* [Chronicle of the women's movement abroad, Britain]).

23   On this occasion, the *Soyuz Zhenshchin* notes as an aside that the matter of universal suffrage is 'practically never raised at present' in Britain. The energetic agitation and activity of the British social-democratic party around this demand, the resolutions adopted by the Labour Party, the interest with which the entire working class follows the outcome of this struggle - all of this is dismissed or, more accurately, ignored by our equal rights campaigners. *Soyuz Zhenshchin* ought to be better informed on the subject of the proletarian women's movement.

24   'Given the differences in the tactics adopted by the NUWSS and the WSPU, one might expect that there would be a split between them, with deleterious effects on the course of the women's movement as a whole. Fortunately, both organisations have been able to avoid this risk. A sort of tacit agreement has been reached between them: Both organisations continue to go their own ways, but come together at times for joint actions. One external sign of this agreement is the magazine *Women's Franchise*, which is jointly published by both organisations. Apparently, this rapprochement has had an effect on both organisations. The WSPU has moved to the right, and the NUWSS to the left' (*Союзъ Женщинъ*, 1907, no. 4, article by I. Mirovich).

25 As is known, Stanger's bill was passed by 271 votes to 92 in the House of Commons in February of this year. Of course, the further fate of the bill is entirely dubious; it will inevitably face an insurmountable obstacle in the form of the House of Lords. But, for now, it is the first victory of the feminist 'principle' in Britain.

26 C. Zetkin, *Zur Frage des Frauenwahlrechts*, p. 31.

27 See *Die Gleichheit*, 1906, no. 252, p. 17.

28 Keir Hardie justifies his position on property-qualified voting rights as follows:
'Some see in this modern reform a fatal attempt to extend the property qualification and, by granting voting rights to properties women, aid in uniting them with reactionaries by opposing voting rights for working-class women. Needless to say, a significant part of the Liberal press adopts and emphasises this false assertion, with all the inventiveness of which a rich and flawless imagination is capable . . . Anyone who reads the aforementioned bill will see that it does not propose any property qualification, but calls for women to be granted voting rights on the same basis as men. This bill merely proposes to destroy the disenfranchisement that excludes women, on the basis of their sex, from exercising the right to vote. If a property qualification exists for men, let it apply to women, as well. Even if a woman is as intelligent as Bacon, as talented as Shakespeare, as eloquent as Demosthenes, as rich as Croesus, even with all these qualities she, as a woman, cannot give her vote for a member of Parliament. The bill proposed eliminates the disenfranchisement that prevents her being a citizen, removes her from the sphere of "idiots, imbeciles, and paupers", and recognises in woman the human essence that is capable of citizenship.' (Keir Hardie, *Женщина-гражданка* [*Zhenshchina-grazhdanka*, Original title: *The Citizenship of Women*], *Союзъ Женщинъ*, 1908, no. 2)
[In the original: 'There are those who see in this innocent-looking measure a sinister attempt to extend and strengthen the property qualification, and by enfranchising propertied women enable these to range themselves on the side of the reactionaries in opposing the enfranchisement of working-class women. Needless to add, as strong section of the Liberal Press adopts and enforces this mis-statement with all the ingenuity which a fertile and untrained imagination can lend to a bad cause . . . .
Any one who takes the trouble to read the Bill quoted above will note that it does not oppose any franchise qualification, but asks that, whatever the qualification, women shall enjoy the franchise on the same basis as men. It is a Bill which only proposes to do one thing, and that is, to remove the sex disability which debars a woman, because she is a woman, from becoming a voter. If the qualification for men be a property one, it shall be the same for women, no more and no less; and if it be a manhood suffrage, it shall also be a womanhood. A woman may have the brain of a Bacon, the talent of a Shakespeare, the eloquence of a Demosthenes, and the wealth of a Croesus all combined, but being a woman she may not vote for a member of Parliament, and this Bill proposes to remove the disability which stands in the way of her becoming a citizen; to remove her from the sphere of 'idiots, lunatics, and paupers', and to recognize that, woman though she be, she is a human being who may now become a citizen.' Full text at https://bora.uib.no/bora-xmlui/bitstream/handle/1956/4517/The%20citizenship%20of%20women. pdf?sequence=6&isAllowed=y —Trans.]

29 Sachse, *Die Frage des Frauenwahlrechts in England, Neue Zeit*, 1908, no. 51.

30 *Die Gleichheit*, 1908, no. 10.

31   It is curious that even our Russian feminists do not shy away from hurling know-ingly hurling false accusations at social democracy on this issue. In praising the invaluable contributions of Independent Labour Party member Keir Hardie to the women's movement, they contrast him with the 'perfidy' of the social democrats: 'Just recently, in 1906, at the conference of the Labour Party in Belfast, Keir Har-die stood decisively in support of universal suffrage without distinction as to sex, throwing down the gauntlet at the majority of the voices of his party, who wish to have universal suffrage only for men' (*С.Ж.*, 1908, no. 1). Meanwhile, as we have already shown, Keir Hardie defended political rights only for *some* women, whilst the soc-dems defended them for *all*.

32   'Electoral reform is only progressive—indeed, it only makes sense at all in the pres-ent time—if it transfers a share of political power from the propertied classes to the propertyless. An electoral form that maintains the status quo in this regard or even increases the political power of the propertied classes is useless, or even worse than useless, even if it appears to be an "extension" of the franchise. But that is the very essence of the bill on extending limited suffrages to women.' (Sachse, *Zur Frage des Frauenwahlrechts in England, Neue Zeit*, 1908, no. 51, p. 914)

    [In the original: *Eine Wahlreform bedeutet nur dann einen Fortschritt, hat heutzutage überhaupt nur einen Sinn, wenn sie einen Teil der politischen Macht von den besitzenden Klassen auf die besitzlosen Klassen überwälzt. Eine Wahlreform, welche in dieser Beziehung alles beim alten läßt oder gar die politische Macht der besitzenden Klassen steigert, ist nutzlos und schlimmer als nutzlos, auch wenn sie nach einer Wahl-rechts-"Erweiterung" aussieht. Dies ist aber der Fall bei der Limited Bill . . .* (Electoral reform only constitutes progress, only has any purpose at all in the present time, if it transfers a share of political power from the propertied classes to the propertyless classes. An electoral reform that maintains the status quo in this regard, or even increases the political power of the propertied classes, is useless and worse than useless, even if it appears to be an ‚extension' of the franchise. However, this is true of the Limited Bill . . .). Full text available at https://play.google.com/books/reader?id=x-czAQAAMAAJ&pg=GBS.PA914&hl=en_GB —Trans.]

33   Sachse's article in *Neue Zeit*, 1908, no. 51.

34   C. Zetkin, *Zur Frage*, p. 54.

35   C. Zetkin, *Zur Frage*, p. 34.

36   For details on the nature of feminist organisations in France, see *Женскій календарь* (1903) and the article *Женское движеніе* (The women's movement) by T. Bogdanovich (*Міръ Божій*, 1905).

37   See *Союзъ Женщинъ*, no. 1, 1907, *Хроника загр. движ.* (Chronicle of movements abroad).

38   Over the last two years, the French socialist party has begun carrying out more or less systematic work amongst women of the working class, similar to that which plays a decisive role in all countries with socialist parties.

39   See *Союзъ Женщинъ*, 1908, no. 5, *Хроника женскаго движенія за-границей, Франція* (Chronicle of the women's movement abroad, France).

40   *Союзъ Женщинъ*, no. 7, 8, 1908.

41   C. Zetkin, *Zur Frage*, p. 14.

42   *Союзъ Женщинъ*, 1907, no. 3, *Хроника загр. движ.* It should not be overlooked that even this moderate feminist organisation in Germany is feeling the influence

of the growing power of the working-class women's movement and increasingly becoming an advocate of social reformism. At the Hamburg congress, they discussed in good faith the matters of the length of the working day for women, holiday leave, protection for working mothers, legislative standards for the labour of female agricultural workers, etc.

43 C. Zetkin, *Zur Frage* etc., p. 16.

44 *Die Gleichheit*, 1907, no. 13.

45 *Союзъ Женщинъ*, 1908, no. 4, *Хроника женскаго движенія за-границей*, p. 19.

46 *Die Gleichheit*, 1908, no. 10.

47 *Союзъ Женщинъ*, no. 5, 1907.

48 See the 1906 edition of *Zhenskiy Kalendar (Женскій календарь)*, p. 552, which reproduces the full text of the resolution that was adopted at the time. The first mass meeting of women provoked a lively exchange of views in the periodical press, in *Nasha Zhizn (Наша Жизнь)*, *Rus (Русь)*, *Prava (Права)*.

49 *Женскій Вѣстникъ*, 1906, p. 324. [*До прошлаго (т. е. 1905 г.).— сообщаетъ „Женскій Календарь",—вопросъ объ избирательныхъ правахъ весьма мало интересовалъ женщинъ; по крайней мѣрѣ, этотъ интересъ рѣшительно ничѣмъ не выразился. Въ то время какъ въ 1903 году цѣлый рядъ земствъ, начиная съ либеральныхъ и кончая самыми консервативными, поднималъ вопросъ объ избирательныхъ правахъ, одни за активное и пассивное избирательное право, другія за расширеніе существующихъ по передовѣрію правъ женщинъ, послѣднія ничѣмъ не проявили своего отношенія къ этому дѣлу, какъ будто оно не касалось ихъ насущныхъ, кровныхъ интересовъ. Но вотъ въ прошломъ, 1905 году, сразу проявился не только интересъ къ этому вопросу, но необыкновенный подъемъ и воодушевленіе, которые, безъ всякой пропаганды, безъ всякаго общаго плана и организаціи, съ замѣчательнымъ единодушіемъ стали обнаруживаться въ разныхъ самыхъ, противоположныхъ, углахъ нашего отечества.]*

50 Ibid, p. 327.

51 *Женскій календарь*, 1906, p. 327.

52 At the initiative of the president of the Society, Dr Shabanova, aid for those amnestied was even organised.

53 'We firmly hope,' this petition reads, 'that a time is beginning in our homeland in which the initiative and energy of all citizens will have an opportunity to be applied. It is time to put an end to the abnormal legal position of woman, which restricts her even in the sphere of property rights. Though she is subject all duties and pays taxes, she has no voice in their allocation and distribution, and is deprived of an opportunity to provide that benefit to her homeland of which she feels capable.

Firmly believing in the power of public opinion and the feeling of justice inherent in the progressive elements of the Russian people, the undersigned call for women to be granted active and passive suffrage for city and zemstvo government bodies in the next review of *zemstvo* and city bylaws' (*Первый Женскій календарь (Pyervyi zhenskiy kalyendar'*, 1906, p. 325). [In the original:

Мы твердо надѣемся, что наступаетъ время для нашей родины, когда иниціатива и энергія всѣхъ гражданъ получатъ возможность примѣненія. Пора устранить ненормальность правового положенія женщины, ограничивающаго се даже въ имущественныхъ правахъ. Неся повинности и платя налоги, она не имѣетъ голоса въ ихъ назначеніи и распредѣленіи и лишена возможности приносить ту пользу родинѣ, на которую чувствуетъ себя способной.

Твердо вѣруя въ силу общественнаго мнѣнія и въ чувство справедливости, присущее прогрессивнымъ элементамъ русскаго народа, нижеподписавшіяся заявляютъ требованіе, чтобы при предстоящемъ пересмотрѣ земскаго и городового положеній женщинамъ было предоставлено активное и пассивное избирательное право въ городскомъ и земскомъ самоуправленіи. —Trans.]

54   This statement is typical in that the women who signed it, like women in Britain, based their demands on the property qualification, i.e., 'no taxation without representation' (see *Женскій календарь*, 1906, p. 329).

55   'For, even if we allow that the women's movement has only political equality as its task, what prevents us and the social democrats approaching this immediate objective together?' (*Ибо, допустивъ даже, что женское движеніе имѣетъ задачей только политическое равноправіе, что мѣшаетъ намъ и соц.-д.-тамъ итти къ этой ближайшей цѣли вмѣстѣ?*), asks Mrs Kalmanovich. 'After all, we can part ways once universal suffrage has been attained. Surely, if we – let us imagine for a moment – were locked in a stale, stuffy room, in which we all risked suffocation, it would not make sense if, instead of uniting all our forces to open a window or a door to let fresh air in and at least somewhat improve the atmosphere in the room, we were first to ask what side each of us should go in order to suffocate more comfortably?' (*Вѣдь успѣемъ-же мы разойтись, когда всеобщее избирательное право будетъ достигнуто. Неужели-же было-бы разу'мно, если-бы мы—представимъ себѣ на минутку такой случай—будучи запертыми въ душномъ и затхломъ помѣщеніи, въ которомъ мы рисковади-бы всѣ задохнуться, вмѣсто того чтобы напречь всѣ свои силы и открыть окно или дверь и дать проникнуть чистому воздуху и хоть нѣсколько оздоровить помѣщеніе, стали-бы раньше спрашивать, въ какую сторону каждая изъ насъ пойдетъ, когда получитъ возможность легче вздохнуть?*) Isn't the style of argument rather familiar, reminiscent of the discourse of our esteemed Cadets?

56   *Отчеты и протоколы Союза Равнопр.*, 1906, p. 5.

57   *Бюллетень*, no. 3, p. 3.

58   *Бюллетень*, no. 3, p. 3.

59   *Отчеты и протоколы Союза Равнопр.*, 1906, p. 33–34.

60   *Отчеты и Протоколы Союза Равнопр.*, 1906.

61   *Отчеты и протоколы*, pp. 16–17.

62   *Отчеты и протоколы*, p. 12.

63   *Отчеты и протоколы*, 1906, p. 32.

64   *Отчеты и протоколы*, 1906, p. 24.

65   *Союзъ Женщинъ*, 1907, no. 2.

66   *Союзъ Женщинъ*, 1907, no. 1.

67   *Союзъ Женщинъ*, 1907, no. 1.

68   *Союзъ Женщинъ*, 1908, no. 9.

69 'In the West, the women's movement has split into two tendencies – the socialist tendency and the bourgeois tendency. In Russia, the women's movement remains in the state of primordial chaos from which worlds are created. Different tendencies are only just beginning to become visible. But, one way or another, the movement already attracts broad democratically minded circles, and we must take up and formulate their demands.' (*На Западѣ женское движеніе раскололось на дна теченія — соціалистическое и буржуазное. Женское движеніе въ Россіи находится еще въ состояніи первобытнаго хаоса, изъ котораго созидаются міры. Въ немъ едва начинаютъ обозначаться различныя теченія. Но, такъ или иначе, движеніе это уже захватываетъ широкіе демократическіе круги, и мы обязаны уловить и формулировать ихъ запросы.*)

70 *Союзъ Женщинъ*, 1907, no. 5.

71 *Союзъ Женщинъ*, 1908, no. 3, March.

72 *Союзъ Женщинъ*, 1908, no. 9.

73 *Союзъ Женщинъ*, 1907, no. 5.

74 'In vain, the social democrats . . . ascribe to us feminists a desire to subject voting rights to a property qualification. We *never* intended to do such a thing. We Russian feminists do not even understand how it is possible to permit restrictions of any kind to anyone's rights!!?? Indeed, that is the difference between the feminists and women of all the other parties, that there is no intolerance in our ranks; as I have said more than once, we invite *everyone* to join our alliance, both Greeks and Jews, without preventing anyone acting in accordance with their convictions.' (*Напрасно с.-д-ки... приписываютъ намъ, феминисткамъ, желаніе провести избирательное право по цензу. Никогда мы этого не имѣли въ виду. Мы, русскія феминистки, даже не понимаемъ, какъ можно допустить какія-бы то ни было ограниченія въ чьихъ-бы то ни было правахъ!!?? Въ томъ-то и заключается отличіе феминистокъ отъ женщинъ всѣхъ другихъ партій, что у насъ нѣтъ нетерпимости; ыы, какъ я уже не разъ говорила, приглашаемъ въ нашъ союзъ всѣхъ, какъ эллиновъ, такъ и іудеевъ, не мѣшая въ то-же время никому дѣйствовать по своему усмотрѣнію.*) (M. Vakhtina, *Рефераты по женскому вопросу* (Presentations on the female question, p. 20). [Full text available in Russian at https://db.rgub.ru/youthlib/3/Vahtina_M.L._Referaty_po_zhenskomu_voprosu.pdf —Trans.]

75 O. Klirikova, *Законъ о равноправности женщинъ* (The Women's Equality Act), *Союзъ Женщинъ*, 1907, no. 1.

76 *Женскій Вѣстникъ*, 1905, no. 12, pp. 354–355.

77 M. Vakhtina, *Рефераты по женскому вопросу* (*Referaty po zhenskomu voprosu*, Presentations on the female question, p. 6).

78 M. Pokrovskaya, *Экономическій хаосъ* (*Ekonomicheskiy khaos*, Economic Chaos)—*Женскій Вѣстникъ*; 1906, no. 10 and 11. [*Покровская предлагаетъ рабочимъ заняться коопераціями, которыя однѣ въ состояніи спасти человѣчество отъ современнаго ."экономическаго хаоса* —Trans.]

79 *Отчеты и Протоколы Союза Равн.*, 1906, p. 30.

80 *Союзъ Женщинъ*, 1908, no. 2.

81 *Женскій Вѣстникъ*, 1905, issue 5, p. 131.

82   The declaration of the Women's Society was joined by 22 other women's organisations in Russia. In all, the Women's Society and the Progressive Party collected some 9,000 signatures on the declaration.

83   *Союзъ Женщинъ*, 1907, no. 2, and *Женскій Вѣстникъ*, 1905, no. 12.

84   See, e.g., *Женское движеніе*, 1905.

85   *Женское движеніе*, 1905, pp. 14–15.

86   *Отчеты и протоколы*, p. 3.

87   *Женское движеніе*, p. 2.

88   *Отчеты и протоколы*, p. 3.

89   'In the newly formed Cadet party, which a significant number of the members of the *zemstvo* congress joined, the mention of women was again struck out of the party platform, and it took increased agitation both at the party congresses and locally to include those rights as a binding point in the party platform. This concession was doubtlessly made under the pressure of public opinion. In promoting it, women found a great deal of support from the socialist parties' (*Отчеты и протоколы*, 1906, p. 5). (In original: *Во вновь-образовавшійся партіи кадетъ, куда вошла значительная часть членовъ земскаго съѣзда, напоминаніе о женщинахъ опять было вычеркнуто изъ платформы партій, и потребовалась усиленная агитація и на съѣздахъ партіи, и на мѣстахъ для включенія правъ обязательнымъ пунктомъ программы партіи. Несомнѣнно, эта уступка сдѣлана была подъ напоромъ общественнаго мнѣнія. Въ муссированіи его женщины нашли большую поддержку со стороны соціалистическихъ партій.* —Trans.)

90   *Союзъ Женщинъ*, 1907 no. 1, *Вопросъ о равноправіи женщины въ крестьянской средѣ* (The matter of women's equality in the peasant milieu), L. Gurevich.

91   C. Zetkin, *Zur Frage*, p. 27.

92   'The extremely low percentage of proxies issued by women can only be explained by the fact that their options were severely restricted by the related provisions of the *zemstvo* ordinance on whom they could grant proxies. The practical upshot of this restriction is that the overwhelming majority of female property owners are deprived of the right to representation of their property interests. It is this circumstance, in relation to the desire somehow to do away with the abnormal situation in elections, in which the number of voters in the overwhelming majority of cases is smaller than the number of electors to be elected, that led to the board's desire to extend women's right to issue proxies for participation on their behalf in electoral assemblies to all persons meeting the conditions for personal participation in electoral assemblies set forth in §§ 16 and 17 of the *Zemstvo* Institutions Ordinance (*Положеніе о земскихъ учрежденіяхъ* —Trans.), thus putting them in an equal position in this regard to persons of male sex who have reached the civil age of majority but have not reached the age of 25' (*Союзъ Женщинъ*, 1908, no. 4, pp. 3–4). (*Чрезвычайно низкій % выданныхъ женщинами довѣренностей-можно объяснить только тѣмъ, что онѣ сильно стѣснены въ выборѣ своихъ довѣренныхъ существующими на этотъ счетъ статьями дѣйствующаго земскаго положенія. Такое стѣсненіе сводится фактически къ лишенію громаднаго большинства женщинъ - владѣлицъ нрава представительствовать свои имущественные интересы. Вотъ это»го обстоятельство, въ связи съ желаніемъ выйти какъ-нибудь*

изъ ненормальнаго положенія при выборахъ, гдѣ число избирателей въ громадномъ большинствѣ случаевъ оказывается меньше числа подлежащихъ избранію гласныхъ, и привело управу къ пожеланію, чтобы право женщинъ выдавать довѣренности для участія вмѣсто себя въ избирательныхъ собраніяхъ было распространено на всѣхъ лицъ, удовлетворяющихъ условіямъ, опредѣленнымъ статьями 16 и 17. Положенія о земскихъ учрежденіяхъ", для личнаго участія въ избирательныхъ собраніяхъ, и, такихъ образомъ, уравнять ихъ въ этомъ отношеніи съ лицами мужского пола, достигшими гражданскаго совершеннолѣтія, но не достигшими 25-ти-лѣтняго возраста. —Trans.)

93 M. Bezobrazov, *Новыя Права (Novye Prava)*, (*Союзъ Женщинъ*, 1908, no. 3).

94 'We are not spoilt with open appeals to our civic achievements by political actors; as such, we were happy for our Moscow women: It is, after all, pleasant time and again to feel like an influent citizen called upon to participate in elections: Such appeals also force those issuing them to rely on women's influence in the future. Nonetheless, the resolute tone of the moderate elements leads to quite sad thoughts. Would it not be a mistake for "property-qualified male and female citizens" to take a snake-oil salesman for a skilled physician and have him treat their sicked loved ones with patent remedies and incantations?' (*Союзъ Женщинъ*, 1908, no. 3). (*Мы не избалованы открытыми обращеніями политическихъ дѣятелей къ нашимъ гражданскимъ заслугамъ и потому порадовались за нашихъ москвичекъ: все-таки пріятно еще и еще разъ почувствовать себя вліятельными гражданками, призываемыми къ участію на выборахъ: такое обращеніе обязываетъ и призывающихъ и впредь считаться съ вліяніемъ женщинъ. Тѣмъ не менѣе, рѣшительный тонъ умѣренныхъ элементовъ наводитъ на весьма грустныя размышленія. Не ошибутся-ли „граждане и гражданки съ цензомъ", если, принявъ за искуснаго врача—знахаря, вручать его подкуриваньямъ и нашептываньямъ своего дорогого больного? —Trans.)*

95 *Союзъ Женщинъ*, 1907, no. 4.

96 *Союзъ Женщинъ*, 1908, no. 4.

97 Ibid, pp. 2–5.

98 The bill in question is reproduced in all its essential particulars in no. 1 of *Soyuz Zhenshchin* (1908).

99 A. von Rutzen, *Избирательныя права женщинъ въ Госуд. Думу* (Izbiratel'nye prava zhenshchin v Gosud. Dumu, Women's suffrage in the State Duma), *Союзъ Женщинъ*, 1908, no. 3.

100 A. Lasserre, *Коллективное участіе женщинъ во французской революціи* (*Kollektivnoye uchastiye zhenshchin vo frantsuzkoy revolyutsii*, Women's collective participation In the French Revolution). [Full Russian text at https://istmat.org/node/37749 —Trans.]

101 'The women of Grenoble were the first to throw down the gauntlet at the *ancien régime* and resist it openly. The famous order dissolving the parliaments agitated the inhabitants of Grenoble. On 7 June 1788, the members of parliament, complying with the governor's order, were already about to leave the city, but the women of the province of Dauphiné proved to be in a more revolutionary mood than even the men. A mass of traders from the bazaar, peasant women, artisans, all those women who had been brought to the point of desperation by the ancien regime,

threw themselves at the speaker, the members of parliament who had been about to depart, unbridled their carriages, and physically forced them to remain in the city. After organising a special guard, went off to guard the city gates, and took possession of the keys to the city of Grenoble. The women's enthusiasm caught on amongst the men, who joined them; it was they, who with fanatical vitality, rang the tocsin, rallying the defenders of liberty from the surrounding villages; it was they who answered Barnave's call to defend the cause of liberty; it was they who were the first to fight openly against the forces of the crown; it was they who forced the governor to send the speaker a proposal to immediately assemble the parliament. Not surrendering their weapons, they continued to demand the removal of a company of soldiers responsible for bloody battles from the city over the following days. However, of course, the royal government responded to this proposal by sending in two new regiments . . . The reaction intensified, but the mood in Dauphiné did not die down. It was decided to restore the previous estates and convoke the deputies of the three Estates on 27 July. Outraged, the court hastened to drown the province of Dauphiné in soldiers and entrust this 'punitive expedition' to the cruel Marshal de Vaux . . . But Dauphiné did not quieten down, and the women, who had first raised the banner of revolt, responded to the violence of the court with remarkable equanimity by donning belts in the golden blue colours of the flag of Dauphiné, an emblem of the independence of the province. And, in January 1789, they sent the king an address, in which they declared: 'We can no longer give life to children who are condemned to live in a land of despotism' (*Histoire du Dauphiné, par Chapuys-Montlaville, tome II*, p. 484). [Original at https://books.google.com/books?id=f-5AAAAAcAAJ&printsec=frontcover&source=gbs_ge_summary_r&cad=0#v=onepage&q=vaux&f=false —Trans..

102 Lily Braun, *Женскій вопросъ*, p. 72.

103 Adrien Lasserre, *Коллект. участ. женщинъ въ великой французской революціи* (Women's participation in the Great French Revolution), p. 10. [Full text in Russian at https://books.google.com/books?id=rf6QnQAACAAJ&printsec=frontcover&source=gbs_ge_summary_r&cad=0#v=onepage&q&f=false —Trans.]

104 See the speech of Finnish deputy Furuhjelm at the Copenhagen congress. *Женское движеніе*, p. 45.

105 Reeves, *Политич. права женщинъ въ Австраліи* (*Politich. prava zhenshchin v Avstraliyy*, Women's political rights in Australia), p. 3.

106 Ibid, p. 13.

107 W. Reeves, ibid., p. 38. (In original: ' . . .and at the first election of Federal representatives, Free-trade and Labour scored conspicuous successes, while the Forrest party, then fighting without its chief, was ejected from office' [full text at https://books.google.com/books?id=AUivvwEACAAJ&printsec=frontcover&source=gbs_ge_summary_r&cad=0#v=onepage&q=forrest&f=false —Trans.]

108 Reeves, *Политич. права женщинъ въ Австраліи*, p. 9 (in original: But the new labour element was strongly in favour of the reform, and, pledge or no pledge, supported it purely out of personal conviction. In this way, it easily sailed through the Lower House).

109 Ibid, p. 29.

110 It is worth noting that, of all the regions of Australia, Victoria has the strongest feminist movement, but, as is known, it is here of all places that Australian women do not have suffrage.

111 *Die Gleichheit*, 1908, no. 18.

112 See *Die Gleichheit*, no. 11, 1908.

113 *Союзъ Женщинъ*, 1907, no. 1, article by L. Gurevich.

114 *Женскій Вѣстникъ*, 1906, no. 11, p. 399.

115 Much valuable information depicting the degree of participation of the masses of working-class women in the events of 1905 to 1906 is scattered throughout the periodical and other press. It would be extraordinarily instructive to collate all this information, given that, alongside what is known about the participation of heroic individuals in the Russian liberation movement, this mass participation of women in the struggle for the renewal of our social and state structure shows better than anything that Russian women deserve the equality to which they aspire.

116 See the propaganda literature of the Alliance, *Мiръ Труда (Mir Truda); e.g., the brochure Къ крестьянкамъ и работницамъ (K kryest'yankam i rabotnitsam,* To Peasant and Working Women).

117 *Обновленіе мира (Obnovlyenie mira,* Renewing the World) (*Мiръ Труда*), p. 3.

118 See my article: *Два теченія на женск. межд.-соц. конгрессѣ въ Штуттгартѣ (Dva techeniya na zhensk. mezhd.-sots. Kongresse v Shtutgartye,* Two tendencies at the International Socialist Women's Congress in Stuttgart). (*Образованіе [Obrazovanie],* 1907, September).

ABOUT THE TRANSLATOR

Élise Hendrick has worked as a freelance translator since the late 1990s, translating a wide range of medical, legal, technical, literary, and political materials. She works with more than twenty languages, including Russian, Japanese, German, Spanish, French, Italian, and Norwegian, among others, and continues to expand her linguistic repertoire.

Her English translation of Juan Domingo Sánchez Estop's *Althusser and Spinoza: Detours and Returns* (ed. Dan Taylor) is forthcoming from Edinburgh University Press in November 2025.

In addition to her translation work, Hendrick is also a writer and editor, whose projects include the structural and developmental editing of Jay Spencer Green's award-winning novel *Breakfast at Cannibal Joe's*. She maintains an active online presence through *Hyperpolyglotting with Élise* (language discussion and game streaming) and *The Untitled Anarchist Seagull Channel* (political satire and analysis). She is currently completing her first novel, an absurdist queer antifascist road thriller, excerpts of which are available on her Patreon page (https://patreon.com/elisehendrick). Her recent creative work, including the web comics *La Gaviota Brava* and *Lesser Cryptids*, can be found on her Substack (https://uascelise.substack.com/). For translation inquiries, visit her ProZ.com profile (https://www.proz.com/profile/8689).

ABOUT HAYMARKET BOOKS

Haymarket Books is a radical, independent, nonprofit book publisher based in Chicago. Our mission is to publish books that contribute to struggles for social and economic justice. We strive to make our books a vibrant and organic part of social movements and the education and development of a critical, engaged, and internationalist left.

We take inspiration and courage from our namesakes, the Haymarket Martyrs, who gave their lives fighting for a better world. Their 1886 struggle for the eight-hour day—which gave us May Day, the international workers' holiday—reminds workers around the world that ordinary people can organize and struggle for their own liberation. These struggles—against oppression, exploitation, environmental devastation, and war—continue today across the globe.

Since our founding in 2001, Haymarket has published more than nine hundred titles. Radically independent, we seek to drive a wedge into the risk-averse world of corporate book publishing. Our authors include Angela Y. Davis, Arundhati Roy, Keeanga-Yamahtta Taylor, Eve L. Ewing, aja monet, Mariame Kaba, Naomi Klein, Rebecca Solnit, Mohammed El-Kurd, José Olivarez, Noam Chomsky, Winona LaDuke, Robyn Maynard, Leanne Betasamosake Simpson, Howard Zinn, Mike Davis, Marc Lamont Hill, Dave Zirin, Astra Taylor, and Amy Goodman, among many other leading writers of our time. We are also the trade publishers of the acclaimed Historical Materialism Book Series.

Haymarket also manages a vibrant community organizing and event space in Chicago, Haymarket House, the popular Haymarket Books Live event series and podcast, and the annual Socialism Conference.

www.ingramcontent.com/pod-product-compliance
Lightning Source LLC
Jackson TN
JSHW071453111225
95322JS00001B/1